Solaris 7 System Administrator

The Cram Sheet

This Cram Sheet contains the distilled, key facts about the Solaris 7 System Administrator exams. Review this information last thing before you enter the test room, paying special attention to those areas where you feel you need the most review. You can transfer any of these facts onto a blank sheet of paper before beginning the exam.

PART I

INSTALLATION AND MAINTENANCE

1. Software Distribution
   - *Software Groups*—Core, End-User System Support, Developer System Support, Entire Distribution, Entire Distribution Plus OEM Support.
   - *Clusters* are collections of packages; *packages* are installable applications or products; *patches* are updated software used to fix problems.
   - **pkgadd** *package* installs a package, **pkgrm** *package* removes a package, and **pkginfo** lists installed packages. Default spool directory is /var/spool/pkg. Packages can also be installed using **admintool**.
   - **patchadd** *patch* installs a patch, **patchrm** *patch* removes a patch, and **showrev -p** or **patchadd -p** list installed patches. No default spool directory. You can get patches from the Web (**sunsolve.sun.com**) or by CD-ROM.

2. Hardware Requirements
   - SPARC 64MB memory, 1GB hard disk, CD-ROM drive or network interface.
   - Intel 486DX compatible or better, 32MB memory, 895MB hard disk, CD-ROM or network interface.

3. Installation Process
   - Methods are interactive (SunInstall and WebStart) or automatic (JumpStart or Custom JumpStart).

BOOTING AND SHUTTING DOWN

4. SPARC OpenBoot Firmware
   - Display commands are **banner**, **devalias**, **module-info**, **printenv**, and **.version**.

- Test commands are **probe-scsi**, **test-all**, **test floppy**, **test /memory**, and **test net**.
- Device aliases (nonvolatile) are set using **nvalias** *name value* and deleted using **nvunalias** *name*.
- View and modify OpenBoot parameters from Solaris 7 using **eeprom**.
- SPARC keyboard commands are **stop** to bypass POST, **stop+a** to abort the operating system, and **stop+d** to enter diagnostic mode.

5. Boot Process
   - Kernel modules are configured by /etc/system. Modules are located in /platform/sparc/kernel or /platform/i86pc/kernel, /kernel, and /usr/kernel.
   - **init** is last in boot process and starts programs listed in /etc/inittab.

6. Run Level Control
   - The eight run levels are **0** (power down), **s** (single user), **1** (administrative), **2** (multiuser), **3** (multiuser with NFS), **4** (not used), **5** (power down), and **6** (reboot).
   - Commands are **init** and **shutdown**. Use **who -r** to determine the current or last run level.

FILE PERMISSIONS

7. File Permissions
   - Use **chmod** or **setfacl** to set file permissions and modify ACLs. Use **getfacl** to view ACLs.

USER ENVIRONMENT

8. User Accounts
   - /etc/passwd fields are name, password, UID, GID, comment, home directory, and login shell.

- /etc/shadow fields are UID, password, last changed, minimum change, maximum change, warning, inactivity, expiration, and a flag (reserved for future use).
- /etc/group fields are name, password, GID, and a list of comma-separated user accounts.

9. Initialization Files
   - Bourne shell uses .profile for login initialization; C shell uses .login, .cshrc (shell startup), and .logout; korn shell uses .profile and a user-defined shell startup file using the exported ENV variable.
   - The system profile (/etc/profile) is called before the user login initialization file.
   - Templates are the /etc/skel/local.profile, /etc/skel/local.login, and /etc/skel/local.cshrc files.

PROCESS CONTROL

10. Viewing And Terminating Processes
   - **ps** and **pgrep** are used to view process attributes and **kill** (process ID required—default signal is SIGTERM) and **pkill** are used to terminate.

11. Scheduling Processes
   - **cron** access is controlled by /etc/cron.d/cron.allow and /etc/cron.d/cron.deny. The **crontab** command is used to edit crontabs.
   - The **crontab** format is minute, hour (0-23), day, month, weekday (0-6), command.
   - The **at** command allows one time execution using AM/PM or 24-hour time.

DISK ADMINISTRATION

12. Device Names
   - Physical is used by the system, logical (raw and block) is used for disk/tape devices, and instance provides simplified names.
   - The /etc/path_to_inst file provides mapping between physical and instance names.
   - Commands that display names are **df** (logical block), **dmesg** (physical and instance), **format** (physical and logical), **mount** (logical raw), **prtconf** (instance), and **sysdef** (instance).

13. Disk Partitioning
   - The disk label or volume table of contents (VTOC) contains disk geometry and the partition table.
   - The partition table defines partition location and size.
   - **fmthard** or **format** create a partition table and **prtvtoc** displays it.

FILE SYSTEM ADMINISTRATION

14. File System Basics
   - File system types are HSFS (CD-ROM), PCFS (diskette), S5 (obsolete hard disk format), and UFS (default hard disk).

- Mount points are / (kernel files), /usr (system files), /home, /var, /opt, /tmp, and /proc.
- File system commands are **mkfs** or **newfs** to create UFS, **fsck** to check, and **mount** to make available (all commands except **mount** use raw devices).
- Monitoring commands are **df** to list free space, **du** to list disk used space, and **quot** to list the disk used by each user.

15. Back Up And Restore Commands
   - Use **mt -f** *device command* to control magnetic tape. If no *device* is given, then /dev/rmt/0n is assumed. Commands are: **asf** to position tape, **bsf** *n* skip *n* EOF to mark backward, **fsf** skip *n* EOF to mark forward, **rewind**, **erase**, and **status**.
   - Use **ufsdump** *commands raw_device* to back up a file system. Commands are **0-9** for dump level (0 for file system), **f** to output file, and **v** to verify backup. If no *commands* are given, **9uf** /dev/rmt/0 is assumed.
   - Use **ufsrestore f** *backup_device* to restore file system or selected files. If no *backup_device* is given, **/dev/rmt/0** is assumed.
   - **tar** *commands backup_device directory* Commands: **c** to create, **r** to replace, **x** to extract, and **v** for verbose. Use **f** to specify an input/output file or device.

PRINTING

16. LP Print Service
   - Supported clients are Solaris 2.x and 7, SunOS 4.x and 5.x, and HP-UX.
   - Print models are /etc/lp/model/standard (local printer) and /etc/lp/model/netstandard (remote printer).
   - Printer characteristics are stored in *terminfo database* under /usr/share/lib/terminfo.

17. Print Commands
   - Use **/usr/lib/lpsched** or **/etc/init.d/lp start** to start LP Print Service; use **/usr/lib/lpshut** or **/etc/init.d/lp stop** to stop it.
   - Use **lpadmin -p** *printer* **-v** *port* to create a printer, **lpadmin -p** *printer* **-c** *class* to define a printer class, **lpadmin -r** *class* to remove a class, and **lpadmin -d** *printer* to define a default printer or to set the LPDEST or PRINTER variable and export.
   - Use **lp -d** *printer file1 file2* . . . to print files, and **-q** *number* or **-H immediate** to change priority.
   - Use **lpstat** (**-a -o -t -u -c**) to monitor print requests.
   - Use **cancel** *request* to cancel a request and **lpmove** *from to* to move request between printers.

Solaris 7 System Administrator

Darrell L. Ambro

Solaris 7 System Administrator Exam Cram

Limits Of Liability And Disclaimer Of Warranty

Trademarks

The Coriolis Group, LLC
14455 N. Hayden Road
Suite 220
Scottsdale, Arizona 85260

480/483-0192
FAX 480/483-0193
http://www.coriolis.com

Library of Congress Cataloging-in-Publication Data
Ambro, Darrell
  Solaris 7 system administrator exam cram / by Darrell Ambro.
     p. cm.
  Includes index.
  ISBN 1-57610-547-4
    1. Electronic data processing personnel--Certification.   2. Operating systems (Computers) Certification--Study guides.   3. Solaris (Computer file)   I. Title.
QA76.3. A525 2000
005.4'469--dc21   99-085710
                                                          CIP

President, CEO
Keith Weiskamp

Publisher
Steve Sayre

Acquisitions Editor
Jeff Kellum

Marketing Specialist
Cynthia Caldwell

Project Editor
Toni Zuccarini Ackley

Technical Reviewer
Jason Bahga

Production Coordinator
Wendy Littley

Cover Designer
Jesse Dunn

Layout Design
April Nielsen

Printed in the United States of America
10 9 8 7 6 5 4 3

CORIOLIS

14455 North Hayden Road • Suite 220 • Scottsdale, Arizona 85260

Coriolis: The Training And Certification Destination™

Thank you for purchasing one of our innovative certification study guides, just one of the many members of the Coriolis family of certification products.

Certification Insider Press™ has long believed that achieving your IT certification is more of a road trip than anything else. This is why most of our readers consider us their *Training And Certification Destination*. By providing a one-stop shop for the most innovative and unique training materials, our readers know we are the first place to look when it comes to achieving their certification. As one reader put it, "I plan on using your books for all of the exams I take."

To help you reach your goals, we've listened to others like you, and we've designed our entire product line around you and the way you like to study, learn, and master challenging subjects. Our approach is *The Smartest Way To Get Certified ™*.

In addition to our highly popular *Exam Cram* and *Exam Prep* guides, we have a number of new products. We recently launched Exam Cram Live!, two-day seminars based on *Exam Cram* material. We've also developed a new series of books and study aides—*Practice Tests Exam Crams* and *Exam Cram Flash Cards*—designed to make your studying fun as well as productive.

Our commitment to being the *Training And Certification Destination* does not stop there. We just introduced *Exam Cram Insider,* a biweekly newsletter containing the latest in certification news, study tips, and announcements from Certification Insider Press. (To subscribe, send an email to **eci@coriolis.com** and type "subscribe insider" in the body of the email.) We also recently announced the launch of the Certified Crammer Society and the Coriolis Help Center—two new additions to the Certification Insider Press family.

We'd like to hear from you. Help us continue to provide the very best certification study materials possible. Write us or email us at **cipq@coriolis.com** and let us know how our books have helped you study, or tell us about new features that you'd like us to add. If you send us a story about how we've helped you, and we use it in one of our books, we'll send you an official Coriolis shirt for your efforts.

Good luck with your certification exam and your career. Thank you for allowing us to help you achieve your goals.

Keith Weiskamp
President and CEO

For my parents, wife, and kids.

About The Author

Darrell Ambro is a Distinguished Member of Technical Staff with Lucent Technologies. He has been with Lucent and its predecessors for 22 years and has been using various forms of Unix since 1977.

During his career, Darrell has been involved in a variety of projects supporting both military and civilian organizations of the U.S. government. These projects involved local area network (LAN) design, operation, implementation, and troubleshooting; application development and systems integration; system security and intrusion detection; database design; system administration; system testing; proposal development; acceptance test/sales support; software maintenance; and tier 2 support.

In addition to being a Sun Certified System Administrator for Solaris 2.6 and Solaris 7, Darrell is also a Novell Certified NetWare Engineer (CNE) and a Microsoft Certified System Engineer (MCSE).

Darrell is a 2nd Degree Black Belt in Tae Kwon Do under the training of Grand Master Seung Gyoo Dong (The Rebel Grand Master) of Richmond, VA, and Master Scott McSwain of Jamestown, NC.

Acknowledgments

Thanks to:

Jeff Kellum, Toni Zuccarini Ackley, Wendy Littley, April Nielsen, Jesse Dunn, and others at The Coriolis Group who provided guidance and assistance in the development and production of my first book.

My wife, Lilli, and my kids, Shane and Eva, for giving me the time to get it done. I love you.

My supervisor at Lucent Technologies, David Bradley, for keeping me in town during most of the writing effort.

Professor Betty Brewer of A&T State University (Greensboro, NC), whose ever-growing disgust with Microsoft products fuels a fiery motivation for anything Unix.

Herb Fish of NCR (a fellow Flashman fan), who traveled to Communist China with me on one of the most interesting assignments of my career. Herb continues to keep me laughing with his humor and wit.

Contents At A Glance

Table Of Contents

Part I Exam 310-009

Introduction

· ·

Welcome to *Solaris 7 System Administrator Exam Cram*. This book will help you get ready to take—and pass—the two exams required to obtain the Sun Certified System Administrator for Solaris 7 certification. In this Introduction, I talk about Sun's certification program in general and how the *Exam Cram* series can help you prepare for the Solaris 7 certification exams.

Exam Cram books help you understand and appreciate the subjects and materials you need to pass Solaris certification exams. The books are aimed strictly at test preparation and review. They do not teach you everything you need to know about a topic. Instead, I present and dissect the questions and problems that you're likely to encounter on a test.

Nevertheless, to completely prepare yourself for any Solaris test, I recommend that you begin by taking the Self-Assessment included in this book immediately following this Introduction. This tool will help you evaluate your knowledge base against the requirements for a Solaris 7 System Administrator under both ideal and real circumstances.

Based on what you learn from that exercise, you might decide to begin your studies with some classroom training or by reading one of the many system administration guides available from Sun and third-party vendors. I also strongly recommend that you install, configure, and fool around with Solaris 7 and other software that you'll be tested on, because nothing beats hands-on experience and familiarity when it comes to understanding the questions you're likely to encounter on a certification test. Book learning is essential, but hands-on experience is the best teacher of all!

The Sun Certified System Administrator For Solaris 7

The certification program currently includes two separate tests. A brief description of each test follows:

➤ *Sun Certified System Administrator for Solaris 7, Part 1 (Exam 310-009)*—The first exam (Part 1) covers basic system administration. Knowledge tested includes installing the operating system, software package administration, patches, the boot process, system security and file permissions, account administration, disk and file system management, backup, and recovery, along with using and managing the LP Print Service.

➤ *Sun Certified System Administrator for Solaris 7, Part 2 (Exam 310-010)*—The second exam (Part 2) covers advanced topics and several add-on software packages that are used to enhance system administration capabilities. Knowledge tested includes the Solaris 7 network environment and network clients; device administration; virtual disk management systems; Network File System (NFS), along with automounting and caching; naming services such as DNS, NIS, and NIS+; automated installation using JumpStart; and configuring the Common Desktop Environment (CDE).

To become a certified system administrator, an individual must pass both exams. You do not have to take the tests in any particular order. However, it is usually better to take the examinations in order because the knowledge tested builds from the first exam to the second.

It's not uncommon for the entire process to take a year or so, and many individuals find that they must take a test more than once to pass. The primary goal of the *Exam Cram* series is to make it possible, given proper study and preparation, to pass both of the exams on the first try.

Because certification is associated with a particular version of the Solaris operating system, there is no requirement to ever recertify. However, once a Solaris version becomes obsolete, being certified on that version will have very little value. It would be in your best interest to work on the certification for the next version of Solaris.

In the past, Sun has used the certification requirements and test objectives from the previous version as a starting point for the next version. Therefore, once certified on a version of Solaris, you should be very familiar with most of the test objectives for certification in the next version of Solaris. I estimate that about 20 percent of the test objectives changed between Solaris 2.6 and Solaris 7.

The best place to keep tabs on Sun's certification program is on the Sun Web site. The current URL for Sun's System Administrator program is at **http://suned.sun.com/USA/certification/solarismain.html**. Sun's certification Web site changes frequently, so if this URL doesn't work, try using the Search tool on Sun's site (**www.sun.com**) with either "certification" or the quoted phrase "certified system administrator" as the search string. This will help you find the latest and most accurate information about the company's certification programs.

Taking A Certification Exam

Alas, testing is not free. You'll be charged $150 for each test you take, whether you pass or fail. In the United States and Canada, tests are administered by Sylvan Prometric.

First, you must purchase an examination voucher from Sun Educational Services. In the U.S., they can be contacted at 1-800-422-8020. This requires the use of a credit card. The voucher can be used for up to one year from the date of purchase.

Next, contact Sylvan Prometric to register for the exam. In the U.S., their number is 1-800-795-3926. You can also use the Sylvan Web site (**www.2test.com**).

To schedule an exam, call at least one day in advance. To cancel or reschedule an exam, you must call at least one day before the scheduled test time (or you may be charged the $150 fee). When calling Sylvan Prometric, please have the following information ready for the telesales staffer who handles your call:

➤ Your name, organization, mailing address, and social security number.

➤ The name of the exam you want to take.

➤ The number of the Sun voucher. (This information may not be needed, because the Sylvan Prometric staffer may already have it.)

An appointment confirmation will be sent to you by mail if you register more than five days before an exam, or will be sent by fax if less than five days before the exam. A Candidate Agreement letter, which you must sign to take the examination, will also be provided.

On the day of the test, try to arrive at least 15 minutes before the scheduled time slot. You must supply two forms of identification, one of which must be a photo ID.

All exams are completely closed book. In fact, you will not be permitted to take anything with you into the testing area. I suggest that you review the most critical information about the test you're taking just before the test. (*Exam Cram* books provide a brief reference—The Cram Sheet, located inside the front of this book—that lists the essential information from the book in distilled form.) You will have some time to compose yourself, to mentally review this critical information, and even to take a sample orientation exam before you begin the real thing. I suggest you take the orientation test before taking your first exam; they're all more or less identical in layout, behavior, and controls, so you probably won't need to do this more than once.

When you complete a Solaris 7 certification exam, the testing software will tell you whether you've passed or failed. Results are broken into several topical areas. Whether you pass or fail, I suggest you ask for—and keep—the detailed report that the test administrator prints for you. You can use the report to help you prepare for another go-round, if necessary, and even if you pass, the report shows areas you may need to review to keep your edge. If you need to retake an exam, you'll have to call Sylvan Prometric, schedule a new test date, and pay another $150.

Tracking Certification Status

Sun maintains a database that indicates the exams you have passed and your corresponding test scores. This database is accessible at **www.galton.com/~sun**. After you pass both exams, you'll be certified as a System Administrator for Solaris 7. Official certification normally takes anywhere from four to six weeks (generally within 30 days), so don't expect to get your certificate overnight. Once certified, you will receive a package with a Welcome Kit that contains a number of elements:

➤ A System Administrator for Solaris 7 certificate, suitable for framing

➤ A logo sheet, which includes camera-ready artwork, for use on letter-head, business cards, etc.

➤ A Sun Certified System Administrator lapel pin

Many people believe that the benefits of certification go well beyond the perks that Sun provides to newly anointed members of this elite group. I am starting to see more job listings that request or require applicants to have a Solaris certification, and many individuals who complete the program can qualify for increases in pay and/or responsibility. As an official recognition of hard work and broad knowledge, Solaris certification is a badge of honor in many IT organizations.

How To Prepare For An Exam

At a minimum, preparing for Solaris 7 exams requires that you obtain and study the following materials:

➤ The Solaris 7 documentation in printed form, on CD-ROM as delivered with Solaris 7 (AnswerBook2), or on the Web at **docs.sun.com**.

➤ The exam test objectives and sample questions on the Sun certification page (**http://suneducation.sun.com/USA/certification/solarismain.html**).

➤ This *Exam Cram* book. It's the first and last thing you should read before taking the exam.

In addition, you'll probably find any or all of the following materials useful in your quest for Solaris 7 system administration expertise:

➤ *Classroom Training*—Sun offers classroom and computer-based training that you will find useful to help you prepare for the exam. But a word of warning: These classes are fairly expensive (in the range of $440 per day of training). However, they do offer a condensed form of learning to help you "brush up" on your Solaris knowledge. The tests are closely tied to the classroom training provided by Sun, so I would suggest taking the classes to get the Solaris-specific (and classroom-specific) terminology under your belt.

➤ *Other Publications*—You'll find direct references to other publications and resources in this book, and there's no shortage of materials available about Solaris; however, many are not written specifically for Solaris 7. For that reason, I have not referenced a large number of these publications. To help you sift through some of the publications out there, I end each chapter with a "Need To Know More?" section that provides pointers to more complete and exhaustive resources covering the chapter's subject matter. This section tells you where to look for further details.

These required and recommended materials represent a nonpareil collection of sources and resources for Solaris 7 System Administrator topics and software. In the section that follows, I explain how this book works and give you some good reasons why this book should also be on your required and recommended materials list.

About This Book

Each topical *Exam Cram* chapter follows a regular structure, along with graphical cues about especially important or useful material. Here's the structure of a typical chapter:

➤ *Opening Hotlists*—Each chapter begins with lists of the terms, tools, and techniques that you must learn and understand before you can be fully conversant with the chapter's subject matter. I follow the hotlists with one or two introductory paragraphs to set the stage for the rest of the chapter.

➤ *Topical Coverage*—After the opening hotlists, each chapter covers a series of topics related to the chapter's subject. Throughout this section, I highlight material most likely to appear on a test using a special Exam Alert layout, like this:

This is what an Exam Alert looks like. Normally, an Exam Alert stresses concepts, terms, software, or activities that will most likely appear in one or more certification test questions. For that reason, any information found offset in Exam Alert format is worthy of unusual attentiveness on your part. Indeed, most of the facts appearing in The Cram Sheet appear as Exam Alerts within the text.

Even if material isn't flagged as an Exam Alert, *all* the contents of this book are associated, at least tangentially, to something test-related. This book is tightly focused for quick test preparation, so you'll find that what appears in the meat of each chapter is critical knowledge.

I have also provided tips that will help build a better foundation of system administration knowledge. Although the information may not be on the exam, it is highly relevant and will help you become a better test-taker.

This is how tips are formatted. Keep your eyes open for these, and you'll become a test guru in no time!

➤ *Practice Questions*—This section presents a series of mock test questions and explanations of both correct and incorrect answers.

➤ *Details And Resources*—Every chapter ends with a section titled "Need To Know More?". This section provides direct pointers to Sun and third-party resources that offer further details on the chapter's subject matter. In addition, this section tries to rate the quality and thoroughness of each topic's coverage. If you find a resource you like in this collection, use it; but don't feel compelled to use all these resources. On the other hand, I recommend only resources I use on a regular basis, so none of my recommendations will be a waste of your time or money.

The bulk of the book follows this chapter structure slavishly, but there are a few other elements that I would like to point out. Chapters 11 and 23 include sample tests that provide a good review of the material presented throughout the book to ensure you're ready for the exam. Chapters 12 and 24 provide answer keys to the sample tests. Additionally, you'll find an appendix on configuration files and formats; two Glossaries, which explain terms and commmands; and an index that you can use to track down terms as they appear in the text.

Finally, look for The Cram Sheet, which appears inside the front of this *Exam Cram* book. It is a valuable tool that represents a condensed and compiled collection of facts, figures, and tips that I think you should memorize before taking the test. Because you can dump this information out of your head onto a piece of paper before answering any exam questions, you can master this information by brute force—you need to remember it only long enough to write it down when you walk into the test room. You might even want to look at it in the car or in the lobby of the testing center just before you walk in to take the test.

How To Use This Book

If you're prepping for a first-time test, I've structured the topics in this book to build on one another. Therefore, some topics in later chapters make more sense after you've read earlier chapters. That's why I suggest you read this book from front to back for your initial test preparation.

If you need to brush up on a topic or you have to bone up for a second try, use the index or table of contents to go straight to the topics and questions that you need to study. Beyond the tests, I think you'll find this book useful as a tightly focused reference to some of the most important aspects of topics associated with being a system administrator, as implemented under Solaris 7.

Given all the book's elements and its specialized focus, I've tried to create a tool that you can use to prepare for—and pass—both of the Solaris 7 System Administrator examinations. Please share your feedback on the book with me, especially if you have ideas about how I can improve it for future test-takers. I'll consider everything you say carefully, and I try to respond to all suggestions. You can reach me via email at **solaris@unixcert.net**. Or you can send your questions or comments to **cipq@coriolis.com**. Please remember to include the title of the book in your message.

For up-to-date information on certification, online discussion forums, sample tests, content updates, and more, visit the Certification Insider Press Web site at **www.certificationinsider.com**.

Thanks, and enjoy the book!

Self-Assessment

I've included a Self-Assessment in this *Exam Cram* to help you evaluate your readiness to tackle Sun Certified System Administrator for Solaris 7 certification. It should also help you understand what you need to master the topic of this book—namely, Exam 310-009, "Sun Certified System Administrator for Solaris 7, Part 1" and Exam 310-010, "Sun Certified System Administrator for Solaris 7, Part 2." But before you tackle this Self-Assessment, let's talk about the concerns you may face when pursuing a Solaris 7 System Administrator certification, and what an ideal candidate might look like.

Solaris 7 System Administrators In The Real World

In the next section, I describe an ideal Solaris 7 System Administrator candidate, knowing full well that only a few actual candidates meet this ideal. In fact, my description of that ideal candidate might seem downright scary. But take heart, because, although the requirements to obtain a Solaris 7 System Administrator certification may seem pretty formidable, they are by no means impossible to meet. However, you should be keenly aware that it does take time, require some expense, and consume a substantial effort.

You can get all the real-world motivation you need from knowing that many others have gone before you. You can follow in their footsteps. If you're willing to tackle the process seriously and do what it takes to obtain the necessary experience and knowledge, you can take—and pass—the certification tests. In fact, this *Exam Cram* is designed to make it as easy as possible for you to prepare for these exams. But prepare you must!

The same, of course, is true for other Solaris certifications, including:

➤ Solaris 7 Network Administrator, which concentrates on the networking aspects of Solaris 7. This certification requires only one exam. The Solaris 7 System Administrator certification is a prerequisite.

➤ Solaris 2.6 System Administrator, which is similar to the Solaris 7 exam, but addresses the previous version of Solaris. This certification requires two exams.

➤ Solaris 2.6 Network Administrator, which concentrates on the network-ing aspects of the Solaris 2.6 environment. This certification requires only one exam.

The Ideal Solaris 7 System Administrator Candidate

Just to give you some idea of what an ideal Solaris 7 System Administrator candidate is like, here are some relevant statistics about the background and experience such an individual might have. Don't worry if you don't meet these qualifications (or, indeed, if you don't even come close), because this world is far from ideal, and where you fall short is simply where you'll have more work to do. The ideal candidate will have:

➤ Academic or professional training in Unix operating systems, and more specifically the AT&T System V Release 4 (SVR4) Unix operating system on which Solaris is based.

➤ Three-plus years of professional system administration experience, including experience installing and upgrading operating systems, perfor-mance tuning, troubleshooting problems, creating users, and managing backup and recovery scenarios.

I believe that well under half of all certification candidates meet these require-ments. In fact, most probably meet less than half of these requirements (that is, at least when they begin the certification process). But, because all those who have their certifications already survived this ordeal, you can survive it, too—especially if you heed what this Self-Assessment can tell you about what you already know and what you need to learn.

Put Yourself To The Test

The following series of questions and observations is designed to help you figure out how much work you'll face in pursuing Solaris certification and what kinds of resources you may consult on your quest. Be absolutely honest in your answers, or you'll end up wasting money on exams you're not ready to take. There are no right or wrong answers, only steps along the path to certifi-cation. Only you can decide where you really belong in the broad spectrum of aspiring candidates.

Two things should be clear from the outset, however:

➤ Even a modest background in computer science will be helpful.

➤ Hands-on experience with Solaris operating system and technologies is an essential ingredient to certification success.

Educational Background

1. Have you ever taken any computer-related classes? [Yes or No]

   If yes, proceed to question 2; if no, proceed to question 4.

2. Have you taken any classes on the Unix operating system? [Yes or No]

   If yes, you will probably be able to handle the discussions that relate to the Solaris operating system and system administration. If you're rusty, brush up on the basic Unix concepts and networking. If the answer is no, consider some basic reading in this area. I strongly recommend a good Solaris system administration book such as the two-volume *System Administration Guide* for Solaris 7 (Sun, 1998) or *Solaris Essential Reference* by John Mulligan (New Riders, 1999). Or, if these titles doesn't appeal to you, check out reviews for other, similar titles at your favorite online bookstore. However, don't expect a long list. Solaris 7 is still new in terms of available titles.

3. Have you taken any networking concepts or technologies classes? [Yes or No]

   If yes, you will probably be able to handle the networking terminology, concepts, and technologies (but brace yourself for frequent departures from normal usage). If you're rusty, brush up on basic networking concepts and terminology. If your answer is no, you might want to check out some titles on the Transmission Control Protocol/Internet Protocol (TCP/IP), such as *Internetworking With TCP/IP, Volume I* by Douglas E. Comer (Prentice-Hall, 1991).

4. Have you done any reading on Unix or networks? [Yes or No]

   If yes, review the requirements from Questions 2 and 3. If you meet those, move to the next section, "Hands-On Experience." If you answered no, consult the recommended reading for both topics. This kind of strong background will be of great help in preparing you for the Solaris exams.

Hands-On Experience

Another important key to success on all of the Solaris tests is hands-on experience. If I leave you with only one realization after taking this Self-Assessment, it should be that there's no substitute for time spent installing, configuring, and using the various Solaris commands and tools upon which you'll be tested repeatedly and in depth.

5. Have you installed, configured, and worked with Solaris 7? [Yes or No]

If yes, make sure you understand the basic concepts as covered in Exam 310-009.

You can obtain the exam objectives, practice questions, and other information about Solaris exams from Sun's Training and Certification page on the Web at **http://suned.sun.com**.

If you haven't worked with Solaris 7, you must obtain a copy of it for either SPARC or Intel x86 compatible platforms. Then, learn about the installation and administration.

If you have the funds or your employer will pay your way, consider taking a class at a Sun training and education center.

Before you even think about taking any Solaris exam, make sure you've spent enough time with Solaris 7 to understand how it may be installed and configured, how to maintain such an installation, and how to troubleshoot that software when things go wrong. This will help you in the exam—as well as in real life.

Testing Your Exam-Readiness

Whether you attend a formal class on a specific topic to get ready for an exam or use written materials to study on your own, some preparation for the Solaris certification exams is essential. At $150 a try, pass or fail, you want to do everything you can to pass on your first try. That's where studying comes in.

I have included in this book several practice exam questions for each chapter and two sample tests, so if you don't score well on the chapter questions, you can study more and then tackle the sample tests at the end of each part. If you don't earn a score of at least 75 percent on the Part I test and 70 percent on the Part II test, you'll want to investigate the practice tests provided at **www.learnsolaris.com** or other practice test resources as they become available. Of course, more hands-on experience and re-reading selected chapters in this book would also be worthwhile.

For any given subject, consider taking a class if you've tackled self-study materials, taken the test, and failed anyway. If you can afford the privilege, the opportunity to interact with an instructor and fellow students can make all the difference in the world. For information about Sun classes, visit the Certification Program page at **http://suned.sun.com**.

If you can't afford to take a class, visit the Certification Program page anyway, because it also includes free sample questions. Even if you can't afford to spend much at all, you should still invest in some low-cost practice exams from commercial vendors, because they can help you assess your readiness to pass a test better than any other tool. Check with the **www.unixcert.net** Web site for available resources.

6. Have you taken a practice exam on your chosen test subject? [Yes or No]

   If yes—and you scored 75 percent or better on Part I and 70 percent or better on Part II—you're probably ready to tackle the real thing. If your score isn't above that crucial threshold, keep at it until you break that barrier. If you answered no, obtain all the free and low-budget practice tests you can find (or afford) and get to work. Keep at it until you can comfortably break the passing threshold.

There is no better way to assess your test readiness than to take a good-quality practice exam and pass with a score of 75 percent or better on Part I and 70 percent or better on Part II. When I'm preparing, I shoot for 80-plus percent, just to leave room for the "weirdness factor" that sometimes shows up on Solaris exams.

Assessing Your Readiness For Exams 310-009 And 310-010

In addition to the general exam-readiness information in the previous section, other resources are available to help you prepare for the exams. Two Web sites come to mind: **www.solarisguide.com** and **www.solariscentral.org**. These are great places to ask questions about topics you are having trouble understanding and get good answers, or simply to observe the questions that others ask (along with the answers, of course).

I'd also like to recommend that you check out one or more of these books as you prepare to take the exam:

➤ Sobell, Mark G. *A Practical Guide to Solaris*. Addison-Wesley, 1999.

➤ Winsor, Janice. *Solaris System Administrator's Guide, Second Edition.* Macmillan, 1998.

➤ Winsor, Janice. *Advanced Solaris System Administrator's Guide, Second Edition.* Macmillan, 1998.

Note: Keep in mind that some of these titles and others were written for Solaris 2.6 and previous versions of Solaris. All the information in these books may not be applicable to Solaris 7. If there is a discrepancy between the information presented in a book covering a previous version of Solaris and the information presented in this Exam Cram, chances are the information has changed in Solaris 7. In this case, stick with the information in this Exam Cram.

One last note: Hopefully, it makes sense to stress the importance of hands-on experience in the context of the exams. As you review the material for the exams, you'll realize that hands-on experience with Solaris 7 commands, tools, and utilities is invaluable.

Onward, Through The Fog!

Once you've assessed your readiness, undertaken the right background studies, obtained the hands-on experience that will help you understand the products and technologies at work, and reviewed the many sources of information to help you prepare for a test, you'll be ready to take a round of practice tests. When your scores come back positive enough to get you through the exam, you're ready to go after the real thing. If you follow my assessment regime, you'll not only know what you need to study, but when you're ready to make a test date at Sylvan. Good luck!

Part I

Solaris 7
Certification Exams

Terms you'll need to understand:

√ Radio button

√ Checkbox

√ Exhibit

√ Multiple-choice question formats

√ Fill in the blank

√ Careful reading

√ Process of elimination

Techniques you'll need to master:

√ Assessing your exam-readiness

√ Preparing to take a certification exam

√ Practicing (to make perfect)

√ Making the best use of the testing software

√ Budgeting your time

√ Saving the hardest questions until last

√ Guessing (as a last resort)

As experiences go, test-taking is not something that most people anticipate eagerly, no matter how well they're prepared. In most cases, familiarity helps ameliorate test anxiety. In plain English, this means that you probably won't be as nervous when you take your fourth or fifth certification exam as you will be when you take your first one.

Whether it's your first test or your tenth, understanding the exam-taking particulars (how much time to spend on questions, the setting you'll be in, and so on) and the testing software will help you concentrate on the material rather than on the environment. Likewise, mastering a few basic test-taking skills should help you recognize—and perhaps even outfox—some of the tricks and gotchas you're bound to find in some of the test questions.

In this chapter, I'll explain the testing environment and software, as well as describe some proven test-taking strategies that you should be able to use to your advantage.

Assessing Exam-Readiness

Before you take any Solaris exam, I strongly recommend that you read through and take the Self-Assessment included with this book (it appears just before this chapter). This will help you compare your knowledge base to the requirements for obtaining the Solaris 7 System Administrator certification and will help you identify parts of your background or experience that might be in need of improvement, enhancement, or further learning. If you get the right set of basics under your belt, obtaining Solaris certification will be that much easier.

Once you've gone through the Self-Assessment, you can remedy those topical areas where your background or experience might not measure up to that of an ideal certification candidate. But you can also tackle subject matter for individual tests at the same time, so you can continue making progress while you're catching up in some areas.

Once you've worked through this *Exam Cram*, have read the supplementary materials, and have taken the practice tests in Chapters 11 and 23, you'll have a pretty clear idea of when you should be ready to take the real exam. Although I strongly recommend that you keep practicing until your scores top the 75 percent mark on Part I and the 70 percent mark on Part II, 80 and 75 percent, respectively, would be a good goal to give yourself some margin for error in a real exam situation (where stress will play more of a role than when you practice). Once you hit that point, you should be ready to go. But if you get through the practice exam in this book without attaining that score, you should keep taking practice tests and studying the materials until you get there. You'll find more information about other practice test vendors in the Self-Assessment along with even more pointers on how to study and prepare. But now, on to the exam itself!

The Testing Situation

When you arrive at the Sylvan Prometric Testing Center where you scheduled your test, you'll need to sign in with a test coordinator. He or she will ask you to produce two forms of identification, one of which must be a photo ID. Once you've signed in and your time slot arrives, you'll be asked leave any books, bags, or other items you brought with you, and you'll be escorted into a closed room. Typically, that room will be furnished with anywhere from one to half a dozen computers, and each workstation will be separated from the others by dividers designed to keep you from seeing what's happening on someone else's computer.

You'll be furnished with a pen or pencil and a blank sheet of paper or, in some cases, an erasable plastic sheet and an erasable felt-tip pen. You're allowed to write down any information you want on this sheet, and you can write stuff on both sides of the page. I suggest that you memorize as much as possible of the material that appears on the Cram Sheet (inside the front of this book) and then write that information down on the blank sheet as soon as you sit down in front of the test machine. You can refer to the sheet any time you like during the test, but you'll have to surrender it when you leave the room.

Most test rooms feature a wall with a large window. This allows the test coordinator to monitor the room, to prevent test-takers from talking to one another, and to observe anything out of the ordinary that might be going on. The test coordinator will have preloaded the Solaris certification exam that you've signed up for, and you'll be permitted to start as soon as you're seated in front of the machine.

Each Solaris certification exam permits you to take up to 120 minutes to complete the test (the test itself will tell you, and it maintains an on-screen counter/clock so that you can check the time remaining whenever you like). Part I consists of 81 questions and Part II consists of 94 questions, randomly selected from a pool of questions.

The passing score varies per exam. For Exam 310-009, the passing score is 75 percent, and for Exam 310-010, the passing score is 70 percent.

All Solaris certification exams are computer-generated and use a multiple-choice or fill-in-the-blank format. Although this might sound easy, the questions are constructed not just to check your mastery of basic Solaris system administration, but also require you to evaluate one or more sets of circumstances or requirements. Often, you'll be asked to give more than one answer to a question; likewise, you might be asked to select the best or most effective solution to a problem from a range of choices, all of which technically are correct. The tests are quite an adventure, and they involve real thinking. This book will show you what to expect and how to deal with the problems, puzzles, and predicaments that you're likely to find on the exams.

Test Layout And Design

A typical test question is depicted in Question 1. It's a multiple-choice question that requires you to select a single correct answer. Following the question is a brief summary of each potential answer and why it was either right or wrong.

Question 1

Which of the following is the last phase in the Solaris boot process?

○ a. init

○ b. Boot PROM

○ c. BIOS

○ d. Kernel initialization

○ e. Boot programs

The correct answer is a. All of these are phases of either the SPARC or the Intel x86 boot process. The boot PROM and BIOS phases test hardware. Therefore, answers b and c are incorrect. The boot programs phase locates and loads boot programs, and then the kernel initialization phase loads the kernel. Therefore, answers d and e are incorrect. Only then can the init phase occur to initialize the operating system services.

This sample question corresponds closely to those you'll see on Solaris certification exams. To select the correct answer during the test, you would position the cursor over the radio button next to answer a and click the mouse to select that particular choice. The only difference between the questions on the certification exams and questions such as this one is that the real questions are not immediately followed by the answers.

The following is a question for which one or more answers are possible. This type of question provides checkboxes rather than radio buttons for marking all the appropriate selections.

Question 2

Which of the following commands can be used to list all installed patches?
[Select all that apply]

❑ a. **showrev -p**

❑ b. **patchinfo**

❑ c. **patchlist all**

❑ d. **patchadd -p**

The correct answers are a and d. Answers b and c do not exist.

For this type of question, one or more answers must be selected to answer the question correctly. For Question 2, you would have to position the cursor over the checkboxes next to items a and d and click on both to obtain credit for a correct answer.

These two types of questions can appear in many forms and constitute the foundation on which most of the Solaris certification exam questions rest. More complex questions might include so-called exhibits, which are usually tables or data-content layouts of one form or another. You'll be expected to use the information displayed in the exhibit to guide your answer to the question.

Other questions involving exhibits might use charts or diagrams to help document a workplace scenario that you'll be asked to troubleshoot or configure. Paying careful attention to such exhibits is the key to success—be prepared to toggle between the picture and the question as you work. Often, both are complex enough that you might not be able to remember all of either one.

The remaining questions are fill in the blank. This involves entering the name of a command, file name, command line argument, or Solaris-related terminology. A typical fill-in-the-blank question is shown in Question 3. This question provides a box in which to enter the answer.

Question 3

> Enter the full pathname to the file used to modify the configuration of the kernel.
>
> _____

The correct answer is /etc/system.

Be sure to read this type of question very carefully. Without having any answers in front of you, there is nothing to jog your memory and it makes guessing almost impossible. Because this question specifically asked for the full pathname, an answer such as *system*, which might be considered technically correct, will be marked as wrong. Try to be as specific as possible.

Using The Test Software Effectively

A well-known test-taking principle is to read over the entire test from start to finish first, but to answer only those questions that you feel absolutely sure of on the first pass. On subsequent passes, you can dive into more complex questions, knowing how many such questions you have to deal with.

Fortunately, the test software makes this approach easy to implement. At the bottom of each question, you'll find a checkbox that permits you to mark that question for a later visit. (Note that marking questions makes review easier, but you can return to any question by clicking the Forward and Back buttons repeatedly until you get to the question.) As you read each question, if you answer only those you're sure of and mark for review those that you're not, you can keep going through a decreasing list of open questions as you knock the trickier ones off in order.

There's at least one potential benefit to reading the test over completely before answering the trickier questions: Sometimes, you find information in later questions that sheds more light on earlier ones. Other times, information you read in later questions might jog your memory about facts, figures, or behavior that also will help with earlier questions. Either way, you'll come out ahead if you defer those questions about which you're not absolutely sure of the answer(s).

Keep working on the questions until you're absolutely sure of all your answers or until you know you'll run out of time. If unanswered questions remain, you'll want to zip through them and guess. No answer guarantees that no credit will be given for a question, and a guess has at least a chance of being correct. (Blank answers and incorrect answers are scored as equally wrong.)

 At the very end of your test period, you're better off guessing than leaving questions blank or unanswered.

Taking Testing Seriously

The most important advice I can give you about taking any test is this: Read each question carefully. Some questions are deliberately ambiguous, some use double negatives, and others use terminology in incredibly precise ways. I've taken numerous practice tests and real tests myself, and in nearly every test I've missed at least one question because I didn't read it closely or carefully enough.

Here are some suggestions on how to deal with the tendency to jump to an answer too quickly:

➤ Make sure you read every word in the question. If you find yourself jumping ahead impatiently, go back and start over.

➤ As you read, try to restate the question in your own terms. If you can do this, you should be able to pick the correct answer(s) much more easily.

➤ When returning to a question after your initial read-through, re-read every word again—otherwise, your mind can fall quickly into a rut. Sometimes, seeing a question afresh after turning your attention elsewhere lets you see something that you missed, but the strong tendency is to see what you've seen before. Try to avoid that tendency at all costs.

➤ If you return to a question more than twice, try to articulate to yourself what you don't understand about the question, why the answers don't appear to make sense, or what appears to be missing. If you chew on the subject for a while, your subconscious might provide the details that are lacking or you might notice a "trick" that will point to the right answer.

Above all, try to deal with each question by thinking through what you know about being a Solaris system administrator—commands, characteristics, behaviors, facts, and figures involved. By reviewing what you know (and what you've written down on your information sheet), you'll often recall or understand things sufficiently to determine the answer to the question.

Question-Handling Strategies

Based on the tests I've taken, a couple of interesting trends in the answers have become apparent. For those questions that take only a single answer, usually two or three of the answers will be obviously incorrect, and two of the answers will be plausible. But, of course, only one can be correct. Unless the answer leaps out at you (and if it does, re-read the question to look for a trick; sometimes those are the ones you're most likely to get wrong), begin the process of answering by eliminating those answers that are obviously wrong.

Things to look for in the "obviously wrong" category include spurious command choices or file names, nonexistent software or command options, and terminology that you've never seen before. If you've done your homework for a test, no valid information should be completely new to you. In that case, unfamiliar or bizarre terminology probably indicates a totally bogus answer. As long as you're sure what's right, it's easy to eliminate what's wrong.

Numerous questions assume that the default behavior of a particular Solaris command is in effect. It's essential to know and understand the default settings for the various commands. If you know the defaults and understand what they mean, this knowledge will help you cut through many Gordian knots.

Likewise, when dealing with questions that require multiple answers, you must know and select all the correct options to get credit. This, too, qualifies as an example of why careful reading is so important.

As you work your way through the test, another counter that the exam provides will come in handy: the number of questions completed and questions outstanding. Budget your time by making sure that you've completed one-fourth of the questions one-quarter of the way through the test period. Check again three-quarters of the way through. For Exam 310-009 with 81 questions, that's about 20 questions after 30 minutes and 60 questions after 90 minutes (30 minutes remaining). For Exam 310-010 with 94 questions, that's about 24 questions after 30 minutes and 72 questions after 90 minutes (30 minutes remaining).

If you're not through after 110 minutes, use the last 10 minutes to guess your way through the remaining questions. Remember, guesses are potentially more valuable than blank answers because blanks are always wrong, but a guess might turn out to be right. If you haven't a clue about any of the remaining questions, pick answers at random or choose all a's, b's, and so on. The important thing is to submit a test for scoring that has an answer for every question.

Mastering The Inner Game

In the final analysis, knowledge breeds confidence, and confidence breeds success. If you study the materials in this book carefully and review all the questions at the end of each chapter, you should be aware of those areas where additional studying is required.

Next, follow up by reading some or all of the materials recommended in the "Need To Know More?" section at the end of each chapter. The idea is to become familiar enough with the concepts and situations that you find in the sample questions to be able to reason your way through similar situations on a real test. If you know the material, you have every right to be confident that you can pass the test.

Once you've worked your way through Part I, take the practice test in Chapter 11. Likewise, after studying Part II, take the practice test in Chapter 23. The tests will provide a reality check and help you identify areas that you need to study further. Make sure that you follow up and review materials related to the questions you miss before scheduling the real tests. Only when you've covered all the ground and feel comfortable with the whole scope of the practice tests should you take the real tests.

 If you take the practice test in Chapter 11 and don't score at least 75 percent correct or don't score at least 70 percent on the practice test in Chapter 23, you'll want to practice further.

Armed with the information in this book and with the determination to augment your knowledge, you should be able to pass the certification exam. But if you don't work at it, you'll spend the test fee more than once before you finally do pass. If you prepare seriously, the exam should go flawlessly. Good luck!

Additional Resources

By far, the best source of information about Solaris certification exams comes from Sun itself. Because its products and technologies—and the tests that go with them—change frequently, the best place to go for exam-related information is online.

If you haven't already visited the Solaris certification pages, do so right now. As I'm writing this chapter, the certification home page resides at **http:// suned.sun.com/USA/certification/solarismain.html**.

Note: It might not be there by the time you read this, or it might have been replaced by something new and different, because things change regularly on the Sun site. Should this happen, please read the section titled "Coping With Change On The Web" later in this chapter.

The pull-down menu options below the Sun Certified System Administrator for Solaris, Part I and Part II headings point to additional information in the certification pages. Here's what to check out:

➤ *Overview*—An overview of the certification process and exams.

➤ *Supporting Courseware*—Classroom courses and self-paced computer-based training offered by Sun that cover the information listed in the exam objectives.

➤ *Exam Objectives*—A detailed list of the topics that will be covered on the exams.

➤ *Sample Questions*—A limited number of sample questions and answers.

➤ *Registration*—Information on purchasing a Sun voucher and registering with Sylvan Prometric to schedule the exams.

➤ *FAQs*—Frequently Asked Questions; yours might get answered here.

As you browse through them—and I strongly recommend that you do—you'll probably find other things that I didn't mention here that are every bit as interesting and compelling.

Coping With Change On The Web

Sooner or later, all the specifics I've shared with you about the Solaris certification pages, and all the other Web-based resources I mention throughout the rest of this book, will go stale or be replaced by newer information. In some cases, the URLs that you find here might lead you to their replacements; in other cases, the URLs will go nowhere, leaving you with the dreaded "404 File not found" error message.

When that happens, please don't give up. There's always a way to find what you want on the Web—if you're willing to invest some time and energy. To begin with, most large or complex Web sites—and Sun's qualifies on both counts—offer a search engine. As long as you can get to

Sun's home page (and I'm sure that it will stay at **www.sun.com** for a long while yet), you can use this tool to help you find what you need.

The more focused you can make a search request, the more likely it is that the results will include information you can use. For example, you can search for the string "training and certification" to produce a lot of data about the subject in general, but if you're looking for the details on the Sun Certified System Administrator tests, you'll be more likely to get there quickly if you use a search string such as this:

```
"Administrator" AND "certification"
```

Likewise, if you want to find the training and certification downloads, try a search string such as this:

```
"training and certification" AND "download page"
```

Finally, don't be afraid to use general search tools such as **www.search.com**, **www.altavista.com**, or **www.excite.com** to search for related information. Even though Sun offers information about its certification exams online, there are plenty of third-party sources of information, training, and assistance in this area that do not have to follow a party line like Sun does. The bottom line is this: If you can't find something where the book says it lives, start looking around. If worse comes to worse, you can always email me! I just might have a clue. My email address is **solaris@unixcert.net**.

2

System Concepts

Terms you'll need to understand:

√ Kernel

√ Shell

√ File system

√ Multitasking

√ Multiuser

√ Client

√ Server

√ Host

√ Hostname

√ Network

√ IP address

Techniques you'll need to master:

√ Distinguishing between the parts of the operating system

√ Distinguishing between the three shells

√ Identifying a network address by class

√ Understanding host-naming guidelines

This chapter provides some introductory information, including a description of the three parts of the operating system and the three common variations of user interfaces (shells) available with the Solaris 7 operating system. This chapter also defines several computer- and networking-related concepts and several frequently used terms.

The Three Parts Of The Operating System

Solaris 7, like all variations of the Unix operating system, consists of three parts: the kernel, the shell, and the file system. Each of these will be discussed in the next few sections.

The Kernel

The kernel is a collection of software that manages the physical and logical resources of the computer. These management services include controlling the allocation of memory and other storage devices, controlling the access to peripheral devices (input/output), and controlling the scheduling and execution of processes or tasks. For the most part, these services are transparent to the user. The user issues a fairly simple request to perform a task, and the operating system deals with the complexity of manipulating the underlying hardware and allocating logical resources to accomplish the task.

The physical resources are controlled by means of software modules, referred to as *device drivers*, that understand how to communicate with hardware devices and control their operation. Typically, each device has a unique driver that is provided with the hardware and identified by hardware manufacturer, model, and sometimes hardware version.

The logical resources include *processes* and *memory*. A process is a task or program. The kernel maintains internal data structures that are used to define and control the processes, and also controls the scheduling, execution, and termination of processes. Other important kernel services are *memory management* and *interprocess communication*. Memory management involves keeping track of available memory, allocating it to processes as needed, and reclaiming it as processes release it or terminate. Interprocess communication involves handling the cooperative communication between processes.

The Shell

The shell is a software module that provides the interface between users and the kernel. It accepts user requests and submits them to the kernel. It also accepts status and data from the kernel and presents them to the user. Typically, the shell accepts user input from a terminal or network connection;

however, the input can be taken from a file, a device, or even another process. In addition, output from the kernel is typically sent to the user's terminal or network connection. Likewise, this output can be redirected to a file, a device, or another process.

The shell also provides a built-in programming language that can be used to automate repetitive tasks. This includes flow control along with the ability to manipulate numeric and string data.

Solaris 7 provides several different shells, each with unique strengths. Some shells provide a history/recall mechanism that allows the user to reexecute a previous command by entering a few control sequences instead of reentering the command. Other shells provide built-in math manipulation.

The File System

A *file* is a group of bytes treated as a unit for storage, retrieval, and manipulation. The *file system* is a collection of files stored on a disk drive in a hierarchical structure. A special type of file, called a *directory*, serves as a folder and is used to organize files. A file system can be thought of as an inverted tree, with the directories being the branches and the files being the leaves. The name for the top-level directory of a Unix system, "root," comes from this analogy.

The Unix operating system supports the file system concept by providing utilities to create, mount (make accessible), check, repair, duplicate, and back up file systems. The storage space that is accessible on a Unix system usually is divided into multiple file systems. This allows for easier maintenance and improves performance.

The Three Most Common Shells

The Solaris 7 environment provides several shells. The three most common shells are the Bourne shell (sh), the C shell (csh), and the Korn shell (ksh). The Bourne shell is the default.

The Bourne shell was developed by Steven Bourne at AT&T Bell Laboratories and was the shell provided with the original Unix operating system. The Unix operating system was designed and developed by Ken Thompson and Dennis Ritchie at Bell Labs during the 1970s. The most popular version was Unix System V.

The C shell was developed by Bill Joy of the University of California, Berkeley and was provided with a version of the Unix operating system that was developed at the university and referred to as Berkeley Software Distribution (BSD) Unix.

The Korn shell was designed and developed by David G. Korn at AT&T Bell Laboratories. The Korn shell was derived from the Bourne shell by adding many features from the C shell along with new features of its own. Table 2.1 compares the features of the three shells.

Table 2.1 Features of Solaris 7 shells.

Feature	sh	csh	ksh	Function
Aliasing	No	Yes	Yes	The ability to assign a short, simple name to a complex string and then use the name in place of the string in commands. This gives the appearance of being able to add custom commands to the shell.
Bourne shell–compatible syntax	Yes	No	Yes	Because the Korn shell is an enhanced version of the Bourne shell, they use the same syntax. The C shell was developed separately, and its syntax is based on the C programming language.
Default prompt	$	%	$	The default prompt for both the Bourne and the Korn shells is the "$" character, whereas the default prompt for the C shell is the system hostname followed by the "%" character.
History capability	No	Yes	Yes	The history capability of the C and Korn shells keeps track of a user-defined number of previous commands. Instead of reentering a command, it can be copied from the history and then executed.
History editing	No	Yes	No	Modify then reuse previous commands.
History execution	No	!n	fc	Repeat previous command with few keystrokes.
Initialization file: login	.profile	.login	.profile	Stores any commands that should be executed once, when a user logs into the system.
Initialization file: shell startup	No	.cshrc	User defined	Stores commands that are executed every time the user starts a shell to execute a command. With the Korn shell, the user can specify the name of the shell startup initialization file using the ENV parameter.

(continued)

Feature	sh	csh	ksh	Function
Table 2.1				**Features of Solaris 7 shells (continued).**
Inline editing	No	No	Yes	Allows you to edit a command that has been entered but not yet executed. This allows you to correct typographical errors instead of being forced to retype the entire command. Either emacs or vi editing commands can be used.
Logout file	No	.logout	No	Stores commands that should be executed when user logs out.
Overwrite protect	No	Yes	Yes	Prevents files from being accidentally overwritten; can be set by using the **noclobber** parameter.
Repeat last command	No	!!	No	Handy shortcut for reexecuting the last command with only a few keystrokes.
Restricted version	rsh	No	rksh	Intended for users who need limited access to the Unix system. Provides enhanced security by confining the user to a single directory and preventing the redirection of shell output. Be sure not to confuse the restricted Bourne shell (/usr/lib/rsh) with the remote shell (/usr/bin/rsh), which is used to execute commands on a remote system. The restricted version of the Korn shell is /usr/bin/rksh.
Source	AT&T	Berkeley	AT&T	Both the Bourne and Korn shells originated at AT&T Bell Labs, while the C shell came from the University of California at Berkeley.

Use of the initialization files for each shell is an important concept that is helpful when setting up user accounts on a Solaris 7 system. Be sure that you understand their usage and associate the file names correctly with the appropriate shells.

Some Basic Concepts

This section introduces a couple of basic concepts. The first relates to computer operating systems, and the second covers the networking model or paradigm.

Multitasking Vs. Multiuser

Solaris 7 supports multiple users, each of which can be executing one or more processes or tasks. Thus, Solaris 7 is both a multiuser and a multitasking system. Solaris 7 accomplishes this by allowing a task to have access to system resources for a small slice of time. A task is allowed to execute for one or more time slices and then is suspended to allow another task to execute. This provides time-sharing among all active tasks and gives the appearance that all tasks are running simultaneously.

The Client/Server Relationship

Solaris 7 supports operations that use the client/server model. A *server* is a computer system that is configured or designed to provide one or more services to other computers via the network. A *client* is a computer system that is configured or designed to interact with a user and to provide an interface to one or more services running on a server via the network. The main function of the client is to provide a presentation by which the user can interact with the services. This presentation is typically a graphic user interface (GUI) but can be data in a known format. Some of the services that use the client/server model are file sharing, print sharing, and accessing a centralized database.

Some Basic Terms

Several terms related to naming systems and identifying networks are covered in the following paragraphs. You should be familiar with these terms for both the Part I and Part II exams.

Host

A host is a computer system that provides resources to locally and/or remotely logged on users. The distinction between a host and a server is somewhat blurred. By convention, a host is accessed through a terminal locally and through a terminal emulation remotely; both users are logged into the system and use a shell to interact with the system. A server typically provides services to users that are not logged into the system, and interaction is through a software module other than a shell. However, even this distinction might not hold true for every situation.

Hostname

A name assigned to a host. The hostname is usually short and easy to remember and type. Solaris 7 will support a system name up to 257 characters in length. However, to provide maximum interoperability on the Internet, the hostname should be compliant with the guidelines defined in the Internet

Request For Comments (RFC) 952, DOD Internet Host Table Specification. The RFC 952 guidelines are summarized as follows:

➤ A hostname should be a text string up to 24 characters.

➤ A hostname consists of letters (A–Z), digits (0–9), and dashes (-).

➤ No tab or space characters are allowed.

➤ The name should not be case sensitive.

➤ The first character must be a letter.

➤ The last character must not be a dash.

Periods are also allowed, but only to separate the hostname from the domain name and to separate the portions of the domain name.

Network

A network is a shared medium used by computers to communicate and exchange information. To uniquely identify the computers that are accessible through a network, each network is assigned a unique address.

IP Address

An IP address is a unique 32-bit (4-byte or 4-octet) address assigned to a networked computer using the IP addressing scheme as defined by Internet RFC 1700, Assigned Numbers. The IP address consists of four numbers between 0 and 255 and typically is written in dotted decimal notation, such as 192.168.99.27. The IP addresses are grouped into five classes or network types on the basis of the value of the first octet. They are actually divided into network octets and host octets, depending on the class. Classes A, B, and C are used for unicast addressing. See Table 2.2 for a summary of IP address classes.

Class D (224–239) is reserved for multicast addressing, and Class E (240–255) is reserved for future use. With the adoption of classless addressing, the notion of network and host portions of an address is of less importance.

Table 2.2 IP address classes.			
Class	**First Octet**	**Network/Host**	**Max Theoretical Hosts**
A	1–126	network.host.host.host	16,777,216
B	128–191	network.network.host.host	65,536
C	192–223	network.network.network.host	256

A few reserved or restricted addresses have special meanings and should not be used for addressing:

➤ 0.0.0.0 is used to identify the current host on the network.

➤ 255.255.255.255 is used for limited broadcasts on the current network.

➤ Class A 0.h.h.h or Class B 0.0.h.h or Class C 0.0.0.h (that is, the network portion is 0) is used to identify host h on the current network.

➤ Class A n.0.0.0 or Class B n.n.0.0 or Class C n.n.n.0 (that is, the host portion is 0) is used to denote networks and are not used for IP addresses.

➤ Class A n.255.255.255 or Class B n.n.255.255 or Class C n.n.n.255 (that is, the bits of the host portion are all ones) is used for directed broadcasts to all systems on network/subnet n.

➤ Any address starting with 127 is used for internal loopback. By convention, the address 127.0.0.1 is used for the loopback.

Many people overlook these restrictions when determining the maximum number of hosts that can be on a network. Applying these restrictions, the actual maximum number of hosts on a network is less than the theoretical maximum. A Class C network can only have 254 hosts as opposed to its theoretical maximum of 256, because host 0 is not used for IP addressing and host 255 represents a directed broadcast. The same also applies to the other classes of networks.

Practice Questions

Question 1

What are the three parts of the Solaris 7 operating system?

❑ a. Disk drive

❑ b. Kernel

❑ c. File system

❑ d. System console

❑ e. Memory management

❑ f. Shell

❑ g. Process control

The correct answers are b, c, and f. The disk drive and system console are hardware devices. Therefore, answers a and d are incorrect. Memory management and process control are functions of the kernel. Therefore, answers e and g are incorrect.

Question 2

What is the commonly used shell provided by the Solaris 7 system?

○ a. Corn shell

○ b. Sea shell

○ c. Bourne shell

○ d. Berkeley shell

The correct answer is c. Answers a and b are incorrect because they sound similar to the Korn and C shells, but are spelled differently. Answer d, Berkeley shell, does not exist.

Question 3

> Which of the following files are used to store commands that should be executed when a user logs into the system?
>
> ○ a. The .cshrc file
>
> ○ b. The .Profile file
>
> ○ c. The .startup file
>
> ○ d. The profile file
>
> ○ e. The .login file

The correct answer is e. The .login file is the login initialization file for the C shell. The .cshrc file is the shell startup initialization file for the C shell. Therefore, answer a is incorrect. Answer b is similar to the name of the Bourne and Korn login initialization file, but the correct file uses a lowercase p. In Unix, file names are case sensitive, so answer b is incorrect. The file .startup is not a standard initialization file. Therefore, answer c is incorrect. Answer d would be correct if it were to start with a period.

Question 4

> What is a Solaris 7 system feature? [Select all that apply]
>
> ❑ a. Single threaded
>
> ❑ b. Multitasking
>
> ❑ c. Single user
>
> ❑ d. Multiuser

The correct answers are b and d. Solaris 7 is both multitasking and multiuser. Single threaded and single user apply to DOS but not to Solaris 7. Therefore, answers a and c are incorrect.

Question 5

> An account is set up to use the Bourne shell. Which file is used to store commands to be executed when the user logs into the system?
>
> ○ a. The .cshrc file
>
> ○ b. The .profile file
>
> ○ c. The .startup file
>
> ○ d. The .logon file
>
> ○ e. The .login file

The correct answer is b. The .profile file is used to store commands that are executed when the user logs into the system. .cshrc is the shell startup initialization file for the C shell. Therefore, answer a is incorrect. Answers c and d are incorrect because they are not standard names for login initialization files. Answer e is the login initialization file for the C shell.

Question 6

> Which of the following are functions of the kernel? [Select all that apply]
>
> ❑ a. Process control
>
> ❑ b. Hardware interface and control
>
> ❑ c. Memory management
>
> ❑ d. Interprocess communication

Answers a, b, c, and d are all functions of the kernel.

Question 7

> Which of the following shells are available in a restricted version? [Select all that apply]
>
> ❑ a. C shell
>
> ❑ b. Korn shell
>
> ❑ c. Bourne shell

The correct answers are b and c. The C shell does not provide a restricted version. Therefore, answer a is incorrect.

Question 8

What does multitasking mean?

○ a. To support more than one user at a time

○ b. To support more than one process at a time

○ c. To support more than one processor at a time

○ d. To support more than one network connection at a time

The correct answer is b. Supporting more than one user at a time is the definition of multiuser. Therefore answer a is incorrect. Supporting more than one processor at a time is the definition of multiprocessor. Therefore, answer c is incorrect. Supporting more than one network connection at a time is the definition of multiconnection. Therefore, answer d is incorrect.

Need To Know More?

 Bach, Maurice J., *The Design of the Unix Operating System* (Prentice-Hall, Englewood Cliffs, NJ, 1986), ISBN 0-13-201799-7.

 Bolsky, Morris I., and Korn, David G., *The Kornshell Command and Programming Language* (Prentice-Hall, Englewood Cliffs, NJ, 1995), ISBN 0-13-182700-6.

 Kernighan, Brian W., and Pike, Rob, *The Unix Programming Environment* (Prentice-Hall, Englewood Cliffs, NJ, 1984), ISBN 0-13-937681-X.

 Sun Microsystems, *System Reference Manual, Section 1 - User Commands*, are available in printed form (ISBN 805-3172-10), on the Web at **docs.sun.com**, and from online system documentation, AnswerBook2, provided with the Solaris 7 operating system.

 Harrenstien, K., Stahl, M., and Feinler, E., Request For Comments 952, *DOD Internet Host Table Specification* (October 1985), is available at **www.nic.mil/ftp/rfc/rfc952.txt**.

Reynolds, J., and Postel, J., Request For Comments 1700, *Assigned Numbers* (October 1994), is available at **www.nic.mil/ftp/rfc/rfc1700.txt**.

Installing And
Maintaining Solaris 7

3

Terms you'll need to understand:

√ Software groups

√ Software clusters

√ Packages

√ Patches

Techniques you'll need to master:

√ Installing Solaris 7 using SunInstall

√ Upgrading a system to Solaris 7

√ Adding and removing packages

√ Listing installed packages

√ Adding and removing patches

√ Listing installed patches

This chapter addresses topics related to loading software on a Solaris 7 system, including:

➤ Initial installation of the Solaris 7 operating system on a standalone workstation

➤ Adding software using the software packaging utilities

➤ Updating software and fixing problems with patches

The Solaris 7 Distribution

Both Solaris 7 system and application software are delivered as collections of files and directories, referred to as *packages*. These packages can be copied onto the system from CD-ROM or magnetic tape as a single compressed file and uncompressed for installation.

Included with the package is information regarding the package, such as title, storage requirements, and version. Also included are any custom scripts needed to properly install the software.

Sometimes system software is distributed in more than one package, but the packages need to be distributed and installed as a unit. A collection of two or more related packages is referred to as a *software cluster*. A software cluster is a logical grouping of packages.

The Solaris 7 operating system is preconfigured into *software groups* that consist of different collections of software clusters and packages. The five software groups are shown in Table 3.1.

> *Note: Some Solaris 7 documents refer to the software groups as software configuration clusters or simply clusters. Because the term software cluster is used to refer to a collection of packages, this creates some confusion. In this book, the term software groups will be used, as this is the term used in the Solaris 7 Advanced Installation Guide.*

Table 3.1 Solaris 7 software groups.

Software Group	Contents
Core	Required operating system files
End-User System Support	Core plus windowing environments
Developer System Support	End User plus development environment
Entire Distribution	Developer System plus enhanced features
Entire Distribution Plus OEM	Entire Distribution plus third-party hardware drivers; available only for SPARC platforms

Installing Solaris 7

Solaris 7 can be installed in four ways. Two of the methods are interactive: the Solaris Interactive Installation program (SunInstall) and Solaris Web Start. These are objectives for Exam 310-009 and are covered in this chapter. The other two methods are automatic: JumpStart and Custom JumpStart. These are objectives for Exam 310-010 and are covered in Chapter 14.

SunInstall is a text-based interactive installation program that can be used to install the Solaris 7 software but does not support installation of copackaged software. Any copackaged software can be installed using the installation programs provided with the copackaged software after installation of the Solaris 7 software is completed.

Web Start allows installation of Solaris 7 using a Web browser interface instead of the text-based interface used by SunInstall. By default, all Solaris and copackaged software are installed; however, this can be changed to allow specific software to be selected.

Web Start creates a profile that reflects the selected software and then uses the JumpStart utility to read the profile and perform the installation automatically. The JumpStart installation method is described in Chapter 14.

By default, Web Start sets up the system disks, including the root and swap partitions. It also allows the size of the system partitions to be changed and provides access to the Layout File Systems utility to set up other disks. The /opt partition is created automatically for copackaged software. It also allows additional partitions and file systems to be created.

Hardware Requirements

Solaris 7 can be installed on both Sun SPARC platforms and Intel x86 or compatible platforms. The hardware requirements for both are similar.

Solaris 7 On SPARC Hardware

Solaris 7 can be installed on most sun4c, sun4u, and sun4m platform groups. The *Solaris 7 Sun Hardware Platform Guide* should be consulted to determine whether a particular platform is supported along with other devices and peripherals, such as disk drives, CD-ROM drives, tape drives, diskette drives, SCSI/PCI host adapters, graphic accelerators, network interfaces, and board/mouse components.

In addition, the Flash PROM on some sun4u platforms might need to be upgraded. The *Solaris 7 Sun Hardware Platform Guide* provides a procedure for determining whether the Flash PROM for a particular system needs to be upgraded and another procedure for updating the Flash PROM.

Solaris 7 requires a minimum of 64MB of memory. The recommended space for the smallest Solaris 7 software group (End User System with 32-bit support) is 438MB of hard disk space. For the largest software group (Entire Distribution Plus OEM with 64-bit support), 909MB of hard disk space is required. Use of at least a 1 GB hard disk is recommended. Installing the system by using Web Start requires a minimum of 48MB of memory and 2GB of hard disk space. Either a CD-ROM drive or the appropriate environment for a network installation is required.

Solaris 7 On Intel Hardware

Solaris 7 can be installed on most 486DX or better Intel-compatible CPUs, including AMD and Cyrix processors. The *Solaris 7 (Intel Platform Edition) Hardware Compatibility List* should be consulted to determine whether a particular CPU is supported along with other devices and peripherals, such as system buses, disk drives, CD-ROM drives, tape drives, diskette drives, SCSI/PCI host adapters, graphic accelerators, network interfaces, and board/mouse components.

Solaris 7 requires a minimum of 32MB of memory, but 64MB is recommended. The recommended space for the smallest Solaris 7 software group (End User System with 32-bit support) is 438MB of hard disk space. For the largest software group (Entire Distribution), 895MB of hard disk space is recommended. Installing the system by using Web Start requires a minimum of 48MB of memory and 2GB of hard disk space. Either a CD-ROM drive or the appropriate environment for a network installation is required.

Upgrading An Existing System To Solaris 7

Upgrading a system allows you to merge the existing system configuration with the new Solaris 7 operating system. However, planning and sometimes intervention might be required to accomplish the upgrade successfully.

 SunInstall and custom JumpStart (see Chapter 14) can be used to upgrade a system. Web Start and the standard JumpStart cannot be used to upgrade an existing system.

Before The Upgrade

There are a number of tasks you should complete before you upgrade your system:

1. Check the Solaris Release Notes to determine whether any Solaris 7 changes or enhancements affect the current operation. This includes software that might no longer be provided with Solaris or patches that might need to be installed.

2. Verify that the hardware is supported, as described in the previous section.

3. Install Solaris either using a CD-ROM or via the network. Depending on the method, verify either the proper operation of the CD-ROM drive or network connectivity.

4. Some Sun applications, such as DiskSuite, cannot be upgraded automatically. Manual configuration changes are required before the software can be used. Check the documentation provided with the applications.

5. If any third-party software is installed on the system, check with the software manufacturer to verify that the software will run on Solaris 7. It might be necessary to purchase new versions of third-party software.

6. Back up the existing system. If the upgrade fails, it might be necessary to restore to the original system until the reasons for failure can be determined and resolved.

7. Collect any configuration information that might be prompted for during the upgrade, such as hostname, network interface, IP address, subnet mask, and domain name. The need to respond to prompts during installation can be avoided by preconfiguring system configuration information.

8. Set up a backup medium for possible use during the upgrade. In the event that disk space needs to be reallocated, file systems will need to be copied to a backup medium, then reloaded after the space on the system disk(s) has been adjusted. Local devices, such as an unused system disk, a tape, or a diskette, along with remote files systems, can be used for the backup medium.

9. If using the Solaris 7 distribution CD, insert the CD in the system CD-ROM drive. For x86 platforms, also insert the Device Configuration Assistant diskette into the A: drive. If installation is to be performed over the network, set up an install server and possibly a boot server.

10. Reboot the system.

During The Upgrade

If the current layout of the system disks does not provide enough space for the upgrade, the Solaris Interactive Installation (SunInstall) will use the auto-layout feature to reallocate disk space as required. If the auto-layout fails or a different layout is desired, the disk layout must be manually specified.

If the system configuration information was not preconfigured, you will need to provide the appropriate information when prompted.

After The Upgrade

Merging of the existing system configuration with the Solaris 7 operating system might not have been completely successful, and it might be necessary to perform some manual cleanup. Check the /a/var/sadm/system/data/ upgrade_clean file to determine any configuration problems that need to be reviewed and possibly modified before the system can be rebooted.

After resolving any cleanup issues, reboot the system.

Installing An Initial Solaris 7 System

Installing Solaris 7 is similar for both SPARC and x86 platforms. This procedure describes how to perform an installation on a standalone workstation or server.

Before Installation

Before you begin your installation, perform the following steps:

1. If appropriate, back up the existing system.

2. Check that the hardware components are supported.

3. Verify that the system has enough disk space, and add more disk space if required.

4. Decide whether to use the default disk layout or to plan a custom disk layout.

5. Decide whether to supply system configuration information when prompted or to preconfigure system configuration information. This information includes hostname, network interface, IP address, subnet mask, and domain name.

6. If using the Solaris 7 distribution CD, insert the CD in the system CD-ROM drive. For x86 platforms, also insert the Device Configuration Assistant diskette into the A: drive. If installation is to be performed over the network, set up an install server and possibly a boot server.

7. Reboot the system.

For SPARC platforms, enter the appropriate command at the **ok** prompt, depending on the desired installation program and the Solaris boot device (source of Solaris software):

➤ For network install using Web Start—**boot net - browser**

➤ For CD install using Web Start—**boot cdrom - browser**

➤ For network install using SunInstall—**boot net**

➤ For CD install using SunInstall—**boot cdrom**

For x86 platforms, select NET, DISK, or CD as the Solaris boot device. Then select either Solaris Interactive (SunInstall) or Solaris Web Start as the installation program, and wait for booting to complete.

During Installation

If prompted, enter the appropriate system configuration information. Follow the instructions displayed on the screen to finish installation.

After Installation

If you are using SunInstall, and if space was allocated for diskless clients or AutoClients, use Solstice Host Manager to complete the client setup.

Preconfiguring System Configuration Information

Preconfiguring the system configuration information required for installation can be done in two ways: the name service method or the sysidcfg file method:

➤ *Name service method*—This method adds the system information to an available name service (NIS or NIS+). During installation, the information is retrieved from the name service and used to configure the system. This is the recommended method for SPARC installations.

➤ *Sysidcfg method*—This method creates a file named sysidcfg that contains the configuration information. The file must conform to a defined format (keywords and syntax). The file must be available on a local drive, and the local diskette drive on the remote drive must be accessible via the network.

Over-The-Network Installation

Typically, a system is installed with the Solaris 7 distribution CD using a local CD-ROM drive. However, software can be installed over the network if the appropriate systems are set up. These systems are:

➤ *Install server*—A server created by copying the contents of the Solaris 7 distribution CD to its disk drive or that has the distribution CD available in its CD-ROM drive.

➤ *Boot server*—A server used for installing clients that are located on a different subnet than the install server. The boot server should be located on the same subnet as the clients.

Systems to be installed over the network are set up either by using Solstice Host Manager to add (preconfigure) information about the systems to NIS/NIS+ or by adding the information to configuration files of an install server or boot server.

Software Package Administration

Both Sun Microsystems and third-party vendors deliver software as easily manipulated collections of files and executable installation/removal procedures referred to as *packages*.

Software packages can be installed on or removed from standalone systems or servers in a fairly straightforward manner, as both the root and /usr file systems are local.

Package Tools

Solaris 7 package tools provide a convenient mechanism for installing and removing packaged software. These are standard Unix commands and are accessible through the shell command line interface. In addition, the system administration tool, **admintool**, provides a graphical user interface (GUI) for installing and removing packages.

The most commonly used command line package tools are:

➤ pkgadd—Used to install packages

➤ pkginfo *and* pkgparam—Used to display information about packages

➤ pkgrm—Used to remove a package

➤ pkgchk—Used to check the proper installation of a package

Installing A Package Using The **pkgadd** Command

The **pkgadd** command can install a package from disk or CD-ROM. Typically, software obtained through the network or from magnetic tape or diskette is copied into a spool directory on the system before installation. The default package spool directory is /var/spool/pkg, but any location with adequate free space can be used.

To install one or more packages located in the default spool directory using the **pkgadd** command, only the package names need to be specified as command line arguments. For example, to install the SUNWast package, the following command is used:

```
# pkgadd SUNWast

Processing package instance <SUNWast> from </var/spool/pkg>
Automated Security Enhancement Tools
(i386) 11.7.0,REV=1998.09.01.04.53
Copyright 1998 Sun Microsystems, Inc. All rights reserved.
Using </> as the package base directory.
## Processing package information.
## Processing system information.
1 package pathname is already properly installed.
## Verifying package dependencies.
## Verifying disk space requirements.
## Checking for conflicts with packages already installed.
## Checking for setuid/setgid programs.

This package contains scripts which will execute with super-user
permission during the process of installing this package.

Do you want to continue with installation of <SUNWast> [y,n,?] y

Installing Automated Security Enhancement Tools as <SUNWast>
## Installing part 1 of 1.
Installation of <SUNWast> was successful.
#
```

If a package was spooled onto the system into a different directory, the alternate spool directory is specified using the -d command line argument. For example, if the /tmp directory was used to spool the SUNWast package onto the system, use the following command to install the package:

```
pkgadd -d /tmp SUNWast
```

To install a package located on a CD-ROM, the -d command line argument is used to specify the pathname to the CD-ROM drive. For example, the **pkgadd** command can be used to install package SUNWast from a CD-ROM mounted at /cdrom/cdrom0.

```
pkgadd -d /cdrom/cdrom0 SUNWast
```

Actually, the **pkgadd** command does not require the name of a package. If no package name is specified, the **pkgadd** command will prompt with a list of packages that are available in the specified spool directory or on the CD-ROM.

The -s command line argument is used to spool a package into a spool directory instead of installing it. The following command will spool the SUNWast package in from CD-ROM to the /var/spool/pkg directory.

```
pkgadd -s /var/spool/pkg -d /cdrom/cdrom0 SUNWast
```

When using the default spool directory, just the phrase *spool* can be specified with the -s command line argument.

Installing A Package Using **admintool**

After starting **admintool**, select Software from the Browse pull-down menu. The Software window is displayed as shown in Figure 3.1.

To install a package, select Add from the Edit pull-down menu. The Set Source Media window is displayed to allow selection of either CD-ROM or Hard Disk. Figure 3.2 shows the Set Source Media Software Location set to CD With Volume Management. The other choices are CD Without Volume Management and Hard Disk. If a CD-ROM is being used, fill in the appropriate CD Path.

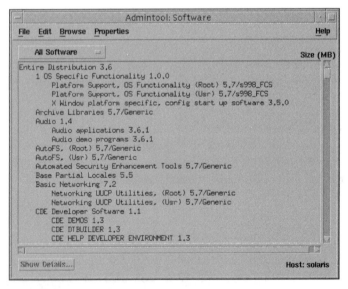

Figure 3.1   The Admintool: Software window.

Figure 3.2   The Admintool: Set Source Media (CD-ROM) window.

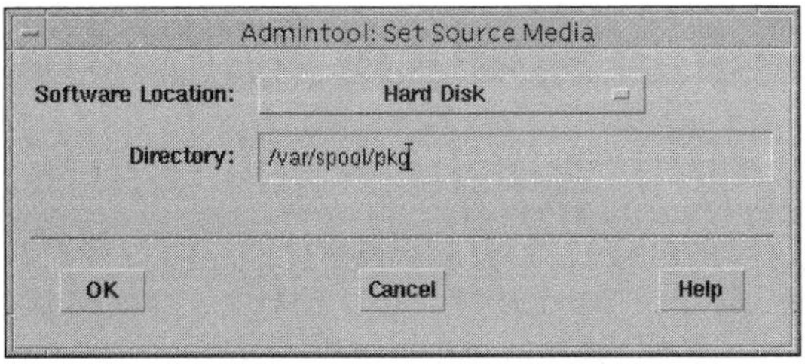

Figure 3.3   The Admintool: Set Source Media (Hard Disk) window.

If the package has been spooled onto disk, change the Software Location selection to Hard Disk (as shown in Figure 3.3) and specify the spool directory if necessary.

After selecting the appropriate source media, click on OK. The Add Software window is displayed as shown in Figure 3.4.

The available packages on the CD-ROM or in the spool directory are listed. Figure 3.4 shows two packages in the /var/spool/pkg directory: Netscape Communicator and the Automated Security Enhancement Tools. To install one or more packages, select the checkbox to the left of the package title and click on the Add button. **admintool** calls the **pkgadd** command and opens a window to display the results.

Obtaining Package Information Using The **pkginfo** Command

The **pkginfo** command with no command line arguments displays a list of installed packages. The following example shows a partial listing of installed packages:

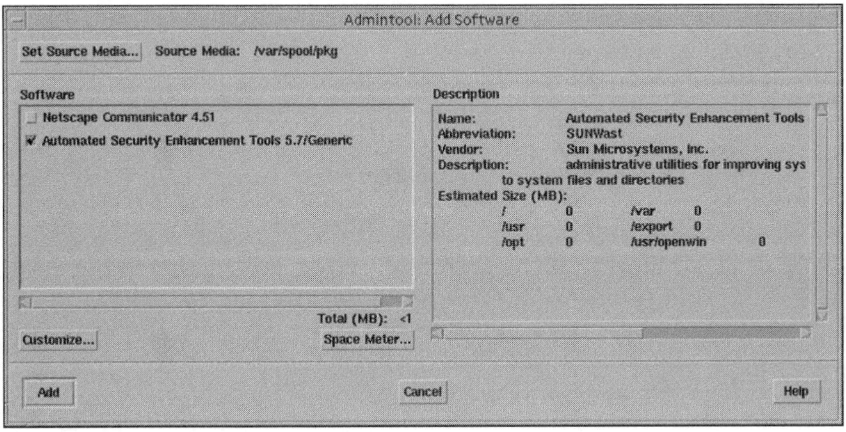

Figure 3.4   Admintool: Add Software window.

```
# pkginfo
system        NCRos86r  NCR Platform Support, OS Functionality (Root)
.
.
.
system        SUNWadmr  System & Network Administration Root
application SUNWakcs  KCMS Collection
application SUNWaman  Solaris 7 Reference Manual Collection
system        SUNWapppr PPP/IP Daemon configuration files
system        SUNWapppu PPP/IP Demon and PPP login service
system        SUNWarc   Archive Libraries
system        SUNWarrf  X11 Arabic required fonts
system        SUNWast   Automated Security Enhancement Tools
system        SUNWatfsr AutoFS, (Root)
system        SUNWatfsu AutoFS, (Usr)
system        SUNWaudio Audio applications
system        SUNWaudmo Audio demo programs
system        SUNWbnur  Networking UUCP Utilities, (Root)
system        SUNWbnuu  Networking UUCP Utilities, (Usr)
.
.
.
#
```

Each software package includes a file named pkginfo that contains various information about the package. It is also used to store information generated during and after installation, such as installation date and a list of any patches applied to the package. To view the contents of the pkginfo file for a particular package, use the **pkginfo** command and specify the -l command line argument along with the name of the package. For example, to display the pkginfo file for the SUNWast package, use the following **pkginfo** command:

```
# pkginfo -l SUNWast
   PKGINST:  SUNWast
      NAME:  Automated Security Enhancement Tools
  CATEGORY:  system
      ARCH:  i386
   VERSION:  11.7.0,REV=1998.09.01.04.53
   BASEDIR:  /
    VENDOR:  Sun Microsystems, Inc.
      DESC:  administrative utilities for improving system
             security by monitoring or restricting access to
             system files and directories
    PSTAMP:  kapow19980901051652
  INSTDATE:  Dec 19 1998 20:14
```

```
HOTLINE:  Please contact your local service provider
 STATUS:  completely installed
  FILES:     40 installed pathnames
             1 shared pathnames
             8 directories
            28 executables
           227 blocks used (approx)
#
```

Obtaining Package Information
Using **admintool**

The same information obtained from the **pkginfo** command can also be obtained using the **admintool** utility. To display a list of installed packages, select Software from the Browse pull-down menu. For a sample list, see Figure 3.1.

To view selected contents of the pkginfo file for a particular package, highlight the package name in the list and click on the Show Details button. The Software Details window is displayed (see Figure 3.5).

 The pkginfo file, along with other package-related files for each installed package, is located under the /var/sadm/pkg directory in subdirectories with the same name as the packages.

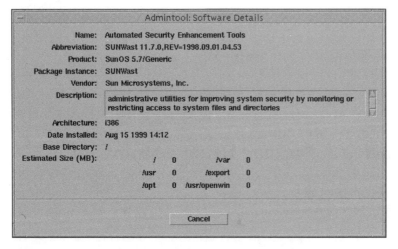

Figure 3.5   The Admintool: Software Details window.

Removing A Package Using The **pkgrm** Command

The **pkgrm** command is used to remove installed packages. To remove one or more packages, only the package name needs to be specified as a command line argument. For example, to remove the SUNWast package, the following command is used:

```
# pkgrm SUNWast

The following package is currently installed:
   SUNWast         Automated Security Enhancement Tools
                   (i386) 11.7.0,REV=1998.09.01.04.53

Do you want to remove this package? y

## Removing installed package instance <SUNWast>
## Verifying package dependencies.
## Processing package information.
## Removing pathnames in class <none>
/usr/aset/util/taskstat
/usr/aset/util/str_to_mode
.
.
.
/usr/aset/asetenv
/usr/aset/aset.restore
/usr/aset/aset
/usr/aset/archives
/usr/aset
/usr <shared pathname not removed>
## Updating system information.

Removal of <SUNWast> was successful.
#
```

Removing A Package Using **admintool**

An installed package can also be removed using the **admintool** utility. First, to display a list of installed packages, select Software from the Browse pull-down menu. For a sample list, see Figure 3.1.

To delete a package, highlight the package name in the list and select Delete from the Edit pull-down menu. A Warning window is displayed to confirm removal of the package (see Figure 3.6). Click on the Delete button to delete the package. **admintool** calls the **pkgrm** command and opens a window to display the results.

Figure 3.6   The Admintool: Warning window.

Patch Administration

A patch is a collection of files intended to update or fix problems with installed software. For example, a patch might be required to fix Year 2000 (Y2K) problems or address a security issue. Because most system and application software is installed as packages, patches are applied against one or more packages. Actually, patches are special packages that are used to update other packages. Like packages, a collection of patches can be grouped together into a patch cluster.

The ability to obtain and install patches, keep track of installed patches, and occasionally remove patches are key skills of a competent system administrator.

Obtaining Patches And Patch Information

Patches can be obtained from Sun Microsystems in several ways. The two most common methods are by purchasing a service contract from Sun or by downloading the patches yourself from Sun's Web or FTP site.

Sun Service customers have access to an online patch database and an extended set of patches. The patches can be downloaded from Sun's Web site or FTP site. In addition, Sun Service customers receive a CD-ROM of patches every six to eight weeks.

For everyone else, recommended and security patches for supported systems can be obtained on the Web at **sunsolve.sun.com** or through anonymous FTP from **sunsolve1.sun.com/pubs/patches**.

 Sun provides a bimonthly report that summarizes recommended and security patches for each supported system. Like the patches, the information is available at **sunsolve.sun.com**, along with other system support information.

Patches are identified with an eight-digit number. The first six digits identify the base patch, and the last two digits identify the revision. For example, patch number 107588-01 is the Y2K update for the x86 version of Solaris 7.

Installing A Patch

Patches are installed using the **patchadd** command. The appropriate type of system configuration must be specified using a **patchadd** command line argument. It might also be necessary to specify a target directory. In addition, a single **patchadd** command can be used to install more than one patch.

Regardless of the type of system configuration being patched, the **patchadd** command is typically executed locally on the system where the software being patched resides (target directory). However, patches can be installed remotely over the network if the target directory can be accessed through Network File System (NFS) services.

If the patch is on a CD-ROM, it can be installed directly from the CD-ROM. A patch downloaded from the Sun Web or FTP site must reside on a system hard disk. This area where patches are stored before they are installed is referred to as the *spool directory*.

 Although patches have no required spool directory, the most commonly used location is the /var/spool/patch directory. However, anywhere on the system where adequate free space exists can be used.

If a patch was obtained via download, chances are good that the patch is zipped (compressed) to make it easier and quicker to download. Some patches (mainly for SPARC platforms) are compressed using the **gzip** command and have file names that end with the .gz suffix. Others (mainly for Intel x86 platforms) are compressed using the **zip** command and have file names that end with the .zip suffix. For example, to unzip the x86 Y2K patch (107588-01), which is located in the current directory, use the **unzip** command as shown in the following listing:

```
unzip 107588-01.zip
```

A subdirectory with the same name as the patch will be created under the current directory and the unzipped files placed in this subdirectory.

The **patchadd** command is then used to install a patch. Because patches have no default spool directory, the full pathname to the patch must be specified as a command line argument. The following example shows the installation of the x86 Y2K patch on a standalone system:

```
# patchadd /var/spool/patch/107588-01
Checking installed patches...

Verifying sufficient filesystem capacity (dry run method)...
Installing patch packages...
Patch number 107588-01 has been successfully installed.
See /var/sadm/patch/107588-01/log for details
Patch packages installed:
SUNWaccu
```

Note that the patch modified the SUNWaccu package (system accounting and reporting utilities). The **patchadd** command is actually a ksh script that calls the **pkgadd** command to install the patch.

To apply a patch to the bootable root image of a diskless client or AutoClient, use the -**R** command line argument and specify the path to the client's root image. For example, applying the Solaris 7 x86 Y2K patch to a diskless client that uses a root image stored under the /export/root/client on the current system requires the following command:

```
patchadd -R /export/root/client /var/spool/patch/107588-01
```

To apply a patch to an operating system (OS) service, use the -**S** command line argument and specify the service. For example, applying the Solaris 7 Y2K patch to an x86 Solaris 7 OS service named Solaris_7x86 on the OS server requires the following command:

```
patchadd -S Solaris_7x86 /var/spool/patch/107588-01
```

To apply a patch to an install server configuration, use the -**C** command line argument and specify the pathname to the install server image. For example, applying the Solaris 7 Y2K patch to an x86 Solaris 7 image named Solaris_7x86 on an install server requires the following command:

```
patchadd -C /export/Solaris_7x86/Tools/Boot
    /var/spool/patch/107588-01
```

Multiple patches can be installed by specifying a directory where all the patches are located along with a list of the patch numbers. For example, to install patches 106542-05, 106794-01, and 106961-01 that are all located in the /var/spool/ patch directory, the following command can be used:

```
patchadd -M /var/spool/patch 106542-05 106794-01 106961-01
```

Instead of listing a large number of patches on the command line, a text file can be created that contains a list of patches. The name of the text file can then be specified on the command line in place of all the individual patch names.

For example, to install the 106542-05, 106794-01, and 106961-01 patches located in the /var/spool/patch directory; create a text file with the name /var/spool/patch/patchlist that contains the name of the three patches (separated by spaces or returns). Then use the following command to install the patches:

```
patchadd -M /var/spool/patch /var/spool/patch/patchlist
```

The **-M** command line argument can be used to install patches for client, services, or install servers by specifying the previously described **-R**, **-S**, or **-C** command line arguments. This should be specified after the -M patch spool directory and patch names or patch list command line arguments.

By default, any files that will be changed by installing the patch are copied to one or more backup directories. This allows the patch to be removed and the system returned to its original state; that is, before the patch was installed. However, if the **-d** command line argument is specified on the **patchadd** command, the files are not backed up, and the patch cannot be removed.

The default backup directories are located under /var/sadm/pkg and are based on the installed package or packages being modified by the patch and the patch number. For example, the x86 Y2K patch (107588-01) modified the SUNWaccu package. Any files changed by installing this patch will be saved under the /var/sadm/pkg/SUNWaccu/107588-01 directory. A different backup directory can be specified by using the **-B** command line argument.

The **patchadd** command will fail if any of the following occur:

➤ A package being patched is not installed or is only partially installed.

➤ The patch requires another patch that is not installed.

➤ The patch is incompatible with another patch already installed.

➤ The current version or a higher version of the patch is already installed.

➤ The architecture of the patch and the system do not match.

 After unzipping a patch, the zip file can be deleted to save space. Likewise, after installing a patch, the files associated with the patch in the patch spool directory can be deleted to save space.

Determining Installed Patches

Two commands can be used to generate a list of installed patches for a standalone system:

➤   showrev -p

➤   patchadd -p

Both commands generate almost identical lists. The following example illustrates the use of the **showrev** command (the output is formatted for readability):

```
$ showrev -p
Patch: 106542-05
        Obsoletes: 106914-04, 106977-01, 107440-01
        Requires:
        Incompatibles:
        Packages: SUNWkvm, SUNWcsu, SUNWcsr, SUNWcsl, SUNWcar,
                  SUNWesu, SUNWarc, SUNWatfsr, SUNWdpl, SUNWhea,
                  SUNWtoo, SUNWpcmci, SUNWtnfc, SUNWvolr
Patch: 106794-01
        Obsoletes:
        Requires:
        Incompatibles:
        Packages: SUNWcsu, SUNWhea
$
```

When a patch is installed, information regarding the patch is added to the pkginfo files of the package(s) that are updated by the patch. The pkginfo files are located in subdirectories under the /var/sadm/pkg directory. The **showrev** and **patchadd** commands extract and format information from the pkginfo files. In addition to the patch number and the package(s) that the patch updates, any appropriate dependency information, such as other required patches or incompatible patches, are listed.

The **patchadd** command can be used to display a list of installed patches for other system configurations using the -C, -R, and -S command line arguments, as previously described. For example, to display the patches applied to an OS service named Solaris7x86, the following **patchadd** command can be used:

```
patchadd -S solaris7x86 -p
```

A list of patches applied to a particular package can be displayed by using the **pkgparam** command. The following example lists the patches applied to the SUNWaccu package:

```
$ pkgparam SUNWaccu PATCHLIST
107588-01
$
```

Removing A Patch

The **patchrm** command is used to remove or back out a patch. The system configurations supported by the **patchadd** command are also supported by the **patchrm** command. The same -**C**, -**R**, and -**S** command line arguments, as previously described, are used. For example, to remove patch 106961-01 from the bootable root image of a diskless client named client5, the following **patchrm** command can be used:

```
patchrm -R /export/root/client5 106961-01
```

Because the default backup directory could have been changed during installation using the -**B** command line argument to the **patchadd** command, the **patchrm** command also supports the -**B** argument.

In addition, the **patchrm** command can be forced to remove a patch that has been superseded by another patch by using the -**f** command line argument.

Installed patches can be removed and the system returned to the state it was in before the patch was installed as long as the following conditions are met:

➤ The patch is not required by another patch or has been made obsolete by a later patch.

➤ The patch was not installed using **patchadd -d**, which informs **patchadd** not to save a copy of files before they are updated or replaced.

Practice Questions

Question 1

Which of the following can be used to install multiple patches? [Select all that apply]

❑ a. **patchadd -M /var/spool/patch 104567-03 106583-10 103276-04**

❑ b. Use **patchadd** to install each patch separately

❑ c. **patchadd -M /var/spool/patch patchlist**

All the answers are correct and can be used to install multiple patches. Answer a would install three patches located in the /var/spool/patch directory. Answer c uses a file named patchlist that contains a list of patches to install. Of course the **patchadd** command can be used to install several patches, one at a time (answer b).

Question 2

Which of the following can be used to install packages? [Select all that apply]

❑ a. **admintool**

❑ b. **pkgtool**

❑ c. **pkgadd**

❑ d. **pkgrm**

❑ e. **pkginfo**

The correct answers are a and c. **pkgtool** does not exist. Therefore, answer b is incorrect. **pkgrm** is used to remove packages, and **pkginfo** is used to display information about packages. Therefore, answers d and e are incorrect.

Question 3

> What are the two most commonly used methods for installing Solaris 7?
>
> ❑ a. Tape
>
> ❑ b. CD-ROM
>
> ❑ c. Network
>
> ❑ d. Diskette
>
> ❑ e. Web

The correct answers are b and c. A tape and a diskette are valid boot devices but are not used for installation. Therefore answers a and d are incorrect. Answer e, the Web, is not feasible.

Question 4

> Which of the following is the default spool directory for packages?
>
> ○ a. /var/spool
>
> ○ b. /var/sadm/pkg
>
> ○ c. /tmp
>
> ○ d. /var/spool/pkg

The correct answer is d. Answer a is the system spool directory. Answer b is the directory that contains information about installed packages. Answer c is the temporary directory.

Question 5

> Solaris 7 *cannot* be installed on which of the following?
>
> ○ a. Macintosh system
>
> ○ b. Sun SPARC
>
> ○ c. Intel x86
>
> ○ d. AMD or Cyrix x86 compatibles

The correct answer is a. Solaris 7 can be installed on Sun SPARC, Intel x86, or Intel x86 compatibles (AMD and Cyrix). Therefore, answers b, c, and d are incorrect.

Question 6

Which commands will display selected information from the SUNWast pkginfo file? [Select all that apply]

- ❏ a. **pkginfo SUNWast**
- ❏ b. **pkginfo –I SUNWast**
- ❏ c. **display pkginfo SUNWast**
- ❏ d. Highlighting SUNWast in the Admintool Software window and clicking on Show Details

The correct answers are a, b, and d. Although the command in answer a provides only package title and type of software, the pkginfo file is the only place this information can be obtained from. Answer c does not exist.

Question 7

Which of the following commands can be used to remove a patch?

- ○ a. **rmpatch**
- ○ b. **patchrm**
- ○ c. **pkgrm -p**
- ○ d. **patchadd -d**

The correct answer is b. Answer a (**rmpatch**) is not a valid command. Answer c (**pkgrm**) is used to remove packages (and no -p command line argument exists). Answer d (**patchadd -d**) is used to add a patch without saving files before they are updated or replaced.

Question 8

Which of the following commands can be used to list all installed patches? [Select all that apply]

- ❏ a. **showrev -p**
- ❏ b. **patchinfo**
- ❏ c. **patchlist all**
- ❏ d. **patchadd -p**

The correct answers are a and d. Answers b and c do not exist.

Question 9

During an upgrade, the disk space needs to be reallocated. Which of the following can be used as the backup media? [Select all that apply]

❑ a. Unused system disk

❑ b. Tape

❑ c. Diskette

❑ d. CD-ROM

❑ e. Remote file system

The correct answers are a, b, c, and e. All of these media can be used as the backup media during an upgrade, assuming that they provide enough storage space. A CD-ROM, as the name implies, is read-only (Compact Disk–Read Only Media). Read-only media cannot be used for backup. Therefore, answer d is incorrect. On the other hand, a writable CD could probably be used, but it was not provided as a choice.

Need To Know More?

Sun Microsystems, *Solaris 7 (Intel Platform Edition) 5/99 Hardware Compatibility List*, is available in printed form (ISBN 806-0269-10), on the Web at **docs.sun.com**, and from online system documentation, AnswerBook2, provided with the Solaris 7 operating system.

Sun Microsystems, *Solaris 7 3/99 Sun Hardware Platform Guide*, is available in printed form (ISBN 806-7391-10), on the Web at **docs.sun.com**, and from online system documentation, AnswerBook2, provided with the Solaris 7 operating system.

Sun Microsystems, *Solaris 7 Reference Manual, Section 1M - User Commands*, is available in printed form (ISBN 805-3172-10), on the Web at **docs.sun.com**, and from online system documentation, AnswerBook2, provided with the Solaris 7 operating system.

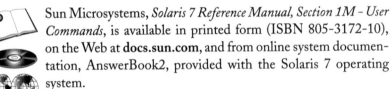

Sun Microsystems, *Solaris 7 Reference Manual, Section 1 - System Administration Commands*, is available in printed form (ISBN 805-3173-10), on the Web at **docs.sun.com**, and from online system documentation, AnswerBook2, provided with the Solaris 7 operating system.

Sun Microsystems, *Solaris 7 System Administration Guide, Volume 1*, is available in printed form (ISBN 805-3727-10), on the Web at **docs.sun.com**, and from online system documentation, AnswerBook2, provided with the Solaris 7 operating system.

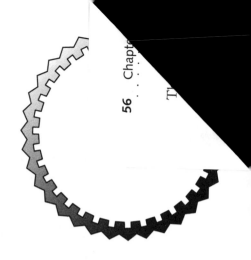

Booting And Shutting Down The System

. . . .

Terms you'll need to understand:

√ OpenBoot

√ Nonvolatile RAM (NVRAM)

√ Device aliases

√ The init program

√ Kernel modules

√ The boot process

√ System run levels

√ The rc scripts

Techniques you'll need to master:

√ Creating and deleting a device alias

√ Troubleshooting boot problems

√ Changing system run levels

√ Adding system services using rc scripts

This chapter addresses three topics related to booting and shutting down the system. The first section covers key aspects of the system firmware on Sun SPARC platforms. The second section summarizes the boot process for both SPARC and Intel x86 platforms. The third section describes system run levels, the services available at the different run levels, and how to change between the run levels. Also included is a description of how to add custom services at a selected run level.

The Boot PROM Firmware (OpenBoot)

The boot Programmable Read-Only Memory (PROM) of a system is used to store the firmware that is executed immediately after the system hardware finishes the Power On Self Test (POST). This firmware is called OpenBoot and is the standard firmware for Sun Systems. OpenBoot firmware pertains only to SPARC platforms, but some limited functionality is available on Intel x86 platforms.

OpenBoot is used to boot the operating system, run diagnostics, modify boot-related parameters stored in nonvolatile RAM (NVRAM), and provide a Forth interpreter.

Currently, two supported versions of OpenBoot are available: version 2.x and version 3.x. OpenBoot 2.x was introduced with SPARCstation 2 and SPARCstation IPX systems. OpenBoot 3.x is an enhanced version OpenBoot 2.x and is based on IEEE Standard 1275-1994, Standard for Boot Firmware. OpenBoot 3.x is used on Sun Ultra series and newer SPARC platforms.

OpenBoot provides a command line interface for the system console. The command line interface has two modes:

➤ *Restricted Monitor*—Allows the administrator to boot the operating system, continue a suspended operation, or start the Forth Monitor. The prompt for the Restricted Monitor is the ">" symbol.

➤ *Forth Monitor*—Allows the administrator to boot the operating system, run diagnostics, and modify system configuration parameters. The prompt for the Forth Monitor is the word "ok" and is typically referred to as the *OpenBoot prompt*.

System configuration parameters are stored in the system NVRAM. These parameters determine the initial configuration and related communication characteristics of the system and retain their value even if the power to the system is shut off.

The value of these parameters can be viewed using the OpenBoot **printenv** command and modified by using the OpenBoot **setenv** command.

Important OpenBoot Commands

Some of the more important OpenBoot commands are used to display system configuration information, perform hardware testing, and control the system booting. All these commands are entered at the Forth Monitor or OpenBoot **ok** prompt.

Table 4.1 lists the OpenBoot commands that are used to display system configuration data, and Table 4.2 lists the OpenBoot commands that are used to perform basic hardware testing. Table 4.3 lists the variations of the OpenBoot **boot** command that are used to select different boot devices.

Table 4.1	OpenBoot commands for displaying system configuration data.
Command	**Description**
banner	Displays the power-on banner
devalias	Lists all device aliases
.enet-addr	Displays Ethernet address
.idprom	Displays formatted ID PROM contents
module-info	Displays CPU speed (multiprocessor 2.x only)
printenv	Lists all NVRAM parameters and default values
show-devs	Lists installed devices
.speed	Displays CPU and bus speeds (3.x only)
.traps	Lists types of SPARC traps
.version	Displays boot PROM version and data

Table 4.2	OpenBoot commands for performing hardware testing.
Command	**Description**
pcia-probe-list	Test PCI
probe-scsi	Tests built-in SCSI for connected devices
probe-scsi all	Tests all SCSI buses
test-all	Tests a group of install devices
test floppy	Tests diskette drive

(continued)

Table 4.2	OpenBoot commands for performing hardware testing (continued).
Command	**Description**
test /memory	Tests system memory
test net	Tests the on-board Ethernet interface
watch-clock	Monitors system clock
watch-net	Monitors network connection

Table 4.3	OpenBoot commands for selecting different boot devices.
Command	**Description**
boot cdrom	Boots from the local CD-ROM
boot disk	Boots from the default hard disk
boot floppy	Boots from the diskette drive
boot net	Boots from the network
boot tape	Boots from the SCSI tape drive

The **boot** command supports a couple of options that might be useful. The -a option requests an interactive boot so that information will be prompted for when needed. In addition, the -s option causes booting to single-user mode instead of the default system run level. When booting from the hard disk, the default device is specified by the boot-device NVRAM configuration parameter. From the OpenBoot **ok** prompt, use the following command to display the default device:

```
ok printenv boot-device
boot-device = disk
ok
```

The default device can be changed as required. For example, to change the default boot device to a device with the alias of **disk2**, use the following command. Then use **reset** to save the new value and reboot:

```
ok setenv boot-device disk2
ok reset
```

Device Aliases

OpenBoot identifies system hardware using a full device pathname that represents the type of device and its location in the system. A device pathname consists of system buses, addresses, and possibly driver names. The following is an example of a full device name for a partition of a SCSI disk drive:

```
/sbus@1f,0/SUNW,fas@e,8800000/sd@3,0:a
```

For more details on device names, see Chapter 8. Because device names are typically long, complex, and awkward to enter, OpenBoot provides the ability to assign a short, easy-to-remember-and-type name or device alias to a full device name.

Creating A Device Alias

A device alias can be created in two ways. The first method uses the **devalias** command. Aliases created with this command are lost when the system is rebooted. The second method uses the **nvalias** command. Aliases created with this command are stored in nonvolatile memory and remain there until removed by the use of other OpenBoot commands. Both commands use the same syntax.

For example, both of the following commands, entered at the OpenBoot **ok** prompt, will assign the alias disk2 to the device named /sbus/esp/sd@2,0 which is a SCSI disk:

```
ok devalias disk2 /sbus/esp/sd@2,0
ok nvalias disk2 /sbus/esp/sd@2,0
ok
```

Whenever the device name is required in the OpenBoot environment, the alias can be used instead.

> *Note: Because the Solaris 7 certification requirements specifically address the use of **nvalias**, the remainder of this section will concentrate on it— but remember that an alias can also be defined using **devalias**.*

When the **nvalias** command is entered, it is actually stored in nonvolatile memory. This portion of memory is treated as an OpenBoot parameter called the **nvramrc** parameter. The contents of the nvramrc parameter are called the *script*. In addition to storing user-defined commands, this parameter is used by device drivers to save startup configuration variables, to patch device driver code, and to store bug patches or other installation-specific device configuration information.

If the OpenBoot **use-nvramrc** parameter is set to **true**, the script is executed during system boot. Any aliases defined in **nvramrc** using the **nvalias** command will be set, and then the aliases can be used in a later part of the script or as the value of one or more other OpenBoot parameters.

Deleting A Device Alias

An alias defined by the **nvalias** command is stored in the script and remains there until it is removed by using the **nvunalias** command, or until the system configuration is restored to its original defaults using the **set-defaults** command.

For example, to delete the device alias **disk2**, which was stored in the script, enter the following command at the OpenBoot **ok** prompt:

```
ok nvunalias disk2
ok
```

 When deleting an alias, be certain that the alias is not used anywhere; otherwise, a possibly critical system parameter might become undefined.

Viewing And Modifying NVRAM Parameters From Solaris

Typically, the NRAM parameters are viewed and modified using OpenBoot commands. It is possible to view and modify the NVRAM parameters from the Solaris 7 environment using the **eeprom(1M)** command. However, only the superuser can modify NVRAM parameters using the **eeprom** command.

To view the value of the **auto-boot?** NVRAM parameter, enter the following **eeprom** command at the system prompt:

```
# eeprom auto-boot?
auto-boot?=true
#
```

To view all NVRAM parameters, enter the **eeprom** command without any command line arguments.

The **eeprom** command can also be used to modify a NVRAM parameter. To set the value of **auto-boot?** to **false**, enter the following command at the system prompt:

```
# eeprom auto-boot?=false
#
```

Troubleshooting Boot Problems

When reset or powered on, a SPARC system typically runs the POST. After this, the system boots automatically (if **auto-boot?** is **true**) or enters the Forth Monitor.

The boot process or OpenBoot initialization sequence performs various checks and loads the appropriate modules. Status messages regarding this initialization sequence can be viewed in the /var/adm/messages file after the system has successfully loaded and started the operating system.

However, if a boot problem occurs, the Solaris 7 system will not be started, and the messages cannot be viewed. To get around this situation, OpenBoot has the ability to send the initialization sequence messages to tty serial port A (TTYA). This is accomplished by setting the **diag-switch?** OpenBoot parameter to **true** and using the **setenv** command before starting the system boot, as in the following example:

```
ok setenv diag-switch? true
ok
```

By attaching a terminal or PC to TTYA, the messages generated by the OpenBoot initialization sequence can be observed and the boot problem identified.

Emergency Keyboard Commands (SPARC Only)

Sometimes it is necessary to take control over a system regardless of its state. From the keyboard of a SPARC system, it is possible to immediately enter the Forth Monitor. Table 4.4 lists the emergency keyboard commands supported by OpenBoot.

When it is necessary to recover a system that has stopped responding, after the **stop+a** sequence, be sure to enter the OpenBoot **sync** command to synchronize the system disks and write a crash dump before issue the appropriate **boot** command.

Table 4.4 Emergency keyboard commands (SPARC only).	
Sequence	**System Response**
stop	Bypasses the POST
stop+a	Aborts the operating system or boot process (returns to OpenBoot **ok** prompt)
stop+d	Enters diagnostic mode
stop+f	Enters the Forth Monitor on TTYA (instead of the system console)
stop+n	Resets NVRAM contents to default values

The Boot Process

The boot PROM stores firmware that is responsible for booting the operating system. Because the SPARC boot process is somewhat different than the Intel x86 boot process, they are covered separately here.

The SPARC Boot Process

The SPARC boot process consists of the following phases:

1. *Boot PROM*—The Boot PROM phase displays system information and then runs the POST diagnostics. After the completion of the diagnostics, the primary boot program, bootblk, is loaded. Its function is to locate the secondary boot program, ufsboot, on the boot device.

2. *Boot Programs*—In the Boot Programs phase, bootblk loads the ufsboot program into memory and executes it.

3. *Kernel Initialization*—In the Kernel Initialization phase, the ufsboot program loads the core kernel into memory and causes it to execute. The kernel initializes its data structures and begins loading other kernel modules on the basis of the /etc/system file using the ufsboot program. After all the necessary modules are loaded and initialized, the kernel starts the /sbin/init program.

4. *init*—In the init phase, the init program starts other processes on the basis of the information contained in the /etc/inittab file. These include a program that calls the run control (rc) scripts that set up various system services.

The Intel x86 Boot Process

The Intel x86 boot process consists of the following phases:

1. *BIOS*—During the BIOS phase, the POST diagnostics are executed. Then the master boot record, mboot, is read from disk to locate the active partition that contains the pboot program.

2. *Boot Programs*—In the Boot Programs phase, the pboot program is loaded, and in turn locates and loads the primary boot program, bootlbk. Then the secondary boot program, either boot.bin or ufsboot, is located in the root file system and loaded.

3. *Kernel Initialization*—In the Kernel Initialization phase, the boot.bin or ufsboot program loads the core kernel into memory and causes it to execute. The kernel initializes its data structures and begins loading other kernel modules. After all the necessary modules are loaded and initialized, the kernel starts the /sbin/init program.

4. *init*—In the init phase, the init program starts other processes on the basis of the information contained in the /etc/inittab file. These include a program that calls the rc scripts that set up various system services.

Kernel Modules

Kernel software is divided into groups of related functions referred to as *modules*. Some modules are part of a small, common core of the operating system. Some modules provide platform-specific operations, whereas other modules are device drivers. This architecture allows portions of the kernel to be included or excluded on the basis of the desired functionality or allows portions of the kernel to be updated without replacing the entire kernel. The device drivers are loadable or dynamic kernel modules that are loaded when the device is accessed.

The kernel modules are stored in three directories—two under the root file system and one under the /usr file system:

➤ */platform/sparc/kernel for SPARC platforms or /platform/i86pc/kernel for x86 platforms*—This directory is used for modules that are specific to the platform.

➤ */kernel*—This directory is used for common kernel modules required for booting.

➤ */usr/kernel*—This directory is used for common kernel modules used by platforms with a particular instruction set.

The /etc/system file is used to determine which kernel modules are loaded and to define various kernel parameters. The format of this file takes the form of one or more keywords followed by one or more parameters. The supported keywords are:

➤ *exclude*—Prevents modules from loading

➤ *forceload*—Forces a module to load

➤ *moddir*—Changes the common kernel module directories

➤ *rootdev*—Sets the physical pathname to the root device

➤ *rootfs*—Defines the type of root file system

➤ *set*—Sets kernel or module variables

The init Program

The last phase of the boot process is the init program. The init program is used to control system processes and services. Its primary purpose is to create or stop processes on the basis of the current state of the system. The system state is referred to as a *system run level*. Several run levels are defined on the basis of the type of activities that the system should be supporting while at a particular run level, such as maintenance, a single user, multiple users, and so on. Information regarding which processes and services should be running at a particular run level is stored in the /etc/inittab file.

Every run level (except 4) has an entry in the /etc/inittab file that identifies an rc program to execute. In addition, each run level has a directory associated with it, which contains rc scripts that should be executed by the rc program to start or stop processes and services when that run level becomes the current run level.

The init program also sets the default environment variables as defined in /etc/default/init. These include local variables and system parameters based on location, such as time zone.

System Run Levels

To provide a convenient way for the system administrator to shut down or reboot the system and control system services and resources, eight system run levels (also referred to as *init states*) are defined and assigned specific functionality. Table 4.5 describes the eight run levels.

Table 4.5   The eight system run levels.

Run Level	init State	Functionality
0	Power Down	The system is being shut down. All users are forced off the system. All operating system services are stopped in an orderly manner. When complete, the system is at firmware (OpenBoot) mode. It is safe to turn off the power to the system and peripherals.
s or S	Single User	The system is prepared for maintenance. Any users are logged off the system. Any services except the most basic operating system services are stopped in an orderly manner. Any mounted file systems remain mounted. A command line interface (with superuser privileges) is started and associated with the system console. This allows the system administrator to perform maintenance, such as system backup, without interference from users or applications.
1	Administrative	Any logged-on users are not affected. Multiple users can log on and use available system resources. All services except the most basic operating system services are stopped in an orderly manner. Any mounted file systems remain mounted. A command line interface (with superuser privileges) is started and associated with the system console. This allows the system administrator to perform maintenance while allowing users to access the system.
2	Multiuser	The system is set up for normal operations. Multiple users can log on and use the system resources. All services, except the Network File System (NFS) service, are started. All default file systems are mounted.
3	Multiuser with NFS	The system is set up for normal operations. This is typically the default system state. Multiple users can access and use the system resources. All services, including resource sharing (NFS), are started. All default file systems are mounted.
4	Alternative Multiuser	Currently, this state is not used and is unavailable.

(continued)

Table 4.5	The eight system run levels (continued).	
Run Level	init State	Functionality
5	Power Down	The system is shut down. All users are logged off the system. All operating system services are stopped in an orderly manner. When complete, it is safe to turn off the power to the system and peripherals. If supported by the system hardware, the power to the system is automatically turned off.
6	Reboot	The system is shut down (run level 0) and then restarted and brought back up to the default run level (as defined in the inittab file, typically 3).

Solaris has eight run levels, of which seven are used. Even though no functionality is defined for run level 4, it is still considered a valid run level.

Changing The System Run Level

Occasionally, it is necessary to change the system run level. This includes shutting down the system to add or remove hardware, performing backups, preparing for an expected power outage, or preparing to physically move the system to another location. Table 4.6 lists the commands that are used to change the system run level from the command line.

The **halt**(1M) command normally logs the shutdown to the system log, writes a shutdown record to the system accounting file, performs a call to the **sync**(1M) command to write out any pending information to the disks, and halts the processor(s). The system and account logging along with disk syncing can be prevented by the use of command line arguments. The **halt** command changes to run level 0 but does not execute the rc scripts associated with run level 0 as the **shutdown**(1M) and **init**(1M) commands do.

The **init** and **telinit**(1M) commands can be used to change to any of the eight run levels. The commands identified in the /etc/inittab for each run level are executed, and any running process not in /etc/inittab is sent a SIGTERM and possibly a SIGKILL to cause them to terminate. For each run level, an entry in the /etc/inittab runs the appropriate rc scripts to start and stop processes.

The **poweroff**(1M) command changes the system to run level 5. Normally, it logs the shutdown to the system log, writes a shutdown record to the system

Table 4.6	Commands used to change the system run level.		
Command	**Path**	**Run Level(s)**	**Description**
halt	/usr/sbin	0	Stops the processor(s)
init	/sbin	0123456s	Processes control initialization
poweroff	/usr/sbin	5	Stops the processor(s) and powers off the system (if possible)
reboot	/usr/sbin	6	Reboots the system
shutdown	/etc	0123456s	Used for compatibility (symbolically linked to /usr/sbin/shutdown)
shutdown	/usr/sbin	0123456s	Changes system run level
telinit	/etc	0123456s	Used for compatibility (symbolically linked to /usr/sbin/init)
uadmin	/sbin	056	Used for administrative control

accounting file, performs a call to **sync** to write out any pending information to the disks, and halts the processor(s) and if possible shuts the power off. The **poweroff** command is equivalent to the init 5 command.

The **reboot**(1M) command changes the system to run level 6. Normally, it logs the reboot to the system log, writes a shutdown record to the system accounting file, performs a call to the **sync** to write out any pending information to the disks, and initiates a multiuser reboot.

The **shutdown** command (both under the /usr/sbin and /etc directories) provides a grace period and warning message capability along with executing the appropriate rc scripts. Like the **init** command, this command can be used to change to any of the eight run levels.

The **shutdown** command without any command line arguments will result in a 1-minute grace period with a warning message at 1 minute, 30 seconds, and now. The **shutdown** command will prompt for confirmation to continue before the "shutdown now" message is broadcast and the run level change continues. The system is then changed to run level s.

The **uadmin**(1M) command provides basic administrative functions, such as shutting down or rebooting a system. Typically, it is called by various system administration procedures and not intended for general use.

The **who -r** command can be used to determine the current run level of the system and the date on which the change to that run level occurred.

The **init** And **shutdown** Commands

The most frequently used commands to change system run levels are the **init** and **shutdown** commands. Both can be used to change to any of the eight run levels. Both use the /etc/inittab to determine the processes to start and stop, and both execute the appropriate rc scripts on the basis of system run level.

In addition, the **shutdown** command provides a user-friendly warning message and grace period to allow users to close files and log out before the system changes run levels.

Run Control (rc) Scripts

As previously stated, every run level (except 4) has an entry in the /etc/inittab file that identifies an rc program to execute. In addition, each run level has a directory associated with it.

The directory contains rc scripts that should be executed by the rc program to start or stop processes and services when that run level becomes the current run level. These rc programs and rc script directories use a standard naming convention based on the run level.

For run level 0, the rc program is /etc/rc0, and /etc/rc0.d is the rc script directory. Likewise, for run level 1, the rc program is /etc/rc1, and /etc/rc1.d is the rc script directory. The same naming convention is applied for run levels 2, 3, and s. Run levels 5 and 6 do not have separate rc directories but rather use the run level 0 rc directory.

Typically, both the rc program and the scripts under the rc script directories are referred to as rc scripts. Referring to the script called directly from the /etc/inittab as the rc program helps avoid confusion.

The rc scripts are shell scripts (typically Bourne) that have been written to start and stop various processes and services. An rc script is usually written in two portions: a start portion and a stop portion. As the name implies, the start portion is executed to start a service, whereas the stop portion is called to stop a service. This allows a single script to control the service. When the rc script is called by the rc program, it provides either a start or a stop command line argument to the rc script, depending on whether the service should be started or stopped at a particular run level. The decision to start or stop a particular service is based on the name of the rc script in the appropriate rc directory.

For example, the standard Unix utility to execute maintenance commands automatically is the **cron** program. It is usually started at run level 2 and stopped at run levels 0, 1, 5, 6, and s. To start **cron** at run level 2, the cron rc script is copied (or linked) into /etc/rc2.d and given the name S75cron. The **S** at the beginning of an rc script causes the rc program to start the service at the particular run level (in this example, run level 2) by calling the rc script with the start argument.

Likewise, the same cron rc script is copied (or linked) into the /etc/rc0.d, /etc/rc1.d, and /etc/rcS.d directories and given the name K40cron. The **K** at the beginning of an rc script causes the rc program to stop the service at the particular run level by calling the rc script with the stop argument.

Note that the number included in the names of the cron rc script files are different. The number provides a method for the rc program to start or stop services in a particular and consistent order. The rc scripts with lower numbers are executed before the rc scripts with higher numbers. This is necessary, as some services might require the presence of other services to operate properly.

For example, a networking application requires that the networking services be available. This means that the rc script to start the application should have a higher number than the rc script to start the networking. In addition, services should be stopped in reverse order. In the case of a networking application, the rc script to stop the application should have a lower number than the rc script to stop the networking.

A copy of all rc scripts are placed in the /etc/init.d directory. To start or stop a particular service, the system administrator only has to locate the appropriate rc script in a single directory.

Adding rc Scripts

The following procedure should be used to add rc scripts for a new service:

1. Write a shell script that will accept the command line arguments **start** and **stop** along with the appropriate actions to perform those functions.

2. As superuser, copy the new rc script to the /etc/init.d directory.

3. Determine the run level at which to start the service (typically 2).

4. Determine the two-digit number to control the start sequence (00 through 99). Look at the other startup scripts in the appropriate rc directory and choose a number that is not being used: one that is greater than any required services but less than any services that will use the new service.

5. Copy or link the new script from the /etc/init.d directory to one or more of the rc directories, giving it a name starting with S followed by the selected two-digit number and then the service name.

6. Determine the run level(s) at which the service should stop (typically, 0, 1, and s), meaning that the script needs to be linked to the appropriate directory.

7. Determine the two-digit number to control the stop sequence (00 through 99). Look at the other stop rc scripts in the appropriate rc directories and choose a number that is not being used: one that is less than any required services but greater than any services that were using the service.

8. Copy or link the new script from the /etc/init.d directory to the appropriate rc directories, giving it a name starting with K followed by the selected two-digit number and then the service name.

Practice Questions

Question 1

Which of the following versions of OpenBoot are currently supported by Sun Microsystems? [Select all that apply]

❏ a. 1.x

❏ b. 2.x

❏ c. 3.x

❏ d. 4.x

The correct answers are b and c. Answer a, version 1.x, is no longer supported. Answer d, version 4.x, currently does not exist.

Question 2

Which OpenBoot command can be used to view system configuration information?

○ a. **env**

○ b. **display**

○ c. **banner**

○ d. **list**

○ e. **show**

The correct answer is c. Answer a is a Solaris 7 command that lists shell variables in the current environment. Answers b, d, and e do not exist, although a **show-dev** OpenBoot command does.

Question 3

Which of the following OpenBoot commands are used to test hardware? [Select all that apply]

❑ a. **probe-scsi**

❑ b. **test floppy**

❑ c. **test net**

❑ d. **watch-clock**

❑ e. **test memory**

Answers a, b, c, and d are correct. These commands test the SCSI controller, the floppy diskette drive, the network interface, and the system clock, in that order. **test /memory** (note the "/" before "memory") is the correct command to test memory. Therefore, answer e is incorrect.

Question 4

Name the OpenBoot command used to delete a nonvolatile device alias.

The correct answer is either **nvunalias** or **set-defaults**.

Question 5

Which emergency keyboard command is used to abort the boot process?

○ a. **stop**

○ b. **stop+a**

○ c. **stop+b**

○ d. **stop+s**

○ e. **stop+!**

The correct answer is b. Answer a bypasses the POST. Answers c, d, and e do not exist.

Question 6

Provide the OpenBoot command to boot a system from the CD-ROM.

_____

The correct answer is **boot cdrom.**

Question 7

Which of the following is the last phase in the Solaris boot process?

○ a. init

○ b. Boot PROM

○ c. BIOS

○ d. Kernel Initialization

○ e. Boot Programs

The correct answer is a. All of these are phases of either the SPARC or Intel x86 boot process. The Boot PROM and BIOS phases (answers b and c) test hardware. The Boot Programs phase (answer e) locates and loads boot programs, then the Kernel Initialization phase (answer d) loads the kernel. Only then can the init phase occur to initialize the operating system services.

Question 8

Which of the following default directories are used to store kernel modules? [Select all that apply]

❏ a. /kernel

❏ b. /usr/kernel

❏ c. /var/kernel

❏ d. /etc/system

❏ e. /etc/kernel

The correct answers are a and b. Answers c and e do not exist. Answer d is used to configure the system kernel.

Question 9

Which of the following commands can be used to change to any of the system run levels? [Select all that apply]

☐ a. **init**

☐ b. **reboot**

☐ c. **shutdown**

☐ d. **poweroff**

☐ e. **uadmin**

☐ f. **halt**

The correct answers are a and c. Answer b, **reboot,** can be used only to change to system run level 6. Answer d, **poweroff,** can be used only to change to system run level 5. Answer e, **uadmin,** can be used only to change to run levels 0, 5, and 6. In addition, this command is not intended for direct use. Answer f, **halt,** can be used only to change to system run level 0.

Question 10

How many run levels are there in Solaris 7?

○ a. 6

○ b. 7

○ c. 8

○ d. 9

The correct answer is c. Answer b might be assumed to be correct, as run level 4 is not used, but run level 4 is counted even though it is not used.

Need To Know More?

 Sun Microsystems, *OpenBoot 2.x Command Reference Manual*, is available in printed form (ISBN 802-5836-10), on the Web at **docs.sun.com**, and from the online documentation, AnswerBook2, provided with the Solaris 7 operating system.

 Sun Microsystems, *OpenBoot 3.x Command Reference Manual*, is available in printed form (ISBN 802-5837-10), on the Web at **docs.sun.com**, and from the online documentation, AnswerBook2, provided with the Solaris 7 operating system.

 Sun Microsystems, *System Administration Guide, Volume 1*, is available in printed form (ISBN 805-3727-10), on the Web at **docs.sun.com**, and from the online documentation, AnswerBook2, provided with the Solaris 7 operating system.

 Sun Microsystems, *System Reference Manual, Section 1M - Administration Commands*, is available in printed form (ISBN 805-3173-10), on the Web at **docs.sun.com**, and from the online documentation, AnswerBook2, provided with the Solaris 7 operating system.

System Security And File Permissions

Terms you'll need to understand:

√ User and group accounts

√ The superuser account

√ The /etc/passwd, /etc/shadow, and /etc/group formats

√ Absolute and symbolic access modes

√ Access Control Lists (ACLs)

Techniques you'll need to master:

√ Restricting and monitoring the superuser account

√ Identifying and monitoring users

√ Changing default and existing file permissions

√ Setting and displaying Access Control Lists

√ Changing file ownership

This chapter covers system security and file permissions. System security addresses controlling access to the system by using passwords and restricting/monitoring the use of the administrative user accounts. The file permissions portion addresses controlling the access to the data in files by using both basic and extended access controls.

System Security

Unix system security is based on controlling access to files (programs and data). Access is controlled by defining user accounts and granting the user accounts different levels of file access. The user accounts are protected by passwords.

Administrative accounts are given access to system data and tools that allow them to perform system maintenance. These include accounts such as root, sys, bin, and adm. Several account administration files are used to store the information associated with user accounts, such as account name and password.

Solaris 7 provides several commands that can be used to identify the user accounts currently logged into the system and to monitor their activities.

The Superuser (root) Account

The root, or superuser, account is a special administrative account that provides the ultimate in terms of access to data and services, as it can override any file permissions on the system. To enforce good system security, access to the superuser account must be restricted and monitored as closely as possible. Solaris 7 provides several capabilities that support this activity, which are discussed in the following sections.

Restricting And Monitoring The Superuser Account

Logging into the system as root can be restricted to the console. That is, the root account cannot log in remotely but is allowed only from the system console. This restriction can be enforced by the following entry in the /etc/default/login file:

```
CONSOLE=/dev/console
```

By default, the root account is restricted. To disable this feature, edit the /etc/default/login file and put the shell comment character (#) at the beginning of the entry.

Restricting the root login to the console forces anyone accessing the superuser account remotely to log in with a regular system account and then use the **su**(1M) command to become the superuser. The use of the **su** command can be monitored and logged in several ways. The /etc/default/su file controls this monitoring and logging.

The usage of the **su** command can be displayed on the system console by adding the following entry in the /etc/default/su file:

```
CONSOLE=/dev/console
```

Both failed and successful attempts to use the **su** command will be displayed on the console. By default, the use of the **su** command is not displayed on the console. To enable this feature, edit the /etc/default/su file and remove the shell comment character (#) at the beginning of the entry. Note that this entry is identical to the entry used in the /etc/default/login file to restrict root login to the system console.

The following listing shows the messages displayed on the console for two uses of the **su** command. The first shows a successful use of **su** to become root on the system named unix from the login dla. The second shows an unsuccessful attempt to become the guest account on the system named unix from the login dla:

```
Aug 23 06:57:11 unix su: 'su root' succeeded for dla on /dev/pts/4
SU 08/23 06:57 + pts/4 dla-root

Aug 23 06:57:47 unix su: 'su guest' failed for dla on /dev/pts/4
```

The use of the **su** command can be logged to a file dedicated for su logging and through the system logging facility (syslog) by adding the following entry in the /etc/default/su file. (Although the default is shown here, any file can be used for the sulog.):

```
SULOG=/var/adm/sulog
```

Both failed and successful attempts to use the **su** command are logged. By default, the use of the **su** command is logged to the sulog. To disable this feature, edit the /etc/default/su file and add the shell comment character (#) at the beginning of the entry.

The following listing shows the contents of the /var/adm/sulog file:

```
SU 07/25 19:09 + console root-daemon
SU 07/25 19:49 + pts/4 dla-root
SU 07/25 19:52 + pts/4 dla-root
SU 08/01 08:49 + pts/4 dla-root
```

```
SU 08/05 21:18 + console root-daemon
SU 08/15 13:21 + pts/4 dla-root
SU 08/22 17:08 + pts/4 dla-root
SU 08/23 06:57 + pts/4 dla-root
SU 08/23 06:57 - pts/4 dla-shlog
```

The "+" or "-" following the date and time indicates success or failure, respectively. The next field indicates where the command was entered, and the next field lists the from and to user accounts.

The use of the **su** command can also be logged using the syslog facility. This is enabled by adding the following entry to the /etc/default/su file:

```
SYSLOG=YES
```

However, the syslog facility must be properly configured to capture and log these messages. The syslog facility is an objective for Part II (Exam 310-010) and is covered in Chapter 15.

By default, the use of the **su** command is logged to the syslog facility. To disable this feature, edit the /etc/default/su file and add the shell comment character (#) at the beginning of the SYSLOG entry.

The sysadmin Group

User accounts that are a member of the sysadmin group (numerical group 14) can perform some selected system administration activities using **admintool**(1M) without being granted full superuser privileges. This allows basic system administration (adding and deleting users, printers, and software, and so on) to be performed by more than one person without compromising system security. This is accomplished by configuring the setuid to root permission for **admintool** and making membership in the sysadmin group a requirement for using **admintool**. Additional information about groups and the setuid permission is provided later in this chapter.

User Account Administration Files

Three administrative files are used to define and manage user accounts:

➤ /etc/passwd

➤ /etc/shadow

➤ /etc/group

/etc/passwd

The /etc/passwd file is an ASCII file that is used to define user accounts on the local system. Each line represents a user account and consists of seven colon-delimited fields. Table 5.1 lists the fields of an entry in the /etc/passwd file.

The following listing shows the default contents of a Solaris 7 /etc/password file:

```
root:x:0:1:Super-User:/:/sbin/sh
daemon:x:1:1::/:
bin:x:2:2::/usr/bin:
sys:x:3:3::/:
adm:x:4:4:Admin:/var/adm:
lp:x:71:8:Line Printer Admin:/usr/spool/lp:
uucp:x:5:5:uucp Admin:/usr/lib/uucp:
nuucp:x:9:9:uucp Admin:/var/spool/uucppublic:/usr/lib/uucp/uucico
listen:x:37:4:Network Admin:/usr/net/nls:
nobody:x:60001:60001:Nobody:/:
noaccess:x:60002:60002:No Access User:/:
nobody4:x:65534:65534:SunOS 4.x Nobody:/:
```

Table 5.1   /etc/passwd fields.

Field	Purpose
user name	The unique name assigned to the user account.
password	In earlier versions of Unix, the password field contained the encrypted account password. For security reasons, the passwords have been moved to the /etc/shadow file. The letter "x" is typically placed in this field to indicate that the password is in /etc/shadow.
UID	A unique numeric identification assigned to the user account. Any processes or files created by the user account will be owned by this UID. The system administrator account, root, is assigned the UID of 0. This is the UID of a superuser account. System maintenance accounts are usually assigned a UID of less than 100, whereas user accounts typically start at 1001.
GID	The numeric identification of the default group that the user account has been assigned to as a member. Groups are defined in the /etc/group file.

(continued)

Table 5.1 /etc/passwd fields (continued).	
Field	**Purpose**
comment field	Information about the owner of the user account, such as real name, phone number, mailing address, and so on. An ampersand in this field is interpreted as the contents of the user name field.
home directory	The full path to the directory where the user is initially located after logging in.
login shell	The full pathname of the initial shell used as a command interpreter. If empty, the default is /usr/bin/sh.

/etc/shadow

The /etc/shadow file is an ASCII file that is used to store passwords for local user accounts along with any password restrictions or aging. Access is restricted to superusers to protect the passwords. Each line represents the password of a user account and consists of nine colon-delimited fields. Table 5.2 lists the fields of an entry in the /etc/shadow file.

Table 5.2 /etc/shadow fields.	
Field	**Purpose**
UID	Used to relate the /etc/shadow entry to a user account defined in the /etc/passwd file.
password	A 13-character encrypted password for the associated user account. If the field contains "NP," this account is used only to own processes or files (setuid) and cannot be used to log in to the system. If the field contains "*LK*," the account is locked and cannot be used to access the system. If the field is empty, no password exists, and the user is forced to enter a password the first time the account is used.
last changed	The number of days between January 1, 1970, and the last date the password was changed.
minimum	The minimum number of days required to pass before the user is allowed to change the password again.
maximum	The maximum number of days the password is valid.
warning	The number of days the user is warned before the password expires.

(continued)

Table 5.2 /etc/shadow fields (continued).	
Field	**Purpose**
inactivity	The number of days the account can be inactive before the password must be changed.
expiration	The number of days between January 1, 1970, and the date on which the account expires.
flag	Reserved for future use.

The following listing shows the guest entry from a Solaris 7 /etc/shadow file that uses all the fields (except flag):

```
guest:on7GbE18yYAek:10688:5:30:5:20:10844:
```

/etc/group

The /etc/group file is an ASCII file that is used to store information about groups on the local system. Each line represents a group and consists of four colon-delimited fields. Table 5.3 lists the fields of an entry in the /etc/group file.

The following listing shows the partial default contents of a Solaris 7 /etc/group file:

```
root::0:root
other::1:
bin::2:root,bin,daemon
sys::3:root,bin,sys,adm
adm::4:root,adm,daemon
uucp::5:root,uucp
mail::6:root
```

Table 5.3 /etc/group fields.	
Field	**Purpose**
group name	The unique name of the group.
password	The password associated with the group. If a password is present, the **newgrp**(1) command prompts users to enter it.
GID	The unique numeric group identification.
users	A comma-separated list of user accounts that belong to the group.

Identifying And Monitoring Users

Several commands can be used to identify and monitor users:

➤ id(1M)—Displays the real and effective UID and GID

➤ last(1)—Displays login and logout information

➤ who(1)—Displays the users currently logged into the system

➤ whodo(1M)—Displays who is doing what

In addition, failed login attempts can be logged.

The **id** command

The **id** command is used to display the real and effective UID and GID for the invoking process or specified user account. If invoked with -a as an option, all groups in which the user ID is a member will be returned. The following listing shows the results of executing the **id** command:

```
# id -a
uid=0(root) gid=1(other)groups=1(other),0(root),2(bin),
3(sys),4(adm),5(uucp),6(mail),7(tty),8(lp),9(nuucp),12(daemon)
#
```

The **last** command

The **last** command is used to display login and logout activity. This is useful because it can identify users that currently are on the system and those that have been on the system recently. The following listing shows the results of the **last** command:

```
$ last
dla       console       :0          Sun Aug 22 17:26   still logged in
dla       ftp           winnt40     Sun Aug 15 14:43 - 14:43  (00:00)
reboot    system boot               Thu Aug  5 21:17
dla       ftp           win95       Sat Jul 10 07:42 - 07:50  (00:08)
root      console       :0          Mon Jun  7 20:14 - down   (3+09:29)
root      console                   Sat Apr 10 13:01 - 13:01  (00:00)
guest     ftp           solaris     Wed Apr  7 17:27 - 17:42  (00:15)
guest     pts/6         solaris     Wed Apr  7 17:15 - 17:16  (00:01)
root      console       :0          Sat Jan 23 14:55 - 19:31  (9+04:36)
reboot    system boot               Sat Jan 23 14:50
root      console       :0          Tue Jan 12 15:59 - 16:05  (00:06)
root      console       :0          Thu Dec 24 08:59 - 10:27  (01:27)
guest     pts/4         solaris     Sun Dec 20 15:17 - 15:18  (00:00)
```

```
reboot system boot          Sun Dec 20 00:03
reboot system boot          Sat Dec 19 20:35

wtmp begins Sat Dec 19 20:35
$
```

The **who** command

The **who** command is used to display the users currently logged into the system and, optionally, information about processes, system reboots, and so on. The following listing shows the results of two **who** commands:

```
# who
dla         console     Aug 22 17:26    (:0)
dla         pts/4       Aug 22 16:54    (winnt40)
# who -a
NAME        LINE        TIME            IDLE    PID     COMMENTS
   .        system boot Aug  5 21:17
   .        run-level 3 Aug  5 21:18    3         0     S
rc2            .        Aug  5 21:18    old      78     id=  s2
rc3            .        Aug  5 21:18    old     262     id=  s3
sac            .        Aug  5 21:18    old     291     id=  sc
LOGIN       console     Aug  5 21:18    0:08    292
zsmon          .        Aug  5 21:18    old     294
dla       + console     Aug 22 17:26    0:08  12399          (:0)
root        pts/3       Aug 22 17:23    1:38    396     id=    3
dla       + pts/4       Aug 22 16:54    .      12268   (winnt40)
root        pts/6       Aug 15 15:32    old    5639     id=    6
root        pts/7       Aug 15 15:32    old    7891     id=    7
.telnet     /dev/pts/3  Aug 22 17:28    12551   id=t100 term=0
#
```

The **whodo** command

The **whodo** command allows the system administrator to combine the information from **who** with process information to produce a list of what users are doing. The following listing shows the results of a **whodo** command:

```
# whodo
Sun Aug 22 19:13:17 EDT 1999
solaris

console     dla         17:26
    ?                 12399     0:00 Xsession
    ?                 12431     3:52 java
```

```
pts/2          12445    0:00 sdt_shell
pts/2          12448    0:00 sh
pts/2          12465    0:02 dtsession
  ?            12681    0:00 dtscreen
  ?            12488    0:03 dtfile

pts/4     dla       16:54
  pts/4        12268    0:00 sh
  pts/4        12655    0:00 sh
  pts/4        12685    0:00 whodo
```

Failed Login Attempts

Failed login attempts are saved in the /var/adm/loginlog file after five unsuccessful attempts. This file is enabled by creating the login log file and disabled by deleting it. The file should be created with read/write permissions for root only.

File Permissions And Ownership

File permissions determine the operations that can be performed on files and directories along with who can perform these operations. There are two types of file permissions: standard, which provide basic security, and extended, which expand the standard permissions.

Standard File Permissions

Files and directories can have read, write, and execution permissions. Permissions can be assigned to three classes of system accounts: the user account that owns the file, the group account that has group permissions, and everyone else. These are referred to as *user*, *group*, and *other* permissions. The read, write, and execution for user, group, and other can be set independently of one another.

Two types of notation are used to specify file permissions (also known as the *file access mode*): absolute mode and symbolic mode. Absolute mode is also referred to as *octal mode*. Absolute mode is a numeric value assigned to each permission per account class. Table 5.4 lists the absolute modes.

The access mode of a file is determined by adding the following absolute modes together:

```
user permissions + group permissions + other permissions
```

For example, a file with user read (400) and user write (200) without any other permissions for group or other would have an access mode of 400 + 200, or 600. Adding group read (040) and group write (020) to this file would result in

Table 5.4	Absolute file permission modes.
Absolute Mode	**Description**
001	other execution
002	other write
004	other read
010	group execution
020	group write
040	group read
100	user execution
200	user write
400	user read

an access mode of 600 + 060, or 660. Adding other read (004) and other write (002) would result in 666. Adding user execution (100) results in a file access mode of 766.

The other type of notation is symbolic mode. Using this mode, read access is represented by the letter "r," write by the letter "w," and execution by the letter "x." The ls(1) command, which is used to list files, uses symbolic mode. The following listing shows the output of an **ls** command:

```
# ls -l
total 18
-rw-rw-rw-  1 root    other      120 Aug 28 07:38 data
-rwxrw-rw-  1 root    other     6528 Aug 28 07:38 junk
-rw-r--r--  1 root    other      636 Aug 28 07:39 list
#
```

The **ls** command lists three sets of **rwx** permissions: one for user, one for group, and one for other. In the absence of a permission, the "-" character is displayed. In the previous listing, the file named "data" has read/write access for user, group, and other (absolute mode of 666). The "junk" file has read/write/execute for user and read/write for group and other (absolute mode of 766). The "list" file has read/write for user and read only for group and other (absolute mode of 644).

Default File Permissions

When a file is created, a set of default permissions are assigned to it. The default permissions are defined using the **umask**(1) command. The **umask** command sets a mask of the permissions that should *not* be included in the file access mode by default. It should be added to the contents of the user's login initialization file to provided a consistent permission mask.

For example, to allow full permission for owner and to remove write permission for group and other, the **umask** would be 022. This means that 022 should be subtracted from a baseline absolute mode of 666 for files (666 – 022 = 644), which yields the desired file access mode. The baseline absolute mode for directories is 777. The following listing shows the impact of the **umask** command on newly created files:

```
# umask 111
# cp file1 file2
# ls -1
total 4
-rwxrwxrwx   1 sys       other        636 Aug 28 07:39 file1
-rw-rw-rw-   1 root      other        636 Aug 28 11:36 file2
# umask 133
# cp file1 file3
# ls -1
total 6
-rwxrwxrwx   1 sys       other        636 Aug 28 07:39 file1
-rw-rw-rw-   1 root      other        636 Aug 28 11:36 file2
-rw-r--r--   1 root      other        636 Aug 28 11:36 file3
# umask 022
# cp file1 file4
# ls -1
total 8
-rwxrwxrwx   1 sys       other        636 Aug 28 07:39 file1
-rw-rw-rw-   1 root      other        636 Aug 28 11:36 file2
-rw-r--r--   1 root      other        636 Aug 28 11:36 file3
-rwxr-xr-x   1 root      other        636 Aug 28 11:36 file4
#
```

Changing File Permissions

The access mode of existing files and directories can be modified using the **chmod**(1) command. The **chmod** command can use either absolute mode or symbolic mode.

Absolute mode is straightforward, as shown in the following listing:

```
# ls -1 file1
-rwxrwxrw-   1 sys       other        636 Aug 28 07:39 file1
# chmod 645 file1
# ls -1 file1
-rw-r--r-x   1 sys       other        636 Aug 28 07:39 file1
#
```

When using symbolic mode, the class of system account (user, group, or other) is defined using the letters "u," "g," and "o." Permissions are added using the "+" character, whereas permissions are removed using the "-" character. Multiple changes can be specified by separating them with commas. The following listing shows using the **chmod** command with symbolic mode:

```
# ls -l file1
-rwxrwxrw-  1 sys      other        636 Aug 28 07:39 file1
# chmod u-x,g-w,g-x,o-w,o+x file1
# ls -l file1
-rw-r--r-x  1 sys      other        636 Aug 28 07:39 file1
#
```

Special Permissions

Several special permissions impact security and allow a user account or group account to temporarily become another user account or group account during the execution of a program. These are set effective UID to owner on execution (setuid) and set effective GID to group on execution (setgid). The setuid and setgid permissions are controlled using the **chmod** command, like the read, write, and execute file permissions.

The setuid permission has an absolute mode of 4000 and a symbolic mode of **s** when used with the **chmod** command. The user execution permission must be set in order for the setuid to be effective. This permission is shown as **s** in the user account execution permission field in the output of an **ls** command. The following listing shows the **chmod** command being used to add and remove the setuid permission from a file:

```
# ls -l list
-rwxr--r--  1 sys      other        636 Aug 28 07:39 list
# chmod 4744 list
# ls -l list
-rwsr--r--  1 sys      other        636 Aug 28 07:39 list
# chmod u-s list
# ls -l list
-rwxr--r--  1 sys      other        636 Aug 28 07:39 list
#
```

The setgid permission has an absolute mode of 2000 and a symbolic mode of **s** when used with the **chmod** command. The group execution permission must be set in order for the setgid to be effective. This permission is shown as **s** in the group account execution permission field in the output of an **ls** command. The following listing shows using the **chmod** command to add and remove the setgid permission from a file:

```
# ls -l list
-rwxr-xr--   1 sys        other          636 Aug 28 07:39 list
# chmod g+s list
# ls -l list
-rwxr-sr--   1 sys        other          636 Aug 28 07:39 list
# chmod 754 list
# ls -l
-rwxr-xr--   1 sys        other          636 Aug 28 07:39 list
#
```

Another special file permission is the sticky bit. Originally, this was used to indicate programs that should be left in memory after execution. When set for frequently used programs, this saved time and CPU cycles by using the image left in memory instead of loading it from disk again.

When the sticky bit is set on a directory that allows write permission for everyone, only the user account that created files and subdirectories under the directory can remove those files and subdirectories. This is especially useful for the /tmp directory, which is available from any user account.

The sticky bit permission has an absolute mode of 1000 and a symbolic mode of **t** when used with the **chmod** command. This permission is shown as **t** in the other account execution permission field in the output of an **ls** command, but it is considered a user account (owner) permission. The following listing shows using the **chmod** command to remove and then add the sticky bit permission to a directory:

```
# ls -ld /tmp
drwxrwxrwt   7 sys        sys            410 Aug 28 03:30 /tmp
# chmod u-t /tmp
# ls -ld /tmp
drwxrwxrwx   7 sys        sys            410 Aug 28 03:30 /tmp
# chmod 1777 /tmp
# ls -ld /tmp
drwxrwxrwt   7 sys        sys            410 Aug 28 03:30 /tmp
#
```

Extended File Permissions: Access Control Lists

Solaris 7 extends the standard Unix file permissions by adding an Access Control List (ACL) capability. ACLs provide the ability to add permissions for specific users and groups along with a default permission (mask).

In addition to supporting the standard read/write/execute permission for the standard file user account (owner), ACLs can be used to set read/write/execute permissions for additional user accounts. Likewise, ACLs support read/write/execute permissions for the standard file group account and allow read/write/execution permissions for additional group accounts. In addition, ACLs support the read/write/execution permission for the standard others (everyone else).

ACLs also include a mask capability that controls the maximum allowed permissions given to user and group accounts other than the standard file user account and the standard file group account.

For example, root owns a file and sets its ACL mask to read/execute. Later, root adds read/write/execute permission to the file ACL for the guest user account. Because of the mask, the write permission is overridden, and the effective permissions for the guest account are read/execute.

The ACL for a directory includes default entries that determine the permissions assigned to files and subdirectories created under the directory. Default permissions can be defined for the standard Unix user, group, and other along with a default mask and default permissions for specific users or groups.

Two commands are used to manage ACLs: The **setfacl**(1) command is used to set ACLs, and the **getfacl** command is used to display ACLs.

Setting ACLs Using **setfacl**

The **setfacl** command is used to set and modify ACLs. It supports three command line arguments:

➤ -d—Deletes the specified ACL entries

➤ -m—Adds/changes the specified ACL entries

➤ -s—Replaces the whole ACL with the specified entries

ACL entries for the standard user and group permissions are specified using the format *entry::permissions* (note the two colons), where *entry* is the keyword **user** or **group** (or the single-letter abbreviations **u** or **g**) and *permissions* is the appropriate combination of **r**, **w**, **x**, and "-" needed to define the permission.

ACL entries for the standard other permission and the mask used for maximum permissions use a slightly different syntax. The format is *entry:permissions* (note the single colon), where *entry* is the keyword **other** or **mask** (or the single-letter abbreviations **o** or **m**) and *permissions* is the appropriate combination of **r**, **w**, **x**, and "-" needed to define the permission.

The following listing shows the **setfacl** command used to set the user permission to read/write, and to set the group and other permission to read-only:

```
# setfacl -s u::rw-,g::r--,o:r-- file1
```

ACL entries for the user and group permissions are specified using the format *entry:id:permissions*, where *entry* is the keyword **user** or **group** (or the single-letter abbreviations **u** or **g**); *id* is a user name, UID, group name, or GID; and *permissions* is the appropriate combination of **r**, **w**, **x**, and "-" needed to define the permission.

The following listing shows the **setfacl** command used to add read/write permission for user account guest and read-only permission for group account staff:

```
# setfacl -m u:guest:rw-,g:staff:r-- file1
```

In addition to all the previously described ACL entries, additional entries can be defined for directories. These entries specify the default ACL entries for files and subdirectories created under the directory. Defaults can be established using the same previously described formats by adding "d:" at the beginning of the "entry" field. All the standard user, group, and other defaults, along with default mask, must be defined initially at the same time.

For example, to define the default ACL entries for the directory shlog, the following **setfacl** command can be used:

```
# setfacl -m d:u::rw-,d:g::rw-,d:o:r--,d:m:r-- /shlog
```

Displaying ACLs Using **getfacl**

The ACLs for a file or directory can be displayed using the **getfacl** command. The following listing displays the ACLs for the shlog directory using the **getfacl** command:

```
# getfacl shlog

# file: shlog
# owner: shlog
# group: staff
user::rwx
group::r-x              #effective:r-x
mask:r-x
other:r-x
default:user::rw-
default:group::rw-
default:mask:r--
default:other:r--
#
```

When using the **ls** command, files that have ACLs are shown with a "+" in front of the file entry.

Changing File Ownership

Two commands are used to control the file ownership:

➤ chown(1M)—Changes file user account ownership

➤ chgrp(1M)—Changes file group account ownership

Changing File User Account

The **chown** command is used to change the file user account that is the owner of a file or directory. By default, only the superuser account (root) is allowed to change file ownership, but this can be modified to allow the current owner of the file to change file ownership as well.

The user account name or associated UID is specified along with the name of one or more files that should be owned by the specified user account. The following listing shows using the **chown** command to change the ownership of several files to the guest user account, which has a UID of 1001. Each **chown** command is preceded and followed by the **ls** command, which is used to list the ownership and permissions of files:

```
# ls -l
total 18
-rw-rw-rw-   1 root      other        120 Aug 28 07:38 data
-rw-rw-rw-   1 root      other       6528 Aug 28 07:38 junk
-rw-r--r--   1 root      other        636 Aug 28 07:39 list
# chown guest junk
# ls -l
total 18
-rw-rw-rw-   1 root      other        120 Aug 28 07:38 data
-rw-rw-rw-   1 guest     other       6528 Aug 28 07:38 junk
-rw-r--r--   1 root      other        636 Aug 28 07:39 list
# chown 1001 data list
# ls -l
total 18
-rw-rw-rw-   1 guest     other        120 Aug 28 07:38 data
-rw-rw-rw-   1 guest     other       6528 Aug 28 07:38 junk
-rw-r--r--   1 guest     other        636 Aug 28 07:39 list
#
```

The **chown** command supports a recursive command line argument, **-R**. When used to change the owner of a directory, the ownership of any files or sub-directories under the directory is also changed.

Even though a separate command exists to change file group account owner-ship, the **chown** command can be used to change group ownership at the same time by following the user account name or UID with the colon char-acter and a group account name or GID. The following example shows using the **chown** command to change both user account ownership and group account ownership:

```
# ls -l
total 18
-rw-rw-rw-   1 guest    other         120 Aug 28 07:38 data
-rw-rw-rw-   1 guest    other        6528 Aug 28 07:38 junk
-rw-r--r--   1 guest    other         636 Aug 28 07:39 list
# chown sys:staff data junk list
# ls -l
total 18
-rw-rw-rw-   1 sys      staff         120 Aug 28 07:38 data
-rw-rw-rw-   1 sys      staff        6528 Aug 28 07:38 junk
-rw-r--r--   1 sys      staff         636 Aug 28 07:39 list
#
```

If the **chown** command is used by anyone other than root to change the own-ership of a file that has the set UID on execution (setuid) special permission, the setuid special permission is cleared. This prevents a user from setting up a setuid file, changing the ownership to someone else, and then using the file to gain access to another user account.

As an enhanced security feature of Solaris 7, the use of the **chown** command is restricted to the superuser account. This restriction can be removed by clearing the following kernel parameter in the /etc/system file and rebooting the system:

```
set rstchown = 0
```

Setting **rstchown** to 1 and rebooting the system will enforce the restriction again.

Changing The File Group Account

The **chgrp** command is used to change the file group account associated with a file or directory. Only the user account that currently owns the file or the superuser account (root) can change file ownership. By default, the owner of a file can change only a group account to which the user belongs.

The group account name or associated GID is specified along with the name
of one or more files that should be owned by the specified group account. The
following listing shows the **chgrp** command being used to change the ownership of several files to the other group account, which has a GID of 1. Each
chgrp command is preceded and followed by the **ls** command, which is used to
list the ownership and permissions of files:

```
# ls -l
total 18
-rw-rw-rw-  1 sys       staff       120 Aug 28 07:38 data
-rw-rw-rw-  1 sys       staff      6528 Aug 28 07:38 junk
-rw-r--r--  1 sys       staff       636 Aug 28 07:39 list
# chgrp other junk
# ls -l
total 18
-rw-rw-rw-  1 sys       staff       120 Aug 28 07:38 data
-rw-rw-rw-  1 sys       other      6528 Aug 28 07:38 junk
-rw-r--r--  1 sys       staff       636 Aug 28 07:39 list
# chgrp 1 data list
# ls -l
total 18
-rw-rw-rw-  1 sys       other       120 Aug 28 07:38 data
-rw-rw-rw-  1 sys       other      6528 Aug 28 07:38 junk
-rw-r--r--  1 sys       other       636 Aug 28 07:39 list
#
```

Like the **chown** command, the **chgrp** command supports a recursive command line argument, **-R**. When used to change the group ownership of a
directory, the group ownership of any files or subdirectories under the directory is also changed.

If the **chgrp** command is used by anyone other than root that does not have the
appropriate permissions and the file has the setuid special permission and/or
the setgid special permission, the setuid and/or getuid special permission is
cleared. This prevents a user from setting up a setuid and/or setgid file, changing the ownership to someone else, and then using the file to gain access to
another user account and/or group account.

As an enhanced security feature of Solaris 7, the use of the **chgrp** command is
restricted by requiring the user account attempting to change group ownership
to be a member of the new group. This restriction can be removed by clearing
the following kernel parameter in the /etc/system file and rebooting the system:

```
set rstchown = 0
```

Setting **rstchown** to 1 and rebooting the system will enforce the restriction again.

Practice Questions

Question 1

> Which command is used to determine the default access mode for files when
> they are created?
>
> ○ a. **setfacl**
>
> ○ b. **chmod**
>
> ○ c. **umask**
>
> ○ d. **getfacl**
>
> ○ e. **ls**

The correct answer is c. The **setfacl** and **chmod** commands are used to set
access modes of existing files. The **getfacl** and **ls** commands are used to display
access modes of existing files.

Question 2

> If a user account is a member of the sysadmin group, the user account can
> be used to perform which of the following types of system administration?
> [Select all that apply]
>
> ❑ a. Add/remove printers
>
> ❑ b. Add/remove user account
>
> ❑ c. Reboot or shut down the system
>
> ❑ d. Add/remove software
>
> ❑ e. Install patches

The correct answers are a, b, and d. Being a member of the sysadmin group
allows the user account to run the **admintool** command. This tool can be
used for many system administration functions, but rebooting/shutting down
the system (answer c) and adding patches (answer e) are not included in its
capability.

Question 3

Enter the command (without command line arguments) used to add read/write permission for user account fred to a file owned by user account george.

_____

The correct answer is **setfacl.**

Question 4

To restrict logging in directly as root to the system console, which file needs to be modified?

○ a. /dev/console

○ b. /etc/passwd

○ c. /etc/default/login

○ d. /etc/default/su

The correct answer is c. Answer a is the pathname for the console, answer b is the password file, and answer d is the file that controls the behavior of the **su** command.

Question 5

What is the /var/adm/loginlog file used to log?

○ a. Logins

○ b. Logouts

○ c. Failed logins

○ d. Successful logins

○ e. All logins and logouts

The correct answer is c. The **last** command is used to determine logins (answers a and d), logouts (answer b), and both logins and logouts (answer e). In addition, the **who** command can be used to identify users currently logged onto the system.

Question 6

> Enter where user account passwords are stored.
>
> _____

The correct answer is /etc/shadow.

Question 7

> The file /etc/default/su controls the behavior of the **su** command, which in-cludes which of the following? [Select all that apply]
>
> ❏ a. Displaying **su** usage on the system console
>
> ❏ b. Restricting **root** usage to the system console
>
> ❏ c. Logging failed **su** attempts
>
> ❏ d. Enabling the logging **su** usage through syslog
>
> ❏ e. Logging successful **su** attempts

The correct answers are a, c, d, and e. Answer b is accomplished by editing the /etc/default/login file.

Question 8

> Which of the following shows the access mode of a file that has the setuid enabled?
>
> ○ a. srwxrwxrwx
>
> ○ b. -rwsrwxrwx
>
> ○ c. -rwxrwsrwx
>
> ○ d. -rwxrwxrws
>
> ○ e. -rwxrwxrwt

The correct answer is b. Answers a and d are not valid file access modes. An-swer c shows setgid, and answer e shows the sticky bit set.

Question 9

> Which command shows all the users that are currently logged into the system?
> [Select all that apply]
>
> ❑ a. **who**
>
> ❑ b. **last**
>
> ❑ c. **whodo**
>
> ❑ d. **id**

The correct answers are a, b, and c. Answer d shows the real and effective UID, GID, and groups for a specified user account.

Question 10

> The file "test" currently has the access mode 644. Which of the following will add write access for the group owner? [Select all that apply]
>
> ❑ a. **chmod test 664**
>
> ❑ b. **chmod 664 test**
>
> ❑ c. **chmod test g+w**
>
> ❑ d. **chmod g+w test**
>
> ❑ e. **setfacl -s u::rw-,g::rw-,o:r--**

The correct answers are b, d, and e. Even though the **setfacl -s** command replaces the existing ACLs, the original access mode is reinstated along with the added group write access. Using **setfacl -m** would also have worked, but was not specified as an answer. Answers a and c do not follow the correct syntax.

Need To Know More?

Sun Microsystems, *System Administration Guide, Volume 2*, is available in printed form (ISBN 805-3728-10), on the Web at **docs.sun.com,** and from the online documentation, AnswerBook2, provided with the Solaris 7 operating system.

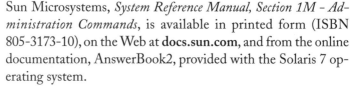

Sun Microsystems, *System Reference Manual, Section 1 - User Commands*, is available in printed form (ISBN 805-3172-10), on the Web at **docs.sun.com,** and from the online documentation, AnswerBook2, provided with the Solaris 7 operating system.

Sun Microsystems, *System Reference Manual, Section 1M - Administration Commands*, is available in printed form (ISBN 805-3173-10), on the Web at **docs.sun.com,** and from the online documentation, AnswerBook2, provided with the Solaris 7 operating system.

6

The User Environment

Terms you'll need to understand:

√ User and group accounts

√ The **admintool** command

√ Password aging

√ Initialization files and templates

√ The system profile

Techniques you'll need to master:

√ Creating and deleting user accounts

√ Administering passwords

√ Creating group accounts

√ Using the **admintool** command

√ Customizing initialization files and templates

This chapter covers the Part I Exam objectives that address the user environment, including administering user accounts and the initialization files associated with user accounts.

User Accounts

User accounts control access to the system. The administration of user accounts and the passwords associated with these accounts are a key system administration activity.

Account Administration

User accounts can be added, modified, or deleted manually or by using the **admintool**(1M) command. The preferred method is the **admintool** command, as this reduces or eliminates the possible introduction of typos and other errors that might affect all the user accounts.

Creating An Account Using The **admintool** Command

When the **admintool** command is started, the Users window is displayed as shown in Figure 6.1. To display the Add User window, select Add from the Edit pull-down menu. The Add User window, shown in Figure 6.2, consists of three portions: User Identity, Account Security, and Home Directory.

The User Identity portion provides the information that needs to be defined to add a user account. All this information is stored in the /etc/passwd file except secondary groups information, which is stored in the /etc/group file. Table 6.1 lists the fields of the User Identity section.

The Account Security portion provides the information used to determine how the password should be defined and to set up password aging. All this information is stored in the /etc/shadow file. Table 6.2 lists the fields of the Account Security section.

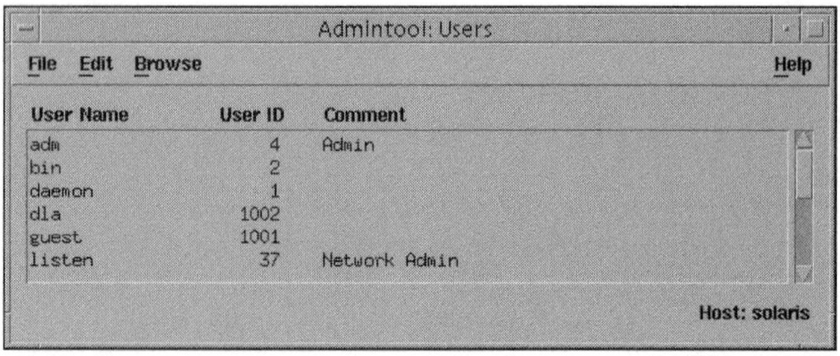

Figure 6.1   The Admintool: Users window.

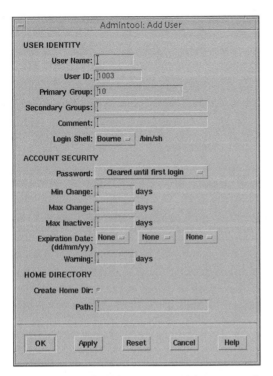

Figure 6.2   The Admintool: Add User window.

Table 6.1	User identity fields of the Admintool: Add User window.
Field	**Description**
User Name	A unique user account name consisting of a maximum of eight upper- and lowercase letters and/or numbers.
User ID	The UID associated with the user account. This is a unique number, typically between 1,000 and 60,000. The next available number starting at 1,000 is provided automatically.
Primary Group	The group to which the user should be assigned. By default, 10 (staff) is provided. Any specified group must exist before members can be added.
Secondary Groups	Additional groups (separated by commas) to which the user should be assigned. Specified groups must exist before members can be added.
Comment	Any text that should be placed in the /etc/passwd gcos field.
Login Shell	The Bourne (default), C, or Korn shell can be selected. Another shell can be specified by selecting "other" from the pull-down menu and entering the name of the shell in the field.

Table 6.2   Account Security fields of the Admintool: Add User window.

Field	Description
Password	The choices are: Cleared until first login, Account is locked, No password–setuid only, Normal password.
Min Change	Minimum days required between password changes
Max Change	Maximum days password is valid
Max Inactive	Maximum number of days account can be inactive before password must be changed
Expiration Date	Date account expires
Warning	Number of days user is warned before password expires

The Home Directory portion is used to define the home directory of the account and to create it if necessary. This path is stored in the /etc/passwd file. The appropriate initialization files are created in the home directory on the basis of the type of login shell selected.

Creating A Group Using The **admintool** Command

To create a group account, start the **admintool** command if it is not already active. Display the Groups window by selecting Groups from the Browse pull-down menu. The Groups window is shown in Figure 6.3.

Then, display the Add Group window by selecting Add from the Edit pull down menu. The Add group window is shown in Figure 6.4.

Enter a unique group name in the Group Name field. Use the next available GID number or enter a unique GID in the Group ID field. In the Members

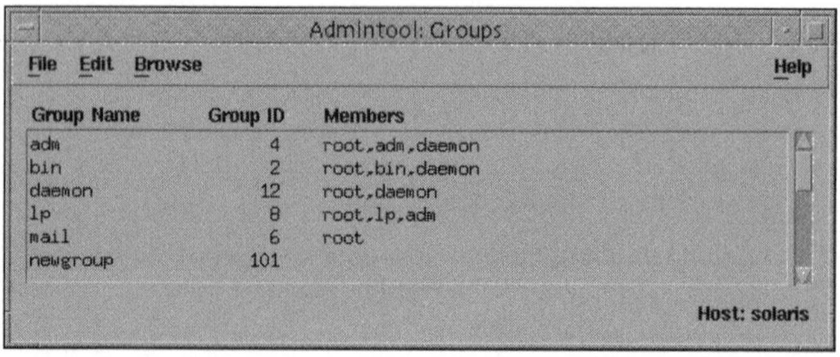

Figure 6.3   The Admintool: Groups window.

Figure 6.4   The Admintool: Add Group window.

List field, enter one or more user account names separated by commas. Using the mouse, click on OK. The new group is displayed in the Groups window.

Deleting An Account Using the **admintool** Command

To delete a user account, start the **admintool** command if it is not already active. Display the Users window by selecting Users from the Browse pull-down menu (see Figure 6.1).

With the mouse, click on the desired account entry to highlight it, and then select Delete from the Edit pull-down menu. The Warning window shown in Figure 6.5 will display.

Password Administration

Password administration involves setting parameters to control password aging, changing a user's password as needed, and possibly locking a user account to prevent use.

Password Aging

The parameters of the /etc/shadow file set through the Account Security fields of the **admintool** command Add Or Modify User Account window determine the password aging policy. This includes how long a password is valid (Max Change), how often it can be changed (Min Change), and how long an account can be inactive before the password must be changed (Max Inactive). These parameters enforce a policy for protecting the integrity of passwords.

Figure 6.5   The Admintool: Warning window.

Changing Passwords Using The **admintool** Command

To change the password of a user account, start the **admintool** command if it is not already active. Display the Users window by selecting Users from the Browse pull-down menu.

The user account can be selected in two ways: by double-clicking on the account entry or by clicking on the account entry to highlight it and then selecting Modify from the Edit pull-down menu. Using either method, the Modify User window is displayed as shown in Figure 6.6.

To modify the account password, position the mouse cursor over the Password field and hold down the left button. Then move the mouse cursor over the Normal Password item and release the mouse button. The Set User Password window is displayed as shown in Figure 6.7.

Enter the same password for both the Enter Password and the Verify Password fields. Asterisks are displayed in the place of each character entered. Using the mouse, click on OK. To save the password, click on OK in the Modify User window. Other than using the **admintool** command, the **passwd**(1) command is the only other way to change the password for a user account.

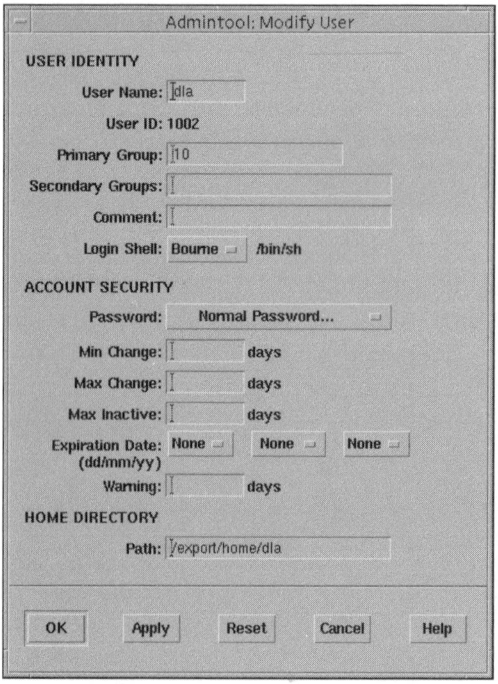

Figure 6.6   The Admintool: Modify User (Normal Password) window.

Figure 6.7   The Set User Password window.

Locking A User Account Using The **admintool** Command

An account can be locked to prevent it from being used. Start the **admintool** command if it is not already active. Display the Users window by selecting Users from the Browse pull-down menu.

The user account can be selected in two ways: by double-clicking on the account entry or by clicking on the account entry to highlight it and then selecting Modify from the Edit pull-down menu. Using either method, the Modify User window is displayed as shown in Figure 6.8.

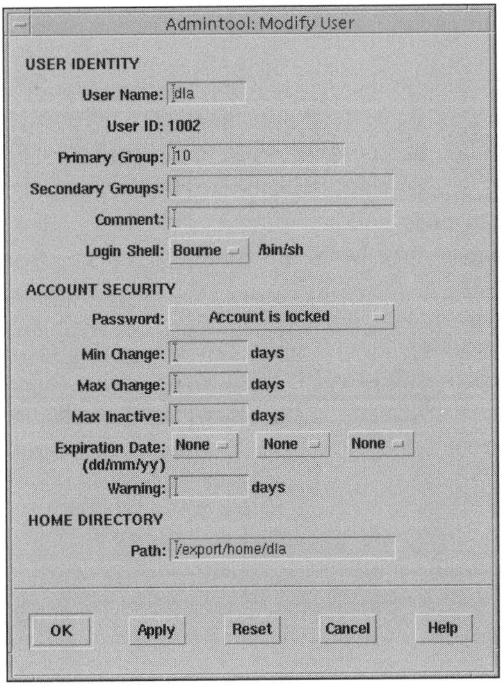

Figure 6.8   The Admintool: Modify User (Account Is Locked) window.

To lock the account, position the mouse cursor over the Password field and hold down the left button. Then move the mouse cursor over the Account Is Locked item and release the mouse button. The Account Is Locked item is displayed in the Password field as shown in Figure 6.8. To save the change, click on OK in the Modify User window.

Initialization Files

Several initialization (or startup) files are associated with each user account home directory. These files are used to specify commands to be executed when the associated event occurs. Depending on the login shell being used, there might be a login initialization file, a shell startup file, or a logout file. Table 6.3 lists the various initialization files.

Commands in the login initialization file are executed when the user logs in. All three common shells provide a login initialization file. Commands in the shell startup file are executed whenever the logged-in user starts a shell. Both csh and ksh provide this capability. The **ENV** parameter is used to define the ksh shell startup initialization file. Only csh provides a file for automatic execution of commands when a user logs out.

The System Profile

For user accounts that use sh (Bourne shell) or ksh as a login shell, commands in the system profile are executed before the user's login initialization file. This file is named /etc/profile and, when executed, sets a default terminal type (TERM) and then calls **umask**(1) to set the default file permission mask to 022. If the user's home directory does not include a file by the name of .hushlogin, the user's storage quota is displayed using **quot**(1M), the message of the day (if any) is displayed, and a notification message is displayed if new email has arrived for the user.

Table 6.3 Initialization files.			
File	**sh**	**csh**	**ksh**
Login initialization file	.profile	.login	.profile
Shell startup initialization file	N/A	.cshrc	user-defined
Logout file	N/A	.logout	N/A

The following listing shows the default contents of /etc/profile:

```
trap ""  2 3
export LOGNAME PATH
if [ "$TERM" = "" ]
then
        if /bin/i386
        then
                TERM=AT386
        else
                TERM=sun
        fi
        export TERM
fi
# Login and -su shells get /etc/profile services.
# -rsh is given its environment in its .profile.
case "$0" in
-sh | -ksh | -jsh)
        if [ ! -f .hushlogin ]
        then
                /usr/sbin/quota
                # Allow the user to break the motd only.
                trap "trap '' 2"  2
                /bin/cat -s /etc/motd
                trap "" 2
                /bin/mail -E
                case $? in
                0)
                        echo "You have new mail."
                        ;;
                2)
                        echo "You have mail."
                        ;;
                esac
        fi
esac
umask 022
trap  2 3
```

Initialization File Templates

When a user account is created and a home directory specified, part of setting up the user account is copying the appropriate default initialization files to the user's home directory. These initial files or templates are stored in the /etc/skel directory.

For user accounts that use sh or ksh as the login shell, the /etc/skel/local.profile file is copied to the .profile file in the user's home directory. The following listing shows the default contents of the /etc/skel/local.profile file:

```
#
# @(#)local.profile 1.6 98/02/06 SMI
#
stty istrip
PATH=/usr/bin:/usr/ucb:/etc:.
export PATH
#
# If possible, start the windows system
#
if [ "`tty`" = "/dev/console" ] ; then
        if [ "$TERM" = "sun" -o "$TERM" = "AT386" ] ; then
                if [ ${OPENWINHOME:-""} = "" ] ; then
                        OPENWINHOME=/usr/openwin
                        export OPENWINHOME
                fi
                echo ""
                echo "Starting OpenWindows in 5 seconds"
sleep 5
                echo ""
                $OPENWINHOME/bin/openwin
                clear # get rid of annoying cursor rectangle
                exit # logout after leaving windows system
        fi
fi
```

For user accounts that use csh as the login shell, the /etc/skel/local.login file is copied to the .login file in the user's home directory. The following listing shows the default contents of the /etc/skel/local.login file:

```
# @(#)local.login 1.4      98/02/06 SMI
stty -istrip
#
if ( "`tty`" == "/dev/console" ) then
        if ( "$TERM" == "sun" || "$TERM" == "AT386" ) then
                if ( ${?OPENWINHOME} == 0 ) then
                        setenv OPENWINHOME /usr/openwin
                endif
                echo ""
                echo -n "Starting OpenWindows in 5 seconds"
                sleep 5
                echo ""
```

```
                $OPENWINHOME/bin/openwin
                clear # get rid of annoying cursor rectangle
                logout # logout after leaving windows system
        endif
endif
```

In addition, for user accounts that use csh as the login shell, the /etc/skel/ local.cshrc file is copied to the .cshrc file in the user's home directory. The following listing shows the default contents of the /etc/skel/local.cshrc file:

```
# @(#)cshrc 1.11 89/11/29 SMI
umask 022
set path=(/bin /usr/bin /usr/ucb /etc .)
if ( $?prompt ) then
        set history=32
endif
```

Customizing The User Environment

The initialization file templates can be modified to provide a custom environment for new user accounts. In addition, the system profile (/etc/profile) can be modified to customize the environment for all users during login initialization.

Keep in mind that the system profile, /etc/profile, is executed before the user's profile. This provides the ability to control and restrict the user environment before the user has an opportunity to make any modifications.

To customize individual user accounts, the initialization files in the user's home directories can be modified. For the most part, this will consist of adding commands to be automatically executed or defining shell parameters.

Defining Shell Variables In .profile

Variables defined and exported in the .profile become part of the user's environment. These variables are available to programs and shells executed by the user.

A common shell variable defined in the .profile is **LPDEST**, which is used to specify a default printer. To define the printer HPLaser as the default printer, include the following lines in the .profile for a user account:

```
LPDEST=HPLaser
export LPDEST
```

An alternate way to define this is to specify both commands on the same line and separate the commands with a semicolon:

```
LPDEST=HPLaser; export LPDEST
```

A similar syntax can be used for a user account that uses the Korn shell as a login shell. ksh also supports the following variation:

```
export LPDEST=HPLaser
```

Although defining variables for csh user accounts is not a certification requirement, the syntax for two csh methods of defining variables is shown in the following listing:

```
set LPDEST=HPlaser
setenv LPDEST HPlaser
```

Changes made to the user's login initialization file do not take effect until the user logs in again, or the .profile is executed by preceding it with a dot separated by a space. This executes the .profile and makes it part of the current environment.

Sourcing .profile

For user accounts that use the Solaris Common Desktop Environment (CDE), the /usr/dt/bin/Xsession command that starts the desktop can be configured to read and process the .login (csh) or .profile (sh and ksh) login initialization file in the user's home directory as part of the startup process.

The first user-specific file that Xsession calls is .dtprofile in the user's home directory. The last line of the default .dtprofile file is:

```
DTSOURCEPROFILE=true
```

This will cause the .login or .profile file to be executed (or sourced) automatically. To change this default behavior and prevent the login initialization file from being sourced, change **true** to **false**.

Practice Questions

Question 1

> Where are the user account initialization file templates stored?
>
> ○ a. Under the user account home directories
>
> ○ b. In the /etc/skel directory
>
> ○ c. In the /usr/skel directory
>
> ○ d. In the /skel directory

The correct answer is b. Answer a is incorrect because the user's copy of the templates (not the templates themselves) are stored under the home directories. The directories in answers c and d do not exist.

Question 2

> Which of the following are valid settings for the **admintool** command password field? [Select all that apply]
>
> ❑ a. Normal password
>
> ❑ b. Account is locked
>
> ❑ c. Cleared until first login
>
> ❑ d. No password—setuid only
>
> ❑ e. One-time password

The correct answers are a, b, c, and d. Solaris 7 does not provide a one-time password capability. Therefore, answer e is incorrect.

Question 3

> Enter the command used to add a user-defined Bourne shell variable to the user environment so that other programs can use the variable.
>
> _____

The correct answer is **export**.

Question 4

> The **admintool** provides a graphical user interface for adding and modifying group accounts. Which of the following fields are displayed on the **admintool** command Add Group and Modify Group windows? [Select all that apply]
>
> ❏ a. Group name
>
> ❏ b. Group ID (GID)
>
> ❏ c. Group alias
>
> ❏ d. Member list

The correct answers are a, b, and d. Answer c is incorrect because groups cannot have an alias.

Question 5

> Using the **admintool** command, how is a user account deleted?
>
> ○ a. Highlighting the user account entry and pressing the Delete key
>
> ○ b. Pressing the Delete key and highlighting the user account to delete
>
> ○ c. Highlighting the user account entry and selecting Delete from the Edit pull-down menu
>
> ○ d. Highlighting the user account entry, selecting Modify from the Edit menu, and then clicking on OK in the Warning window

The correct answer is c. Answers a and b are incorrect because the **admintool** command does not recognize pressing the Delete key as a command. Answer d is incorrect because Delete, not Modify, must be selected from the Edit menu to delete a user account.

Question 6

> Enter the full pathname of the system profile.
>
> _____

The correct answer is /etc/profile.

Question 7

To execute (source) the .profile file in the home directory of a user account automatically during a CDE login, which entry needs to be placed in the user's .dtprofile file?

○ a. **DTSOURCEPROFILE=true**

○ b. **SOURCEPROFILE=.profile**

○ c. **DTSOURCEPROFILE=${HOME}/.profile**

○ d. **SOURCEPROFILE=yes**

The correct answer is a. Answers b and d use an invalid shell variable (SOURCEPROFILE) instead of the correct variable (DTSOURCEPROFILE). Answer c is incorrect because the DTSOURCEPROFILE is used to determine whether to source the .profile file. It is not used to identify the location or name of the .profile file.

Question 8

You decide to enforce password aging for the guest account and want the password to be changed after 20 days. Which field of the **admintool** command Modify User window do you use?

○ a. Password

○ b. Min Change

○ c. Max Change

○ d. Max Inactive

○ e. Expiration Date

○ f. Warning

The correct answer is c. Answer a, the Password field, cannot be modified. Answer b, the Min Change field, contains the minimum number of days that should elapse before the password can be changed again. Answer d, the Max Inactive field, is the maximum number of days the account can be unused before changing the password is required. Answer e, the Expiration Date field, is the date on which the account expires. Answer f, the Warning field, is the number of days the user is warned before the password expires.

Question 9

When using the **admintool** command to create a user account, which of the following can be specified as the login shell? [Select all that apply]

❑ a. Bourne (/bin/sh)

❑ b. C (/bin/csh)

❑ c. Korn (/bin/ksh)

❑ d. Other (specify path)

All the answers are correct.

Question 10

Which commands can be used by root to change a password? [Select all that apply]

❑ a. **admintool**

❑ b. **passmgmt**

❑ c. **usermod**

❑ d. **passwd**

The correct answers are a and d. The **passmgmt** and **usermod** commands (answers b and c) do not provide any facility to specify a password.

Need To Know More?

Sun Microsystems, *System Administration Guide, Volume 1*, is available in printed form (ISBN 805-3727-10), on the Web at **docs.sun.com**, and from the online documentation, AnswerBook2, provided with the Solaris 7 operating system.

Sun Microsystems, *System Reference Manual, Section 1 - User Commands*, is available in printed form (ISBN 805-3172-10), on the Web at **docs.sun.com**, and from the online documentation, AnswerBook2, provided with the Solaris 7 operating system.

Sun Microsystems, *System Reference Manual, Section 1M - Administration Commands*, is available in printed form (ISBN 805-3173-10), on the Web at **docs.sun.com**, and from the online documentation, AnswerBook2, provided with the Solaris 7 operating system.

Controlling Processes

Terms you'll need to understand:

√ Process attributes

√ Signals

√ The **ps** and **pgrep** commands

√ The **kill** and **pkill** commands

√ The **cron** and **crontab** commands

√ The crontab files

Techniques you'll need to master:

√ Viewing process attributes using the **ps** and **pgrep** commands

√ Terminating processes using the **kill** and **pkill** commands

√ Scheduling processes using the **cron** and **at** commands

√ Controlling use of the **cron** and **at** commands

This chapter covers controlling programs or processes running on the system. This consists of viewing the status of processes, killing processes as needed, and scheduling the automatic starting of processes.

Viewing And Terminating Processes

The **ps**(1) and **pgrep**(1) commands are used to view attributes of processes, whereas the **kill**(1) and **pkill**(1) commands are used to terminate processes.

The **ps** Command

The **ps** command is used to display information about active processes. Without any command line arguments, the **ps** command displays processes that have the same effective user ID (UID) of the user account that executed the command. Table 7.1 lists the command line arguments supported by the **ps** command.

A considerable amount of information on processes is available through the **ps** command and its several variations of display formats.

Table 7.1	The ps command line arguments.
Argument	**Description**
-a	Displays all processes except process group leaders and processes not associated with terminals
-A	Displays all processes (identical to -e)
-c	Displays alternate columns
-d	Displays all processes except process session leaders
-e	Displays all processes
-f	Uses the full listing display format
-g *Process Group ID*	Displays processes with the specified process group ID
-G *Group ID*	Displays processes with the specified group ID (GID)
-j	Displays session and process group ID
-l	Uses the long listing display format
-L	Displays information about each lightweight process
-n *Name*	Uses an alternate name list file (ignored)
-o *Format*	Uses an alternate display format
-p *Process ID*	Displays the process with the specified process ID (PID)

(continued)

Table 7.1 The ps command line arguments (continued).	
Argument	**Description**
-P	Displays the number of the processor executing the process (only meaningful on a multiprocessor system)
-s *Process Session ID*	Displays processes with the specified process session ID
-t *Terminal Device Path*	Displays processes associated with the specified terminal device path
-u *Effective User ID*	Displays processes with the specified effective user ID
-U *Real User ID*	Displays processes with the specified real user ID
-Y	Displays alternate columns in long listing

The default information displayed for a process is its process ID (PID), the terminal device it is associated with (TTY), its accumulated execution time (TIME), and the program or command name (CMD). This information is included in all formats unless specifically omitted.

All the command line arguments used to specify an ID—such as process group ID, real group ID, PID, process session ID, effective UID, and real UID—accept multiple IDs (separated by commas). For the real and effective user IDs and the real group ID, either the numeric IDs or the account names can be specified.

The following listing shows the use of the **ps** command with several different command line arguments:

```
$ ps -udla
    PID TTY       TIME CMD
    781 ?         0:19 xterm
    782 pts/5     0:00 sh
    910 pts/5     0:10 telnet
    913 pts/6     0:01 sh
$ ps -tpts/5
    PID TTY       TIME CMD
    782 pts/5     0:00 sh
    910 pts/5     0:10 telnet
$ ps -f -udla
     UID   PID  PPID  C    STIME TTY      TIME CMD
     dla   781     1  0   Aug 28 ?        0:19 xterm -display
     dla   782   781  0   Aug 28 pts/5    0:00 sh
     dla   910   782  0   Aug 28 pts/5    0:10 telnet solaris
     dla   913   911  0   Aug 28 pts/6    0:01 -sh
$
```

The PPID column lists the parent PID of the process, the C column lists processor utilization (obsolete), and the STIME shows the start date.

The kill Command

The **kill**(1) command is used to terminate a process by sending a signal to it that will cause it to exit. Many different types of signals exist. The signals that are typically used to terminate a process are listed in Table 7.2, and a complete listing of base signals can be found in **signal**(5).

The default response of processes that receive these signals is to terminate, but this behavior can be changed on a process-by-process basis.

The signal can be specified using either its symbolic name (excluding the SIG prefix) or its numeric value. If a signal is not specified, SIGTERM (15) is sent by default. The PIDs of the processes to be terminated must be known. The following listing shows sending the KILL signal (9) to several processes using the **kill** command:

```
# kill -KILL 4220 4224 4229
#
4229 Killed
4224 Killed
4220 Killed
# kill -9 4247
#
4247 Killed
```

A PID preceded by a minus sign is interpreted as a process group ID, and the signal is sent to all processes in that process group.

Table 7.2   Signals used to terminate processes.

Symbolic Name	Value	Description
SIGHUP	1	Hangup
SIGINT	2	Interrupt
SIGKILL	9	Kill
SIGTERM	15	Terminate
SIGUSR1	16	User signal 1
SIGUSR2	17	User signal 2

The **pgrep** And **pkill** Commands

The **pgrep**(1) and **pkill**(1) commands support viewing and terminating processes by name or other attributes, such as UID, GID, and so on. Table 7.3 lists the command line arguments supported by both the **pgrep** and the **pkill** command.

The *pattern* is a regular expression that is used to select processes based on the program name. The following listing shows the difference between obtaining

Table 7.3 Common pgrep and pkill command line arguments.	
Argument	**Description**
pattern	Regular expression to match against program name and/or arguments
-f	Matches pattern against full arguments instead of program name
-g *Process Group ID*	Matches processes with the specified process group ID
-G *Real Group ID*	Matches processes with the specified real group ID
-n	Matches only the newest process that meets the specified criteria
-P *Parent Process ID*	Matches processes with the specified parent process ID
-s *Process Session ID*	Matches processes with the specified process session ID
-t *Terminal Device Path*	Matches processes associated with the specified terminal device path
-u *Effective User ID*	Matches processes with the specified effective user ID
-U *Real User ID*	Matches processes with the specified real user ID
-v	Matches all processes except those that meet specified criteria
-x	Matches only processes that exactly match the pattern

the PID of the **admintool** command using the **ps** and **grep**(1) commands versus the **pgrep** command:

```
$ ps -eaf|grep admintool
root  2898  1096  0  Sep 04 pts/7   0:02 admintool
$ pgrep adm*
2898
$
```

When the -f command line argument is specified along with the *pattern*, the *pattern* is compared against the program arguments instead of the program name. In addition, if the -x command line argument is specified, the regular expression interpretation of *pattern* is disabled, and *pattern* must match the program name or program arguments exactly.

All the ID types of command line arguments accept multiple IDs (separated by commas). In the case of real and effective user IDs and real group ID (-G), either the numeric IDs or the account names can be specified.

The **pgrep** command supports two additional command line arguments. The -d command line argument is used to specify a delimiter for separating PIDs when the specified **pgrep** criteria match more than one PID. By default, this delimiter is the newline character. The following listing shows using the **pgrep** command to list the processes owned by the dla user account and the effect of specifying the space character as the delimiter:

```
$ pgrep -u dla
781
782
910
913
$ pgrep -d' ' -u dla
781 782 910 913
$
```

The delimiter command line argument allows the output of the **pgrep** command to be used as the input to other commands or shell scripts.

The other command line argument is -l, which includes the name of the program with the PIDs of matched processes. The following listing shows the use of the -l command line argument:

```
$ pgrep -l -u dla
  781 xterm
  782 sh
  910 telnet
  913 sh
$
```

The **pkill** command is similar to the **pgrep** command, but instead of displaying information on matched processes, the matched processes are terminated using the SIGTERM (15) signal.

All the command line arguments listed in Table 7.3 are supported, allowing processes to be selected on the basis of regular expression pattern matching and/or various IDs. In addition, the **pkill** command supports a command line argument to specify a signal to be used instead of SIGTERM. This command line argument is the minus sign followed by a symbolic name (not including the SIG prefix) or the signal number. The following listing shows the use of the SIGKILL signal to terminate all processes associated with the dla user account:

```
# pkill -KILL -u dla
#
```

Scheduling Processes

Two commands are available for scheduling automatic execution of processes: cron(1M) and at(1).

The **cron** Command

The **cron** command is a daemon started during system boot. It is responsible for executing commands at a future time and perhaps periodically on a scheduled basis. The commands to be executed are specified in a standardized tabular format and stored in files referred to as *crontab files*. These files are located under the /var/spool/cron/crontabs directory.

Commands that are executed automatically by being placed in a crontab file are referred to as *cron jobs*. Commands to be executed only once at a future time can be submitted using the **at** command instead of modifying the crontabs. The **at** command is described in the next section.

The two general classes of crontabs are system crontabs, which are owned by system accounts such as root, lp, and so on, and user crontabs, which are created and maintained by nonadministrative user accounts.

Default **cron** Settings

Like other system utilities, parameters can be set to control the behavior of the **cron** command. These settings are listed in the /etc/default/cron file.

The **cron** command will log its activities in the /var/cron/log file if the following entry is contained in the /etc/default/cron file:

```
CRONLOG=YES
```

This is the default. To disable logging, change **YES** to **NO** and reboot the system or restart cron using the /etc/init.d/cron run control (rc) script.

Other entries that can be added to the /etc/default/cron is **PATH**, which sets the PATH shell environment parameter for user cron jobs, and **SUPATH**, which sets the PATH shell environment variable for root cron jobs. The following listing shows the **PATH** and **SUPATH** settings:

```
PATH=/usr/bin:/usr/ucb:
SUPATH=/usr/sbin:/usr/bin:
```

The crontab Files

The /var/spool/cron/crontabs directory contains both the system and the user crontab files. These files have the same name as the account name of the owner. For example, the crontab for the guest user account is named guest.

The crontab file contains entries that specify a command to execute along with a time and frequency of execution. Commands can be executed daily, weekly, or monthly at any time of the day.

A crontab entry consists of six fields separated by spaces or tabs. An asterisk (*) is used as a placeholder in a field that is not used. Table 7.4 lists the fields of a crontab entry.

The following listing shows the contents of a typical root crontab file:

```
10 3 * * 0,4 /etc/cron.d/logchecker
10 3 * * 0   /usr/lib/newsyslog
15 3 * * 0 /usr/lib/fs/nfs/nfsfind
1 2 * * * [ -x /usr/sbin/rtc ] && /usr/sbin/rtc -c
30 3 * * * [ -x /usr/lib/clean ] && /usr/lib/clean
```

Table 7.4   The fields of a crontab entry.

Field	Values	Description
minute	0–59	Minutes of the hour
hour	0–23	Hour of the day
day	1–31	Day of the month
month	1–12	Month of the year
weekday	0–6	Day of the week (0 = Sunday)
command	N/A	The command to execute

Note that multiple values in a field can be specified by separating them with a comma as shown in the crontab entry for logchecker. In this example, logchecker will be executed at 3:10 A.M. every Sunday and Thursday morning.

 A critical skill for system administrators is the ability to understand and use crontabs to schedule log maintenance, system backups, and other routine maintenance.

Manipulating crontabs

The **crontab**(1) command can be used to create, list, edit, and delete crontabs. One capability of the **crontab** command (the ability to edit the crontab files of other users) is available only to the superuser.

When **crontab** is executed without any command line arguments, it reads the standard input (typically the keyboard). When terminated with Ctrl+d, the entered data is used to create the crontab (or overwrite an existing crontab) for the user account that executed the **crontab** command. When a file name is specified as a command line argument, the contents of the specified file are used to create/overwrite the user crontab.

When **crontab** is executed with a -e command line argument, the editor specified by the shell environment parameter EDITOR is invoked on the user crontab. If the EDITOR parameter is not set, the **ed**(1) text editor is used. This allows editing of the crontab associated with the invoking user account.

The **crontab -l** command can be used to display the contents of the user's crontab, and the **crontab -r** command can be used to delete the user's crontab.

 When the **cron** daemon starts, it reads all existing crontabs. Because it normally does not re-read the crontabs, it will not be aware of any changes made unless they are made using the **crontab** command. The **crontab** command notifies the **cron** daemon that a crontab has changed or been added. The **cron** daemon then updates its information.

The superuser can specify a user account name after the **crontab** command argument to control the crontab of another user account. This can be used with the -l or -r command line arguments to list or delete the crontab of another user account; however, do not specify a user account name with the -e command line argument.

If the superuser attempts to modify the crontab of another user account using the **crontab -e** command and specifying the user account name as a command line argument, the results will be unpredictable. Instead, use the **su**(1) command to become the other user account and then use the **crontab -e** command.

Access Control

Access to the **crontab** command is controlled by two files: cron.allow and cron.deny, both of which reside under the /etc/cron.d directory. These text files contain lists of user account names (one per line) that are allowed or denied access.

Users are allowed access to the **crontab** command if their user account name is listed in the /etc/cron.d/cron.allow file. If the cron.allow file does not exist, users will be allowed access if their user account name is not listed in the /etc/cron.d/cron.deny file. In addition, users will be denied access if neither file exists.

These access rules also apply to the root account if either the cron.allow or the cron.deny file exists. By default, the /etc/cron.d/cron.deny file is created and contains all initial nonadministrative user accounts.

The **at** Command

A simple way to execute one or more commands once without modifying a crontab is to use the **at**(1) command. Commands submitted for later execution are grouped together as an at-job and are assigned an at-job ID.

The basic format of the **at** command is **at** *time*, where *time* specifies the time at which the command(s) should be executed. The time can be specified using any combination of either A.M./P.M. or 24-hour format, plus month and day in conjunction with the keywords **now, today, tomorrow,** and so on. The following listing shows several different types of time specifications:

```
at now
at 10am
at 2pm
at noon
at 3pm + 1 week
at 3pm next week
at 2am jan 24
at 1400 tomorrow
```

The command(s) to be executed can be entered from the standard input and ended with Ctrl+d or can be read from a file that is specified by using the -f *file* command line argument. The at-jobs are stored under the /var/spool/cron/ atjobs directory.

The **at** command supports other command line arguments to specify that the commands should be executed using the Bourne shell (**-b**), the C shell (**-c**), or the Korn shell (**-k**) and whether the user should be notified by mail when the command is executed (**-m**). Like the **crontab** command, the **at** command supports the -l and -r command line arguments and allows at-jobs to be listed and removed by at-job ID.

The **batch**(1) command is equivalent to **at -m now** and allows a batch job to be entered by means of the standard input.

Use of the **at** and **batch** commands is controlled by the /usr/lib/cron/at.allow and /usr/lib/cron/at.deny files. These files function similarly to the **cron** access control files except that, if neither file exists, only the superuser can submit jobs, and an empty at.deny allows access to everyone.

Practice Questions

Question 1

Which of the following criteria can be used to select processes using the **pkill** command? [Select all that apply]

❑ a. Program name

❑ b. Start time

❑ c. Real or effective UID

❑ d. Associated terminal device

The correct answers are a, c, and d. Answer b, the start time, is not supported as a criterion for either the **pkill** or the **pgrep** command.

Question 2

Enter the command that can be used to list, edit, and delete crontab files.

_____

The correct answer is **crontab**.

Question 3

If a signal is not specified when using the **kill** command, by default, which signal is sent to the specified processes?

○ a. SIGHUP

○ b. SIGINT

○ c. SIGKILL

○ d. SIGTERM

The correct answer is d. All of these signals can typically be used to terminate processes, but SIGTERM is the default signal used by the **kill** and **pkill** commands.

Question 4

> What is the order of the fields in a crontab file?
>
> ○ a.   month, day, hour, minute, weekday, command
>
> ○ b.   command, weekday, minute, hour, day, month
>
> ○ c.   minute, hour, day, month, weekday, command
>
> ○ d.   second, minute, hour, day, month, weekday, command

The correct answer is c. Answers a and b contain all the correct fields but are not in the correct order. Answer d lists an extra field (second), which is not a valid field of a crontab file.

Question 5

> Which command can be used to schedule command execution using A.M./P.M. time notation?
>
> _____

The correct answer is **at**.

Question 6

> Which of the following criteria can be specified to select processes using the **pgrep** command? [Select all that apply]
>
> ❏ a.   Program name
>
> ❏ b.   Process ID (PID)
>
> ❏ c.   Real or effective UID
>
> ❏ d.   Associated terminal device

The correct answers are a, c, and d. Answer b, process ID, cannot be specified as a criterion because the **pgrep** command is used to determine process IDs.

Question 7

The /etc/cron.d/cron.deny file exists, but the /etc/cron.d/cron.allow file does not. Which of the following statements are true regarding access to the cron capability? [Select all that apply]

❑ a. Without a cron.allow file, no one, including root, is allowed to create, edit, or delete crontab files.

❑ b. Without a cron.allow file, only root is allowed to create, edit, or delete crontab files.

❑ c. Any user account not listed in the cron.deny file can create, edit, or delete their crontab file.

❑ d. Any user account listed in the cron.deny file cannot create, edit, or delete their crontab file.

The correct answers are c and d. Answers a and b are incorrect because if a cron.deny exists and a cron.allow does not exist, any account not listed in the cron.deny file can use the cron facility.

Question 8

What information is provided on all process listings generated by the **ps** command? [Select all that apply]

❑ a. Program or command name

❑ b. Parent process ID

❑ c. Process ID

❑ d. Associated terminal device

Answers a, c, and d are correct. Answer b, parent process ID, is provided only on the full (-f) and long (-l) listing formats.

Need To Know More?

Sun Microsystems, *System Administration Guide, Volume 2*, is available in printed form (ISBN 805-3728-10), on the Web at **docs.sun.com,** and from the online documentation, AnswerBook2, provided with the Solaris 7 operating system.

Sun Microsystems, *System Reference Manual, Section 1 - User Commands*, is available in printed form (ISBN 805-3172-10), on the Web at **docs.sun.com,** and from the online documentation, AnswerBook2, provided with the Solaris 7 operating system.

Sun Microsystems, *System Reference Manual, Section 1M - Administration Commands*, is available in printed form (ISBN 805-3173-10), on the Web at **docs.sun.com,** and from the online documentation, AnswerBook2, provided with the Solaris 7 operating system.

Sun Microsystems, *System Reference Manual, Section 5 - Headers, Tables and Macros*, is available in printed form (ISBN 805-3177-10), on the Web at **docs.sun.com,** and from the online documentation, AnswerBook2, provided with the Solaris 7 operating system.

8

Disk Administration

Terms you'll need to understand:

√ Physical device names

√ Logical device names (raw and block disk devices)

√ Instance names

√ The /etc/path_to_inst file

√ The **df, dmesg, format, mount, prtconf, prtvtoc**, and **sysdef** commands

√ Disk label (volume table of contents)

√ Partitions and the partition table

Techniques you'll need to master:

√ Displaying physical, logical, and instance names

√ Partitioning disks using the **format** utility

√ Displaying the partition table

√ Using raw and block logical device names

The first part of this chapter describes the three naming conventions used to identify system devices and then focuses on the device names associated with disks and the commands used to display these names. The second part of this chapter defines the logical structure of a disk, referred to as a *partition*, and describes how to create and display partition-related data.

Disk Device Names

Disks, like other devices of the Solaris 7 operating system, can be referenced using three naming conventions:

➤ Physical device name

➤ Logical device name

➤ Instance name

Physical Device Names

When the system is booted, the kernel builds a device hierarchy, referred to as the *device tree*, to represent the devices attached to the system. This tree is a hierarchy of interconnected buses with the devices attached to the buses as nodes. The root node is the main physical address bus.

Each device node can have attributes such as properties, methods, and data. In addition, each node typically has a parent node and might have children nodes. A node with children is typically another bus, whereas a node without children is a device attached to a bus.

The *full device pathname* identifies a device in terms of its location in the device tree by identifying a series of *node names* separated by slashes with the root indicated by a leading slash. Each node name in the full device pathname has the following form:

```
driver-name@unit-address:device arguments
```

driver-name identifies the device name, *@unit-address* is the physical address of the device in the address space of the parent, and *:device arguments* is used to define additional information regarding the device software. For example, the following full device address represents a slice (or partition) of a SCSI disk drive on a SPARC system:

```
/sbus@1f,0/esp@0,4000/sd@3,0:a
```

This identifies a device attached to the sbus with a main system bus address of 1f,0; an esp device (SCSI bus) attached at SBus slot 0, offset 4000; and an sd device (SCSI disk) with a SCSI bus target of 3, a logical unit of 0, and an argument of a, which represents slice a of the disk.

Devices can also be referenced using physical device names. These are located under the /devices directory. Although these physical names define the exact location of devices within the system, they are difficult to remember and use.

Logical Device Names

Another naming convention that is easier to use is logical device names. Logical device names are used to identify disk, tape, and CD-ROM devices and provide either *raw access* (one character at a time) or *block access* (via a buffer for accessing large blocks of data).

The logical name of SCSI disk devices on a SPARC system identifies the SCSI controller (bus), SCSI target (location on bus), drive (almost always 0), and slice (partition) as in the following logical device name:

```
/dev/dsk/c0t3d0sa
```

All logical device names reside under the /dev directory, and the dsk subdirectory identifies the device as a block disk device (the rdsk subdirectory indicates a raw disk). This block disk device is addressed as SCSI controller 0, SCSI bus target 3, drive 0, and slice (partition) a. Note the similarities (and differences) between this logical device name and its physical device name as described in the previous section. Devices that have direct controllers as opposed to bus-oriented controllers (such as IDE drives) do not include the t# (bus target) portion of the logical device name.

Some commands, such as the **format**(1M) command used to format a disk, the **newfs**(1M) command used to create a file system, and the **fsck**(1M) command used to check a file system, expect raw device names (/dev/rdsk). Other commands, such as the **mount**(1M) command used to make a file system available for use and the **df**(1M) command used to display free file system space, expect block device names (/dev/dsk). A few commands, such as the **prtvtoc**(1M) command, accept either raw or block logical device names.

Instance Names

Instance names are abbreviated names that are mapped to or associated with the physical device names of devices. These allow devices to be quickly and easily identified without requiring the use of the long and typically complicated physical device names. An instance name typically consists of a short driver binding name, such as **sd**, and an instance number. For example, **sd0** could be the instance name of the first SCSI disk or **fd0** could be the instance name of the first diskette drive.

The mapping of physical device names (also known as full device pathnames) with instance names is accomplished using the /etc/path_to_inst file. This file is rebuilt automatically when the system is reconfigured using the **touch /reconfigure** command or the **boot -r** command. The format of the /etc/path_to_inst file consists of three fields separated by tab characters. The fields are described in Table 8.1.

The following listing shows the /etc/path_to_inst file for an x86 Solaris 7 operating system. The tab between each field has been replaced with an appropriate number of spaces to improve readability:

```
"/isa"                                            0   "isa"
"/isa/pnpCTL,0031@pnpCTL,0045,1000775b"           0   "sbpro"
"/isa/pnpTCM,5094@pnpTCM,5094,afe4c17a"           0   "elx"
"/isa/lp@1,378"                                   0   "lp"
"/isa/kd@0,a0000"                                 0   "kd"
"/isa/kdmouse@1,60"                               0   "kdmouse"
"/isa/chanmux"                                    0   "chanmux"
"/isa/asy@1,3f8"                                  0   "asy"
"/isa/asy@1,2f8"                                  1   "asy"
"/isa/fdc@1,3f0"                                  0   "fdc"
"/isa/fdc@1,3f0/fd@0,1"                           1   "fd"
"/isa/fdc@1,3f0/fd@0,0"                           0   "fd"
"/isa/chanmux@1,3b0"                              1   "chanmux"
"/pci@0,0"                                        0   "pci"
"/pci@0,0/pci-ide@7,1"                            0   "pci-ide"
"/pci@0,0/pci-ide@7,1/ata@0"                      0   "ata"
"/pci@0,0/pci-ide@7,1/ata@1"                      1   "ata"
"/pci@0,0/pci-ide@7,1/ata@0/cmdk@0,0"             0   "cmdk"
"/pci@0,0/pci-ide@7,1/ata@0/cmdk@1,0"             1   "cmdk"
"/pci@0,0/pci-ide@7,1/ata@1/st@0,0"               7   "st"
"/pci@0,0/pci-ide@7,1/ata@1/sd@0,0"              16   "sd"
"/options"                                        0   "options"
"/objmgr"                                         0   "objmgr"
"/pseudo"                                         0   "pseudo"
```

Table 8.1   Fields of the /etc/path_to_inst file.

Field	Description
Physical Name	Full physical device name or full path device name
Instance Number	The unique number (typically starting with 0)
Driver Binding Name	Name assigned to the device driver

Determining Disk Device Names

Several commands can be used to identify disk device names. These include the following:

➤ df(1M)

➤ dmesg(1M)

➤ format(1M)

➤ mount(1M)

➤ prtconf(1M)

➤ sysdef(1M)

The df Command

The **df** command lists free blocks (available storage space) and files (number of additional files that can be created) on a file system basis. The file systems are identified using logical block disk device names as shown in the following listing:

```
# df
/proc          (/proc          ):       0 blocks      965 files
/              (/dev/dsk/c0d0s0 ):   56122 blocks    35836 files
/usr           (/dev/dsk/c0d0s6 ):  181578 blocks   168053 files
/dev/fd        (fd             ):       0 blocks        0 files
/var           (/dev/dsk/c0d0s3 ):  307186 blocks   147845 files
/export/home   (/dev/dsk/c0d0s7 ): 1854628 blocks   488829 files
/opt           (/dev/dsk/c0d0s5 ):   15272 blocks   109653 files
/usr/openwin   (/dev/dsk/c0d0s1 ):  232678 blocks   160634 files
/tmp           (swap           ):  332952 blocks     9991 files
```

The dmesg Command

The **dmesg** command collects and displays diagnostic messages from the syslog (typically /var/adm/messages). These messages are generated during system boot and use instance names (and physical names) to identify devices. The following listing shows a partial output from the **dmesg** command:

```
# dmesg
Sun Sep 12 15:56:08 EDT 1999
Aug 25 19:43:51 solaris unix: ISA-device: fdc0
Aug 25 19:43:51 solaris unix: fd0 at fdc0
Aug 25 19:43:51 solaris unix: fd0 is /isa/fdc@1,3f0/fd@0,0
Aug 25 19:44:05 solaris unix: ISA-device: asy0
Aug 25 19:44:05 solaris unix: asy0 is /isa/asy@1,3f8
```

```
Aug 25 19:44:05 solaris unix: ISA-device: asy1
Aug 25 19:44:05 solaris unix: asy1 is /isa/asy@1,2f8
Aug 25 19:44:11 solaris unix: pseudo-device: xsvc0
Aug 25 19:44:11 solaris unix: xsvc0 is /pseudo/xsvc@0
Aug 26 20:58:55 solaris unix: SunOS Release 5.7
Aug 26 20:58:55 solaris unix: mem = 65152K (0x3fa0000)
Aug 26 20:58:55 solaris unix: avail mem = 54063104
```

The **format** Command

The **format** command supports menu selection of disk devices. Both logical device names (minus the /dev/rdsk prefix) and physical device names are displayed:

```
# format
Searching for disks...done
AVAILABLE DISK SELECTIONS:
       0. c0d0 <DEFAULT cyl 614 alt 2 hd 128 sec 63>
          /pci@0,0/pci-ide@7,1/ata@0/cmdk@0,0
       1. c0d1 <DEFAULT cyl 771 alt 2 hd 255 sec 63>
          /pci@0,0/pci-ide@7,1/ata@0/cmdk@1,0
Specify disk (enter its number):
```

Note that in the case of the **format** command, the logical device name does not include the slice/partition portion, as this information is not required to identify the disk drive.

The **mount** Command

The **mount** command lists mounted file systems. The file systems are identified using logical block disk device names as shown in the following listing:

```
# mount
/proc on /proc read/write on Sat Sep 11 17:02:51 1999
/ on /dev/dsk/c0d0s0 read/write on Sat Sep 11 17:02:51 1999
/usr on /dev/dsk/c0d0s6 read/write on Sat Sep 11 17:02:51 1999
/dev/fd on fd read/write on Sat Sep 11 17:02:51 1999
/var on /dev/dsk/c0d0s3 read/write on Sat Sep 11 17:02:51 1999
/opt on /dev/dsk/c0d0s5 read/write on Sat Sep 11 17:02:54 1999
/tmp on swap read/write on Sat Sep 11 17:02:54 1999
#
```

The **prtconf** Command

The **prtconf** command displays system configuration information. Devices are identified using the driver binding name and instance number, which compose the instance name. The following listing shows the output from the **prtconf** command on an x86 Solaris 7 system:

```
# prtconf
System Configuration:  Sun Microsystems   i86pc
Memory size: 96 Megabytes
System Peripherals (Software Nodes):
i86pc
    +boot (driver not attached)
        memory (driver not attached)
    aliases (driver not attached)
    chosen (driver not attached)
    i86pc-memory (driver not attached)
    i86pc-mmu (driver not attached)
    openprom (driver not attached)
    options, instance #0
    packages (driver not attached)
    delayed-writes (driver not attached)
    itu-props (driver not attached)
    isa, instance #0
        motherboard (driver not attached)
        asy, instance #0
        lp (driver not attached)
        asy, instance #1
        fdc, instance #0
            fd, instance #0
            fd, instance #1 (driver not attached)
        kd (driver not attached)
        bios (driver not attached)
        bios (driver not attached)
        pnpTCM,5094, instance #0
        kd, instance #0
        chanmux, instance #0
    pci, instance #0
        pci8086,1250 (driver not attached)
        pci8086,7000 (driver not attached)
        pci-ide, instance #0
            ata, instance #0
                cmdk, instance #0
            ata, instance #1
                sd, instance #16
        pci1002,80 (driver not attached)
    used-resources (driver not attached)
    objmgr, instance #0
    pseudo, instance #0
```

The **sysdef** Command

The **sysdef** command displays the system configuration or definition that lists all hardware devices, including pseudo and system devices, loadable modules, and tunable kernel parameters. Like the **prtconf** command, devices are identified using the driver binding name and instance number, which compose the instance name. The following listing shows the partial output of the **sysdef** command:

```
# sysdef
*
* Hostid
*
  04eaa94c
*
* i86pc Configuration
*
*
* Devices
*
+boot (driver not attached)
        memory (driver not attached)
aliases (driver not attached)
chosen (driver not attached)
i86pc-memory (driver not attached)
i86pc-mmu (driver not attached)
openprom (driver not attached)
options, instance #0
packages (driver not attached)
delayed-writes (driver not attached)
itu-props (driver not attached)
isa, instance #0
        motherboard (driver not attached)
        asy, instance #0
        lp (driver not attached)
        asy, instance #1
        fdc, instance #0
                fd, instance #0
                fd, instance #1
        kd (driver not attached)
        bios (driver not attached)
        pnpTCM,5094, instance #0
        kd, instance #0
        chanmux, instance #0
 pci, instance #0
        pci8086,1250 (driver not attached)
        pci8086,7000 (driver not attached)
```

```
        pci-ide, instance #0
                ata, instance #0
                        cmdk, instance #0
                ata, instance #1
                        sd, instance #16
        pci1002,80 (driver not attached)
used-resources (driver not attached)
objmgr, instance #0
```

Partitioning Disks

The Solaris 7 operating system requires that disk drives support a logical structure in order to use its storage space. The logical structure consists of a small *disk label*, also called a *volume table of contents (VTOC)*, with the remainder of the disk being divided into *slices* or *partitions*. Once a partition is defined, a file system can be created within the partition. The physical and logical device name associated with a file system is actually the name of the partition in which it resides.

The Disk Label, Or VTOC

The disk label, or VTOC, contains various geometry data about the disk, such as sectors per track, tracks per cylinder, available cylinders, and so on. In addition, the disk label contains the *partition table*.

Partitions

A partition, or disk slice, is a contiguous collection of disk sectors as defined by the partition table. Once a partition is defined in the partition table, a file system can be created within the partition. The partition table contains an entry for each partition on the disk. Table 8.2 describes the fields of the partition table.

When partitions are defined, they can be assigned a hexadecimal tag that identifies the intended use of the partition. These tags can be used during system maintenance to quickly identify and select partitions. The tags are stored in the tag field of the partition table. Table 8.3 provides a list of partition tags.

The partition table can be created using either the **format** command or the **fmthard**(1M) command. It can be displayed using the **format** command or the **prtvtoc**(1M) command.

Once the partition table has been populated with the appropriate information (the disk partitions have been defined), file systems can be created within the partitions; however, not all partitions are intended to hold a file system.

Table 8.2 Fields of the partition table.	
Field	**Description**
Partition Name	Single hexadecimal character used as a name for the partition (0 through f)
Tag	Intended use of the partition—obsolete (see Table 8.3)
Flags	A value of 1 indicates that the partition is not mountable; a value of 10 indicates that the partition is read-only—obsolete
First Sector	Number of the first sector in the partition
Sector Count	Number of sectors in the partition
Last Sector	Number of the last sector assigned to the partition
Mount Directory	The directory where the partition (actually file system) was last mounted

Table 8.3 Partition tags.	
Partition Type	**Tag Value**
unassigned	0
boot	1
root	2
swap	3
usr	4
backup	5

Using The **format** Command To Partition A Disk

The **format** command can be used to create or modify a partition table. After selecting a disk, the FORMAT MENU is displayed. From this menu, select partition to display the PARTITION MENU as shown in the following listing:

```
PARTITION MENU:
        0       - change '0' partition
        1       - change '1' partition
        2       - change '2' partition
        3       - change '3' partition
        4       - change '4' partition
        5       - change '5' partition
        6       - change '6' partition
        7       - change '7' partition
        select - select a predefined table
```

```
modify - modify a predefined partition table
name   - name the current table
print  - display the current table
label  - write partition map and label to the disk
!<cmd> - execute <cmd>, then return
quit
```

Existing partitions can be modified by selecting the partition number (0 through 7) and then entering tag, flags, starting cylinder, and a partition size in bytes or cylinders. A predefined table can be selected and used. Alternatively, an existing partition table can be used as a starting point to create a custom table. Custom tables can be saved using the save item of the FORMAT MENU.

Using The **prtvtoc** Command To Display The VTOC

The **prtvtoc** command is used to display the VTOC of a physical disk drive. In addition to displaying the partition table, it also displays the disk geometry. The following listing shows the output of the **prtvtoc** command for an x86 IDE disk drive:

```
# prtvtoc /dev/rdsk/c0d0s0
* /dev/rdsk/c0d0s0 partition map
*
* Dimensions:
*     512 bytes/sector
*      63 sectors/track
*     128 tracks/cylinder
*    8064 sectors/cylinder
*     616 cylinders
*     614 accessible cylinders
*
* Flags:
*   1: unmountable
*  10: read-only
*
*                       First     Sector    Last
* Partition Tag Flags  Sector      Count   Sector  Mount Directory
          0    2   00    24192     104832   129023  /
          1    4   00   129024     693504   822527  /usr/openwin
          2    5   00        0    4951296  4951295
          3    7   00   822528     620928  1443455  /var
          4    3   01  1443456     306432  1749887
          5    0   00  1749888     411264  2161151  /opt
          6    4   00  2161152     741888  2903039  /usr
          7    8   00  2903040    2048256  4951295  /export/home
          8    1   01        0       8064     8063
          9    9   01     8064      16128    24191
#
```

Practice Questions

Question 1

Which of the following activities can be performed using the **format** command? [Select all that apply]

❑ a. Display a partition table

❑ b. Modify a single partition in a partition table

❑ c. Replace the entire partition table

❑ d. Copy the partition table from one disk to another

The correct answers are a, b, and c. Although a partition table can be created, saved, and used on another disk, the **format** command does not provide a method for copying a table from one disk to another.

Question 2

Enter the command that can be used to display the date and time the file systems were mounted.

_____

The correct answer is **mount**.

Question 3

The **dmesg** command lists devices using what?

○ a. Logical raw device names

○ b. Logical block device names

○ c. Instance names

The correct answer is c. Answers a and b (logical device names) are not displayed by the **dmesg** command.

Question 4

Enter the full pathname of the file used to map between physical device names and instance name (driver binding name and instance number).

The correct answer is /etc/path_to_inst.

Question 5

What command can be used to display both the physical device name and the (partial) logical device name of disks?

The correct answer is **format**.

Question 6

Devices can be addressed using physical device names. Under which directory are these physical device names listed?

○ a. /dev

○ b. /etc

○ c. /devices

○ d. /phy

The correct answer is c. Answer a, the /dev directory, is used for logical device names. Answer b, the /etc directory, is not used for devices, and answer d, the /phy directory, does not exist.

Question 7

Which of the following commands either display or expect logical device names? [Select all that apply]

❑ a. **format**

❑ b. **newfs**

❑ c. **fsck**

❑ d. **mount**

❑ e. **df**

❑ f. **prtvtoc**

All the answers are correct.

Question 8

Enter the command used to display a list of free blocks and number of files on a file system basis.

The correct answer is **df**.

Question 9

Which of the following are fields of a partition table? [Select all that apply]

❑ a. Partition name

❑ b. Partition tag

❑ c. Disk label

❑ d. Volume table of contents

❑ e. Number of sectors in partition

The correct answers are a, b, and e. Answer c, the disk label, is the portion of the disk that contains the partition table. Answer d, the volume table of contents, is another name for the disk label.

Question 10

Which of the following information is displayed by the **prtvtoc** command?
[Select all that apply]

❑ a. Disk dimensions (geometry)

❑ b. Partition table

❑ c. Disk label

❑ d. Volume table of contents

All the answers are correct. The **prtvtoc** command displays the disk label
(otherwise known as the volume table of contents), which consists of the
disk geometry and the partition table.

Need To Know More?

Sun Microsystems, *System Administration Guide, Volume 1*, is available in printed form (ISBN 805-3727-10), on the Web at **docs.sun.com**, and from the online documentation, AnswerBook2, provided with the Solaris 7 operating system.

Sun Microsystems, *System Reference Manual, Section 1 - User Commands*, is available in printed form (ISBN 805-3172-10), on the Web at **docs.sun.com**, and from the online documentation, AnswerBook2, provided with the Solaris 7 operating system.

Sun Microsystems, *System Reference Manual, Section 1M - Administration Commands*, is available in printed form (ISBN 805-3173-10), on the Web at **docs.sun.com**, and from the online documentation, AnswerBook2, provided with the Solaris 7 operating system.

Sun Microsystems, *System Reference Manual, Section 4 - File Formats*, is available in printed form (ISBN 805-3176-10), on the Web at **docs.sun.com**, and from the online documentation, AnswerBook2, provided with the Solaris 7 operating system.

File System Administration

Terms you'll need to understand:

√ File system

√ Types of file systems

√ Default Solaris 7 file systems

√ The **mkfs**, **mkfs_ufs**, and **newfs** commands

√ The **fsck** command

√ The **mount** and **umount** commands

√ The **mountall** and **umountall** commands

√ The **df**, **du**, and **quot** commands

√ The /etc/mnttab and /etc/vfstab files

√ The **mt** command

√ The **ufsdump** and **ufsrestore** commands

√ The **tar** command

Techniques you'll need to master:

√ Creating (making) file systems

√ Checking and repairing file systems

√ Mounting and unmounting file systems

√ Monitoring file system usage

√ Backing up and restoring file systems, directories, and files

√ Recovering the root or /usr file system

The first part of this chapter reviews some basic information about file systems, including creating, checking, repairing, monitoring, mounting, unmounting, and monitoring usage. The second part of this chapter describes the commands used to back up and restore files, directories, and file systems.

File System Basics

A file system is a logical collection of files and directories contained in a partition. It can be treated as a single entity when making it available for use (mounting), checking, and repairing.

The three types of file systems supported by the Solaris 7 environment are disk based, memory based (virtual), and network based. The Part I exam concentrates on disk-based files systems and touches on virtual file systems. The Part II exam covers network-based file systems. We'll be discussing network-based file systems in Chapter 18.

Disk-based file systems are stored on physical disks, CD-ROMs, and diskettes on the local system. Table 9.1 lists the disk-based file systems' formats.

Virtual file systems are memory based and provide access to special system information, such as processes. Several virtual file system formats are used, including CacheFS for system cache, TMPFS for the temporary file system, and PROCFS for the process file system.

Default Solaris 7 File Systems

The disk space available for use with a Solaris 7 operating system is a collection of mounted file systems. The top directory is the location where the root file system is mounted. The locations where other file systems are mounted, called *mount points*, are typically subdirectories of the root file system, and normally are used to refer to the file systems themselves. For example, the file system mounted at /usr normally is referred to as the *usr file system*. Table 9.2 lists the default file systems of a Solaris 7 operating system.

Table 9.1 Disk-based file systems.

Format	Description
HSFS (High Sierra file system)	The default format for CD-ROM file systems
PCFS (PC file system)	The default format for diskette file systems; same as the DOS disk format
S5 (System V file system)	An older format used for hard disk file systems
UFS (Unix file system)	The default format for hard disk file systems

Table 9.2   Default file systems.

File System	Use
root (/)	The top of the hierarchical file system tree. Contains critical system files, such as the kernel and device drivers.
/usr	System files, such as commands and programs, used to administer and use the system.
/home	User home directories. On some systems, it might be /export/home or a network-based file system.
/var	System files that change or grow, such as logs, queues, and spooling areas.
/opt	Third-party software and applications.
/tmp	Temporary files cleared each time the system boots.
/proc	Information on active processes.

All the disk-based file systems are UFS. The two memory-based file systems (/tmp and /proc) are type TMPFS and PROCFS, respectively.

 Because kernel files reside in the root file system and system files reside in the /usr file system, these two file systems are required to boot a usable system.

Creating UFS File Systems

The **mkfs**(1M), **mkfs_ufs**(1M), and **newfs**(1M) commands can be used to create a UFS file system. The **mkfs_ufs** command is typically not used directly. It is called by the **mkfs** command when it is used to create a UFS file system. The **newfs** command is the preferred method for creating a UFS file system, as it provides a user-friendly interface to the **mkfs** command.

The **newfs** command calculates the appropriate parameters and calls the **mkfs** command to create the file system. Command line arguments can be specified to override the calculated parameters. The only required command line argument is the raw logical device name of the partition in which the file system should be created. The following listing shows using the **newfs** command to create a UFS in a 1GB partition. The -v command line argument is *verbose mode*, which causes the **newfs** command to display its actions:

```
# newfs -v /dev/rdsk/c0d1s7
newfs: construct a new file system /dev/rdsk/c0d1s7: (y/n)? y
mkfs -F ufs /dev/rdsk/c0d1s7 2104515 63 240 8192 1024 . . . 8 7
```

```
Warning: 12286 sector(s) in last cylinder unallocated
/dev/rdsk/c0d1s7: 2104514 sectors in 140 cylinders of 240 tracks,
        63 sectors
        1027.6MB in 24 cyl groups (6 c/g, 44.30MB/g, 10688 i/g)
super-block backups (for fsck -F ufs -o b=#) at:
 32, 90816, 181600, 272384, 363168, 453952, 544736, 635520,
 726304, 817088, 907872, 998656, 1089440, 1180224, 1271008,
 1361792, 1452576, 1543360, 1634144, 1724928, 1815712,
 1906496, 1997280, 2088064,
#
```

If using the **mkfs** command directly, the -F command line argument should be included to identify the type of file system to create. If not specified, the file system type listed in the /etc/default/fs file is used by default. The default type for local (disk-based) file systems is UFS. Additional parameters, such as block size and disk geometry (sectors per track, tracks per cylinder, and so on) can also be specified.

The commands used to create file systems expect raw (character) logical device names. In addition, the only type of disk-based file system that can be created on a standard Solaris 7 operating system is UFS. However, when a diskette is formatted, the PCFS is created on the diskette automatically, because the PCFS format is the DOS disk format.

Checking And Repairing File Systems

File systems are damaged when the data that defines the file systems is corrupted. This can be caused by either software errors or failures of the underlying physical disk hardware. The **fsck**(1M) command checks (audits) the logical consistency of a file system and attempts to make the repairs necessary to eliminate any inconsistency. The **fsck** command checks the superblock, inodes, indirect blocks, and directory data block.

The **fsck** command is typically executed when a file system is mounted automatically as part of system boot. It can also be executed manually on one or more file systems. Only unmounted file systems should be checked and repaired, because changes can effect programs accessing the file system, in turn causing even more damage. One or more raw logical device names (partitions) can be specified as command line arguments. Like the **mkfs** command, the -F command line argument should be used to specify the type of file system being checked. The following listing shows using the **fsck** command to check the 1GB file system previously created:

```
# fsck -F ufs /dev/rdsk/c0d1s7
** /dev/rdsk/c0d1s7
```

```
** Last Mounted on
** Phase 1 - Check Blocks and Sizes
** Phase 2 - Check Pathnames
** Phase 3 - Check Connectivity
** Phase 4 - Check Reference Counts
** Phase 5 - Check Cyl groups
2 files, 9 used, 1019783 free
#
```

If the -F command line argument is not specified, the type of file system defined in the /etc/default/fs file is used by default. In addition, if no partitions (raw logical device names) are specified, all the file systems listed in the /etc/vfstab file are checked.

 Like the commands used to create file systems, the **fsck** command expects raw logical device names. The **fsck** command can be used to check and repair CacheFS, UFS, and S5 file systems.

Mounting And Unmounting File Systems

File systems are made accessible using the **mount**(1M) command. This command associates the file system with a subdirectory of a currently mounted file system.

The **mount** command is typically called with two command line arguments: a logical block device name (partition) associated with a file system and a mount point where the file system should be mounted. In addition, the -F command line can be specified to identify the type of file system being mounted. Mounted file systems are listed in the /etc/mnttab file. If the **mount** command is used with no command line arguments, a list of all currently mounted file systems is displayed.

The **mount** command supports several options specified as command line arguments. One significant option is UFS large file support. By default, UFS file systems support large files (greater than 2GB in size). This is the same as specifying -o **largefiles** as a command line argument. To disable large file support, specify -o **nolargefiles** as a command line argument to the **mount** command. If this option is specified and a large file exists on the file system, the mount will fail. The following (abbreviated) listing shows the use of the **mount** command:

```
# mount
/proc on /proc read/write
/ on /dev/dsk/c0d0s0 read/write/largefiles
/usr on /dev/dsk/c0d0s6 read/write/largefiles
```

```
/var on /dev/dsk/c0d0s3 read/write/largefiles
/opt on /dev/dsk/c0d0s5 read/write/largefiles
/tmp on swap read/write
# mount -F ufs -o nolargefiles /dev/dsk/c0d1s7 /usr2
# mount
/proc on /proc read/write
/ on /dev/dsk/c0d0s0 read/write/largefiles
/usr on /dev/dsk/c0d0s6 read/write/largefiles
/var on /dev/dsk/c0d0s3 read/write/largefiles
/opt on /dev/dsk/c0d0s5 read/write/largefiles
/tmp on swap read/write
/usr2 on /dev/dsk/c0d1s7 read/write/nolargefiles
#
```

 The **mount** command can be used to mount CacheFS, HSFS, NFS, PCFS, TMPFS, and UFS file systems. Unlike the other file system commands, the **mount** command expects a logical block device name of a partition in which the file system resides.

The **umount**(1M) command is used to unmount a file system. The file system cannot be unmounted if it is busy (a program that resides on the file system is being executed or the current directory of a logged-in user account is within the file system). Either the logical block device name or the mount point can be specified as a command line argument.

The **mountall**(1M) command is used to mount all file systems listed in the /etc/vfstab file. This file is also used to determine the file systems to automatically mount during system boot. You can add or remove file systems in the /etc/vfstab file by using any standard text editor. Table 9.3 lists the (tab-separated) fields of an entry in the /etc/vfstab file. A hyphen (-) is used to indicate no entry in a field.

The **umountall**(1M) command is used to unmount all the file systems listed in the /etc/mnttab file, except root, /proc, /var, and /usr.

Table 9.3   Fields of the /etc/vfstab file.

Field	Description
Device To Mount	Logical block device name of the file system partition to mount.
Device To fsck	Logical raw device name used for the **fsck** command.
Mount Point	Subdirectory where the file system should be mounted.
FS Type	File system type.

(continued)

Table 9.3 Fields of the /etc/vfstab file (continued).	
Field	**Description**
fsck Pass	Flag used to indicate whether the **fsck** command should be executed automatically (a nonzero numeric value indicates yes).
Mount At Boot	A "yes" indicates that the file system should be mounted at boot or when the **mountall** command is executed; otherwise, "no".
Mount Options	Any mount options that are desired and appropriate for the file system.

Monitoring File System Usage

Several commands can be used to monitor file system usage. These are the **df**(1), **du**(1), and **quot**(1M) commands.

The **df** command (without command line arguments) displays the mount point, logical block device name, number of free 512-byte blocks, and number of files that can be created for each file system. (The -**k** command line argument lists sizes in 1024-byte blocks (kilobytes) instead of 512-byte blocks.) The command can also be used to display the disk space used by file systems. The following listing shows the use of the **df** command:

```
# df
/proc          (/proc          ):        0 blocks       948 files
/              (/dev/dsk/c0d0s0 ):    56098 blocks     35834 files
/usr           (/dev/dsk/c0d0s6 ):   181578 blocks    168053 files
/var           (/dev/dsk/c0d0s3 ):   307080 blocks    147835 files
/export/home   (/dev/dsk/c0d0s7 ):  1854626 blocks    488828 files
/opt           (/dev/dsk/c0d0s5 ):    15272 blocks    109653 files
/tmp           (swap            ):   311360 blocks      9985 files
/usr2          (/dev/dsk/c0d1s7 ):  2039566 blocks    256508 files
#
```

The **du** command lists the number of 512-byte blocks allocated to each subdirectory and the total for the current directory. Several frequently used command line arguments include -**a** to list all nondirectory files, -**k** to list sizes in terms of 1,024-byte blocks (kilobytes) instead of 512-byte blocks, and -**s** to report only the total sum of the specified files. The following listing shows using the **du** command to determine the amount of storage space allocated to the /etc/openwin directory and its contents:

```
# cd /etc/openwin
# du
```

```
4          ./etc/devdata/SUNWaccel/monitors/pnp
6          ./etc/devdata/SUNWaccel/monitors
8          ./etc/devdata/SUNWaccel
10         ./etc/devdata
12         ./etc
10         ./server/etc
12         ./server
2          ./devdata/profiles
4          ./devdata
30         .
#
```

The **quot** command is used to list the number of 1,024-byte blocks of a file system owned by each user. Either a file system (mount point) or **-a** (all mounted file systems) needs to be specified as a command line argument. Another useful command line argument is **-f**, which displays the number of files in addition to the amount of space available. The following listing shows using the **quot** command:

```
# quot /export/home
/dev/rdsk/c0d0s7:
17627   root
  133   dla
    2   guest
    1   sys
#
```

Backing Up And Restoring

Solaris 7 provides utilities to back up and restore not only entire file systems but also directories and even selected files. A magnetic tape is typically used to back up data, but other media, such as hard disks, writable CDs, and even diskettes, can be used.

A magnetic tape can contain more than one grouping of data, or *data set*. In some cases a data set might be a single file. Usually, the data set is a collection of files written to a tape as a single unit. The data sets are separated by an *End Of File (EOF)* mark and are composed of any number of records or blocks. The size of the block is determined by the command used to store the data on the tape.

The mt Command

The **mt**(1) command is used to control magnetic tape operations. This includes positioning the tape to the beginning of a data set, rewinding the tape, and even erasing the tape. Table 9.4 lists the **mt** operations that are specified as

Command	Description
Table 9.4 The mt operations.	
asf *count*	Positions the tape after the *count*–1 EOF mark
bsf *count*	Skips backward over *count* EOF marks
bsr *count*	Skips backward over *count* records
eof *count*	Writes *count* EOF marks
eom	Skips forward to a position after the last data set
erase	Erases the entire tape
fsf *count*	Skips forward over *count* EOF marks
fsr *count*	Skips forward over *count* records
rewind	Rewinds the tape
status	Displays status of tape drive

command line arguments. Most operations expect a value as another command line argument that specifies the number of times the operation should be repeated (shown in the table as *count*). If *count* is not specified, the operation is performed once.

If a raw tape device is not specified following the -f command line argument, the default tape device /dev/rmt/0n is assumed. The following listing shows positioning a tape to the fifth data set (that is, skipping over four EOF marks):

```
# mt -f /dev/rmt/0n fsf 4
#
```

The **ufsdump** And **ufsrestore** Commands

The **ufsdump**(1M) and **ufsrestore**(1M) commands are used to back up and restore UFS file systems or specified files/directories. These commands can perform incremental backup and restore using the file modification date as the selection criterion.

Dumping A File System Using The **ufsdump** Command

The **ufsdump** command provides several command line arguments. Most of them relate to changing the default characteristics of the backup media. Table 9.5 lists the more significant command line arguments of the **ufsdump** command.

These single-character arguments are specified together as a single group followed by the files (*archive_file, dump_file,* and so on) in the same order as

Table 9.5 The **ufsdump** command line arguments.	
Argument	**Description**
0-9	The dump level (**0** is the entire file system)
a *archive_file*	Uses *archive_file* to store a dump table of contents
c	Uses cartridge tape instead of standard half-inch reel tape
f *dump_file*	Uses *dump_file* instead of /dev/rmt/0
u	Records dump level and date in /etc/dumpdates
v	Verifies dump media after backup

the single-character arguments. Along with the appropriate command line arguments, the files to dump (typically a logical raw device name of a file system) must be specified.

 To ensure a usable backup, the file system should be unmounted or the system should be in the single-user run level before the backup is performed.

If no other command line arguments are specified other than the files to dump, the default is **9uf /dev/rmt/0**, which creates a dump level 9 backup using /dev/rmt/0 as the dump file and records the backup in the /etc/dumpdates file.

The dump level determines which files are backed up. If **0** is specified, the entire file system is backed up; otherwise, all files that have changed since the backup using a lower-numbered dump level are backed up. The following listing shows using **ufsdump** to back up the entire file system identified by its logical raw device name, /dev/rdsk/c0t1d0s5, to the default tape device (/dev/rmt/0):

```
# ufsdump 0u /dev/rdsk/c0t1d0s5
```

Restoring A File System Using The **ufsrestore** Command

The **ufsrestore** command is used to restore a file system backed up using the **ufsdump** command. Like the **ufsdump** command, the **ufsrestore** command supports an **f** *dump_file* command line argument for identifying the media that contains the backup. If not specified, the /dev/rmt/0 device is used by default. The following listing shows using the **ufsrestore** command to restore a file system backup from the /dev/rmt/1 device to the current directory:

```
# ufsrestore f /dev/rmt/1
```

The **ufsrestore** command also supports an interactive restore capability that is enabled using the **i** command line argument.

Restoring Selected Files Using The **ufsrestore** Command

The **ufsrestore** command can be used to restore selected files from a backup instead of the entire file system. The files or directories to be restored from the backup are listed as command line arguments on the **ufsrestore** command. The following listing shows restoring the /etc/password file and the /etc/default directory (and its contents) from a backup of the root file system on the /dev/rmt/1 device:

```
# ufsrestore f /dev/rmt/1 /etc/passwd /etc/default
```

The **tar** Command

The **tar**(1) command is used to create a tape archive and add or extract files from the archive. Table 9.6 lists the five basic functions of the **tar** command.

Along with these functions, the **f** *tar_file* command line argument is used to specify a backup device. If this command line argument is not used, either the backup device specified by the **TAPE** environmental variable or the backup device identified in the /etc/default/tar file is used. The files or directories to be backed up are listed as command line arguments after the function and argument. The **v** option can be used to display the names of files as they are added to or extracted from the archive.

Backing Up A Directory Using The **tar** Command

The following listing shows using the **tar** command to back up the /export/home directory to the /dev/rmt/0 tape drive:

```
# tar cf /dev/rmt/0 /export/home
```

Table 9.6   The tar functions.

Function	Description
c	Creates (overwrites) a tape archive
r	Replaces the named files in a tape archive
t	Lists the files in a tape archive
u	Updates the named files in a tape archive
x	Extracts all the named files from a tape archive

Restoring A Directory Using The **tar** Command

The following listing shows using the **tar** command to restore the /export/ home directory from the /dev/rmt/0 tape drive:

```
# tar xf /dev/rmt/0
```

Recovering The root Or /usr File System

Occasionally, the root or /usr file system needs to be recovered. Assuming that the file system has been backed up and that the backup is available, the following procedure can be used:

1. Select an available partition or, if additional hardware is required, install the new disk in the system and then format and create an appropriately sized partition.

2. Create a file system using the **newfs** command or another command (such as the **mkfs** command).

3. Mount the new file system on a temporary mount point. Then change the directory to the temporary mount point.

4. Use the **ufsrestore** command to restore the root or /usr backup to the new file system.

5. Remove the restoresymtable created by the **ufsrestore** command to check point the restore.

6. Unmount the new file system.

7. Use the **fsck** command to check the new file system.

8. If recovering the root file system, use the **installboot**(1M) command to create a boot block on the new file system.

9. Reboot the system.

Practice Questions

Question 1

> Which of the following can be backed up using the **ufsdump** command? [Select all that apply]
>
> ❑ a. File systems on hard disks
>
> ❑ b. Files on hard disks
>
> ❑ c. File systems on CD-ROMs
>
> ❑ d. Directories on hard disks

The correct answers are a, b, and d. File systems on CD-ROMs (answer c) are not UFS file systems and cannot be backed up using the **ufsdump** command.

Question 2

> Enter the command that can display disk usage by user account.
>
> _____

The correct answer is **quot**.

Question 3

> Which command line argument is used to disable support for files larger than 2GB in size?
>
> ○ a. **-o no2gfiles**
>
> ○ b. **-o nobigfiles**
>
> ○ c. **-o largefiles**
>
> ○ d. **-o nolargefiles**

The correct answer is d. Answers a and b are not valid command line arguments. Answer c would enable (not disable) large file support.

Question 4

> Which of the following file systems is typically used for system commands?
>
> ⭘ a. root
>
> ⭘ b. /usr
>
> ⭘ c. /var
>
> ⭘ d. /home

The correct answer is b. Answer a, root, is used for the kernel and device drivers. Answer c, /var, is used for logging and spooling. Answer d, /home, is used for user home directories.

Question 5

> Which of the following commands can be used to create a UFS file system?
>
> ⭘ a. **newfs /dev/rdsk/c0d1s7**
>
> ⭘ b. **mkfs -t UFS /dev/rdsk/c0d1s7**
>
> ⭘ c. **newfs /dev/dsk/c0d1s7**
>
> ⭘ d. **newfs /dev/dsk/c0t1d1s7**

The correct answer is a. Answer b is incorrect because the correct argument to specify a UFS file system is the -F command line argument. Answers c and d are incorrect because they use logical *block* device names. The **newfs** command requires logical *raw* device names.

Question 6

> Which of the following commands use logical block device names? [Select all that apply]
>
> ❑ a. **mount**
>
> ❑ b. **umount**
>
> ❑ c. **fsck**
>
> ❑ d. **newfs**

The correct answers are a and b. Answer b, **umount,** can also use mount point. Answers c and d, **fsck** and **newfs,** both use logical raw device names.

Question 7

> Which of the following types of file systems can be mounted using the **mount** command? [Select all that apply]
>
> ❑ a. S5
>
> ❑ b. UFS
>
> ❑ c. TMPFS
>
> ❑ d. HSFS

All the answers are correct.

Question 8

> Which of the following **tar** commands can be used to back up the /etc directory?
>
> ○ a. **tar cvf /dev/rmt/0 /etc**
>
> ○ b. **tar cvf /etc /dev/rmt/0**
>
> ○ c. **tar -cvf /dev/rmt/0 /etc**
>
> ○ d. **tar -cvf /etc/ dev/rmt/0**

Answer a is correct. All the other answers do not use proper syntax. In answer b, the command line arguments are in the wrong order. The proper order of command line arguments is function, followed by backup device, followed by the files to back up. The -c in answers c and d is incorrect (no hyphen is required).

Question 9

> Which of the following functions can be performed by the **fsck** command? [Select all that apply]
>
> ❑ a. Mounting file systems
>
> ❑ b. Repairing corrupted file systems
>
> ❑ c. Checking for file system damage
>
> ❑ d. Displaying the amount of space used by each user

The correct answers are b and c. Answer a is the function of the **mount** and **mountall** commands. Answer d is the function of the **quot** command.

Question 10

Which file contains a list of file systems to mount during system boot or when the **mountall** command is used?

O a. /etc/vfstab

O b. /etc/default/fs

O c. /etc/mnttab

O d. /etc/autofs

The correct answer is a. Answer b, /etc/default/fs, contains the default file system type. Answer c, /etc/mnttab, contains the list of currently mounted file systems. Answer d, /etc/autofs, does not exist.

Question 11

Which of the following commands can be used to position a tape loaded in device /dev/rmt/0n to the third data set after the tape has been rewound? [Select all that apply]

❑ a. **mt -f /dev/rmt/0n fsf 2**

❑ b. **mt fsf 2**

❑ c. **mt -f /dev/rmt/0n fsf 3**

❑ d. **mt fsf 3**

❑ e. **mt asf 3**

The correct answers are a, b, and e. Answers c and d would position the tape to the beginning of the fourth data set.

Need To Know More?

 Sun Microsystems, *System Administration Guide, Volume 1*, is available in printed form (ISBN 805-3727-10), on the Web at **docs.sun.com**, and from the online documentation, AnswerBook2, provided with the Solaris 7 operating system.

 Sun Microsystems, *System Reference Manual, Section 1 - User Commands*, is available in printed form (ISBN 805-3172-10), on the Web at **docs.sun.com**, and from the online documentation, AnswerBook2, provided with the Solaris 7 operating system.

 Sun Microsystems, *System Reference Manual, Section 1M - Administration Commands*, is available in printed form (ISBN 805-3173-10), on the Web at **docs.sun.com**, and from the online documentation, AnswerBook2, provided with the Solaris 7 operating system.

Sun Microsystems, *System Reference Manual, Section 5 - Headers, Tables and Macros*, is available in printed form (ISBN 805-3177-10), on the Web at **docs.sun.com**, and from the online documentation, AnswerBook2, provided with the Solaris 7 operating system.

Printing

Terms you'll need to understand:

√ Line Printer (LP) Print Service

√ Print server and print client

√ Local and remote printers

√ terminfo database

√ Printer class

√ Default printer

√ Print request

√ Print queue

√ Print request priority

Techniques you'll need to master:

√ Defining local and remote printers

√ Modifying printer configuration

√ Starting and stopping the LP Print Service

√ Defining a printer class

√ Printing files

√ Setting a default printer

√ Monitoring and canceling print requests

√ Moving print requests to another printer

√ Assigning a priority to print requests

The first part of this chapter covers the concepts and components of the Line Printer (LP) Print Service and the procedures for adding printers using the **admintool** command. The second part of this chapter describes the commands used to start and stop the LP Print Service and modify its configuration; submit, monitor, and cancel print requests; and move print requests and assign print request priorities.

 Printing is the most heavily covered topic on the Part I exam. Be sure to understand the concepts and commands (especially the command line arguments mentioned in this chapter). Make sure you actually use the commands and review the manual pages for them. Thoroughly knowing the contents of this chapter may make the difference between passing or failing the exam.

LP Print Service

The *LP Print Service* is software that allows users to print files. It provides the ability to add, modify, and delete printer definitions; provides print scheduling; and supports both local and remote printers.

A *local printer* is a printer attached directly to the local system by means of a serial or parallel communication port. A *remote printer* is a printer attached to a system (or network interface device) that functions as a print server. Accessing a remote printer from a local system requires defining the local system as a client to the remote printer.

A *print server* is a system that has a local printer attached to it that the system makes available to other systems on the network. A *print client* is a system that sends its print requests to a print server.

Supported Operating Systems

Because the Solaris LP Print Service uses the Berkeley Software Distribution (BSD) protocol as defined by Request For Comment (RFC) 1179, the following operating systems can be supported as print clients:

➤ Solaris 2.x and 7

➤ SunOS 4.x and 5.x

➤ HP-UX

Print Models

A *print model* is a script that defines how the LP Print Service interfaces with the printers. The print model is responsible for initializing the printer port and the printer based on information provided by the terminfo database, printing a banner page and multiple copies if requested.

Generic print models are provided with the Solaris operating system. To make full use of printer capability, a model might be provided with the printer, or a custom model can be written. The default print model for a local printer is /etc/lp/model/standard, and the default model for a remote printer is /etc/lp/model/netstandard.

The terminfo Database

The characteristics of both terminals and printers are defined in a database referred to as the terminfo database. Characteristics include control sequences that switch between typefaces (bold, underline, and so on) and other functionality, such as cursor/print head positioning. Using the name of a terminal or printer, applications can look up the characteristics of a printer or terminal and issue the appropriate commands to initialize and control its operation.

If the terminfo name of a printer is known, the **infocmp**(1M) command can be used to display the terminfo entry for that printer. The following listing shows using the **infocmp** command to display the hplaser terminfo entry:

```
$ infocmp hplaser
# Reconstructed from file: /usr/share/lib/terminfo/h/hplaser
hplaserjet|hplaser|HP Laserjet I,
        bitwin#1, bitype#2, cols#80, lines#60, npins#8,
        orc#12, orhi#120, orl#8, orvi#48, spinh#300,
        spinv#300,
        chr=%?%p1%{0}%>%p1%{127}%<%t\E&k%p1%dH%;,
        cpi=%?%p1%{10}%=%t\E&k0S%e%p1%{17}%=%t\E&k2S%;, cr=\r,
        cud=\E&a+%p1%dR, cud1=\n, cuf=\E&a+%p1%dC, cuf1=\s,
        cvr=%?%p1%{0}%>%p1%{127}%<%t\E&l%p1%dC%;,
        endbi=\E*rB, ff=\f, hpa=\E&a%p1%dC, is2=\EE\E&k2G,
        mgc=\E9, porder=1\,2\,3\,4\,5\,6\,7\,8;0, ritm=\E(s0S,
        rmul=\E&d@, sbim=\E*b%p1%dW, sitm=\E(s1S,
        slines=\E&l%p1P, smgbp=\E&l%p1%{1}%+%dF,
        smglp=\E&a%p1%dL, smgrp=\E&a%p1%dM,
        smgtp=\E&l%p1%{1}%+%dE, smul=\E&dD, u9=\E&l%p1P,
        vpa=\E&a%p1%dR,
$
```

If the terminfo name for a printer is not known, examine the subdirectories under /usr/share/lib/terminfo. Entries for terminals/printers are stored in separate files under one or two levels of subdirectories. For example, the terminfo entry for a Hewlett-Packard (HP) LaserJet printer is stored in the /usr/share/lib/terminfo/h/hplaserjet file.

Although the contents and maintenance of the terminfo database is not a certification requirement, additional information can be found on the terminfo(4) manual pages.

admintool

The **admintool**(1M) command provides a graphical user interface used to simplify several routine system administration operations, such as adding users and printers and installing and removing software.

Adding A Local Printer

To add a local printer using the **admintool** command, follow these steps:

1. Start **admintool**.

2. Select Printers from the Browse pull-down menu. The Printers window is displayed.

3. Select Edit|Add|Local Printer. The Add Local Printer window is displayed (see Figure 10.1).

4. Fill in the following:

   ➤ Printer Name

   ➤ Description

   ➤ Printer Port (/dev/term/a, /dev/term/b, and so on)

   ➤ Printer Type (PostScript, HP, DEC, and so on)

   ➤ File Contents (PostScript, ASCII, Both, None, Any)

   ➤ Fault Notification (Write To Superuser, Mail To Superuser, None)

   ➤ Options (Default Printer, Always Print Banner)

   ➤ User Access List (default is All; use the Add or Delete button to modify)

5. Click on OK.

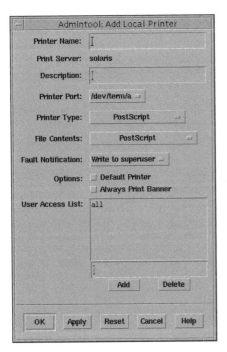

Figure 10.1   The Admintool: Add Local Printer window.

Adding A Remote Printer

To add a remote printer using the **admintool** command, follow these steps:

1. Start **admintool**.

2. Select Printers from the Browse pull-down menu. The Printers window is displayed.

3. Select Edit|Add|Access To Printer. The Add Access To Printer window is displayed (see Figure 10.2).

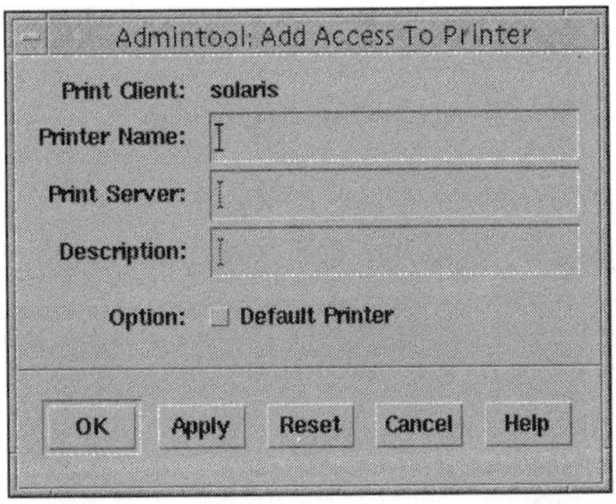

Figure 10.2   The Admintool: Add Access To Printer window.

4. Fill in the following:

> ➤ Printer Name

> ➤ Print Server

> ➤ Description

> ➤ Option (Default Printer)

5. Click on OK.

Modifying A Local Printer Configuration

To modify the configuration of a local printer using the **admintool** command, follow these steps:

1. Start **admintool**.

2. Select Printers from the Browse pull-down menu. The Printers window is displayed, listing the defined printers.

3. Highlight the printer to be modified, then select Modify from the Edit pull-down menu. The Modify Printer window is displayed (see Figure 10.3).

4. The following fields are displayed:

> ➤ Printer Name (cannot be modified)

> ➤ Print Server (cannot be modified)

> ➤ Description

> ➤ Printer Port (/dev/term/a, /dev/term/b, and so on)

> ➤ Printer Type (cannot be modified)

> ➤ File Contents (PostScript, ASCII, Both, None, Any)

> ➤ Fault Notification (Write To Superuser, Mail To Superuser, None)

> ➤ Options (Default Printer, Always Print Banner, Accept Print Requests, Process Print Requests)

> ➤ User Access List (default is All; use the Add or Delete button to modify)

5. After making changes, click on OK.

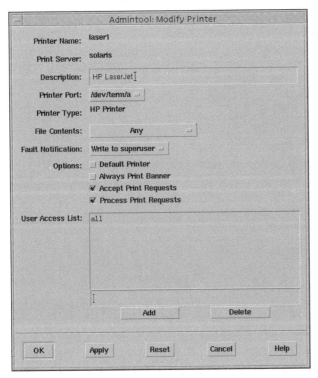

Figure 10.3   The Admintool: Modify (local) Printer window.

Modifying A Remote Printer Configuration

To modify the configuration of a remote printer using the **admintool** command, follow these steps:

1. Start **admintool**.

2. Select Printers from the Browse pull-down menu. The Printers window is displayed, listing the defined printers.

3. Highlight the printer to be modified, then select Modify from the Edit pull-down menu. The Modify Printer window is displayed (see Figure 10.4).

4. The following fields are displayed:

   ➤ Printer Name (cannot be modified)

   ➤ Print Server (cannot be modified)

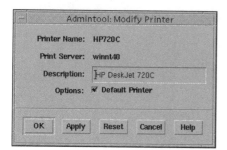

Figure 10.4 The Admintool: Modify (remote) Printer window.

➤ Description

➤ Options (Default Printer)

5. After making changes, click on OK.

Print Commands

Print commands are used to start, stop, and configure the LP Print Service and submit files to be printed.

Starting And Stopping The LP Print Service

The **lpsched**(1M) command is used to start the LP Print Service, whereas the **lpshut**(1M) command is used to stop the service. Both these commands are symbolically linked to the /usr/lib directory. An alternative method is to use the /etc/init.d/lp run control (rc) script, which calls the **lpsched** and **lpshut** commands. The following listing shows using both methods for stopping and starting the LP Print Service:

```
# /usr/lib/lpshut
Print services stopped.
# /etc/init.d/lp start
Print services started.
# /etc/init.d/lp stop
Print services stopped.
# /usr/lib/lpsched
Print services started.
#
```

Defining A Printer

The **lpadmin**(1M) command is used to define a printer by specifying the -p command line argument followed by a printer name and, at a minimum, the

-v command line argument followed by a device (port). The following listing shows defining the printer laser1, which is attached to the /dev/term/a port:

```
# lpadmin -p laser1 -v /dev/term/a
```

Additional command line arguments can be specified to define printer type, content type, and so on.

Controlling Printer Usage

After a printer is defined, its usage can be controlled using the **enable**(1) and **disable**(1) commands and specifying the name of a defined printer as a command line argument. A printer cannot be used for printing until it is enabled.

Printers either accept or reject attempts to place print requests on their queues. This functionality is controlled separately using the **accept**(1M) and **reject**(1M) commands and specifying the name of a defined printer as a command line argument.

Defining Printer Classes

A *printer class* is a group of one or more printers assigned to a printer class name. When a print request is submitted to a printer class instead of a printer, the first available printer in the class is used to print the request. The **lpadmin** command is used to define printer classes by assigning a printer to the class. Additional printers can be assigned using the same command. The following listing shows using the **lpadmin** command to create a printer class by the name of *draft* by assigning the printer laser1 to it:

```
# lpadmin -p laser1 -c draft
#
```

A printer class can also be deleted using the **lpadmin** command as shown in the following listing:

```
# lpadmin -r draft
#
```

Printing Files (Submitting Print Requests)

The **lp**(1) command is used to submit one or more files to be printed. A destination printer can be selected by specifying the **-d** command line argument. The following listing shows using the **-d** command line argument to print the files abc and xyz using the laser2 printer.

```
# lp -d laser2 abc xyz
request id is laser2-3 (2 files)
#
```

If a destination printer is not specified, the appropriate default printer is used. Other commonly used command line arguments are -n followed by a number that specifies the number of copies to print, and -o, which is followed by printer-specific options.

Default Printers

The two types of default printers are a system default printer and a user/application-defined default printer. The *system default printer* is defined by the administrator and is used as the destination for all print jobs that do not specify a printer. It can be overridden by a user/application-defined default printer. Users or applications can define a default printer using special shell variables that have been exported to their environment.

Setting Up A System Default Printer

The system administrator can specify a system default printer by using the **admintool** or the **lpadmin** command. Only previously defined printers can be identified as system default printers. The following listing shows defining the laser1 printer as the system default printer:

```
# lpadmin -d laser1
#
```

The **lpstat** command can be used to determine the system default printer as shown in the following listing:

```
# lpstat -d
system default destination: laser1
#
```

Setting Up A User/Application Default Printer

A user or application can select a printer by specifying a destination printer with the **lp**(1) command or by defining either the **LPDEST** or **PRINTER** shell variable and exporting it to the environment. **LPDEST** and/or **PRINTER** are usually defined in the user's login profile. The following listing shows the contents of a .profile file that sets the user default printer to the laser2 printer:

```
LPDEST=laser2
export LPDEST
```

The following precedence order is used to determine the destination printer:

1. Printer specified on the **lp** command line using the **-d** command line argument

2. Default printer defined by the **LPDEST** variable

3. Default printer defined by the **PRINTER** variable

4. System default printer

When using LP Daemon/BSD commands, such as **lpr**(1), the **LPDEST** and **PRINTER** variables are reversed in the precedence order.

 If a destination printer is not specified and a default printer is not defined, print jobs are rejected.

Monitoring Print Requests

The **lpstat**(1) command is used to check the status of print requests. The **-o** command line argument is used to display the status of print requests, whereas the **-t** command line argument shows all status information. The following listing shows a typical use of the **lpstat** command:

```
# lp -d laser1 abc
request id is laser1-27 (1 file(s))
# lpstat
laser1-27    solaris!root   10281   Oct 03 15:18
# lpstat -t
scheduler is running
system default destination: laser1
device for laser1: /dev/term/a
device for laser2: /dev/term/b
laser1 accepting requests
laser2 accepting requests
laser1-27    solaris!root   10281   Oct 03 15:18
#
```

The **lpstat** command also supports several other commonly used command line arguments. These include **-a** to list printers accepting requests, **-u** to list users that have queued print requests, and **-c** to list printer classes and class members.

Canceling Print Jobs

The **cancel**(1) command is used to cancel one or more queued print requests: the request currently being printed or print requests from a specific user. The following listing shows canceling the print request with the request ID of laser1-27:

```
# cancel laser1-27
laser1-27: cancelled
#
```

Multiple request IDs (separated by spaces) can be specified. To cancel the current request printing on a specific printer, specify the printer name instead of the request ID. To cancel print requests from one or more specific users, use the **-u** command line argument followed by one or more (space- or comma-separated) user account names. If a printer name is specified after the list of user accounts, only the print requests submitted by the specified user account(s) queued on the specified printer are canceled.

Moving Print Requests To Other Printers

The **lpmove**(1M) command is used to move all queued print requests from one printer queue to another. The following listing shows moving all queued print requests from the laser2 printer to the laser1 printer:

```
# lpmove laser2 laser1
```

If a print request ID followed by a printer name are specified as command line arguments instead, only the specified print request is moved to the specified printer.

Assigning Priorities To Print Requests

The priority of a print request can be moved ahead of other print requests in a queue by assigning it a higher priority. Priorities can be assigned using the **lp** command and specifying the priority with the **-q** command line argument. The priority is a number between 0 and 39 (inclusive), where a lower number gives a higher priority and zero moves the print request to the top of the queue. The following listing shows printing the file abc and setting the priority to 10:

```
# lp -q 10 abc
request id is laser1-28 (1 file(s))
```

The priority of a print request can be changed after it has been submitted by using the **lp** command and specifying a print request ID using the **-i** command line argument. The print request ID is displayed when the print request is submitted or can be determined using the **lpstat** command.

Moving A Print Request To The Top
Of The Queue

Moving a print request to the top of the queue using the **lp** command can be done in two ways. The first method is to specify **immediate** special handling using the **-H** command line argument. The following listing shows using the **immediate** special handling method while submitting the abc file for printing:

```
# lp -H immediate abc
request id is laser1-29 (1 file(s))
#
```

The other types of special handling are **hold** to suspend the printing of a job and **resume** to resume the printing of a job.

The second method of moving a print request to the top of the queue is to assign a priority of 0 to the print request using the **-q** command line argument.

Practice Questions

Question 1

> Which of the following can be used to set a default printer?
>
> ○ a. Defining and exporting the **LPDEFAULT** shell variable
>
> ○ b. Using the **lpadmin** command
>
> ○ c. Using the **lp** command
>
> ○ d. Using the **lpdefault** command

The correct answer is b. Answer a, **LPDEFAULT**, is incorrect because the shell variable should be **LPDEST**. Answer c, the **lp** command, uses the default printer but cannot be used to define it. Answer d, the **lpdefault** command, does not exist.

Question 2

> Which of the following commands can be used to start or stop the LP Print Service? [Select all that apply]
>
> ❏ a. /usr/lib/lpsched
>
> ❏ b. /etc/init.d/lp stop
>
> ❏ c. /usr/lib/lpstart
>
> ❏ d. /usr/init.d/lp start
>
> ❏ e. /usr/lib/lpshut

The correct answers are a, b, d, and e. Answer c, /usr/lib/lpstart, does not exist.

Question 3

> Which of the following are default print models? [Select all that apply]
>
> ❏ a. netstandard
> ❏ b. default
> ❏ c. standard
> ❏ d. lpmodel

The correct answers are a and c. Answers b and d do not exist.

Question 4

> Which of the following fields can be filled in when adding a remote printer using the **admintool** command? [Select all that apply]
>
> ❏ a. Printer name
> ❏ b. Print server
> ❏ c. Printer type
> ❏ d. Printer port

The correct answers are a and b. Answers c and d are not fields on the Admintool: Add Access To Printer window.

Question 5

> Which of the following **lp** commands can be used to print one or more files? [Select all that apply]
>
> ❏ a. **lp *file1***
> ❏ b. **lp *file1 file2***
> ❏ c. **lp -d *file1***
> ❏ d. **lp -d *laser1 file1***

The correct answers are a, b, and d. Answer c does not use the proper syntax (the file name is used in place of the destination printer name).

Question 6

Which of the following commands can be used to change the priority of a print request? [Select all that apply]

- ❏ a. **lp -i *laser1-49* -H 0**
- ❏ b. **lp -i *laser1-49* -q 0**
- ❏ c. **lp -d *laser1* -q 0 file1**
- ❏ d. **lp -d *laser1* -H immediate**

The correct answers are b, c, and d. Answer a is incorrect because the -H command line argument requires the keyword **immediate** to work properly.

Question 7

Where are the terminfo files located?

- ○ a. /usr/share/terminfo
- ○ b. /usr/terminfo/lib
- ○ c. /usr/share/lib/terminfo
- ○ d. /usr/lib/terminfo

The correct answer is c. None of the other pathnames are valid.

Question 8

Enter the command that can be used to monitor print requests.

The correct answer is **lpstat**.

Question 9

Which of the following **lpadmin** command line arguments are required to define a printer class? [Select all that apply]

- ❑ a. **-c** *class*
- ❑ b. **-C** *class*
- ❑ c. **-d** *printer*
- ❑ d. **-p** *printer*
- ❑ e. **-P** *printer*

The correct answers are a and d. Answers b and e are not valid command line arguments. Answer c is used to define a printer, not a printer class.

Need To Know More?

Sun Microsystems, *System Administration Guide, Volume 2*, is available in printed form (ISBN 805-3728-10), on the Web at **docs.sun.com**, and from the online documentation, AnswerBook2, provided with the Solaris 7 operating system.

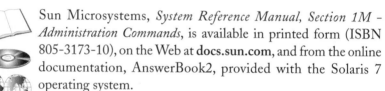

Sun Microsystems, *System Reference Manual, Section 1 - User Commands*, is available in printed form (ISBN 805-3172-10), on the Web at **docs.sun.com**, and from the online documentation, AnswerBook2, provided with the Solaris 7 operating system.

Sun Microsystems, *System Reference Manual, Section 1M - Administration Commands*, is available in printed form (ISBN 805-3173-10), on the Web at **docs.sun.com**, and from the online documentation, AnswerBook2, provided with the Solaris 7 operating system.

Sun Microsystems, *System Reference Manual, Section 4 - File Formats*, is available in printed form (ISBN 805-3176-10), on the Web at **docs.sun.com**, and from the online documentation, AnswerBook2, provided with the Solaris 7 operating system.

Sample Test I

This chapter provides pointers to help you develop a successful test-taking strategy, including how to choose proper answers, how to decode ambiguity, how to work within the Solaris testing framework, how to decide what you need to memorize, and how to prepare for the test. At the end of the chapter are 81 questions on the topics that pertain to Exam 310-009, "Sun Certified System Administrator for Solaris 7, Part I."

Keep in mind that to become certified, you must pass this exam and a second exam (310-010). The sample test for the second exam is in Chapter 23.

Questions, Questions, Questions

There should be no doubt in your mind that you're facing a test full of specific and pointed questions. The Part I exam is a fixed-length exam; it will include 81 questions, and you'll be allotted 120 minutes to complete it. You'll be required to achieve a score of 75 percent or better to pass the exam.

For this exam, questions belong to one of three types:

➤ Multiple choice with a single answer

➤ Multiple choice with multiple answers

➤ Fill in the blank

Always take the time to read a question at least twice before selecting an answer, and always look for an Exhibit button as you examine each question. Exhibits include graphics information related to a question. An exhibit is usually a screen capture of program output or GUI information that you must examine to analyze the question's contents and to formulate an answer. The Exhibit button brings up graphics and charts used to help explain a question, provide additional data, or illustrate program behavior.

Not every question has only one answer; many questions require multiple answers. A large number of multiple-answer questions have been included (probably more than you'll see on the exam). If you don't select all the correct answers, you will not get credit for answering the question correctly. Therefore, you need to read each question carefully to determine how many answers are necessary or possible and to look for additional hints or instructions when selecting answers. Such instructions often occur in brackets immediately following the question itself (as they do for all multiple-choice, multiple-answer questions). Unfortunately, some questions do not have any correct answers and you're forced to find the "most correct" choice.

Picking Proper Answers

Obviously, the only way to pass any exam is to select enough of the correct answers to obtain a passing score. However, the exams are not standardized like the SAT and GRE exams; in some cases, questions are strangely worded, and deciphering them can be a real challenge. In those cases, you might need to rely on answer-elimination skills. Almost always, at least one answer out of the possible choices for a question can be eliminated immediately because it matches one of these conditions:

➤ The answer does not apply to the situation.

➤ The answer describes a nonexistent issue, an invalid option, or an imaginary state.

➤ The answer can be eliminated because of the question itself.

After you eliminate all answers that are obviously incorrect, you can apply your retained knowledge to eliminate further answers. Look for items that sound correct but that refer to actions, commands, or features that are not present or not available in the situation that the question describes.

If you're still faced with a blind guess among two or more potentially correct answers, reread the question. Try to picture how each of the possible remaining answers would alter the situation. Be especially sensitive to terminology; sometimes the choice of words ("remove" instead of "disable") can make the difference between a right answer and a wrong one.

Only when you've exhausted your ability to eliminate answers, but remain unclear about which of the remaining possibilities is correct, should you guess at an answer. An unanswered question offers you no points, but guessing gives you at least some chance of getting a question right; just don't be too hasty when making a blind guess.

Because you're taking a fixed-length test, you can wait until the last round of reviewing marked questions (just as you're about to run out of time or out of unanswered questions) before you start making guesses. Guessing should be your technique of last resort!

Decoding Ambiguity

You'll discover that many exam questions test your knowledge of things that are not directly related to the issue that a question raises. This means that the answers you must choose from—even incorrect ones—are just as much a part of the skill assessment as the question itself. If you don't know something about a variety of system administration topics, you might not be able to eliminate obviously wrong answers because they relate to a different area of system administration than the area that the question at hand is addressing. In other words, the more you know about Solaris system administration, the easier it will be for you to tell a right answer from a wrong one.

Questions often give away their answers, but you have to be alert to see the clues. Often, subtle hints appear in the question's text in such a way that they seem almost irrelevant to the situation. You must realize that each question is a test unto itself and that you need to inspect and successfully navigate each question to pass the exam. Look for small clues, such as a reference to *raw* as opposed to *block* device names and invalid commands. Little things like these can point at the right answer if you properly understand the question; if missed, they can leave you facing a blind guess.

Another common difficulty with certification exams is vocabulary. Be sure to brush up on the key terms presented at the beginning of each chapter. You might also want to read through the Glossary Of Terms and Glossary Of Commands at the end of this book the day before you take the test.

Working Within The Framework

The test questions appear in random order, and many elements or issues that receive mention in one question might also crop up in other questions. It's not uncommon to find that an incorrect answer to one question is the correct answer to another question and vice versa. Take the time to read every answer to each question, even if you recognize the correct answer to a question immediately. That extra reading might spark a memory or remind you about a function or command that helps you on another question elsewhere in the exam.

Because you're taking a fixed-length test, you can revisit any question as many times as you like. If you're uncertain of the answer to a question, check the box that's provided to mark it for easy return later on. You should also mark questions that you think offer information that you can use to answer other questions. The testing software is designed to let you mark every question if you choose; use this framework to your advantage. Everything you'll want to see again should be marked; the testing software can then help you return to marked questions quickly and easily.

Deciding What To Memorize

The amount of memorization that you must undertake for an exam depends on how well you remember what you've read and how well you know Solaris system administration by heart. The tests will stretch your recollection of system administration commands and functions.

At a minimum, you'll want to memorize the following kinds of information:

➤ File system administration and maintenance (checking, mounting, backing up, and restoring)

➤ Commands related to file Access Control Lists (ACLs) and standard access permissions

➤ The basic commands for Line Printer (LP) administration and usage.

If you work your way through this book while logged in as root to a Solaris 7 system and try to manipulate this environment's features and functions as they're discussed throughout the book, you should have little or no difficulty mastering this material. In addition, don't forget that the Cram Sheet at the front of the book is designed to capture the material that's most important to memorize; use this to guide your studies as well.

Preparing For The Test

The best way to prepare for the test—after you've studied—is to take at least one practice exam. One is included in this chapter for that reason; the test questions are located in the pages that follow (and, unlike the preceding chapters in this book, the answers don't follow the questions immediately; you'll have to flip to Chapter 12 to review the answers separately).

Give yourself 120 minutes to take the exam, keep yourself on the honor system, and don't look back at the text in the book or jump ahead to the answer key. When your time is up or you've finished the questions, you can check your work in Chapter 12. Pay special attention to the explanations for the incorrect answers; these can also help reinforce your knowledge of the material. Knowing how to recognize correct answers is good, but understanding why incorrect answers are wrong can be equally valuable.

Also, review all the questions at the end of each chapter. They cover the topics from a different point of view than the questions in this sample test. This should help you better understand the similarities and differences between related topics.

Taking The Test

Relax. Once you're sitting in front of the testing computer, there's nothing more you can do to increase your knowledge or preparation. Take a deep breath, stretch, and start reading that first question.

There's no need to rush; you have plenty of time to complete each question and return to those questions that you skip or mark for return. If you read a question twice and remain clueless, you can mark it. Both easy and difficult questions are intermixed throughout the test in random order. Don't cheat yourself by spending too much time on a difficult question early on in the test, thereby depriving yourself of the time you need to answer the questions at the end of the test.

On a fixed-length test, you can read through the entire test and, before returning to marked questions for a second visit, figure out how much time you have to answer each question. As you answer each question, remove its mark. Continue to review the remaining marked questions until you run out of time or you complete the test.

That's it for pointers. Here are some questions for you to practice on.

Sample Test

Question 1

Enter where group account membership is stored.

_____

Question 2

Which of the following can be backed up using the **ufsdump** command? [Select all that apply]

❑ a. File systems

❑ b. Files

❑ c. Volume table of contents

❑ d. Directories

Question 3

Which of the following **admintool** fields can be modified for a remote printer? [Select all that apply]

❑ a. Printer name

❑ b. Print server

❑ c. Description

❑ d. Options

Question 4

Enter the OpenBoot NVRAM parameter used to send messages from the system initialization sequence to TTYA.

_____

Question 5

Which of the following **cancel** commands can be used to cancel the printing of one or more print requests? [Select all that apply]

❑ a. **cancel -u** *root*

❑ b. **cancel -u** *root laser1*

❑ c. **cancel** *laser1*

❑ d. **cancel** *laser1-37*

Question 6

Which of the following commands display the logical device names of mounted file systems? [Select all that apply]

❑ a. **df**

❑ b. **prtconf**

❑ c. **dmesg**

❑ d. **sysdef**

❑ e. **mount**

Question 7

Which of the following commands can be used to list the amount of disk space used by a file system?

○ a. **du**

○ b. **df**

○ c. **quot**

Question 8

Enter the command used to terminate a process on the basis of its program name.

_____

Question 9

When using **admintool** to create a user account, which of the following can be specified? [Select all that apply]

❑ a. Username

❑ b. User ID (UID)

❑ c. Group ID (GID)

❑ d. User's phone number

❑ e. Secondary groups

Question 10

Which of the following types of files are typically stored in the root file system? [Select all that apply]

❑ a. User home directories

❑ b. System commands

❑ c. Kernel files

❑ d. Device drivers

Question 11

Enter the command used to move requests queued for one printer to another printer.

_____

Question 12

Which command can be used to display the contents of a terminfo entry for printers?

○ a. **infocmp**

○ b. **terminfo**

○ c. **pinfo**

○ d. **printers**

Question 13

Which of the following commands display both instance and physical device names?

○ a. **sysdef**

○ b. **prtconf**

○ c. **mount**

○ d. **dmesg**

○ e. **df**

Question 14

Which of the following functions can be performed by a nonadministrative user with the **crontab** command? [Select all that apply]

❑ a. Delete the user's crontab file

❑ b. Edit the user's crontab file

❑ c. List the user's crontab file

❑ d. List another user's crontab file

❑ e. Edit another user's crontab file

Question 15

Which of the following commands will add a printer to a printer class?

○ a. **lp -p laser1 -c draft**

○ b. **lpadmin -d laser1 -c draft**

○ c. **lpadmin -p laser1 -c draft**

○ d. **lp -d laser1 -c draft**

Question 16

Which of the following is an instance name composed of?

- ○ a. Full pathname and physical device number
- ○ b. Driver binding name and instance number
- ○ c. Logical device name and partition number
- ○ d. Physical device name and instance number

Question 17

Which of the following commands can be used to define a Bourne shell variable?

- ○ a. **setenv PRINTER=lp1**
- ○ b. **env PRINTER lp1**
- ○ c. **PRINTER=lp1**
- ○ d. **set PRINTER lp1**
- ○ e. **define PRINTER as lp1**

Question 18

What must be specified when using the **kill** command to terminate a process?

- ○ a. The signal to send to the process
- ○ b. The process ID (PID) of the process
- ○ c. The owner (UID) of the process
- ○ d. The name of the process

Question 19

Which of the following commands can be used to create a UFS file system? [Select all that apply]

- ❑ a. **mkfs**
- ❑ b. **mkfs -F ufs**
- ❑ c. **mkfs_ufs**
- ❑ d. **newfs**

Question 20

When the **mount** command is entered without any command line arguments, what happens? [Select all that apply]

❑ a. All file systems in /etc/vfstab are mounted

❑ b. All mounted file systems are displayed

❑ c. All file systems in /etc/vfstab are displayed

❑ d. All file systems listed in /etc/mnttab are displayed

Question 21

What does /dev/dsk/c0t3d0s6 identify?

○ a. The logical raw device addressed as Controller 0 Target 3 Disk 0 Partition 6

○ b. The logical block device addressed as Controller 0 Target 3 Disk 0 Partition 6

○ c. The physical raw device addressed as Controller 0 Target 3 Disk 0 Partition 6

○ d. The physical block device addressed as Controller 0 Target 3 Disk 0 Partition 6

Question 22

What is the impact of DTSOURCEPROFILE=true in the .dtprofile of a user account that uses the C shell as the login shell?

○ a. None—only accounts that use the Bourne and Korn shells as login shells are affected.

○ b. The .profile file in the home directory of the user account is sourced.

○ c. The .login file in the home directory of the user account is sourced.

○ d. The .cshrc file in the home directory of the user account is sourced.

Question 23

What does a physical device name consist of? [Select all that apply]

- ❑ a. Slashes
- ❑ b. Instance numbers
- ❑ c. Node names
- ❑ d. SCSI controller numbers

Question 24

To execute the **reducelog** command at 11 P.M. every Sunday evening, which entry should be placed in a crontab file?

- ○ a. 11 00 * * 0 reducelog
- ○ b. 0 23 * * 0 reducelog
- ○ c. * * 23 0 0 reducelog
- ○ d. reducelog 11 00 * * 0

Question 25

Which of the following types of file systems can be checked using the **fsck** command? [Select all that apply]

- ❑ a. S5
- ❑ b. UFS
- ❑ c. TMPFS
- ❑ d. HSFS

Question 26

Which of the following files are used to control access to the **at** command?

- ○ a. /usr/lib/cron/at.allow
- ○ b. /etc/cron/at.allow
- ○ c. /var/spool/cron/atjobs/at.allow
- ○ d. /var/spool/cron/atjobs/at.deny

Question 27

Which of the following commands either display or can use logical raw device names? [Select all that apply]

❑ a. **format**

❑ b. **newfs**

❑ c. **fsck**

❑ d. **mount**

❑ e. **df**

❑ f. **prtvtoc**

Question 28

Which of the following functions can be performed using OpenBoot commands? [Select all that apply]

❑ a. Boot the operating system

❑ b. Change the root password

❑ c. View and modify NVRAM parameters

❑ d. Set the system time

❑ e. Run diagnostics

Question 29

Enter the command used to display the PID of a process if only the program name is known.

_____

Question 30

The /etc/cron.d/cron.deny file exists, but not the /etc/cron.d/cron.allow file. Which of the following statements is true regarding access to the cron capability? [Select all that apply]

❏ a. Without a cron.allow file, no one, including root, is allowed to create, edit, or delete crontab files.

❏ b. Without a cron.allow file, only root is allowed to create, edit, or delete crontab files.

❏ c. Any user account not listed in the cron.deny file can create, edit, or delete crontab files.

❏ d. Any user account listed in the cron.deny file cannot create, edit, or delete crontab files.

Question 31

What information is provided by the **df** command? [Select all that apply]

❏ a. Logical raw device of the file system partition

❏ b. Logical block device of the file system partition

❏ c. Free blocks

❏ d. Number of files that can be created

Question 32

You want to prevent the password for the guest account from being changed frequently. Which field of the Admintool: Modify User window do you use?

○ a. Password

○ b. Min Change

○ c. Max Change

○ d. Max Inactive

Question 33

What information is provided on all process listings generated by the **ps** command? [Select all that apply]

❑ a. Program or command name

❑ b. Parent process ID

❑ c. Process ID

❑ d. Associated terminal device

Question 34

The logical structure of a disk consists of a disk label (volume table of contents) and what?

_____

Question 35

Which of the following files are used to control access to the crontab files? [Select all that apply]

❑ a. /etc/cron.d/cron.deny

❑ b. /etc/cron.d/cron.allow

❑ c. /var/spool/cron/cron.allow

❑ d. /var/spool/cron/cron.deny

❑ e. /usr/lib/cron/cron.allow

❑ f. /usr/lib/cron/cron.deny

Question 36

Enter the command used to change file access modes.

_____

Question 37

At which run level is Network File System (NFS) services typically started?

○ a. 2

○ b. 3

○ c. 4

○ d. 5

Question 38

Enter the command (without command line arguments) used to identify the parent process ID of a process.

_____

Question 39

Which command can be used by the guest account to change its password?

○ a. **admintool**

○ b. **passmgmt**

○ c. **usermod**

○ d. **passwd**

Question 40

The entry "SULOG=/var/adm/sulog" to enable logging of **su** usage is added to which of the following files?

○ a. /dev/console

○ b. /etc/passwd

○ c. /etc/default/login

○ d. /etc/default/su

○ e. /var/adm/loginlog

Question 41

Which of the following can be added in the members list of the Admintool: Add Group window? [Select all that apply]

❑ a. UIDs that are less than 1,000

❑ b. The names of user accounts that are locked or have no password (setuid only)

❑ c. UIDs that are 1,000 or greater

❑ d. The names of user accounts used for system administration

Question 42

When a user account is created, the .profile is copied from which file?

○ a. /etc/skel/default.profile

○ b. /etc/profile

○ c. /etc/skel/local.profile

○ d. /.profile

Question 43

Which is the preferred method to temporarily prevent a user account from being used?

○ a. Delete the user account and all files in the home directory of the user account

○ b. Lock the account using **admintool**

○ c. Modify the user account .profile to change the user environment

○ d. Use **admintool** to change the UID and GID associated with the user account

Question 44

What is the access mode of a file created with the umask set to 123?

○ a. 321

○ b. -rwxrwxrwx

○ c. 345

○ d. rw-r--r--

Question 45

Which of the following can be used to remove packages? [Select all that apply]

❑ a. **admintool**

❑ b. **pkgtool**

❑ c. **pkgadd**

❑ d. **pkgrm**

❑ e. **pkginfo**

Question 46

Which of the following shows the access mode of a file that has the setgid enabled?

○ a. srwxrwxrwx

○ b. -rwsrwxrwx

○ c. -rwxrwsrwx

○ d. -rwxrwxrws

○ e. -rwxrwxrwt

Question 47

Enter the full pathname to the file used to modify the configuration of the kernel.

_____

Question 48

Which commands can be used to install a package from CD-ROM? [Select all that apply]

- ☐ a. **admintool** with Source Media set to CD with Volume Management
- ☐ b. **pkgadd -d /cdrom/cdrom0**
- ☐ c. **admintool** with Source Media set to CD without Volume Management
- ☐ d. **pkgadd -s /cdrom/cdrom0**

Question 49

Which command shows the users that have logged off the system?

- ○ a. **who**
- ○ b. **last**
- ○ c. **whodo**
- ○ d. **id**

Question 50

Which of the following situations will allow a user account to execute **admintool**? [Select all that apply]

- ☐ a. The account is a member of the sysadmin group.
- ☐ b. The account is root.
- ☐ c. The account is logged in at the console.
- ☐ d. The account is a member of the sys group.
- ☐ e. The account is a member of the adm group.

Question 51

Enter the command used to rewind a magnetic tape.

Question 52

Which command is used to change the system boot device?

○ a. **use disk2 as boot-device**

○ b. **set boot-device disk2**

○ c. **setenv boot-device disk2**

○ d. **set boot-dev disk2**

○ e. **setdev boot disk2**

Question 53

Enter the OpenBoot command used to create and store a nonvolatile device alias.

_____

Question 54

Enter a command that can be used to generate a list of installed packages.

_____

Question 55

What is the result of the following command?
setfacl -s u::rw-,g::r--,o:r--file1

○ a. Access mode 644 is added to the existing ACLs for file1.

○ b. Access mode 644 is deleted from the existing ACLs for file1.

○ c. Access mode 644 replaces the existing ACLs for file1.

○ d. Access mode 622 is added to the existing ACLs for file1.

○ e. Access mode 622 replaces the existing ACLs for file1.

Question 56

Which of the following can be used to specify the printer to be used? [Select all that apply]

❑ a. The LPDEST shell variable

❑ b. The **lpadmin** command

❑ c. The **lp** command

❑ d. The PRINTER shell variable

Question 57

Which of the following Solaris 7 commands can be used to modify a NVRAM parameter?

○ a. **setenv**

○ b. **set**

○ c. **setnvram**

○ d. **eeprom**

○ e. **setprom**

Question 58

Enter the name of the /etc/init.d rc script used to start or stop the LP Print Service.

_____

Question 59

Which of the following files can the line "CONSOLE=/dev/console" be included in to increase system security? [Select all that apply]

❑ a. /dev/console

❑ b. /etc/passwd

❑ c. /etc/default/login

❑ d. /etc/default/su

❑ e. /var/adm/loginlog

Question 60

Which of the following can be used to remove multiple patches?

- ○ a. **patchrm -M /var/spool/patch 104567-03 106583-10 103276-04**
- ○ b. Use **patchrm** to remove each patch separately
- ○ c. **patchrm -M /var/spool/patch patchlist**

Question 61

Enter the command that provides the ability to issue a warning message before the system run level is changed.

_____

Question 62

How is logging failed login attempts to /var/adm/loginlog enabled?

- ○ a. Add "FAIL=/var/adm/loginlog" to the /etc/default/login file
- ○ b. Execute the **logfail /var/adm/loginlog** command
- ○ c. Create the /var/adm/loginlog file
- ○ d. Execute the **login -fail /var/adm/loginlog** command

Question 63

Enter a command that can be used to remove an installed package.

_____

Question 64

You enter the **patchrm 108577-03** command, and it fails. Which of the following situations will cause the command to fail? [Select all that apply]

- ❑ a. You are not logged in as root
- ❑ b. Patch 108577-03 is not installed on the system
- ❑ c. Patch 108577-04 is installed on the system
- ❑ d. The patch was installed using **patchadd -d**

Question 65

A patch obtained from Sun Microsystems can be installed using which of the following commands? [Select all that apply]

❑ a. **pkgadd -patch 107588-01**

❑ b. **patchadd 107588-01**

❑ c. **patchadd /var/spool/patch/107588-01**

❑ d. **patch SUNWaccu 107588-01**

Question 66

When is the system profile executed?

○ a. After the .profile in the home directory of the user account

○ b. Before the .profile in the home directory of the user account

○ c. Instead of the .profile in the home directory of the user account

Question 67

Which of the following is the first phase in the Solaris boot process?

○ a. init

○ b. Boot PROM or BIOS

○ c. Boot programs

○ d. Kernel initialization

Question 68

Which of the following operating systems are supported as print clients by the LP Print Service? [Select all that apply]

❑ a. HP-UX

❑ b. Solaris

❑ c. Microsoft Windows

❑ d. Macintosh

Question 69

Enter the command line argument used with the **df** command to display file system sizes in terms of K (1,024) byte blocks.

_____

Question 70

Which of the following commands can be used to back up the entire file system located on the disk drive identified by c0t1d0s5?

○ a. **ufsdump 0u /dev/dsk/c0t1d0s5**

○ b. **ufsdump 0u /dev/rdsk/c0t1d0s5**

○ c. **ufsdump 9u /dev/rdsk/c0t1d0s5**

○ d. **ufsdump 9u /dev/dsk/c0t1d0s5**

Question 71

Three types of naming conventions can be used to reference disks. Two are physical device names and logical device names. Enter the third type of naming convention.

_____

Question 72

Which of the following commands can be used to move a print request to the top of a printer queue? [Select all that apply]

❏ a. **lp -H immediate file1**

❏ b. **lpadmin -t file1**

❏ c. **lp -d laser1 -q 0 file1**

❏ d. **lp -d laser1 -H immediate file1**

Question 73

Which of the following commands can be used to move one or more print requests from printer laser2 to printer laser1? [Select all that apply]

❑ a. **lpmove laser2 laser1**

❑ b. **lpmove laser1 laser2**

❑ c. **lpmove laser2-35 laser1**

❑ d. **lpmove laser2 all laser1**

Question 74

Enter the command used to remove a print request from a print queue.

_____

Question 75

Which of the following commands can be used to cancel one or more print requests? [Select all that apply]

❑ a. **cancel laser1-36**

❑ b. **cancel "laser1-36 laser1-38 laser2 -12"**

❑ c. **cancel -u dla**

❑ d. **cancel -u dla laser1**

Question 76

Enter the command and command line argument used to list all printers accepting requests.

_____

Question 77

Which of the following commands is used to list printer classes and the member printers?

- ○ a. **lp -c**
- ○ b. **lpadmin -c**
- ○ c. **lpstat -c**
- ○ d. **lpadmin -c -m**

Question 78

In terms of default printers, which of the following precedence orders is correct?

- ○ a. The system default, followed by the printer specified by the **lp -d** command line argument, then the LPDEST variable
- ○ b. The printer specified by the **lp -d** command line argument, followed by the LPDEST variable, then the system default
- ○ c. The LPDEST variable, followed by the system default, then the printer specified by the **lp -d** command line argument.

Question 79

Enter the command that allows a printer to print.

_____

Question 80

Enter the command that allows requests to be placed on a printer queue.

_____

Question 81

Which of the following functions can be performed using the **admintool** command? [Select all that apply]

❑ a. Add or modify a local printer

❑ b. Add or modify a remote printer

❑ c. Delete a local printer

❑ d. Delete a remote printer

Answer Key I

1. /etc/group
2. a, b, d
3. c, d
4. **diag-switch?**
5. a, b, c, d
6. a, e
7. b
8. **pkill**
9. a, b, c, d, e
10. c, d
11. **lpmove**
12. a
13. d
14. a, b, c
15. c
16. b
17. c
18. b
19. a, b, c, d
20. b, d
21. b
22. c
23. a, c

24. b
25. a, b, d
26. a
27. a, b, c, f
28. a, c, e
29. **pgrep**
30. c, d
31. b, c, d
32. b
33. a, c, d
34. slices or partitions
35. a, b
36. **setfacl** or **chmod**
37. b
38. **ps**
39. d
40. d
41. b, d
42. c
43. b
44. d
45. a, d

46. c
47. /etc/system
48. a, b, c
49. b
50. a, b
51. **mt**
52. c
53. **nvalias**
54. **admintool** or **pkginfo**
55. c
56. a, b, c, d
57. d
58. **lp**
59. c, d
60. b
61. **shutdown**
62. c
63. **admintool** or **pkgrm**
64. a, b, c, d
65. b, c
66. b
67. b

68. a, b
69. **-k**
70. b
71. instance
72. a, c, d
73. a, c
74. **cancel**
75. a, b, c, d
76. **lpstat -a**
77. c
78. b
79. **enable**
80. **accept**
81. a, b, c, d

Question 1

The correct answer is /etc/group.

Question 2

The correct answers are a, b, and d. The **ufsdump** command can back up files and directories within a UFS file system, including the entire file system. Answer c, volume table of contents, is part of the disk layout and does not physically reside within a file system.

Question 3

The correct answers are c and d. Answers a and b cannot be modified and are defined by the remote print server, not the local print client.

Question 4

The correct answer is **diag-switch?**.

Question 5

All the answers are correct. Answer a cancels all requests submitted by the root account. Answer b cancels all root requests on the laser1 queue. Answer c cancels all the print requests on the laser1 queue. Answer d cancels the print request with the request ID laser1-37.

Question 6

The correct answers are a and e. Answers b, c, and d display the physical device names or instance names of all disk devices whether they are mounted or not.

Question 7

The correct answer is b because it displays the amount of disk space used by a file system. Answer a, the **du** command, is used to list the amount of disk space used by a directory. Answer c, the **quot** command, is used to list the amount of disk space used by a user account.

Question 8

The correct answer is **pkill**.

Question 9

All the answers are correct. Information such as phone numbers can be defined in the Comments field.

Question 10

The correct answers are c and d. Kernel files and device drivers are stored in the root file system. Answer a, user home directories, are stored in the /home file system. Answer b, system commands, are stored in the /usr file system.

Question 11

The correct answer is **lpmove**.

Question 12

The correct answer is a. Answer b is the name of the terminal and printer characteristics database. The commands in answers c and d do not exist.

Question 13

The correct answer is d. Although **sysdef** and **prtconf** display the driver binding name and instance number (which, combined, make up the instance name), they do not display physical device names. Therefore, answers a and b are incorrect. The **mount** and **df** commands use only logical device names. Therefore, answers c and e are incorrect.

Question 14

The correct answers are a, b, and c. Only the superuser can list and edit another user's crontab file. Thus, answers d and e are incorrect.

Question 15

The correct answer is c. Answers a and d use the **lp** command instead of the **lpadmin** command. Answer b should identify the printer with the -p command line argument instead of the -d command line argument.

Question 16

The correct answer is b. The full pathname in answer a could mean several things, and physical device numbers do not exist. Answer c, the logical device name, and answer d, the physical device name, are the other two type of device names used with the Solaris 7 operating system.

Question 17

The correct answer is c. Answer a uses the **setenv** command, which is a C shell command. Answer b uses the **env** command, which is used to display, not set, variables. Answer d, the **set** command, is used to modify shell behavior. Answer e does not exist.

Question 18

The correct answer is b. The system uses the process ID to identify a specific process. Answer a is not required because the SIGTERM signal is used by default if a signal is not specified. Answers c and d could refer to more than one process. Something more unique is required to identify a particular process.

Question 19

All the answers are correct. Because a file system type is not specified with answer a, the default file system type as specified in the /etc/default/fs file, which is UFS, is assumed. All other commands specify file system type UFS or are intended for UFS file systems.

Question 20

Answers b and d are correct. All mounted file systems are listed in the /etc/mnttab file. Answer a is incorrect because this is actually a description of the **mountall** command. Answer c is incorrect because /etc/vfstab does not contain a list of the currently mounted file systems. It contains a list of files to mount automatically on boot.

Question 21

The correct answer is b. Answer a is incorrect because the path is /dev/dsk instead of /dev/rdsk, which identifies a raw device. Answers c and d are incorrect because physical device names are located under the /devices directory, not the /dev directory.

Question 22

The correct answer is c. The .login file is the login initialization file for a C shell account. Answer a is incorrect because the DTSOURCEPROFILE can be used with Bourne, C, and Korn shell accounts. Answer b is incorrect because the C shell does not use the .profile file. Answer d is incorrect because the .cshrc file is used only when a new shell is started.

Question 23

Answers a and c are correct. A physical device name consists of system buses and node names separated by the slash character.

Question 24

Only answer b matches the correct order required by the format of the crontab file. The format of a crontab entry is minutes, hour (24-hour clock), day, month, and weekday and then command.

Question 25

The correct answers are a, b, and d. Answer c, the TMPFS file system, cannot be checked.

Question 26

The correct answer is a. Another file used to control access is the /usr/lib/cron/at.deny file, but it was not listed as a choice. The other choices do not exist.

Question 27

The correct answers are a, b, c, and f. Answers d and e display or expect logical block devices.

Question 28

The correct answers are a, c, and e. Answers b and d can be performed only from the Solaris 7 operating system.

Question 29

The correct answer is **pgrep**.

Question 30

The correct answers are c and d because they accurately describe the crontab access control mechanism. Answer a is incorrect because root can modify crontab files regardless of the cron.allow and cron.deny files. Answer b is incorrect because in the absence of a cron.allow file, any user not listed in the cron.deny file can create, edit, or delete their crontab.

Question 31

Answers b, c, and d are correct. The **df** command displays mounted file systems, which are mounted using the logical block device name, not the logical raw device name. Thus, answer a is incorrect.

Question 32

The correct answer is b. Answer a, the Password field, is incorrect because it contains the password. Answer c, the Max Change field, is incorrect because it determines the maximum length of time a password can be used before it must be changed. Answer d, the Max Inactive field, is incorrect because it determines how long the account cannot be used before the user is forced to change the password.

Question 33

Answers a, c, and d are correct. The purpose of the **ps** command is to identify processes and who owns the processes. Answer a, the program/command name, allows the human user to determine the PID of a process that requires some attention (such as termination using the **kill** command). Answer c, the process ID (PID), uniquely identifies the process. More than one process of the same name might be listed. To uniquely identify who owns a process, either a username (not a choice) or the terminal device associated with the process (answer d) is needed.

Question 34

Either slices or partitions is correct.

Question 35

The correct answers are a and b. All the other files do not exist.

Question 36

Either **setfacl** or **chmod** is correct.

Question 37

The correct answer is b. Answer a, 2, is incorrect because this state is multiuser without remote capabilities enabled. Answer c, 4, is incorrect because it is not used. Answer d, 5, is incorrect because it is used to shut down the system.

Question 38

The correct answer is **ps**.

Question 39

The correct answer is d. Answer a is incorrect because the guest account is not and should not be a member of the sysadmin group. Answer b, the **passmgmt** command, and answer c, the **usermod** command, are incorrect because they do not support changing passwords.

Question 40

The correct answer is d. Answer a, /dev/console, is the pathname for the console. Answer b, /etc/passwd, is the password file. Answer c, /etc/default/login, is the file used to control login behavior. Answer e, /var/adm/loginlog, is the file used to log failed login attempts.

Question 41

The correct answers are b and d. Any valid user account name can be specified. UIDs cannot be specified. Thus, answers a and c are incorrect.

Question 42

The correct answer is c. Answer a, /etc/skel/default.profile, is incorrect because it does not exist. Answer b, /etc/profile, is incorrect because it is the system profile. Answer d, /.profile, is incorrect because it is the profile for the root account.

Question 43

The correct answer is b. All the other answers would cause problems or not prevent the user account from being used.

Question 44

The correct answer is d. Execute permissions in the unmask do not affect files (only directories). The unmask equivalent of 123 for files is 022. This results in $666 - 022 = 664$, which translates to rw- for user, r-- for group, and r-- for others.

Question 45

The correct answers are a and d. Answer b does not exist. Answer c, the **pkgadd** command, is incorrect because it is used to install packages. Answer e, the **pkginfo** command, is incorrect because it is used to display information about packages.

Question 46

The correct answer is c. Answers a and d are not valid file access modes. Answer b shows setuid enabled, and answer e shows the sticky bit set.

Question 47

The correct answer is /etc/system.

Question 48

The correct answers are a, b, and c. Answer d is incorrect because the -s command line argument is used to spool a package, not install it.

Question 49

The correct answer is b. Answers a and c show who is currently logged into the system. Answer d shows the real and effective UID, GID, and groups for a user account.

Question 50

The correct answers are a and b. To execute **admintool**, the account must be root or a member of the sysadmin group. The device used to log in to the system does not affect access. Therefore, answer c is incorrect. Answer d, the sys group, and answer e, the adm group, are incorrect because they do not enable access to the **admintool**.

Question 51

The correct answer is **mt**.

Question 52

The correct answer is c. None of the other answers provided list valid OpenBoot commands.

Question 53

The correct answer is **nvalias**.

Question 54

Either **admintool** or **pkginfo** is correct.

Question 55

The correct answer is c. The access mode rw-r--r-- is 644, and the -s command line argument to **setfacl** causes the ACLs to be replaced as opposed to being added (-m) or deleted (-d).

Question 56

All the answers are correct. Answers a, b, and d can be used to set a default printer to use if a printer is not specified when a file is submitted for printing. Answer c, the **lp** command, can be used to specify a printer to use other than a default printer.

Question 57

The correct answer is d. Answers a and b are used to set shell parameters. Answers c and e do not exist.

Question 58

The only correct answer is **lp**.

Question 59

The correct answers are c and d. Answer a is the pathname for the console. Answer b is the password file, and answer e is the file that is used to log failed login attempts.

Question 60

The correct answer is b. The **patchrm** command does not support the -M command line argument like the **patchadd** command does.

Question 61

The correct answer is **shutdown**.

Question 62

The correct answer is c. All the other answers do not result in anything meaningful.

Question 63

Either **admintool** or **pkgrm** is correct.

Question 64

All the answers are correct because any of the situations will cause the **patchrm** to fail.

Question 65

The correct answers are b and c. If your current working directory is /var/spool/patch, a full pathname is not required. Answer a, the **pkgadd** command, is incorrect because it can be used to install only packages, not patches. Answer d, the **patch** command, is incorrect because it is a user command for updating text files and has nothing to do with system patches.

Question 66

The correct answer is b. The system profile, /etc/profile, is executed before the users .profile in the user's home directory.

Question 67

The correct answer is b. All other phases occur after the Boot PROM (SPARC) or BIOS (x86) phase.

Question 68

The correct answers are a and b. Answers c and d are not supported by the Solaris LP Print Services.

Question 69

The correct answer is -**k**. Without command line arguments, 512-byte blocks are displayed.

Question 70

The correct answer is b. Answer a is incorrect because it uses the block device name (/dev/dsk) instead of a raw device name (/dev/rdsk). Answer c is incorrect because it uses dump level 9 instead of dump level 0. Answer d is incorrect because both the dump level and the device name are incorrect.

Question 71

The correct answer is instance.

Question 72

The correct answers are a, c, and d. The -**H immediate** or the -**q 0** command line argument can be specified with the **lp** command to move a print request to the top of a printer queue. The **lpadmin** command is used to manage printers, not print requests. Therefore, answer b is incorrect.

Question 73

The correct answers are a and c. Answer a moves all print requests queued on laser2 to laser1. Answer c moves only print request laser2-35 to laser1. Answer b is incorrect because it would move all print requests queued on laser1 to laser2. Answer d includes an invalid command line argument (**all**).

Question 74

The correct answer is **cancel**. To remove a print request from a queue use the **cancel** command followed by the name of one or more print requests.

Question 75

All the answers are correct. Answer a cancels a single print request. Answer b cancels three print requests. Answer c cancels all queued print requests submitted by the user account dla. Answer d cancels all print requests submitted by the user account dla that are queued on printer laser1.

Question 76

The correct answer is **lpstat -a**, which lists all printers currently accepting requests.

Question 77

The correct answer is c. The **lp** command is used to submit print requests, not view the status of printers or print requests. Therefore, answer a is incorrect. Likewise, the **lpadmin** command is used to manage printers, not view the status of printers. Therefore, answers b and d are incorrect.

Question 78

The correct answer is b. A printer destination specified using the **-d** command line argument when a file is submitted for printing using the **lp** command will override any other defaults. If not specified, the default printer for the user, specified using the LPDEST shell variable, will be used. If a default printer is not specified for the print request or for the user submitting the request, then the system default is used.

Question 79

The correct answer is **enable**. A printer must be enabled before it can be used for printing.

Question 80

The correct answer is **accept**. A printer queue must be instructed to accept print requests.

Question 81

All the answers are correct. The **admintool** command can add, modify, and delete both local and remote printers.

Part II

The Network Environment

Terms you'll need to understand:

√ Network classes

√ TCP/IP configuration files

√ Servers and clients

√ File servers

√ Diskless clients

√ AutoClients

√ Standalone workstations

Techniques you'll need to master:

√ Configuring TCP/IP on a Solaris 7 system

√ Logging into a remote system

√ Checking the status of a remote system

√ Distinguishing between standalone, diskless, and AutoClient configurations

√ Checking the status of the network interface

t of this chapter covers basic network concepts and terms. Some of
iation was covered in Chapter 2 as it pertained to the Part I exam.
,o lists this information as an examination objective and it is repeated
..e with a slightly different emphasis.

The second part of this chapter covers the concepts and components of the different types of the Solaris 7 configurations, including standalone systems, diskless clients, and AutoClients.

TCP/IP Networking

This section covers a variety of networking related topics including:

➤ Network classes

➤ Solaris 7 TCP/IP configuration files

➤ Checking network connectivity

➤ Accessing remote systems

➤ Identifying logged on users

➤ Viewing network statistics

Classes Of Networks

The three most commonly used IP network classes are A, B, and C. Table 13.1 provides a summary of the characteristics of these different IP network classes.

The subnet mask is used to separate the network portion of an IP address from the host portion. More information on network classes is provided in Chapter 2.

Table 13.1   IP address classes.

Class	First Octet	Default Subnet Mask	Maximum Theoretical Hosts
A	1–126	255.0.0.0	16,777,216
B	128–191	255.255.0.0	65,536
C	192–223	255.255.255.0	256

TCP/IP Configuration Files

Solaris 7 uses several files to configure the TCP/IP environment. These files are used to identify both the hostname and the IP address of the system. The following three files are used to configure TCP/IP:

➤ /etc/inet/hosts

➤ /etc/nodename

➤ /etc/hostname.*interface*

The next few sections look at these files in depth.

The /etc/inet/hosts File

The /etc/hosts file (which is a symbolic link to /etc/inet/hosts) contains a listing of hostnames and their associated IP addresses. This file is used to convert hostnames to IP addresses. Table 13.2 summarizes the format of the /etc/inet/ hosts file.

The columns are separated by one or more tab or space characters. If more than one alias is defined, they should be separated using either spaces or tabs.

 At a minimum, the /etc/inet/hosts file should contain an entry for localhost (IP address 127.0.0.1) and an entry for each network interface installed on the system.

Additional entries can be added to the /etc/inet/hosts file for other systems. This allows access to the remote systems using hostnames instead of IP addresses.

The /etc/nodename File

The /etc/nodename file contains only one entry: the default hostname of the local system. As described in Chapter 2, the hostname or node name should be

Table 13.2 /etc/inet/hosts file format.	
Column	**Description**
IP Address	IP address in dotted decimal notation
Host name	Hostname or node name of the system
Alias	Alternate hostname(s) for the system

ccordance with RFC 952, *DOD Internet Host Table Specification*.
worthwhile to reread the portion of Chapter 2 that deals with the
ing conventions.

The /etc/hostname.*interface* File

One /etc/hostname.*interface* file exists for each network interface installed on
the system. The *interface* portion of the file name reflects the manufacturer and
type of network interface. For example, if an Intel x86–based system has a
single 3COM Etherlink III network interface card installed, the file name
would be /etc/hostname.elx0. For a SPARC 5 platform with two network
interfaces, the file names would be /etc/hostname.le0 and /etc/hostname.le1.

The /etc/hostname.*interface* file(s) should contain only one entry: either the
hostname or the IP address that is assigned to that interface.

If a hostname is used, that hostname must also be listed in the
/etc/inet/hosts file. Also note that if more than one network
interface is installed on the system, the /etc/hostname.*interface*
files will contain different hostnames. Only the hostname (or IP
address) that matches the hostname defined in the /etc/node-
name file is considered the default hostname for the system.

Checking Network Connectivity

Solaris 7 provides two commands for checking network connectivity between
systems and the proper operation of the network interfaces on both systems:
the **ping**(1M) command and the **spray**(1M) command.

The **ping** Command

The **/usr/sbin/ping** command uses the Internet Control Message Protocol
(ICMP) to send ECHO_REQUEST datagrams to another host. When a host
receives an ECHO_REQUEST datagram, it responds with an ECHO_REPLY
datagram. This basic echo mechanism is used to verify both the connectivity
between two hosts and the proper operation of the network interfaces and
protocol stacks (of both hosts) up to the Internet layer where the Internet
Protocol (IP) resides. The following listing shows sending one ICMP
ECHO_REQUEST datagram using the **ping** command:

```
$ /usr/sbin/ping solaris7
solaris7.ambro.org is alive
$
```

Table 13.3 lists the command line arguments supported by the **ping** command.

Table 13.3   The ping command line arguments.

Argument	Description
-d	Sets the SO_DEBUG socket option
-i *interface*	Uses the specified interface address
-I *interval*	Specifies an interval between transmissions (default of 1 second)
-l	Use loose source routing
-L	Turns off loopback of multicast packets
-n	Displays addresses instead of hostnames
-r	Bypasses the routing tables (remote host is on local network)
-R	Records route in IP header
-s	Sends ICMP packets until interrupted
-t *time*	Specifies a time to live (in seconds) for IP packets
-v	Displays detailed information (verbose mode)

At a minimum, a hostname or IP address must be specified. All these command line arguments are specified before the hostname or IP address.

When used without any command line arguments (only a hostname is specified), a time-out can be specified after the host name. The default time-out is 20 seconds.

When used with the -s command line argument, a packet size and a count can be specified after the hostname. The following listing shows using the **ping** command to send five packets (each with 60 bytes of data) to the solaris7 host:

```
$ /usr/sbin/ping -s solaris7 60 5
PING solaris7: 60 data bytes
68 bytes from solaris7 (192.168.99.27): icmp_seq=0. time=1. ms
68 bytes from solaris7 (192.168.99.27): icmp_seq=1. time=0. ms
68 bytes from solaris7 (192.168.99.27): icmp_seq=2. time=0. ms
68 bytes from solaris7 (192.168.99.27): icmp_seq=3. time=0. ms
68 bytes from solaris7 (192.168.99.27): icmp_seq=4. time=0. ms

----solaris7 PING Statistics----
5 packets transmitted, 5 packets received, 0% packet loss
round-trip (ms)  min/avg/max = 0/0/1
$
```

The **spray** Command

The **/usr/sbin/spray** command sends a stream of User Datagram Protocol (UDP) packets to a host using the Remote Procedure Call (RPC) mechanism. On the remote end, the spray daemon, **sprayd**(1M), accepts these packets and acknowledges receiving the packets. The **spray** command, along with the **sprayd** program, is used to verify both the connectivity between two hosts and the proper operation of the network interfaces and protocol stacks (of both hosts) up to the application layer.

The following listing shows using the **spray** command to test network connectivity:

```
$ /usr/sbin/spray solaris7
sending 1162 packets of length 86 to solaris7 ...
        255 packets (21.945%) dropped by solaris7
        1967 packets/sec, 169173 bytes/sec
$
```

Table 13.4 lists the command line arguments supported by the **spray** command.

At a minimum, a hostname or IP address must be specified. All these command line arguments are specified before the hostname or IP address.

> *Note: The sprayd program must be running on the remote system in order for the **spray** command to work properly.*

Accessing Remote Systems

Several commands can be used to access a remote system. Two provide the ability to log in to the system as a local user through the network: the **telnet**(1) command and the **rlogin**(1) command.

Table 13.4 The spray command line arguments.	
Argument	**Description**
-c *count*	The number of packets to send (default is the number of packets required to send a total of 100K)
-d *delay*	The number of microseconds to pause between packets (default is 0)
-l *length*	The length of the Ethernet packet (default is 86)
-t *type*	The class of transport (default is UDP)

The **telnet** Command

The **telnet** command is used to remotely log in to a system through the network. The user must provide a valid user account name and password as defined on the remote system because the **telnet** command uses standard Unix login/ password authentication.

The hostname or IP address of the remote system is typically specified as a command line argument. If not specified, the **telnet** command is placed in an interactive mode.

The **rlogin** Command

The **rlogin** command can also be used to remotely log in to a system through the network. If the *remote authentication database* has been set up properly, the user might be able to log in without providing a valid user account name and password. This capability is described in the next section. If this database has not been set up properly, the user must, as with the **telnet** command, provide a valid user account name and password as defined on the remote system.

Unlike the **telnet** command, the hostname or IP address of the remote system must be specified as a command line argument to the **rlogin** command.

Other Commands

Two other commands provide remote access. The first is the **rcp**(1) command that copies a specified file from the local system to the specified remote system. The destination is specified as *host:path*, where *host* is the name of the remote system and *path* is the full path to where the file should be copied.

The second is the **rsh**(1) command, which executes the specified command on the specified remote system. See the *System Reference Manual* for additional details.

Remote Authentication Database

The remote authentication database is used to determine which remote hosts and users are considered as being trusted. The **rlogin** command, along with the **rsh** command and the **rcp** command, uses the remote authentication database. This database consists of two types of files: the /etc/host.equiv file, which applies to the entire system, and the .rhosts files, which apply to individual user accounts and are located in the home directories of user accounts.

The remote authentication database is used to determine whether a user on a remote system can access the local system using the same user account. For example, if the guest account on a remote system is authorized to access the local system and then does so using the **rlogin** command, the user is automatically logged into the local system as a guest without providing a user account name and a password.

The remote authentication procedure first checks to determine whether the hostname of the remote system is listed in the /etc/host.equiv file. If it is not listed, remote authentication fails and the user is prompted for a local user account name and password.

If the hostname of the remote system is listed, the remote authentication continues. The home directory of the local user account name (that matches the user account name of the remote user) is checked to determine whether the hostname of the remote system is listed in the .rhosts file. If it is listed, remote authentication succeeds and the user is granted access to the local system. If it is not listed, remote authentication fails and the user is prompted for a local user account name and password.

Both files consist of a list of hostnames (one per line). A hostname by itself or preceded by a plus sign (+) is considered a trusted host and allowed access. If a hostname is preceded by a minus sign (-), the host is considered untrusted and denied access.

Optionally, a hostname can be followed by a user account name. If this form is used in the /etc/hosts.equiv file and the remote user account matches the specified user account name, the user is given access as any user. If the user is allowed to access the system using any user account, then the user either provides the user account as a command line option to the **rlogin** command or is prompted for it. If the optional form is used in the .rhosts file, the remote user is given access as the specified user account.

Identifying Users

Two commands are used to identify remote users logged into the local system: the **who**(1) command and the **finger**(1) command.

The **who** command displays the following information about each logged-in user:

➤ Username

➤ Terminal

➤ Login time

➤ Remote hostname

The **finger** command also displays information about users. By default, it lists the following information about each logged-in user:

➤ Username

➤ User's full name (from the /etc/passwd comment field)

➤ Terminal

➤ Idle time

➤ Login time

➤ Remote hostname

One or more user account names can be specified as command line arguments (separated by spaces); this causes the **finger** command to provide a detailed report about the user account(s). The -l command line argument provides a more detailed listing of user information. Also, the -**H** command line argument provides headings for the columns of the listing.

The following listing compares the default outputs of the **who** and **finger** commands as executed on the system named solaris7:

```
# who
root       console      Oct 25 14:52    (:0)
dla        pts/3        Oct 25 14:53    (winnt40)
root       pts/4        Oct 25 14:54    (solaris7:0.0)
dla        pts/5        Oct 25 14:56    (winnt40)

# finger
Login      Name           TTY        Idle    When     Where
root       Super-User     console    4 Mon   14:52    :0
dla        Darrell Ambro  pts/3      3 Mon   14:53    winnt40
#
```

The **finger** command can also be used to view users logged into a remote system by specifying a hostname preceded with the "@" character as a command line argument. The following listing shows using the **finger** command from a remote system to determine who is logged into the system named solaris7:

```
# finger @solaris7
[solaris7]
Login      Name           TTY        Idle     When     Where
root       Super-User     console    30 Mon   14:52    :0
dla        Darrell Ambro  pts/3      29 Mon   14:53    winnt40
#
```

Another command, **rusers**(1), displays users logged into a remote system. By default, only the user accounts currently logged into the system are listed. By specifying the -l command line argument, the **rusers** command provides information similar to the **who** and **finger** commands. The following listing shows using the **rusers** command from a remote system to determine who is logged into the system named solaris7:

```
# rusers solaris7
solaris7            root dla
# rusers -l solaris7
root          solaris7:console      Oct 25 14:52    34 (:0)
dla           solaris7:pts/3        Oct 25 14:53    33 (winnt40)
#
```

Viewing Network Statistics

The **netstat**(1M) command is used to display network statistics. Although several output formats are controlled by command line arguments, only the -i format (used to show the TCP/IP statistics) is specified as a test objective. Other common uses are the **netstat** command without command line arguments, which lists current connections, and the **netstat -r** command, which lists the routing table. Consult the manual page in the System Reference Manual (Section 1M) for details on these uses and other useful command line arguments.

The following listing shows the output of the **netstat -i** command:

```
# netstat -i
Name Mtu   Net/Dest Address   Ipkts Ierrs Opkts Oerrs Collis Queue
lo0  8232  loopback localhost 14891 0     14891 0     0      0
elx0 1500  localnet solaris   5301  0     1463  0     1      0
#
```

Table 13.5 describes the columns of the **netstat -i** output.

Table 13.5	The netstat output format.
Column	**Description**
Name	The interface name.
Mtu	The maximum transmission unit (maximum packet size).
Net/Dest	The local network. (If possible, the network is mapped to a network name using the /etc/networks file or the appropriate name service.)

(continued)

Table 13.5	The netstat output format (continued).
Column	**Description**
Address	The IP address of the interface. (If possible, the address is mapped to a hostname using the /etc/hosts file or the appropriate name service.)
Ipkts	The number of input packets.
Ierrs	The number of input errors.
Opkts	The number of output packets.
Oerrs	The number of output errors.
Collis	The number of network collisions.
Queue	The number of packets waiting in the queue.

The Solaris Network Environment

The Solaris 7 network environment supports several different types of system configurations, including standalone, diskless, and AutoClient. These configurations provide different capabilities and impact deployment and support costs.

Standalone Configuration

A *standalone* system has local disk space that is used to store all operating system files, applications, and user data. This includes the root (/), /usr, /export/home, and /var file systems. Likewise, it provides local swap for the system's virtual memory. A standalone system can function autonomously and can be either networked or nonnetworked. A networked standalone system can be used as a server, such as a file server, to provide remote access to shared or common data.

File Server Concepts

A *file server* is a standalone system that functions as a server and allows clients to access files via the network. There are several variations of file servers.

For Part II of the certification exam, the main file server of interest is the *operating system (OS) server*. The OS server provides access to client systems that do not have all or some of the operating system files available through local file systems on local hard disks.

An OS server can support more than one version of an operating system at a time. This includes not only different releases of an operating system, such as Solaris 7, Solaris 2.6, and SunOS 2.5, but also different hardware platforms, such as SPARC and Intel x86 compatibles.

Diskless Configuration

A *diskless client,* as the name implies, does not have a hard disk for locally storing the operating system or applications. This storage is provided by a *diskless client server* that is accessible via the network. For a diskless client to boot and operate, the client must remotely mount its root (/) and /usr file systems from an OS server.

In addition to providing a common set of operating system files for all the diskless clients (of the same version) through the network, the OS server provides hard disk space assigned for use by each client. This disk space is used for swap space for the diskless client's virtual memory system and the /home file system for user accounts that are unique to each diskless client.

Compared to the standalone configuration, the diskless configuration is cheaper and easier to maintain because only a very small number of systems (the OS servers) require hard disks. Only one copy of common files is required, and this is shared among many clients. In addition, all data unique to each client is stored on an OS server, simplifying backup and restore procedures. Because no data is stored on the clients, the client hardware can be easily replaced or upgraded.

The main disadvantages of the diskless configuration are its dependence on the network and the load that it places on the network. If a diskless client cannot access the OS server via the network, it cannot operate at all. In addition, because all data (including that in swap space) is accessed remotely, the network is extremely loaded even under normal operating conditions.

AutoClient Configuration

An *AutoClient* is similar to a diskless client, except that it has a limited amount of local storage space (minimum of 100MB) that is used for a specific purpose. Like the diskless client, the AutoClient must remotely access its root (/) and /usr file systems from an OS server configured as an AutoClient server. Unlike the diskless client, the AutoClient uses local disk space to store or cache the root (/) and /usr file systems.

In addition, the local hard disk is used for swap space. Like the diskless configuration, the OS server provides hard disk space for the /home and /var file systems that are unique to each diskless client.

Compared to the diskless configuration, the AutoClient configuration is somewhat more expensive because its client requires a hard disk, but the hard disk is small. Like the diskless configuration, only one copy of common files is required, and this is shared among the clients. In addition, all data unique to each client is stored on an OS server, simplifying backup and restore procedures. Thus, in terms of client hardware, AutoClients, like diskless clients, can be replaced or upgraded easily.

The disadvantages of the diskless configuration are reduced and in some cases eliminated by the AutoClient configuration. After the AutoClient has cached the operating system, it no longer requires access to the OS server for those files. In addition, the local swap space eliminates a significant portion of the network load.

Comparison Of Configurations

Table 13.6 provides a comparison of the significant differences among the various system configurations supported in the Solaris 7 network environment.

Standalone systems that function as servers typically provide file systems—such as /export/root, /export/home, and /export/swap—that are used to store the files that are remotely accessed by diskless clients and AutoClients. In addition, servers and standalone systems provide the /opt file system for storing application software.

Table 13.6 A comparison of system configurations.			
System Type	Local Swap	Local File Systems	Remote File Systems
Standalone	Yes	root, /usr, /var, /export/home	None
Diskless client	No	None	root, /usr, /var, /home
AutoClient	Yes	root, /usr	/var, /home

Practice Questions

Question 1

> Which of the following can be used as a file server?
>
> ○ a. AutoClient
>
> ○ b. Diskless client
>
> ○ c. Nonnetworked standalone system
>
> ○ d. Networked standalone system

The correct answer is d. A networked standalone system meets both of the basic requirements of a file server: It is networked, and it has storage space. Answer a, AutoClient, is incorrect because it has only a minimum amount of local storage space. Answer b, diskless client, is incorrect because it does not have any local storage space. Answer c, nonnetworked standalone system, is incorrect because it is not networked and cannot make its storage space available to other systems.

Question 2

> Which of the following commands uses remote authentication?
>
> ○ a. **finger**
>
> ○ b. **telnet**
>
> ○ c. **spray**
>
> ○ d. **rlogin**

The correct answer is d. Answers a and c, the **finger** and **spray** commands, do not require any authentication. Answer b, the **telnet** command, uses the standard Unix user account name and password to authenticate remote users.

Question 3

Enter the name of the command (without command line arguments) used to display network statistics.

The correct answer is **netstat**.

Question 4

Which of the following have local swap space? [Select all that apply]

❑ a. Nonnetworked standalone system

❑ b. AutoClient

❑ c. OS server

❑ d. Diskless client

❑ e. Networked standalone system

The correct answers are a, b, c, and e. All of these systems have a local hard disk that is used for swap space. Only answer d, diskless client, does not have a local disk and thus cannot have local swap space.

Question 5

Which of the following commands can be used to identify users on the local system? [Select all that apply]

❑ a. **who**

❑ b. **ping**

❑ c. **finger**

❑ d. **rusers**

❑ e. **spray**

The correct answers are a, c, and d. Answer a, the **who** command, identifies only users on the local system. Answer c, the **finger** command, can be used to identify users on either the local or a remote system. Answer d, the **rusers** command, typically is used to identify users on a remote system. However, the hostname of the local system can be specified as a command line argument just as the hostname of a remote system can. Thus, the **rusers** command can be used to identify users on the local system as well.

Answers b and e, the **ping** and **spray** commands, are incorrect because they are used to test network connectivity.

Question 6

> Which of the following IP addresses are on a Class B network? [Select all that apply]
>
> ❑ a. 128.34.17.230
>
> ❑ b. 120.56.117.3
>
> ❑ c. 192.186.13.4
>
> ❑ d. 191.255.255.47

The correct answers are a and d. The first octet of a Class B address is between 128 and 191 (inclusive). Answer b is a Class A address, and answer c is a Class C address.

Question 7

> What does the /etc/host.equiv file contain? [Select all that apply]
>
> ❑ a. The names of trusted hosts
>
> ❑ b. The IP addresses of trusted hosts
>
> ❑ c. The names of untrusted hosts
>
> ❑ d. The IP addresses of untrusted hosts

The correct answers are a and c. Hostnames listed in the /etc/host.equiv file that are preceded with a hyphen are denied access because they cannot be trusted. Answers b and d are incorrect because hostnames, not IP addresses, must be used in the /etc/host.equiv file.

Question 8

> Which of the following commands can be used to identify users on a remote
> system? [Select all that apply]
>
> ❑ a. **who**
>
> ❑ b. **ping**
>
> ❑ c. **finger**
>
> ❑ d. **rusers**
>
> ❑ e. **spray**

The correct answers are c and d. Answer a, the **who** command, identifies only
users on the local system. Answers b and e, the **ping** and **spray** commands, are
used to test network connectivity.

Question 9

> Enter the name of the file that is symbolically linked to the /etc/hosts file.
>
> _____

The correct answer is /etc/inet/hosts.

Need To Know More?

Sun Microsystems, *System Administration Guide, Volume 2*, is available in printed form (ISBN 805-3728-10), on the Web at **docs.sun.com**, and from the online documentation, AnswerBook2, provided with the Solaris 7 operating system.

Sun Microsystems, *System Reference Manual, Section 1 - User Commands*, is available in printed form (ISBN 805-3172-10), on the Web at **docs.sun.com**, and from the online documentation, AnswerBook2, provided with the Solaris 7 operating system.

Sun Microsystems, *System Reference Manual, Section 1M - Administration Commands*, is available in printed form (ISBN 805-3173-10), on the Web at **docs.sun.com**, and from the online documentation, AnswerBook2, provided with the Solaris 7 operating system.

Sun Microsystems, *TCP/IP and Data Communications Administration Guide*, is available in printed form (ISBN 805-4003-10), on the Web at **docs.sun.com**, and from the online documentation, AnswerBook2, provided with the Solaris 7 operating system.

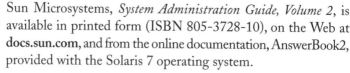

Advanced Installation

Terms you'll need to understand:

√ Installation phases

√ Software packages, clusters, and groups

√ Installation methods

√ Install server

√ Boot server

√ Custom JumpStart

√ JumpStart rules file and profile files

Techniques you'll need to master:

√ Installing systems

√ Preconfiguring system installation information

√ Installing a system using the Solaris interactive installation program

√ Setting up and using over-the-network installation

√ Setting up a JumpStart configuration directory

The first part of this chapter covers concepts and terms related to system installation. Some of this information was covered in Chapter 3 as it pertained to the exam objectives for the Part I exam. Part II also lists this information as an exam objective and it is repeated here with a slightly different emphasis.

The second part of this chapter covers the concepts and components of an over-the-network installation environment. The third part covers automating installation using the JumpStart feature.

Server Installation

The exam objectives for Part II cover installation of a server. This includes the phases of an installation, the hardware requirements for a server, and the software configurations that can be installed on a system.

Installation Phases

Installation consists of three phases: The *system configuration* phase identifies the necessary system information, the *system installation* phase copies the software onto the system, and the *post-installation* phase updates system software as required.

System Configuration Phase

During the system configuration phase, basic information about the system, such as host name and domain, is identified. This information can optionally be set up ahead of time, or *preconfigured*. There are two methods to preconfiguring system information. The first involves using the sysidcfg file, and the second involves using a name service.

For the sysidcfg file method, a file for each system is created that contains a set of lines in the form of *keyword=value*, such as **timezone=US/CENTRAL**. The file can be available either over the network or on diskette.

For the name service method, entries for each system are added to the Network Information Service (NIS) or the Network Information Service Plus (NIS+) database. Naming services are described in Chapter 19.

 If a system is not preconfigured, the **sysidtool**(1M) is executed during installation to prompt for the information. The **sysidtool** command consists of five programs: **sysidnet**, **sysidnis**, **sysidsys**, **sysidroot**, and **sysidpm**.

System Installation Phase

During the system installation phase, the selected Solaris 7 software group (covered later in this chapter) is installed using one of the four installation methods:

➤ SunInstall (standard interactive installation)

➤ WebStart

➤ JumpStart

➤ Custom JumpStart

The two interactive installation methods (SunInstall and WebStart) are Part I exam objectives and were discussed in Chapter 3. The two automatic installation methods (JumpStart and custom JumpStart) are Part II exam objectives and are described later in this chapter.

Post-installation Phase

During the post-installation phase, any appropriate patches are installed along with any separately purchased applications. In addition, any custom configurations, such as user accounts and environments, are applied to the system. Typically, system security hardening is also performed during the post-installation phase.

Hardware Requirements

The hardware requirements for a server are similar to the client hardware requirements for items such as memory, monitor, keyboard, mouse, floppy diskette drive, and network interface. In addition, a server requires enough hard disk space to store the configuration of the operation system and any applications. The recommended storage space required for each available operation system configuration (referred to as a *software group*) is covered in the next section.

Servers typically require a CD-ROM drive, as Solaris 7 and applications can be installed on the server from the CD. In some situations, a server might require a CD-ROM drive to make the contents of a CD available through the network.

Software Configurations

The Solaris 7 system software is distributed in several different configurations. These configurations were described in Chapter 3, but they are also exam objectives for Part II, so they'll be discussed here.

Software Packages

Solaris 7 system and application software are delivered as collections of files and directories, referred to as *software packages*. These packages can be copied onto the system from CD-ROM or magnetic tape as a single compressed file and then uncompressed for installation.

Included with the package is information regarding the package, such as title, storage requirements, and version. Also included are any custom scripts needed to properly install the software.

Software Clusters

Sometimes system software is distributed in more than one package, but the packages need to be distributed and installed as a unit. A collection of two or more related packages is referred to as a *software cluster*. A software cluster is a logical grouping of packages.

Software Groups

Software groups (also referred to as *software configuration clusters*) are collections of software clusters. Depending on the intended use of the system, the most appropriate software group should be selected for installing an operating system. Table 14.1 describes these five software groups. Table 14.2 summarizes the recommended disk space for each software group. The amounts for 32-bit support relate to the Intel x86 platforms, and the amounts for 64-bit support relate to SPARC platforms.

Table 14.1 Solaris 7 software groups.	
Software Group	**Contents**
Core	Minimum files required for the operating system
End User Support System	Typical configuration for a system that supports general users. Consists of the Core software group plus:
	Windowing software: Common Desktop Environment (CDE) and Openwindows
	Basic networking and printer support
	Standard Unix and patch utilities
	Java Virtual Machine
Developer System Support	Intended as a software development environment. Consists of the End User Support System plus:
	Programming tools and libraries
	Extended terminal, X, and kernel probing support
	CDE/Motif developer software and runtimes
	Online manual pages

(continued)

Table 14.1   Solaris 7 software groups (continued).

Software Group	Contents
Entire Distribution	All files included with the Solaris 7 distribution. Consists of the Developer System Support plus:
	AnswerBook2 (online Web-based documentation)
	Enhanced security features, including disk quotas and system accounting
	Enhanced network support, including Unix-to-Unix Copy Protocol (UUCP), Dynamic Host Configuration Protocol (DHCP) server, Point-to-Point Protocol (PPP), and the Network Information Service (NIS)
Entire Distribution Plus OEM System Support	Includes modules and drivers for optional hardware components. Consists of the Entire Distribution plus:
	PCI drivers
	SunFastEthernet and FastWide SCSI adapter drivers

Table 14.2   Solaris 7 software group space recommendations.

Software Group	32-Bit Support (in MB)	64-Bit Support (in MB)
End User Support System	438	532
Developer System Support	716	837
Entire Distribution	787	895
Entire Distribution Plus OEM System Support	801	909

Solaris Interactive Installation Program (SunInstall)

The standard interactive installation program (SunInstall) is probably the most frequently used installation method. The following procedure outlines the use of SunInstall for a SPARC platform:

1. Boot the system. Get the system to the OpenBoot **ok** prompt.

2. If installing from a local CD-ROM drive using a Solaris 7 distribution CD, insert the distribution CD into the CD-ROM drive. Type "boot cdrom", and then press the Enter key. If installing over the network (discussed in the next section), enter "boot net", and then press the Enter key.

3. Wait for booting to complete.

4. If system information was not preconfigured, the **sysidtool** command will prompt for the necessary information at this time. Enter the requested information.

5. The Solaris 7 software is installed on the system. Follow the instructions displayed on the screen to finish the installation.

The following procedure outlines the use of SunInstall for an Intel x86 platform:

1. Insert the Configuration Assistant diskette in the diskette drive. Boot the system. Press the F2 key to scan devices, then press the F2 key again to identify devices. A menu for selecting a boot device (NET, DISK, or CD) is displayed.

2. If installing from a local CD-ROM drive using a Solaris 7 distribution CD, insert the distribution CD into the CD-ROM drive. Check the CD menu item, then press the F2 key to continue. If installing over the network (covered in the next section), check the NET menu item and press the F2 key to continue.

3. A menu for selecting the type of installation (Solaris Interactive, Custom JumpStart, or Solaris WebStart) is displayed. Select Solaris Interactive.

4. Wait for booting to complete.

5. If system information was not preconfigured, the **sysidtool** command will prompt for the necessary information at this time. Enter the requested information.

6. The Solaris 7 software is installed on the system. Follow the instructions displayed on the screen to finish the installation.

Over-The-Network Installation

Typically, Solaris is installed directly from the Solaris distribution CD. This requires that each system be equipped with a CD-ROM drive. However, another approach is available: Solaris can be installed over the network using a remote server that has either the Solaris distribution CD in its CD-ROM drive or a copy of the files from the Solaris distribution CD on its hard disk.

The over-the-network installation can be used with either of the two interactive installation methods (Solaris interactive installation or WebStart, covered in Chapter 3) or the two automatic installation methods (JumpStart and custom JumpStart).

To perform over-the-network installation, one or more network servers must be set up. These consist of an install server and possibly a boot server. In addition, information about the install clients must be added in the local NIS or NIS+ or in the /etc/bootparams file of an install server.

Install Server

An install server is a system that provides the distribution files necessary for the installation of the Solaris operating system on an install client during an over-the-network installation. The files can be provided directly from the Solaris distribution CD mounted in a local CD-ROM drive or from a local hard disk.

By copying the distribution files to a local hard disk, a single install server can be used to provide the files for multiple releases (Solaris 7, Solaris 2.6, and so on) and/or for multiple platforms (SPARC and Intel x86). In addition, a local hard disk typically provides faster access to the distribution files than does a local CD-ROM drive.

To set up a system as an install server, mount the Solaris distribution CD in the local CD-ROM drive. Alternatively, you can use the **setup_install_server** command, under the Solaris_7/Tools directory on the Solaris distribution CD, to copy the distribution files to the local hard disk of the install server. One command line argument is required: the full pathname to a target directory to which the distribution files will be copied. Although any directory can be used, by convention the directory is named /export/install. The following listing shows executing the **setup_install_server** command from the Solaris_7/Tools directory of the distribution CD to set up an install server:

```
# setup_install_server /export/install
```

Boot Server

A boot server is a system that contains the files necessary to boot an install client over the network during an over-the-network installation. After an install client has booted, the boot server has completed its function. The remainder of the installation is supported by an install server.

Typically, an install server and a boot server reside on the same system. However, if install clients are on a different subnet than an install server, a boot server must be set up on the same subnet as the install clients.

To set up a system as a boot server, the system must have access to the Solaris software distribution CD through a local CD-ROM drive or a remotely shared CD-ROM drive.

The **setup_install_server** command, under the Solaris_7/Tools directory on the Solaris software distribution CD, is used to copy the boot software to the boot server. Two command line arguments are required. The first is the **-b** command line argument, which specifies that a boot server is being set up. The second is the full pathname to an empty directory to which the boot files will be copied. Although any directory can be used, by convention the directory is named "boot" and is located under the /export/install directory. The following listing shows executing the **setup_install_server** command from the Solaris_7/Tools directory of the distribution CD to set up a boot server:

```
# setup_install_server -b /export/install/boot
```

Adding Install Clients

When a system or install client is installed over the network, basic information about the install clients needs to be available through a name service (NIS/NIS+) or in the bootparams file under the /etc directory on the install server or boot server.

The Solstice Host Manager program can be used to add this information or, if Host Manager is not available, the **add_install_client** command. However, this command can be used only to update the /etc/bootparams file on an install server or boot server.

The following listing shows using the **add_install_client** command to set up a system for over-the-network installation. This command is executed from the Solaris_7/Tools directory of the distribution CD. The name of the system to be installed is identified by the **host** command line argument followed by the platform group of the system.

In this example, the command line argument **sun4m** is used to identify the system to be installed as a SPARC5 platform:

```
# add_install_client host sun4m
```

For a custom JumpStart installation, the name of the profile server and the custom JumpStart directory are specified by adding the command line argument **-c** *system:directory* to a boot server (instead of an install server). Then, the associated install server and directory of the CD image is specified by the command line argument **-s** *system:directory*. If the system has been pre-configured, the system and directory where the sysidcfg file resides can be specified by the command line argument **-p** *system:directory*.

Automating Installation With JumpStart

The JumpStart feature provides a mechanism to automatically install the Solaris operating system. The two JumpStart methods are JumpStart and custom JumpStart.

 Not only does JumpStart automate installation, it can be used to automate the installation of large numbers of systems that are identically configured. If you need to install 100 servers using the same configuration, JumpStart provides a way to simplify this task.

JumpStart enables automatic installation of the Solaris operating system on new SPARC platforms by inserting the Solaris distribution CD into the local CD-ROM drive and powering on the system or booting via the network. The software that is installed is determined by a default profile. The default profile is selected based on the hardware model and the size of the hard disks. The software installed cannot be manually selected.

All new SPARC platforms have a preinstalled JumpStart boot image. This boot image can be copied to an existing SPARC platform by using the **re-preinstall**(1M) command.

Custom JumpStart enables automatic installation of the Solaris operating system on new SPARC or Intel x86 platforms by inserting the Solaris distribution CD into the local CD-ROM drive and powering on the system or booting via the network. The software that is installed is determined by a custom profile. This provides a method to automatically install groups of systems in an identical manner. The custom profile, along with other JumpStart configuration files, is located in the JumpStart configuration directory.

JumpStart Configuration Directory

The JumpStart configuration directory contains the files used to customize a JumpStart installation. It provides a means to automate the system configuration phase of an installation for groups of similar systems. This directory can reside either on a floppy diskette, referred to as a *profile diskette*, or on a network server, referred to as a *profile server*. The profile server provides access to the custom JumpStart configuration files over the network and eliminates the need to create and distribute multiple profile diskettes during installation of a large number of systems. The two basic types of files in the JumpStart directory are a rules file and one or more profile files.

The Rules File

The rules file is a text file that contains an entry or rule for each system or group of systems that are to be automatically installed. Each rule identifies the system (or group of systems) based on one or more attributes and identifies a unique profile file that provides the configuration details for that system or group of systems.

Each rule consists of one or more keywords and values followed by the name of a begin script, the profile file, and then the finish script (all separated by tabs or spaces). Keywords (and associated values) include the following:

➤ any

➤ arch (followed by a processor-type value)

➤ disksize (followed by a disk name value)

➤ hostaddress (followed by an IP address value)

➤ hostname (followed by a hostname value)

➤ memsize (followed by a physical memory value)

➤ model (followed by a platform name value)

One or more of these keywords and associated values are specified per rule to uniquely identify a system or group of systems. Following the keywords and values is the name of a begin script. This is a Bourne shell script that executes before installation begins. If a begin script is not required, a hyphen (-) should be specified instead. Following the begin script is the name of a profile file in the JumpStart configuration directory that provides the configuration details for that system or group of systems. Following the profile file is the name of the finish script. The finish script is a Bourne shell script that is executed after installation is complete. If a finish script is not required, a hyphen (-) should be specified instead.

The Profile Files

A profile file is a text file that defines how to install the Solaris 7 software on a system. Like the rules file, a profile file contains keywords and associated values that guide the installation. Keywords and associated values include the following:

➤ boot_device (followed by the partition to use as a boot device)

➤ cluster (followed by the name of the software group to install, add, or delete)

➤ filesys (followed by pathname and mount point of a remote file system to mount)

➤ package (followed by the name of a software package to add or delete)

➤ root_device (followed by the partition to use as the root device)

Validation

Before the rules file and profile files can be used, they must be validated by using the **check**(1M) command (located on the Solaris 7 distribution CD under the Tools directory). If the rules file and all the profile files are set up correctly, a rules.ok file is created in the JumpStart configuration directory.

Practice Questions

Question 1

Which of the following commands is used to set up an install server?

○ a. **setup_install_server**

○ b. **setup_install_server -b**

○ c. **install_server_setup**

○ d. **server_setup -i**

The correct answer is a. Answer b is incorrect because the **-b** command line argument is used to install a boot server. Answers c and d are incorrect because these commands do not exist.

Question 2

Which of the following is a reason to set up a boot server on a separate system than an install server?

○ a. A boot server cannot reside on an install server.

○ b. One or more install clients are not on the same subnet as the install server.

○ c. All install clients are not on the same subnet.

○ d. NIS or NIS+ cannot locate a boot server that resides on an install server.

The correct answer is b. Answer a is incorrect because a boot server can reside on an install server. Answer c is incorrect because the location of clients in relation to other clients does not determine the need for boot servers. It is the location of the clients in relation to the install server that determines the need for a separate boot server. Answer d is incorrect because NIS and NIS+ do not locate things but serve only as databases of information.

Question 3

> Enter the name of the command (without command line arguments) used to add install client information to an install or a boot server.
>
> _____

The correct answer is **add_install_client**.

Question 4

> Which of the following install methods can use over-the-network installation resources? [Select all that apply]
>
> ❏ a. Custom JumpStart
>
> ❏ b. WebStart
>
> ❏ c. JumpStart
>
> ❏ d. Interactive installation

All the answers are correct. All four installation methods can use over-the-network installation resources.

Question 5

> Which of the following are automatic installation methods? [Select all that apply]
>
> ❏ a. SunInstall
>
> ❏ b. Custom JumpStart
>
> ❏ c. WebStart
>
> ❏ d. JumpStart

The correct answers are b and d. SunInstall and WebStart are interactive installation methods. Therefore, answers a nd c are incorrect.

Question 6

> Which of the following files should be in a JumpStart configuration directory?
> [Select all that apply]
>
> ❑ a. One or more JumpStart profile files
>
> ❑ b. **check**
>
> ❑ c. rules file
>
> ❑ d. rules.ok file

The correct answers are a, c, and d. The profile files (answer a) and the rules file (answer c) are the two types of files that must be created in the JumpStart configuration directory. If they are set up correctly, the rules.ok file (answer d) is created in the JumpStart configuration directory. The **check** command (answer b), which is located on the Solaris 7 distribution CD, must be executed to validate the rules and profile files.

Question 7

> Enter the file used by a custom JumpStart installation to define how a system is installed.
>
> _____

The correct answer is profile.

Question 8

> Which of the following are Solaris 7 software groups? [Select all that apply]
>
> ❑ a. Entire Distribution
>
> ❑ b. Basic
>
> ❑ c. End User Support
>
> ❑ d. Java Development Environment

The correct answers are a and c. Answers b and d do not exist.

Question 9

Enter the name of the file that is updated by the **add_install_client** command.

_____

The correct answer is /etc/bootparams.

Need To Know More?

Sun Microsystems, *Solaris Advanced Installation Guide*, is available in printed form (ISBN 805-3408-10), on the Web at **docs.sun.com**, and from the online documentation, AnswerBook2, provided with the Solaris 7 operating system.

Sun Microsystems, *System Reference Manual, Section 1 - User Commands*, is available in printed form (ISBN 805-3172-10), on the Web at **docs.sun.com**, and from the online documentation, AnswerBook2, provided with the Solaris 7 operating system.

Sun Microsystems, *System Reference Manual, Section 1M - Administration Commands*, is available in printed form (ISBN 805-3173-10), on the Web at **docs.sun.com**, and from the online documentation, AnswerBook2, provided with the Solaris 7 operating system.

Syslog And
Auditing Utilities

Terms you'll need to understand:

√ The syslog facility

√ The syslog source facilities

√ The syslog severity levels

√ The **who**, **whodo**, **last**, **logins**, and **ps** commands

Techniques you'll need to master:

√ Configuring the syslog facility

√ Enabling syslog messages to track use of the root login account

√ Enabling syslog message for network connections

√ Using the **who**, **whodo**, and **last** commands to audit login account usage

√ Using the **logins** command to audit login account information

√ Using the **ps** command to monitor processes

The first part of this chapter covers the Solaris 7 syslog facility. This mechanism provides the ability to log user and system messages in one or more files on either the local or a remote system.

The second part of this chapter describes five commands (**who, whodo, last, logins,** and **ps**) that are used to audit the usage of the logins, view the attributes of login accounts, and monitor processes.

The syslog Facility

The **syslogd**(1M) command accepts messages sent to it from system and user programs and handles them based on the entries in the /etc/syslog.conf file. These messages can be reporting anything from emergency situations to debugging details. Common uses include monitoring logins and recording hacking attempts. A syslog message is categorized by its source, a *source facility*, and a priority, or *severity level*.

Source Facilities

To provide better control over the handling of log messages, the facilities generating the messages can be used to determine where the messages are sent or stored. This allows separate log files for different types of messages based on the source. Table 15.1 lists the keywords used in the /etc/syslog.conf file to identify the source of messages and control handling.

Table 15.1   The syslog source facilities.

Keyword	Description
auth	Login authentication
cron	The **at**(1) and **cron**(1M) commands
daemon	System daemons
kern	The kernel
lpr	The line printer spooling system
local0-7	As defined locally
mail	System mail
mark	Timestamp produced by **syslogd**(1M)
news	The USENET network news system
user	User programs
uucp	The UUCP system
*	All facilities except mark

The *user* facility is the default and is used if the source does not specify a facility keyword in the syslog message.

Priority (Severity) Levels

Along with the source facility, a syslog message can be identified by priority, or severity. This provides a second mechanism (with finer granularity) for handling messages based on importance. Table 15.2 lists the keywords used in the /etc/syslog.conf file to identify the severity of messages and control handling. These keywords are ordered on the basis of severity (from most severe to least severe).

Customizing System Message Handling

To control the handling of syslog messages, entries are added to the /etc/syslog.conf file. These entries take the form of one or more facility/severity keyword combinations followed by a tab character and an action. The facility and severity identify a particular source facility and message severity, whereas the action determines how the messages are handled.

Facility/Severity Keywords Combinations

The facility and severity keywords are separated by a period (.) and identify a particular source facility and severity of messages. For example, kern.emerg identifies emergency error messages from the kernel.

Table 15.2	The syslog severity levels.
Keyword	**Description**
emerg	Panic conditions
alert	Conditions that need immediate attention
crit	Critical conditions
err	Other errors
warning	Warning messages
notice	Conditions that might require special handling
info	Nonurgent information
debug	Typically generated by debug messages in programs
none	Special keyword used to prevent logging of messages generated by specified sources

Three special cases exist. The first special case is when a facility keyword is specified without being followed by a "." and a severity keyword. This is used to identify all levels of severity. For example, if the facility keyword *mail* is specified by itself, all severity levels of mail messages are processed.

The second special case is when a facility keyword is followed by a "." and the *none* severity keyword. This implies that no messages from the specified facility should be processed. For example, mail.none indicates that no mail messages should be processed.

The third special case is when the asterisk (*) facility is used. This implies that all source facilities (except the mark facility) should be processed. For example, *.notice indicates that all messages of the notice level sent to syslog (from all sources except mark) should be processed.

More than one facility/severity combination can be specified on an /etc/syslog.conf entry by separating them with the semicolon (;) character.

Actions

Each entry has an action associated with it. Table 15.3 lists the four forms of actions.

The /etc/syslog.conf File

Entries in the /etc/syslog.conf file determine the handling of syslog messages. The **syslogd** daemon reads the /etc/syslog.conf file whenever it is started, or when it is sent the SIGHUP (1) signal. Table 15.4 summarizes the default syslog message handling (/etc/syslog.conf contents) for systems that log messages locally.

Table 15.3	The syslog actions.
Action	**Description**
/filename	The identified syslog messages will be appended to the specified file (must begin with a slash [/] character).
@host	The identified syslog messages will be forwarded to the **syslogd** daemon on the specified remote host (must begin with the at [@] character).
login account	The identified syslog messages are written to the standard out (typically the monitor) associated with the specified login account if the account is currently logged onto the system. Multiple login accounts can be specified (separated by commas).
*	The identified syslog messages are written to the standard out of all login accounts currently logged onto the system.

Table 15.4   The default /etc/syslog.conf file.

Facility/Severity	Action	Description
*.err;kern.notice; auth.notice	/dev/sysmsg	All error, kernel notice, and authorization notice messages are written to the /dev/sysmsg file.
*.err;kern.debug; daemon.notice; mail.crit	/var/adm /messages	All error, kernel debug, daemon notice, and critical mail messages are written to the /var/adm/messages file.
*.alert;kern.err; daemon.err	operator	All alert, kernel error, and daemon error messages are written to the operator login account (if currently logged onto the system).
*.alert	root	All alert messages are written to the root login account (if currently logged onto the system).
*.emerg	*	All emergency messages are written to all login accounts currently logged onto the system.
mail.debug	/var/log/syslog	All debug mail messages are written to the /var/log/syslog file.
user.err	/dev/sysmsg	All user error messages are written to the /dev/sysmsg file.
user.err	/var/adm /messages	All user error messages are written to the /var/adm/messages file.
user.alert	root, operator	All user alert messages are written to the root and operator login accounts (if currently logged onto the system).

Unless an entry exists for a particular facility/severity combination, messages generated using that particular combination are discarded. Be careful not to delete any of the existing entries unless those messages are being handled by a new entry. The most commonly used default log file is /var/adm/messages.

Messages Generated By The **login** Command

The **login**(1) command, used to log onto the system, can be configured to generate auth.notice syslog messages when the root account logs onto the system. In addition, multiple failed attempts to log in as root are logged as auth.crit syslog messages. These messages are generated by the **login** command if the /etc/default/login file contains the following entry:

```
SYSLOG=YES
```

Messages Generated By Internet Services

The Internet services daemon, **inetd**(1M), which is used to start the standard Internet services, can be configured to trace incoming TCP connections by logging client IP address, TCP port number, and name of the service as a daemon.notice syslog message. To enable this logging, add the -t command line argument to the **inetd** command at the end of the /etc/init.d/inetsvc file.

Auditing Login Accounts And Processes

Several commands are available to monitor the use of system and user login accounts. In addition, several commands can be used to identify the processes currently running on the system and the associated login accounts.

The **who** Command

The **who**(1) command can be used to determine which system and user accounts are currently logged into the local system. Without arguments, the **who** command lists the login account name, terminal device, login date/time, and an indication of X window or origination:

```
$ who
root          console       Nov  4 16:16    (:0)
root          pts/3         Nov  4 16:17    (solaris:0.0)
dla           pts/4         Nov  5 11:02    (winnt40)
$
```

When the -q command line argument is specified, only the login account names and number of users currently logged on are displayed, as shown in the following listing:

```
$ who -q
root      root      dla
# users=3
$
```

The **whodo** Command

The **whodo**(1M) command is used to determine the processes that each login account is executing. The following listing shows (among other things) that the user dla is using the **vi**(1) command:

```
# whodo
Fri Nov  5 12:18:36 EST 1999
solaris
```

```
console      root      16:16
   ?                423      0:00 Xsession
   pts/2            467      0:00 sdt_shell
   pts/2            483      0:00 ttsession
   pts/2            484      0:01 dtsession
   ?                1091     0:00 dtscreen
   ?                491      0:04 dtwm
   ?                507      0:00 dtaction
   ?                492      0:01 sdtperfmeter
   pts/2            470      0:00 sh
   ?                433      0:00 fbconsole
   ?                468      0:00 dsdm

pts/3        root      16:17
   pts/3            515      0:00 sh

pts/4        dla       11:02
   pts/4            1051     0:00 sh
   pts/4            1097     0:00 vi
```

When the -1 command line argument is specified, additional details are displayed, as shown in the following listing:

```
# whodo -1
 12:23pm  up 1 day(s), 16 hr(s), 35 min(s)  4 user(s)
User    tty        login@ idle  JCPU PCPU what
root    console  Thu 4pm 20:07     1       /usr/dt/bin/sdt_shell
root    pts/3    Thu 4pm  1:36    11       /sbin/sh
dla     pts/4    11:02am     5            vi
dla     pts/5    11:04am     4            whodo -1
#
```

In addition, if the name of a login account is specified after the -1 command line argument, only information on that login account is displayed.

The w(1) command (which is not listed as a test objective) can be used to list the users currently logged into the system. Its output is similar to the **whodo** command.

The **last** Command

The **last**(1) command is used to display login and logout information. This command can be used both to determine which accounts are logged into the system and to display the last time accounts were used (starting with most recent). The following listing shows a partial output from the **last** command:

```
# last
guest   console       :0        Fri Nov  5  8:36 - 12:37  (00:01)
dla     pts/4         winnt40 Fri Nov  5 11:02    still logged in
reboot  system boot             Wed Nov  3 19:47
dla     pts/3         winnt40 Mon Oct 25 14:53 - 13:27 (4+22:33)
root    console       :0        Mon Oct 25 14:52 - 19:36 (9+05:43)
root    console       :0        Mon Oct 18 18:59 - 19:00  (00:00)
```

As shown in the listing, the guest account logged into the system from the console at 8:36 on November 5 and logged out at 12:37 the same day. The listing also shows the dla account as still being logged onto the system. To list information for only a particular login account, specify the account name as a command line argument, as shown in the following listing:

```
# last guest
guest   console   :0     Fri Nov  5  8:36 - 12:37  (00:01)
wtmp begins Sat Dec 19 20:35
#
```

The **logins** Command

The **logins**(1M) command can be used to list user and login information. When used without any command line arguments, the **logins** command displays the following information regarding each login account:

➤ Account name

➤ User ID (UID)

➤ Primary group name

➤ Primary group ID (GID)

➤ Contents of the /etc/passwd comment field

Table 15.5 summarizes the command line arguments supported by the **logins** command.

Table 15.5	Command line arguments for the logins command.
Argument	**Description**
-a	Displays the number of days until the account password expires due to inactivity and the date the password expires
-d	Displays only accounts with identical UIDs
-g group	Displays only accounts that belong to the specified group

(continued)

Table 15.5	Command line arguments for the logins command (continued).
Argument	**Description**
-l *account*	Displays only the specified login account (can be a comma-separated list of account names)
-m	Displays all groups of which an account is a member
-o	Converts the output to a format using colon-delimited fields
-p	Displays only accounts with no passwords
-s	Displays only system (administrative) login accounts
-t	Sorts output by account name instead of UID
-u	Displays only user (nonadministrative) login accounts
-x	Displays extended information, such as home directory, login shell, and password aging

The following listing shows the use of the **logins** command:

```
# logins
root        0       other       1       Super-User
daemon      1       other       1
bin         2       bin         2
sys         3       sys         3
adm         4       adm         4       Admin
uucp        5       uucp        5       uucp Admin
nuucp       9       nuucp       9       uucp Admin
listen      37      adm         4       Network Admin
lp          71      lp          8       Line Printer Admin
guest       1001    staff       10
dla         1002    staff       10      Darrell Ambro
shlog       1003    staff       10
cshlog      1004    staff       10
joe         1005    staff       10
nobody      60001   nobody      60001   Nobody
noaccess    60002   noaccess    60002   No Access User
nobody4     65534   nogroup     65534   SunOS 4.x Nobody
```

The **ps** Command

The **ps**(1) command can be used to identify the processes currently running on the system. This command is also a Part I exam objective and is covered in detail in Chapter 7. Reread this portion of Chapter 7 for information on the command line arguments for the **ps** command.

The following listing shows a partial output from the **ps -eaf** command:

```
# ps -eaf
UID    PID  PPID  C    STIME TTY      TIME CMD
root     0     0  0    Nov 03 ?     0:00 sched
root     1     0  0    Nov 03 ?     0:00 /etc/init -
root     2     0  0    Nov 03 ?     0:00 pageout
root   301   298  0    Nov 03 ?     0:00 /usr/lib/saf/listen tcp
root   298     1  0    Nov 03 ?     0:00 /usr/lib/saf/sac -t 300
root   166     1  0    Nov 03 ?     0:00 /usr/lib/autofs/automountd
root   177     1  0    Nov 03 ?     0:00 /usr/sbin/syslogd
root   151     1  0    Nov 03 ?     0:00 /usr/sbin/inetd -s
root   181     1  0    Nov 03 ?     0:00 /usr/sbin/cron
root   245     1  0    Nov 03 ?     0:00 /usr/sbin/vold
root   287     1  0    Nov 03 ?     0:00 /usr/dt/bin/dtlogin -daemon
root   302   298  0    Nov 03 ?     0:00 /usr/lib/saf/ttymon
root  1468  1092  1 14:13:42 ?     0:00 ps -eaf
root   885     1  0 06:44:56 ?     0:00 /usr/lib/lpsched
root  1049   151  0 11:02:26 ?     0:00 in.telnetd
```

Practice Questions

Question 1

Which of the following commands is used to determine when a particular login account was last used?

- ○ a. **logins**
- ○ b. **last**
- ○ c. **whodo**
- ○ d. **ps**

The correct answer is b. Answer a is incorrect because it displays attributes about login accounts, not the usage of the login accounts. Answers c and d are incorrect because these commands list information regarding processes.

Question 2

The /etc/syslog.conf file was modified to capture messages from a particular user application, but the log file still does not contain any of those messages. Which of the following reasons could explain this? [Select all that apply]

- ❑ a. A typographical error exists in the /etc/syslog.conf entry that was added.
- ❑ b. The **syslogd** program was not restarted.
- ❑ c. The user application does not generate the facility and/or severity of messages being expected.
- ❑ d. The **syslogd** program is not running.
- ❑ e. The wrong log is being examined.

Answers a, b, c, d, and e are all correct. All of these are reasons for the syslog facility not working as expected. Entries with typographical errors are either ignored or cause other entries to be misinterpreted. The **syslogd** command reads the /etc/syslog.conf file only when it is started or it receives the SIGHUP signal. The /etc/syslog.conf entry must match the expected facility/severity being used by the user application to submit the messages. If the **syslogd** command is not running, it cannot receive and handle messages. Be certain that the messages are being sent to the intended log file.

Question 3

Identify the name of the command that combines the **who** command with the **ps** command.

_____

The correct answer is **whodo**.

Question 4

Which of the following are source facilities for syslog messages? [Select all that apply]

❑ a. login

❑ b. news

❑ c. local8

❑ d. kern

Answers b and d are correct. auth (not login) is the source facility associated with logging onto the system; therefore, answer a is incorrect. The eight locally de-fined source facilities are local0 through local7; therefore, answer c is incorrect.

Question 5

Which of the following are valid command line arguments for the **logins** com-mand? [Select all that apply]

❑ a. **-p** (displays account without passwords)

❑ b. **-q** (displays only account names)

❑ c. **-a** (displays administrative login accounts)

❑ d. **-g _group_** (displays login accounts that are a member of the specified group)

The correct answers are a and d. Answers b and c do not exist. The command line argument to display administrative (system) login accounts is -s.

Question 6

Which of the following are valid uses for the asterisk (*) within the /etc/syslog.conf file? [Select all that apply]

❏ a. Represents all source facilities

❏ b. Represents all severity levels

❏ c. Represents all messages

❏ d. Writes message to all logged-on users

The correct answer is d. An asterisk can be used to represent all source facilities except mark; therefore, answer a is incorrect. No symbol or keyword is available to represent all severity levels or all messages; therefore, answers b and c are incorrect.

Question 7

Identify the command used to list the login accounts currently logged into the system.

_____

The correct answer is either the **last** command or the **who** command.

Question 8

Which of the following are severity levels? [Select all that apply]

❏ a. alert

❏ b. notice

❏ c. none

❏ d. mail

The correct answers are a, b, and c. Answer d is a source facility, not a severity level, and therefore is incorrect.

Question 9

Enter the name of the default log file used for most of the syslog messages.

_____

The correct answer is /var/adm/messages.

Need To Know More?

Sun Microsystems, *System Administration Guide, Volume 2*, is available in printed form (ISBN 805-3728-10), on the Web at **docs.sun.com**, and from the online documentation, AnswerBook2, provided with the Solaris 7 operating system.

Sun Microsystems, *System Reference Manual, Section 1 - User Commands*, is available in printed form (ISBN 805-3172-10), on the Web at **docs.sun.com**, and from the online documentation, AnswerBook2, provided with the Solaris 7 operating system.

Sun Microsystems, *System Reference Manual, Section 1M - Administration Commands*, is available in printed form (ISBN 805-3173-10), on the Web at **docs.sun.com**, and from the online documentation, AnswerBook2, provided with the Solaris 7 operating system.

Device Administration

Terms you'll need to understand:

√ Data Communication Equipment (DCE)

√ Data Terminal Equipment (DTE)

√ Modem access modes

√ Service Access Facility (SAF)

√ Service Access Controller (SAC)

√ The **listen** and **ttymon** port monitors

√ The **sacadm**, **pmadm**, and **ttyadm** SAF commands

√ The **tip** command

Techniques you'll need to master:

√ Using the **admintool** command to set up a terminal

√ Using the **admintool** command to set up a bidirectional modem

√ Using the **tip** command to access a remote system

This chapter covers several aspects of communication devices. The first part of the chapter defines terms related to serial devices and communication using serial devices. The second part describes the Service Access Facility (SAF), which is used to administer the serial communication devices (along with some network connectivity). The third part describes how to use the **admintool** command to set up terminals and bidirectional modems. The fourth part describes the **tip** command, which can be used to connect to a remote system using a serial port and a modem (or a hardwired connection).

Serial Devices

Most serial communication conforms to the EIA RS-232 standard (or its revisions RS-232-C or RS-232-D) issued by the Electronics Industries Association. This standard addresses two types of serial communication equipment. The first is Data Communication Equipment, or Data Circuit-Terminating Equipment (DCE), which provides part of the communication network or at least the access point to the network. The second is Data Terminal Equipment (DTE), which is the end device that uses the DCE for communication.

The RS-232 standard defines the interface between the DCE and DTE in terms of electrical signal characteristics, the mechanical interface (connector), and a functional description of the interchange circuits.

Data Communication Equipment (DCE)

The most widely used DCE is probably the modulator/demodulator (modem) used for communication through the Public Switched Telephone Network (PSTN), otherwise known as the phone system.

Over the years, modems have increased in transmission throughput by using more sophisticated modulation techniques and functionality, such as error detection/correction and compression. However, for the external modem, one thing has not changed, namely, the manner in which the modem interfaces to a terminal or computer. This interface has always been defined by the RS-232 standard.

Data Terminal Equipment (DTE)

The most commonly used DTE devices are terminals and computers. Technically, the serial communication port on the terminal or computer that interfaces to the DCE is considered the DTE, but opinions vary, and most accept either view.

Almost every computer made in the last 15 years has at least one serial communication port; most personal computers and desktops have two. These can be used to interface to communication devices such as modems, input devices such as mice, output devices such as printers, and even other computers.

Important Terms

The Part II exam objectives specify that the following terms should be defined. These definitions are brief but should be adequate.

Serial Device

A *serial device* is a device that communicates using the RS-232 standard. This includes communication devices such as modems, input devices such as mice, output devices such as printers, and in some contexts other computers.

 Most Solaris 7 systems (both SPARC and x86) have two serial devices. These are identified as serial ports a and b. Their full pathnames are /dev/term/a and /dev/term/b, respectively.

Port

A *port* is a controlled physical device that can transfer data between entities. The port can be used for input, output, or both.

Serial Port

A *serial port* is a port that conforms to the RS-232 standard. This includes not only the electrical signaling and interchange circuits but also connectors and cables.

Modem

A *modem* is used to convert digital data to and from electrical analog signals. Signals can be transmitted over the PSTN or dedicated lines.

Null Modem Cable

A *null modem cable* is a cable that allows two DTE devices (such as computers) to communicate via serial ports. This is accomplished by cross-wiring the cable so that each DTE appears as a DCE device (or modem) to the other one. This makes it appear as if a modem is being used when actually no (or null) modems are being used.

Data Carrier Detect

One of the interchange circuits defined by the RS-232 standard and transmitted on one of the wires in a serial cable is the *Data Carrier Detect (DCD)*. The DCE (typically a modem) will inform the attached DTE that it has detected a carrier signal from the DCE at the other end of the communication path by placing a voltage on (asserting) the DCD circuit. This informs the DTE that the remote device is present and has answered the call (but is not necessarily ready, which is indicated by a different signal).

DCD has been adapted for other uses. Some serial printers require what is referred to as *receiver handshaking*, which means that the printer expects DCD to be asserted by the computer before it is willing to operate.

Port Monitor Program

The Solaris 7 *port monitor program* monitors the RS-232 interchange circuits (such as DCD) on the serial ports of the system and provides information to applications as to the status of the interchange circuits. Additional port monitor functionality is described later in this chapter.

Modem Access Modes

In the Solaris 7 environment, modems are set up to be used or accessed in one of three configurations: inbound, outbound, or bidirectional:

➤ *Inbound*—With the inbound configuration, the modem is configured to answer incoming calls and negotiate with the originating modem to establish a connection. Once a connection is established, a process such as the **login** command or the Unix-To-Unix Copy Protocol (UUCP) uses the connection to perform some operation.

➤ *Outbound*—With the outbound configuration, the modem is configured to originate an outgoing call on behalf of a service. An outbound configuration can be used to connect to an Internet Service Provider (ISP) or send files using the UUCP capability.

➤ *Bidirectional*—As the name implies, this modem configuration is a combination of the inbound and outbound configurations. It can answer inbound calls and originate outbound calls.

The Service Access Facility

The *Service Access Facility (SAF)* is a two-level facility that provides services for serial ports and network connections. A *service* is defined as a program that monitors and sets up connections using the serial ports and network interfaces.

The first, or top-level, SAF program is the Service Access Controller or **sac**(1M) command. It is responsible for starting and controlling the lower-level SAF programs, or *port monitors*, which monitor one or more ports to handle requests for services.

The Service Access Controller (SAC)

The **sac** command is a program that is started when the system is booted. It first reads the system configuration file, /etc/saf/_sysconfig. This file is used to customize the behavior of the **sac** command. Then the SAC administrative file, /etc/saf/_sactab, is read. This file lists the port monitors that should be started.

By default, two port monitors are defined. These are described in the next section. The **sac** command is defined in the /etc/inittab file to start at system run levels 2, 3, and 4.

 In terms of system operation, starting the **sac** command at run levels 2 or 3 (multiuser and multiuser with NFS) is more appropriate than starting the command at run level 4 because run level 4 is not defined.

Port Monitors

Two types of port monitors are provided with the Solaris 7 operating system: the **ttymon**(1M) command and the **listen**(1M) command.

The **ttymon** Port Monitor

The **ttymon** command is a STREAMS-based TTY port monitor. It monitors serial ports in order to select terminal modes, baud rates, and other communication-related settings. In addition, it connects a specified service to a port when the connection is established. The **ttymon** command can be configured to monitor and set up multiple ports. It runs under the control of the **sac** command as part of the second level of the SAF.

When set up, an instance (executing image) of the **ttymon** command is assigned a unique *port monitor tag*, such as zsmon. The configuration of the services associated with this port monitor is stored in an administrative file by the name of _pmtab under a directory with the same name as the port monitor. For example, the administrative file for the zsmon port monitor is /etc/saf/zsmon/_pmtab.

The **ttymon** port monitors use the information in the /etc/ttydefs file to initialize the baud rate (line speed) and terminal settings for each port.

The **listen** Port Monitor

The **listen** command is a STREAMS-based network listener daemon. It listens for and accepts network service requests. Then it invokes a specified service and associates it with the network connection. The **listen** command runs under the control of the **sac** command as part of the lower level of the SAF.

When set up, an instance (executing image) of the **listen** command is assigned a unique port monitor tag typically associated with the protocol being used, such as tcp. The configuration of the services associated with this port monitor is stored in an administrative file by the name of _pmtab under a directory with the same name as the port monitor. For example, the administrative file for the tcp port monitor is /etc/saf/tcp/_pmtab.

SAF Commands

Two commands are used to administer the SAF. The **sacadm**(1M) command is used to control the behavior of the SAC, whereas the **pmadm**(1M) command is used to control the behavior of port monitors.

The **ttyadm**(1M) command is used with the **pmadm** command to format entries for the port monitor table (_pmtab).

The **sacadm** Command

The **sacadm** command provides administrative control over the top level of the SAF, namely, the SAC. A single command line argument (listed in Table 16.1) specifies the function that the **sacadm** command should perform. This

Table 16.1 The sacadm command line arguments.	
Argument	**Description**
-a	Adds the port monitor defined by the remainder of the command line arguments
-d	Disables the specified port monitor
-e	Enables the specified port monitor
-g	Displays or replaces the per-port configuration script for the specified port monitor
-G	Displays or replaces the per-system configuration script for the specified port monitor
-k	Stops or kills the specified port monitor
-l	Lists information for all port monitors or the specified port monitor or port monitor type
-L	Lists -l information in condensed format
-r	Removes the specified port monitor
-s	Starts the specified port monitor
-x	Rereads the SAC configuration file or port monitor table

command line argument is usually accompanied by the -p command line argument, which specifies a port monitor tag. For example, the following listing shows using the **sacadm** command to disable the zsmon port monitor:

```
# sacadm -d -p zsmon
```

The **pmadm** Command

The **pmadm**(1M) command provides administrative control over the lower level of the SAF, namely, the services provided by a port monitor. A single command line argument (listed in Table 16.2) specifies the function that the **pmadm** command should perform. This command line argument is usually accompanied by the -p command line argument, which specifies a port monitor tag, and the -s command line argument, which specifies the service. For example, the following listing shows using the **pmadm** command to disable the service for ttya provided by the zsmon port monitor:

```
# pmadm -d -p zsmon -s ttya
```

Table 16.2   The pmadm command line arguments.

Argument	Description
-a	Adds the service defined by the remainder of the command line arguments to the specified port monitor
-d	Disables the specified service associated with the specified port monitor
-e	Enables the specified service associated with the specified port monitor
-g	Displays or replaces the per-service configuration script for the specified service associated with the specified port monitor
-i	Defines the owner (a user account) of the service
-l	Lists information for all services or the services of the specified port monitor
-L	Lists -l information in condensed format
-m	Defines port monitor–specific data
-r	Removes the specified service associated with the specified port monitor
-v	Defines the version of the port monitor table

The **ttyadm** Command

The **ttyadm** command is used to format **ttymon**-specific data. Typically, the output of the **ttyadm** command is captured and placed in the **ttymon** port monitor table (_pmtab).

> *Note: The equivalent command to format **listen**-specific data is the **nlsadm** command. However, it is not listed as a Part II exam objective and thus is not discussed here. For additional information, see the nlsadm(1M) manual page in the System Reference Manual, Section 1M - Administration Commands.*

The type of data that the **ttyadm** command generates is controlled by one or more command line arguments. These are listed in Table 16.3.

Table 16.3 The ttyadm command line arguments.	
Argument	**Description**
-b	Sets the bidirectional port flag
-c	Sets the connect-on-carrier flag
-d *device*	Uses the specified *device* as the port
-h	Forces a hangup on disconnect
-i *message*	Displays *message* on connection if service on this port is disabled
-l *ttylabel*	Uses the *ttylabel* entry from the /etc/ttydefs file for setting the baud rate
-m *modules*	Pushes the specified *modules* on the I/O STREAM associated with the port
-p *prompt*	Displays a prompt on connection (such as login:)
-r *count*	Waits until *count* newline characters are received before displaying the prompt
-s *service*	Specifies the *service* to invoke when a connection is established
-S *flag*	Sets the software carrier if *flag* is **y** for the software carrier; otherwise, uses the hardware carrier (*flag* of **n**)
-t *timeout*	Time-outs the port in *timeout* seconds
-T *termtype*	Sets the terminal type to *termtype*
-V	Displays the version number

The following listing shows using the **ttyadm** command to create the necessary **pmadm** command line arguments to add a port monitor service to the zsmon port monitor configuration. Note that this is actually a single line that has been formatted to improve readability:

```
# pmadm -a -p zsmon -s a -i root -v 'ttyadm -V'
  -m "`ttyadm -l contty -d /dev/term/a -s /usr/sbin/login`"
```

In this example, the **ttyadm** command is used to generate most of the data that is added to the _pmtab when a service with the tag of **a** is added to the zsmon port monitor. Note that the output of the first use of the **ttyadm** command becomes the data associated with the -v command line argument of the **pmadm** command and that the second use of the **ttyadm** command becomes the data associated with the -m command line argument of the **pmadm** command.

Using admintool

The **admintool** command can be used to configure the serial ports to support not only inbound, outbound, and bidirectional modem configurations, but also a hardwired terminal. These configurations require different options, but the same **admintool** windows are used for all the configurations.

Adding A Terminal

The following procedure describes how to add a hardwired terminal to the system using the **admintool** command:

1. When the **admintool** command is started, the Admintool: Users window is displayed, as shown in Figure 16.1. Select Serial Ports from the Browse pull-down menu. The Admintool: Serial Ports window shown in Figure 16.2 is displayed.

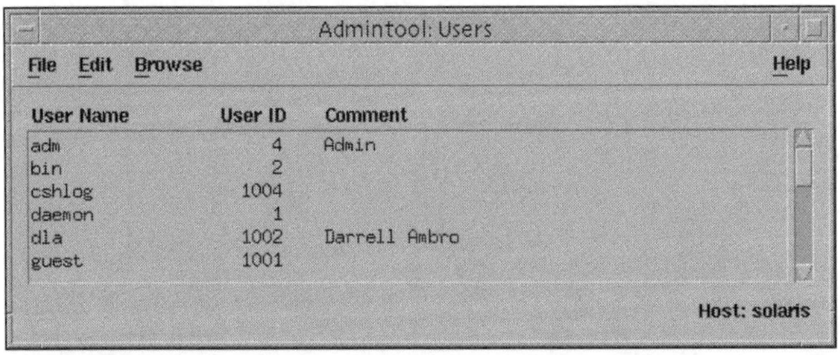

Figure 16.1   The Admintool: Users window.

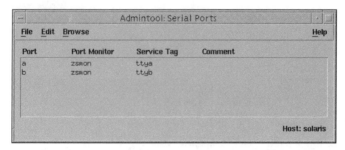

Figure 16.2 The Admintool: Serial Ports window.

2. Determine the serial port to be used for the terminal. With the mouse, click on the desired port entry to highlight it and then select Modify from the Edit pull-down menu. The Admintool: Modify Serial Port window shown in Figure 16.3 is displayed. Typically, only two ports (port a and port b) are listed; however, if additional serial ports have been added to the system, they will be listed as well.

3. To configure a hardwired terminal, position the mouse cursor over the Template field and hold down the left button. Then move the mouse cursor over the Terminal - Hardwired item and release the mouse button.

   By default, only the basic options are displayed in the Admintool: Modify Serial Port window. Additional options are displayed by clicking on the More or Expert radio button. All the serial port options are described in detail later in this chapter.

4. To modify the baud rate for the serial port, position the mouse cursor over the Baud Rate field and hold down the left button. Then move the mouse cursor over the desired baud rate and release the mouse button.

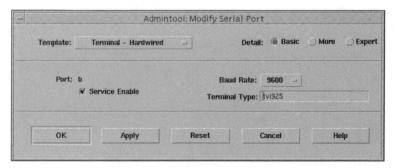

Figure 16.3 The Admintool: Modify Serial Port window (Terminal - Hardwired).

5. To modify the name of the terminal (a terminfo entry), highlight the contents of the Terminal Type field and then enter the name of the desired terminal type. When finished, click on OK.

Adding A Bidirectional Modem

The following procedure describes how to add a bidirectional modem to the system using the **admintool** command:

1. Start the **admintool** command if it is not already active. Display the Admintool: Serial Ports window (shown earlier in Figure 16.2) by selecting Serial Ports from the Browse pull-down menu.

2. Determine the serial port to be used for the modem. With the mouse, click on the desired port entry to highlight it and then select Modify from the Edit pull-down menu. The Admintool: Modify Serial Port window (shown earlier in Figure 16.3) is displayed.

3. To configure a hardwired terminal, position the mouse cursor over the Template field and hold down the left button. Then move the mouse cursor over the Modem - Bidirectional item and release the mouse button. The Admintool: Modify Serial Port window will be similar to Figure 16.4.

   By default, only the basic options are displayed in the Admintool: Modify Serial Port window. Additional options are displayed by clicking on the More or Expert radio button. All the serial port options are described in detail later in this chapter.

4. To modify the baud rate for the serial port, position the mouse cursor over the Baud Rate field and hold down the left button. Then move the mouse cursor over the desired baud rate and release the mouse button.

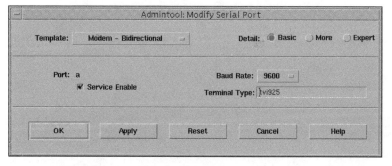

Figure 16.4   The Admintool: Modify Serial Port window (Modem - Bidirectional).

5. To modify the name of a default terminal type for inbound connections (a terminfo entry), highlight the contents of the Terminal Type field and then enter the name of the desired terminal type. When finished, click on OK.

Serial Port Options

The Admintool: Modify Serial Port window of the **admintool** command can display three sets of options: Basic, More, and Expert. Typically, the options are set automatically based on the selected setting of the Template field. Figure 16.5 shows all the options of the Modify Serial Port window, and Table 16.4 describes these options.

Table 16.4	Options of the Admintool: Modify Serial Port window.
Option	**Description**
Service Enable	Indicates that the port should be enabled for use
Baud Rate	Selects the line speed used to communicate with the attached modem or terminal
Terminal Type	Indicates the terminfo entry used to identify the type of terminal attached to the port

(continued)

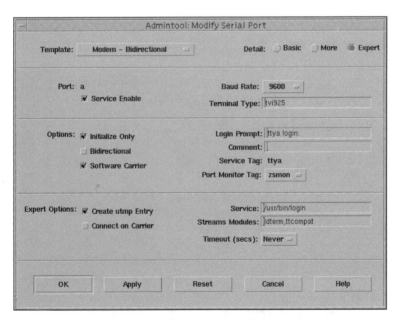

Figure 16.5 The Admintool: Modify Serial Port (Expert option) window.

Table 16.4   Options of the Admintool: Modify Serial Port window (continued).

Option	Description
Initialize Only	Indicates that the port is initialized but not configured
Bidirectional	Indicates that the port is being used for a bidirectional modem configuration
Software Carrier	Indicates that software carrier detection should be used instead of hardware carrier detection
Login Prompt	Specifies the prompt to be transmitted after the connection is established
Comment	Displays a comment describing the use or configuration of the port
Service Tag	Displays the service tag associated with the port
Port Monitor Tag	Specifies the name of the port monitor used to manage the port
Create utmp Entry	Creates an entry in the login account files when a user logs in through the port
Connect on Carrier	Indicates that the program specified in the Service field should be called when a connection is made
Service	Specifies the command or process that should be started to handle I/O through the port
Streams Modules	Specifies the STREAMS modules that need to be pushed onto the stream associated with the serial port
Timeout (secs)	Specifies the number of seconds that the port should wait on input after it has been opened

Even though the options are not covered in detail on the exam, be sure to understand the purpose of these options. Keep in mind that all the options do not apply to all the types of configurations.

The **tip** Command

The **tip**(1) command is used to connect to a remote system through an RS-232 connection. It is a basic terminal emulator designed to communicate over a modem or hardwired serial port.

Typically, anything entered by the user is transmitted to the remote system. However, a set of escape sequences is supported that allows the user to instruct the **tip** command to perform operations such as file transfers. All these escape sequences begin with the tilde (~) character. For additional information, see the manual page for the **tip** command in the *System Reference Manual*.

A command line argument specifies either the name of a remote system or how to connect to the remote system. This argument takes the form of a hostname, a phone number, or a device name:

➤ If a hostname is specified, the /etc/remote(4) file is searched for an entry with a matching name. This entry describes how the **tip** command should attempt to connect with the remote system. The /etc/remote file is discussed in the next section.

➤ If a phone number is specified, default settings, such as serial port and baud rate, are used to connect to the remote system that can be reached by dialing the specified phone number.

➤ If a device is specified, it is assumed that the device is a hardwired connection to another system. The **tip** command interprets any character string beginning with a slash (/) character, such as /dev/term/b, as being a device name.

To override the default baud rate associated with a hostname or to specify a baud rate when using a phone number or device, specify the baud rate preceded with a hyphen (-) as the first command line argument. This actually represents an entry in the /etc/remote file that defines line characteristics. The following listing shows examples of the **tip** command using a hostname, phone number, and device to specify the remote system or connection method:

```
tip gcuxa
tip -9600 1-555-3842
tip /dev/term/a
```

The hostname example uses gcuxa as the hostname. This should be the name of an entry in the /etc/remote file. The phone number example overrides the default baud rate by specifying 9600 baud as the line speed. The device example uses port A (dev/term/a) to connect to a remote system.

The /etc/remote And /etc/phones Files

The /etc/remote file contains information for remote systems and line speed definitions. Entries for remote systems define which device (serial port) to use, modem settings and control strings, baud rate, and phone number.

If the phone number field is defined as an at symbol (@), the **tip** command searches the /etc/phones(4) file. This file contains entries consisting of a hostname (that matches the name of an entry in the /etc/remote file) and a phone number.

Practice Questions

Question 1

Which of the following can be specified as a **tip** command line argument to connect to a remote system? [Select all that apply]

❏ a. IP address

❏ b. Hostname as defined in /etc/remote

❏ c. Hostname as defined in /etc/hosts

❏ d. Phone number

❏ e. System device, such as a serial port

The correct answers are b, d, and e. Answers a and c are valid for network communication but not for communication through a serial port using the **tip** command. Therefore, they are incorrect.

Question 2

Which of the following can be considered Data Termination Equipment (DTE)? [Select all that apply]

❏ a. Modem

❏ b. Computer

❏ c. Terminal

❏ d. Access point to a network

❏ e. Serial port

The correct answers are b, c, and e. Answers a and d are incorrect because they are types of Data Communication Equipment (DCE).

Question 3

Identify the graphical administrative command that can be used to add a terminal or modem to the system configuration.

_____

The correct answer is the **admintool** command.

Question 4

Which of the following modem access modes are supported? [Select all that apply]

- ☐ a. Inbound
- ☐ b. Data carrier detect
- ☐ c. Bidirectional
- ☐ d. Outbound

The correct answers are a, c, and d. Answer b is incorrect because it is an RS-232 interchange circuit.

Question 5

Enter the name of the command used to control the enabling and disabling of services.

_____

The correct answer is the **pmadm** command.

Question 6

Which of the following files does the **sac** command use to determine the port monitors that should be started?

- ○ a. _pmtab
- ○ b. _sactab
- ○ c. _sysconfig
- ○ d. /etc/saf/pmconfig

The correct answer is b. Answer a is incorrect because it defines port monitor services. Answer c is incorrect because it is used to define configuration parameters that control the behavior of the **sac** command. Answer d is incorrect because it does not exist.

Question 7

Which of the following are port monitors? [Select all that apply]

❑ a. **inetd**

❑ b. **listen**

❑ c. **ttymon**

❑ d. **sac**

The correct answers are b and c. Answer a is the Internet Services daemon. Answer d is the Service Access Controller, which is used to start and stop port monitors. Therefore, answers a and d are incorrect.

Question 8

Identify the name of the command that is used to format data for a **ttymon** port monitor table.

The correct answer is the **ttyadm** command.

Question 9

Which of the following is considered the top-level SAF process or program?

○ a. **sac**

○ b. **ttymon**

○ c. **listen**

○ d. **pmadm**

The correct answer is a. **ttymon** and **listen** are lower-level SAF programs. Therefore, answers b and c are incorrect. **pmadm** is not considered part of the two-level SAF; it is a command used to configure the lower-level SAF programs. Therefore, answer d is incorrect.

Need To Know More?

Sun Microsystems, *System Administration Guide, Volume 2*, is available in printed form (ISBN 805-3728-10), on the Web at **docs.sun.com**, and from the online documentation, AnswerBook2, provided with the Solaris 7 operating system.

Sun Microsystems, *System Reference Manual, Section 1 - User Commands*, is available in printed form (ISBN 805-3172-10), on the Web at **docs.sun.com**, and from the online documentation, AnswerBook2, provided with the Solaris 7 operating system.

Sun Microsystems, *System Reference Manual, Section 1M - Administration Commands*, is available in printed form (ISBN 805-3173-10), on the Web at **docs.sun.com**, and from the online documentation, AnswerBook2, provided with the Solaris 7 operating system.

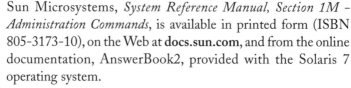

Sun Microsystems, *System Reference Manual, Section 4 - File Formats*, is available in printed form (ISBN 805-3176-10), on the Web at **docs.sun.com**, and from the online documentation, AnswerBook2, provided with the Solaris 7 operating system.

Advanced Disk Management

Terms you'll need to understand:

√ Virtual file systems

√ Striping and concatenation

√ Mirroring

√ Redundant Arrays of Inexpensive Disks (RAID)

√ DiskSuite virtual disk manager

√ Enterprise Volume Manager

Techniques you'll need to master:

√ Identifying RAID levels

√ Identifying virtual file system pathnames

√ Distinguishing between DiskSuite and Volume Manager

This chapter starts with a review of basic disk management in terms of the commands used to perform the management. The next section introduces and describes features of virtual file systems and defines some of the basic terminology.

The last two sections briefly describe the features and capabilities of two Solstice disk management software products that are available for the Solaris 7 operating system: Solstice DiskSuite and Solstice Enterprise Volume Manager.

Basic Disk Management

This section provides a brief review of the basic disk management commands provided with the Solaris 7 operating system. These commands are covered in more detail in Chapter 9.

> *Note: Review of Chapter 9 should be considered part of your preparation for the Part II exam.*

Before creating a file system on a disk, the disk must be formatted using the **format** command. Next, the volume table of contents (VTOC) must be defined using either the **fmthard** or the **format** command. The VTOC includes the partition table that determines the number and size of partitions or disk slices. The **prtvtoc** command can be used to display the VTOC. For x86 platforms, the **fdisk** command is used to create or modify the partition table.

The **mkfs** or **newfs** command is used to create a UFS file system on the partition. The file system must fit within a partition, and only one file system can reside within a partition.

The **fsck** command is used to check and repair file systems. Typically, a file system should be checked before it is made available for use.

The **mount** or **mountall** command is used to mount the file system and make it available for use.

Virtual File Systems

Virtual disk management systems allow the use of physical disks in different ways that are not supported by the standard Solaris file systems. This section summarizes these advantages and describes several techniques used to provide virtual file systems.

Advantages Of Virtual Disk Management Systems

A virtual disk management system can overcome disk capacity and architecture limitations and improve performance and reliability. In addition, manageability is enhanced by the use of a graphical management tool.

Overcoming Disk Limitations

Virtual disk management systems allow partitions on multiple disks to be combined and treated as a single partition. Not only does this allow file systems to be larger than the largest available physical disks, it also allows the entire storage area available on a physical disk to be used.

Improved Performance

Typically, using multiple disks in place of a single disk will increase performance by spreading the load across several physical disks.

Improved Reliabilty

Virtual disk management systems typically support data-redundancy or high-availability features, such as mirroring and Redundant Arrays of Inexpensive Disks (RAID) configurations. In addition, features such as hot sparing and file system logging reduce recovery time.

Enhanced Manageability

Virtual disk management systems typically provide a simple graphical user interface for disk management and administration. This allows simple, almost error-free administration of complex disk configurations and file systems.

The graphical interface usually includes a visual representation of the physical disks and virtual disk file systems. In addition, it typically supports drag-and-drop capabilities that allow quick configuration changes.

Concatented Virtual Devices

Unlike the standard Solaris file system, which consists of a single partition (slice), a concatenated virtual file system consists of two or more slices. The slices can be on the same physical disk or on several physical disks. The slices also can be of different sizes.

Concatenation implies that the slices are addressed in a sequential manner. That is, as space is needed, it is allocated from the first slice in the concatenation. Once this space is completely used, space is allocated from the second slice, and so on.

The main advantage of a concatenated virtual device is that it provides a means for using slices that might otherwise be too small for use. In addition, concatenation using more than one physical disk provides some load balancing between the disks and can result in head movement optimization.

However, using multiple disks increases the chance that a failure of any one disk will result in the failure of the virtual device.

Striped Virtual Device

A striped virtual device, like a concatenated virtual device, can consist of two or more slices. The slices can be on the same physical disk or on several physical disks. The slices can also be of different sizes.

Unlike a concatenated device, the slices are addressed in an interleaved manner. That is, as space is needed, it is allocated as a block from the first slice, then a block from the second slice, and so on.

The main advantage of a striped device is that when the slices are on several physical disks, it provides an increase in performance because it allows multiple simultaneous reads and writes. This is because each physical disk in the striped virtual device can be accessed at the same time. In addition, like concatenated virtual devices, it provides a means for using slices that might otherwise be to small for use.

As with concatenated virtual devices, multiple disks increase the chance that a failure of any one disk will result in the failure of the virtual device.

> *Note: A concatenated striped virtual device is a striped virtual device that has been expanded by concatenating additional slices to the end of the device.*

Mirroring And Duplexing

Mirroring is the technique of copying data being written to an online device to another, offline device. This provides a real-time backup of data that can be brought online to replace the original device in the event that the original device fails. Typically, the two disks share the same controller.

Duplexing is similar to mirroring, except that each disk has its own controller. This provides a little more redundancy.

RAID Configurations

One approach to improving data availability is to arrange disks in various configurations known as Redundant Arrays of Inexpensive Disks. Table 17.1 lists the levels of RAID.

Virtual disk management systems implement one or more of these RAID levels but typically not all of them. The commonly supported RAID levels are 0, 1, and 5.

UFS File System Logging

With UFS file system logging, updates to a UFS file system are recorded in a log before they are applied. In the case of system failure, the system can be restarted, and the UFS file system can quickly use the log instead of having to use the **fsck** command.

The **fsck** command is a time-consuming and not always 100 percent accurate method of recovering a file system. It reads and verifies the information that

Table 17.1	RAID levels.
Level	Description
0	Striping or concatenation
1	Mirroring and duplexing
2	Hamming Error Code Correction (ECC), used to detect and correct errors
3	Bit-interleaved striping with parity information (separate disk for parity)
4	Block-interleaved striping with parity information (separate disk for parity)
5	Block-interleaved striping with distributed parity information
6	Block-interleaved striping with two independent distributed parity schemes
7	Block-interleaved striping with asynchronous I/O transfers and distributed parity information
10	Mirrored striping or striped mirroring (combination of RAID 0 and RAID 1)
53	Similar to RAID 5 except data is taken from RAID 3 disks (the data on a set of RAID 3 disks is copied to another set of disks using RAID 5 methodology)

defines the file system. If the system crashed during an update, the update might have been only partially completed. The **fsck** command must correct the information by removing these partial updates.

With UFS file system logging, only logged updates are actually applied to the file system. If the system crashes, the log has a record of what should be complete and can be used to quickly make the file system consistent.

Solstice DiskSuite

Solstice DiskSuite is a software product that can be used to increase storage capacity and data availability and in some cases increase performance.

DiskSuite uses virtual disks, called *metadevices*, to manage the physical disks. A metadevice is a collection of one or more physical disk slices or partitions. The basic disk management commands, except the **format** command, can be used with metadevices.

Like the standard Solaris file systems that are accessible using raw (/dev/rdsk) and block (/dev/dsk) logical device names, virtual file systems under DiskSuite are accessed using either the raw or the block device name under /dev/md/rdsk or /dev/md/dsk.

Because a metadevice can be built that includes slices from more than one physical disk, it can be used to create a file system that is larger than the largest available physical disk. For SPARC platforms, metadevices can include IPI, SCSI, and SPARCStorage Array drives. For x86 platforms, metadevices can include SCSI and IDE devices. In addition, slices that are too small to be of any use can be combined to create usable storage.

DiskSuite supports four types of metadevices. These are listed in Table 17.2.

Table 17.2 Types of DiskSuite metadevices.	
Metadevice	**Description**
Simple	Used directly or as a building block for mirror and trans metadevices (the three types of simple metadevices are stripes, concatenations, and concatenated stripes)
Mirror	Used to replicate data between simple metadevices to provide redundancy
RAID5	Used to replicate data with parity, allowing regeneration of data
Trans	Used for UFS file system logging

DiskSuite allows metadevices to be dynamically expanded by adding additional slices. Then a UFS file system on that metadevice can be expanded.

Hot Spare Pools

A hot spare pool is a collection of slices that are automatically substituted for slices that fail. When a disk error occurs, DiskSuite locates a hot spare (slice) in the hot spare pool that is at least the size of the failing slice and allocates the hot spare as a replacement for the failing slice. Assuming a mirrored or RAID level 5 configuration, the data from the failed slice is copied to its replacement from the mirrored data or rebuilt using parity information.

Administration

Two methods are available to manage the DiskSuite objects. The first is the DiskSuite Tool, which provides a graphical user interface. The second is a set of commands that are referred to collectively as the DiskSuite *command line interface*.

DiskSuite Tool

The DiskSuite Tool, also known as the **metatool** command, is used to set up and administer a DiskSuite configuration. It provides a graphical view of both the DiskSuite objects and the underlying physical disks. The DiskSuite configuration can be modified quickly by using drag-and-drop manipulation. However, the DiskSuite Tool does not support all DiskSuite operations. These operations must be performed using the command line interface.

DiskSuite Command Line Interface

The command line interface provides a set of commands to create and manage DiskSuite objects. Most of these commands start with the prefix "meta," such as the **metainit** command used to initialize a metadevice. The command line interface includes the following commands:

➤ **growfs**(1M)—Expands a UFS file system

➤ **mdlogd**(1M)—Daemon used to send SNMP messages

➤ **metaclear**(1M)—Deletes metadevices and hot spare pools

➤ **metadb**(1M)—Creates and deletes database replicas

➤ **metadetach**(1M)—Detaches a metadevice from a mirror

➤ **metahs**(1M)—Manages hot spares and hot spare pools

➤ **metainit**(1M)—Configures metadevices

➤ **metaoffline**(1M)—Places mirrors offline

➤ **metaonline**(1M)—Places mirrors online

➤ **metaparam**(1M)—Modifies metadevices

➤ **metarename**(1M)—Renames metadevice names

➤ **metareplace**(1M)—Replaces slices of mirrors and RAID 5 metadevices

➤ **metaroot**(1M)—Sets up files for mirroring the root file system

➤ **metaset**(1M)—Administers disksets

➤ **metastat**(1M)—Displays the status of metadevices or hot spare pools

➤ **metasync**(1M)—Resynchronizes metadevices during reboot

➤ **metatool**(1M)—Runs the DiskSuite Tool graphical user interface

➤ **metattach**(1M)—Attaches a metadevice to a mirror

Solstice Enterprise Volume Manager

Solstice Enterprise Manager is a software product that, like DiskSuite, can be used to increase storage capacity and data availability. Unlike DiskSuite, the Volume Manager includes performance analysis tools and dynamic online tuning to provide optimal use of storage.

> *Note: The Solstice Enterprise Volume Manager is also known as the Veritas Volume Manager. Sun Microsystems has been reselling the Veritas product under the Solstice brand since 1997. The Volume Manager supports the virtual file system referred to as the Veritas File System (vxfs).*

 Like the standard Solaris file systems that are accessible using raw (/dev/rdsk) and block (/dev/dsk) logical device names, virtual file systems under the Volume Manager are accessed using the either the raw or the block device name under /dev /vx/rdsk or /dev/vx/dsk.

The Solstice Volume Manager uses a *VM disk* to manage storage. A VM disk is a physical disk partition that has been assigned to the Volume Manager. Each VM disk consists of a public region from which storage is allocated and a private region used to store configuration information. A disk group is a collection of VM disks that share a common configuration. Initially, a default disk group is used; however, additional groups can be defined to provide better management.

The public region of a VM disk is subdivided into *subdisks* and is the basic unit used by the Volume Manager to allocate storage. A *plex* collection of subdisks can be organized to support the following approaches to data availability:

➤ Concatenated virtual device

➤ RAID level 0 (striping)

➤ RAID level 1 (mirroring)

➤ RAID level 5 (block-interleaved striping with distributed parity information)

➤ RAID 10 (RAID 1 + RAID 0)

A *volume* is a virtual disk device composed of up to 32 plexes. The volume is the virtual object that the operating system and applications view and manipulate.

Hot Relocation

When a subdisk fails, the Volume Manager automatically reacts by reconstructing the failed Volume Manager objects on a spare disk or free space within a disk group and then substituting the rebuilt subdisk for the failed subdisk.

Administration

The Volume Manager provides three methods to manage the disk groups: a graphical user interface (Visual Administrator), a set of command line utilities, and the **vxdiskadm** menu-oriented interface.

Visual Administrator

Visual Administrator, also known as the **vxva** command, is used to set up and administer a Volume Manager configuration. It provides a graphical view of both the Visual Manager objects and the underlying physical disks. The Volume Manager configuration can be modified quickly by using drag-and-drop manipulation.

Visual Administrator allows statistics about the performance and activity levels of the Volume Manager objects to be displayed either graphically with colored icons or numerically with pop-up forms. Statistics that can be monitored include reads and writes, block reads and writes, total I/O, and average read and write times.

Command Line Utilities

The command line utilities provide a set of commands to create and manage Volume Manager objects. Most of these commands start with the prefix "vx," such as the **vxdiskadd** command used to add a physical disk to the Volume Manager configuration. The command line utilities include the following commands:

- ➤ **vxassist**(1M)—Manages volumes

- ➤ **vxbootsetup**(1M)—Sets up system boot information

- ➤ **vxdctl**(1M)—Controls Volume Manager daemons

- ➤ **vxdg**(1M)—Manages disk groups

- ➤ **vxdisk**(1M)—Manages disks

- ➤ **vxdiskadd**(1M)—Adds disks under Volume Manager

- ➤ **vxdiskadm**(1M)—Administrates disks

- ➤ **vxdisksetup**(1M)—Sets up disks

- ➤ **vxedit**(1M)—Edits configuration records

- ➤ **vxencap**(1M)—Encapsulates a partition on a new disk

- ➤ **vxevac**(1M)—Evacuates all volumes on disk

- ➤ **vxinfo**(1M)—Prints volume accessibility information

- ➤ **vxiod**(1M)—Manages kernel daemons

- ➤ **vxmake**(1M)—Creates configuration records

- ➤ **vxmend**(1M)—Mends problems with a configuration record

- ➤ **vxmirror**(1M)—Mirrors a volume on a disk

- ➤ **vxnotify**(1M)—Displays configuration events

- ➤ **vxplex**(1M)—Manages plexes

- ➤ **vxprint**(1M)—Displays configuration records

- ➤ **vxr5check**(1M)—Verifies RAID 5 parity

- ➤ **vxreattach**(1M)—Reattaches a disk

- ➤ **vxrecover**(1M)—Recovers a volume

- ➤ **vxrelocd**(1M)—Relocates failed disks

- ➤ **vxresize**(1M)—Changes the size of a volume

- ➤ **vxrootmir**(1M)—Mirrors a root volume

- ➤ **vxsd**(1M)—Manages subdisks

➤ **vxserial**(1M)—Manages licensing keys

➤ **vxsparecheck**(1M)—Replaces failed disks

➤ **vxstat**(1M)—Displays statistics

➤ **vxtrace**(1M)—Runs a trace operation

➤ **vxva**(1M)—Starts the Visual Administrator

➤ **vxvol**(1M)—Manages a volume

The **vxdiskadm** Menu Interface

The **vxdiskadm** command provides a menu-driven interface to the command line utilities. It eliminates the need to be familiar with the **vx** commands and their command line arguments.

Practice Questions

Question 1

> Which of the following virtual devices or RAID levels does the Volume Manager
> support? [Select all that apply]
>
> ❏ a. Concatenated virtual device
>
> ❏ b. RAID level 0
>
> ❏ c. RAID level 1
>
> ❏ d. RAID level 5
>
> ❏ e. RAID 10

All the answers are correct.

Question 2

> Which of the following are types of virtual file systems? [Select all that apply]
>
> ❏ a. Concatenated
>
> ❏ b. Aggregated
>
> ❏ c. Sliced
>
> ❏ d. Monolithic
>
> ❏ e. Striped

The correct answers are a and e. The other answers do not relate to virtual file
systems; they are simply appropriate sounding words.

Question 3

> Identify the prefix used with most of the commands associated with the DiskSuite
> command line interface.
>
> _____

The correct answer is meta.

Question 4

Which of the following are features of a virtual disk management system? [Select all that apply]

❑ a. Graphical administration tool

❑ b. Improved reliability

❑ c. Improved performance

❑ d. The ability to overcome physical disk limitations

All the answers are correct. Virtual disk management systems provide all these features.

Question 5

Enter the abbreviation for a multilevel system of techniques that is used to improve data reliability.

The correct answer is RAID.

Question 6

Which of the following is a name for a virtual file system that is composed of several partitions and in which the partitions are allocated and used one at a time?

○ a. RAID 5

○ b. Striped

○ c. Concatenated

○ d. Hot spare

The correct answer is c. Answer a is incorrect because it is a configuration that uses a striped file system. Answer b is incorrect because a striped virtual file system uses all the slices in an interleaved fashion. Answer d is incorrect because it is not a type of file system.

Question 7

> Enter the word used to describe the technique of writing data to both an online disk and an offline disk to provide a real-time replacement disk if needed.
>
> _____

The correct answer is mirroring.

Question 8

> Identify the pathname for virtual file systems associated with the DiskSuite disk manager.
>
> ○ a. /dev/dsk
>
> ○ b. /dev/vx/dsk
>
> ○ c. /dev/md/dsk
>
> ○ d. /dev/ds/dsk

The correct answer is c. Answer a is incorrect because it is associated with standard file systems. Answer b is incorrect because it is associated with Volume Manager virtual file systems. Answer d does not exist.

Question 9

> Which of the following is the first command used to prepare a new disk for use?
>
> ○ a. **mount**
>
> ○ b. **newfs**
>
> ○ c. **fsck**
>
> ○ d. **format**

The correct answer is d. The **mount** command is used to mount the file system. Therefore, answer a is incorrect. The **newfs** command is used to create a file system after the disk has been formatted. Therefore, answer b is incorrect. The **fsck** command is used to check the file system. Therefore, answer c is incorrect.

Question 10

Which of the following administration methods can be used with Volume Manager? [Select all that apply]

❏ a. Graphical administration tool

❏ b. Command line utilities

❏ c. Menu-driven command interface

❏ d. Client/server remote utility

The correct answers are a, b, and c. Answer d does not exist.

Need To Know More?

 Sun Microsystems, *Solstice DiskSuite 4.2 Reference Guide*, is available in printed form (ISBN 805-5962-10), on the Web at **docs.sun.com**, and from the online documentation, AnswerBook2, provided with the Solaris 7 operating system.

 Sun Microsystems, *Solstice DiskSuite 4.2 User's Guide*, is available in printed form (ISBN 805-5961-10), on the Web at **docs.sun.com**, and from the online documentation, AnswerBook2, provided with the Solaris 7 operating system.

 Sun Microsystems, *Sun Enterprise Volume Manager 2.5 Administrator's Guide*, is available in printed form (ISBN 805-1607-10), on the Web at **docs.sun.com**, and from the online documentation, AnswerBook2, provided with the Solaris 7 operating system.

 Sun Microsystems, *Sun Enterprise Volume Manager 2.5 Reference Manual*, is available in printed form (ISBN 805-2696-10), on the Web at **docs.sun.com**, and from the online documentation, AnswerBook2, provided with the Solaris 7 operating system.

 Sun Microsystems, *Sun Enterprise Volume Manager 2.5 User's Guide*, is available in printed form (ISBN 805-1603-10), on the Web at **docs.sun.com**, and from the online documentation, AnswerBook2, provided with the Solaris 7 operating system.

Network File
System (NFS)

Terms you'll need to understand:

√ Network File System (NFS)

√ Resource sharing and mounting

√ WebNFS

√ The Auto File System (AutoFS) service

√ The Cache File System (CacheFS) service

Techniques you'll need to master:

√ Sharing and unsharing NFS resources

√ Mounting and unmounting NFS resources

√ Determining NFS resources, shared or mounted

√ Configuring AutoFS maps

√ Configuring a CacheFS cache

This chapter covers some final topics relating to file systems. The first part covers the Network File System (NFS) and the commands used to administer NFS. The next part describes the AutoFS and CacheFS service that support NFS.

The NFS Environment

The Network File System (NFS) service uses the server/client model to allow systems to remotely access the storage of other systems. The NFS protocol is defined by Request For Comment (RFC) 1813, *NFS Version 3 Protocol Specification*.

An NFS server allows computers of different architectures running different operating systems to access its storage space across a network. The NFS service also allows multiple systems to access the same information, eliminating redundancy, improving consistency, and reducing administration.

An NFS client accesses this information in a somewhat transparent mode. That is, the remote resource appears and can be treated as local storage space for most operations and applications.

NFS Administration

Before file systems or directories can be accessed (that is, mounted) by a client through NFS, they must be shared or, in older terminology, advertised. Once shared, authorized NFS clients can mount the resources.

 Another term used for sharing NFS resources is *exporting*. This term appears occasionally in Solaris documentation but is most often seen as a directory name for NFS resources such as /export/home or /export/swap.

Sharing NFS Resources

NFS resources can be shared using the **share**(1M) command and unshared using the **unshare**(1M) command. In addition, any resources identified in the /etc/dfs/dfstab file are automatically shared at system boot or when the **shareall**(1M) command is used. Shared resources are automatically recorded in the /etc/dfs/sharetab file. When the **unshareall**(1M) command is used, all resources listed in the /etc/dfs/sharetab file are automatically unshared.

Actually, the NFS server is started and the identified resources are shared when the system enters system run level 3 as a result of system boot or administrator actions. The resources are unshared and the NFS server is stopped when the system run level changes to any level other than 3.

The **share** Command

The **share** command is used to share NFS resources so that NFS clients can mount and access them. At a minimum, the full pathname of the directory (or mount point of the file system) to be shared is specified as a command line argument.

In addition, three other command line arguments are supported. The -d command line argument is followed by a description of the data being shared. The -**F nfs** command line argument is used to specify the type of file system. If not specified, the default file system type listed in the /etc/dfs/fstypes file (NFS) is assumed. The -**o** command line argument is followed by one or more NFS-specific options (separated by commas). The **share** command options for NFS are listed in Table 18.1. For details on the settings associated with these options, consult the **share** description in the *System Reference Manual*.

Table 18.1 The share command's NFS-specific options.	
Option	**Description**
aclok	Allows access control for NFS Version 2 clients
anon=uid	Assigns anonymous users the specified uid
index=file	Displays the contents of file instead of listing the directory for WebNFS clients
nosub	Prevents clients from mounting subdirectories of shared resources
nosuid	Prevents clients from setting setuid or setgid access modes on files
public	Specifies a public file handle
ro	Allows read-only access
ro=list	Allows read-only access to those clients specified by list
rw	Allows read/write access
rw=list	Allows only read/write access to those clients specified by list
sec=mode	Uses one or more of the security modes specified by mode to authenticate clients
window=value	Sets maximum lifetime for client's credentials to value seconds

The following listing shows using the **share** command to allow NFS clients to mount the /export/home file system, including WebNFS clients. All clients will have read-only access:

```
# share -F nfs -o public,ro /export/home
#
```

If the **share** command is used without any command line arguments, the currently shared resources will be listed.

The **unshare** Command

The **unshare** command is used to stop the sharing of NFS resources so that NFS clients can no longer mount and access them. At a minimum, the full pathname of a directory (or mount point of the file system) that is currently shared is specified as a command line argument.

Only one other command line argument is supported: the **-F nfs** command line argument, which is used to specify the type of file system. If not specified, the default file system type listed in the /etc/dfs/fstypes file (NFS) is assumed.

The following listing shows using the **unshare** command to stop the sharing of the /export/home file system:

```
# unshare -F nfs /export/home
#
```

The /etc/dfs/dfstab File

The /etc/dfs/dfstab file specifies resources that should be shared automatically when the system is changed to run level 3 or when the **shareall** command is used.

This file can be modified using any text editor. To automatically share a resource, add a line to the /etc/dfs/dfstab file that contains the **share** command with the desired command line arguments and options that would have been entered manually. To remove automatic sharing of a resource, delete the appropriate **share** command from the /etc/dfs/dfstab.

> *Note: You might be wondering why some of the directories, files, and even commands associated with NFS use the phrase dfs or df. This comes from the System V (5) version of the Unix operating system. Originally, Distributed File Systems (DFS) had two variations: NFS and the Remote File System (RFS). Directories, files, and commands that used the dfs phrase were used to manage and configure both types of file systems. Since then, RFS has disappeared, leaving behind the DFS legacy.*

The **shareall** And **unshareall** Commands

The **shareall** command is used to share one or more resources. If the **-F nfs** command line argument is not specified, the default file system type (NFS) is assumed. If the name of a file (that contains one or more **share** commands) is not specified as a command line argument, the /etc/dfs/dfstab file is used by default.

The **unshareall** command is used to unshare all currently shared resources. If the **-F nfs** command line argument is not specified, the default file system type (NFS) is assumed.

The **dfshares** Command

The **dfshares**(1M) command is used to list shared resources on either the local or a remote system. If the hostname (or IP address) of a remote system is specified as a command line argument, the resources shared on that system are listed.

In addition, two other command line arguments are supported. The **-F nfs** command line argument is used to specify the type of file system. If not specified, the default file system type listed in the /etc/dfs/fstypes file (NFS) is assumed. If the **-h** command line argument is specified, the header describing the columns of the resource listing is not displayed.

In addition, information on locally shared resources can be obtained from the /etc/dfs/sharetab file. This file is updated by the **share, shareall, unshare,** and **unshareall** commands to reflect the currently shared resources.

Mounting NFS Resources

NFS resources that have be shared by an NFS server can be mounted by an NFS client using the **mount**(1M) command and unmounted using the **umount**(1M) command. In addition, any NFS resources identified in the /etc /vfstab file are automatically mounted at system boot or when the **mountall**(1M) command is used. Likewise, the NFS resources listed in the /etc/mnttab file are unmounted by using the **umountall**(1M) command.

The **mount** Command

The **mount** command is used to mount NFS resources like any other standard Solaris file system so that NFS clients can mount and access them. For NFS, the hostname (or IP address) and pathname of the currently shared directory is specified as a command line argument followed by a mount point. The host- and pathnames are separated by a colon (:).

The generic **mount** command line arguments are listed in Table 18.2. A few of the more significant NFS-specific options (separated by commas) used with the -**o** command line argument are listed in Table 18.3. For additional information, see the **mount_nfs**(1M) page in the *System Reference Manual*.

The following listing shows using the **mount** command to mount the /export/ home file from the solaris system on the /sun_home mount point. The resource is soft mounted (1,000 attempts) with read-only access:

```
# mount -F nfs -o soft,retry=1000,ro solaris:/export/home /sun_home
#
```

Table 18.2　The mount command line arguments.

Argument	Description
-F *fstype*	Specifies the file system type
-m	Mounts the file system without creating an /etc/mnttab entry
-o	Specifies NFS-specific options (see Table 18.3)
-O	Overlays an existing mount point
-r	Mounts the file system read-only

Table 18.3　The mount command's NFS-specific options.

Option	Description
hard	If the server does not respond, returns an error and exits
intr	Allows keyboard interrupts to kill the process while waiting on a *hard* mount
nointr	Does not allow keyboard interrupts to kill the process while waiting on a *hard* mount
public	Specifies a public file handle
retrans=*n*	Retransmits NFS requests *n* times
retry=*n*	Retries the mount operation *n* times
ro	Mounts resource read-only
rw	Mounts resource read/write
soft	If the server does not respond, continues to try to mount the resource
timeo=*n*	Sets NFS time-out to *n* tenths of a second

If the **mount** command is used without any command line arguments, all currently mounted file systems (standard Solaris file systems and NFS resources) are displayed.

The **umount** Command

The **umount** command is used to unmount local file systems and remote NFS resources so that local users can no longer access them. For NFS, one or more *system:path name* pairs (or file system mount points) that are currently mounted are specified as command line arguments.

Two other command line arguments are supported. The first is the **-V** command line argument, which is used to display instead of execute the command line used to actually perform the unmount (used to verify the command line). The second is the **-a** command line argument, which is used to perform parallel unmount operations if possible.

The following listing shows using the **umount** command to unmount the /export/home file system being shared from the solaris host:

```
# umount solaris:/export/home
#
```

The /etc/vfstab File

The /etc/vfstab file, referred to as the *file system table*, specifies resources that should be automatically mounted when the system is booted or when the **mountall** command is used.

This file can be modified using any text editor. To automatically mount an NFS resource, add a line to the /etc/vfstab file that contains the appropriate options that would have been entered manually with a **mount -F nfs** command. To remove automatic mounting of an NFS resource, delete the appropriate line from the /etc/vfstab file.

Table 18.4 lists the (tab-separated) fields and the appropriate values of an entry in the /etc/vfstab file as they pertain to mounting an NFS resource. A hyphen (-) is used to indicate no entry in a field.

The **mountall** And **umountall** Commands

The **mountall** command is used to mount one or more local file systems and/or remote (NFS) shared file systems or directories. If the name of a file (containing information on one or more resources) is not specified as a command line argument, the /etc/vfstab is used by default. The **mountall** command will mount only the resources in the file system table (or specified file) that have the Mount At Boot column set to "yes."

Table 18.4 Fields of an NFS resource /etc/vfstab entry.	
Field	**Description**
Device To Mount	Uses the *system:resource* format, where *system* is a hostname or IP address and *resource* is the full pathname of the shared NFS resource
Device To fsck	Uses a hyphen (-) to indicate no entry, as NFS clients should not check remote NFS resources with the **fsck** command
Mount Point	Specifies the subdirectory where the NFS resource should be mounted
FS Type	Uses "nfs" to indicate an NFS resource
fsck Pass	Uses a hyphen (-) to indicate no entry
Mount At Boot	Uses "yes" to indicate that the resource should be mounted at boot or when the **mountall** command is executed; otherwise, "no"
Mount Options	Specifies any desired NFS mount options; see Table 18.3 or the manual page for the **mount** command

If a file system type is specified using the -F command line option, only file systems of that type are mounted. If the -l command line argument is specified, only local file systems are mounted. If the -r command line argument is specified, only remote shared file systems or directories are mounted.

The **umountall** command is used to unmount all currently mounted resources. It also supports the -F, -l, and -r command line arguments supported by the **mountall** command. In addition, it supports the -h *host* command line argument to specify that only the resources mounted from that host should be unmounted. The -k command line argument can be used to kill processes using the **fuser**(1M) command to allow unmounting and the -s command line argument that prevents unmount operations from being performed in parallel. Currently mounted file resources are listed in the /etc/mnttab file.

The **dfmounts** Command

The **dfmounts**(1M) command is used to list currently mounted resources (and its clients) on either the local or a remote system. If the hostname (or IP address) of a remote system is specified as a command line argument, the resources mounted on that system (and its clients) are listed.

In addition, two other command line arguments are supported. The -F **nfs** command line argument is used to specify the type of file system. If not specified, the default file system type listed in the /etc/dfs/fstypes file (NFS) is assumed. If the **-h** command line argument is specified, the header describing the columns of the listing is not displayed. The following listing shows using the **dfmounts** command to list the NFS resources on the local system named solaris:

```
# dfmounts
RESOURCE  SERVER PATHNAME           CLIENTS
   -         solaris /export/home   uxsys2.ambro.org
```

WebNFS

WebNFS extends the NFS protocol to allow Web browsers or Java applets to access NFS shared resources. This allows client systems to access NFS resources without requiring them to be NFS clients. Browsers can access NFS resources by using an NFS URL that takes the form **nfs://***server/path*. The WebNFS server and client specifications are defined by RFCs 2054 and 2055.

The **share** command supports two NFS-specific options that pertain to WebNFS access. The first is the public option. Each server has one public file handle that is associated with the root file system of the server. NFS URLs are relative to the public file handle. For example, accessing the target directory under the /usr/data shared resource on the host server requires using the **nfs://server/usr/data/target** NFS URL. However, if the public option is specified when the /usr/data directory is shared, the public file handle is associated with the /usr/data directory, and this would allow using the **nfs://server/target** NFS URL to access the same data.

The second option is the **index** option. This is used to specify a file that contains information that should be displayed instead of a listing of the directory. The following listing shows using the **share** command to enable read/write NFS and WebNFS access relative to the /export/home directory:

```
# share -F nfs -o rw,public,index=index.html /export/home
#
```

The Auto File System Service

The Auto File System (AutoFS) service is a client-side service that is used to automatically mount and unmount NFS resources on demand. This simplifies keeping track of resources manually and can reduce network traffic. In addition, AutoFS eliminates the need to add NFS mounts in the /etc/vfstab file. This allows faster booting and shutdown, and users need not know the root password to mount/unmount NFS resources.

The **automount**(1M) command runs when the system is booted (system run level 2) and initializes the AutoFS service. In addition, the **automountd**(1M) command is started at this time. The **automountd** command is a daemon process that runs continuously and provides the automatic mounting and unmounting.

The configuration of the AutoFS service is controlled by *AutoFS maps* that define local mount points and associate remote NFS resources with the mount points. These maps are read by the **automount** command during initialization.

AutoFS Maps

The three types of AutoFS (or automount) maps are auto_master, direct, and indirect. All these maps are under the /etc directory.

The /etc/auto_master File

One auto_master map is located under the /etc directory. The auto_master file associates directories with indirect maps. In addition, the auto_master file references one or more direct maps.

Entries in the auto_master file consist of three fields:

➤ *Mount point*—The mount point is the initial portion of a full pathname to a local directory where an NFS resource should be mounted.

➤ *Map name*—The map name is the file name of a map (direct or indirect) or a special built-in map. The built-in maps are identified by the first character in the name being a hyphen (-).

➤ *Mount options*—The mount options field contains zero or more (comma-separated) NFS-specific mount options as described earlier in Table 18.3.

A special mount point that uses the notation "/-" indicates that the map listed in the map name field is a direct map that actually contains the mount points. In addition, a special entry that consists of only the keyword **+auto_master** is used to include AutoFS maps that are part of Network Information Service (NIS) or NIS+.

The following listing shows the contents of the /etc/auto_master file:

```
# Master map for automounter
#
+auto_master
/net           -hosts          -nosuid,nobrowse
/home          auto_home       -nobrowse
/xfn           -xfn
/-             auto_direct
```

As previously described, the **/net** and **/xfn** entries reference built-in maps. The **/home** entry references the indirect map /etc/auto_home, and the / entry references the direct map /etc/auto_direct.

The **-hosts** built-in map uses the hosts database. The **-xfn** built-in map uses resources shared thorough the Federated Naming Service (FNS).

Direct Maps

A direct map provides both mount point and NFS resources. Entries in a direct map consist of three fields:

➤ *Key*—The key is typically a full pathname that is to be used as a mount point.

➤ *Mount options*—The mount options field contains zero or more (comma-separated) NFS-specific mount options, as described earlier in Table 18.3.

➤ *NFS resource*—The NFS resource files takes the form *server:file system*, which identifies a file system shared by the system server. Because more than one NFS server might be providing the same resource, multiple resources can be specified (separated by spaces). The first available resource is used.

The following listing shows the contents of the /etc/auto_direct file that is referenced in the /etc/auto_master file:

```
/usr/local/bin              nfsserver:/usr/local/bin
/usr/games        -ro       nfsserver:/usr/games
```

In this example, the /usr/local/bin and /usr/games directories shared by the host named nfsserver are mounted on the local system under mount points using the same names.

Indirect Maps

An indirect map provides the remainder of the /etc/auto_master mount point and identifies the NFS resource that should be mounted on the client. Entries in an indirect map consist of three fields:

➤ *Key*—The key is typically a directory that provides the remainder of the mount point.

➤ *Mount options*—The mount options field contains zero or more (comma-separated) NFS-specific mount options, as described earlier in Table 18.3.

➤ *NFS resource*—The NFS resource files takes the form *server:file system*, which identifies a file system shared by the system server.

The following listing shows the contents of the /etc/auto_home file:

```
dla                          solaris:/export/home/dla
guest        -rw,nosuid      nfsserver:/export/home/guest
```

In this example, the indirect map is referenced by the **/home** entry in the auto_master file. It contains two entries. The first entry identifies the /home/ dla mount point, which is used to mount the /export/home/dla directory from the host named solaris. The second entry identifies the /home/guest mount point, which is used to mount the /export/home/guest directory from the host named nfsserver.

Running The **automount** Command

When changes are made to the AutoFS maps, the **automount** command might need to execute manually. Any changes to the /etc/auto_master file require that the **automount** command be executed to put the changes into effect. This also must be done when an addition or a deletion is made to a direct map.

The Cache File System (CacheFS) Service

The Cache File System (CacheFS) is a client-side service that provides the ability to cache a remotely accessed NFS resource locally on the NFS client. This not only speeds up client access to the data but also decreases network traffic and load on the NFS server.

After creating a cache, a remote NFS resource can be mounted "in" the cache. The first time the NFS resource is accessed, data is copied from the remote NFS server into the local cache. Subsequent accesses are from the local cache instead of the remote NFS server. Like other types of file systems, the remote NFS resource can be mounted manually using the **mount** command, at system boot, by adding it to the /etc/vfstab file or as needed using the AutoFS mechanism (described in the previous section).

> *Note: The root (/) and /usr file systems cannot be cached using the CacheFS mechanism. However, these two file systems can be cached using the Auto-Client configuration, which is briefly described in Chapter 13.*

Configuring A Cache

The **cfsadmin**(1M) command is used to create, check, tune, and delete caches. In addition, the **cfsadmin** command is used to list cache contents and statistics. The **cachefsstat**(1M) command can also be used to display additional cache statistics.

The -c command line argument is specified to create a cache, followed by the full pathname of a directory to be used for the cache. In addition, multiple options (separated by commas) can be specified using the -o command line argument. The following listing shows using the **cfsadmin** command to create a cache under the /cache directory. The size of the largest file that can be cached is set to 10MB:

```
# cfsadmin -c -o maxfilesize=10 /cache
#
```

To list the file systems mounted in the cache and statistics, use the -l command line argument. Additional command line arguments include -s to perform a consistency check, -u to update cache parameters, and -d to delete a cache. All of these command line arguments should be followed by the full pathname of the cache directory.

Mounting a remote NFS resource in the cache using the **mount** command requires specifying the remote file system, the local cache, and a local mount point.

The -F command line argument should be used to identify the file system type as cacheFS. In addition, at least two cache-specific mount options need to be specified using the -o command line argument: **backfstype**, which is used to identify the type of file system being mounted (typically nfs), and **cachedir**, which is used to identify the cache directory. The following listing shows using the **mount** command to mount the /export/home file system from the host server on the /home mount point using /cache as the cache directory. The line is wrapped to improve readability:

```
# mount -F cachefs -o backfstype=nfs,cachedir=/cache
    server:/export/home /home
#
```

In addition, the administrator can specify files and directories that should be placed in the cache by using the **cachefspack**(1M) command. The -p command line argument can be used to specify files and directories, or the -f command line argument can be used to identify a packing list. A *packing list* is a file that contains one or more entries that identify files and directories to cache using the syntax defined by **packingrules**(4). The **cachefspack** command can also be used to remove or unpack files and directories by using the -u command line argument and specifying file/directories, specifying -uf and a packing list, or specifying -U and the full pathname of a cache that unpacks all files and directories.

Practice Questions

Question 1

Which of the following commands can be used to mount the /export/home file system from the solaris system (IP address of 192.168.39.7) on the /mnt mount point?

○ a. **mount -F nfs -h solaris /export/home /mnt**

○ b. **mount -F nfs 192.168.39.7:/export/home /mnt**

○ c. **mount -F nfs /mnt solaris:/export/home**

○ d. **mount -F nfs /export/home@solaris /mnt**

The correct answer is b. The first argument following the -F file system type should be the hostname or IP address of the system sharing the resource. None of the other answers use the appropriate syntax or command line arguments.

Question 2

Enter the name of the file system used to temporarily store a remote NFS resource on a local disk.

_____

The correct answer is CacheFS.

Question 3

Which of the following are types of AutoFS maps? [Select all that apply]

❏ a. direct

❏ b. indirect

❏ c. linked

❏ d. auto_master

❏ e. auto_home

The correct answers are a, b, and d. Answer c, linked, is not associated with the AutoFS capability. Answer e is a commonly used name for an indirect map.

Question 4

Which of the following situations requires that the **automount** command be manually executed? [Select all that apply]

❑ a. Addition to auto_master

❑ b. Addition to direct map

❑ c. Addition to indirect map

❑ d. Deletion from auto_master

❑ e. Deletion from direct map

❑ f. Deletion from indirect map

The correct answers are a, b, d, and e. Changes to indirect maps do not require running the **automount** command. Therefore, answers c and f are incorrect.

Question 5

Which of the following commands is used to create a CacheFS configuration?

○ a. **cfsadm**

○ b. **cachefsinit**

○ c. **cfsadmin**

○ d. **newcache**

○ e. **cfscreate**

The correct answer is c. None of the other commands exist.

Question 6

Identify the command used to make an NFS resource available for mounting or to list those already available.

_____

The correct answer is **share**.

Question 7

Which of the following commands can be used to determine any mounted NFS resources? [Select all that apply]

☐ a. **share**

☐ b. **dfmounts**

☐ c. **nfsmounts**

☐ d. **mountall**

☐ e. **mount**

The correct answers are b and e. **share** is used to share NFS resources. Therefore, answer a is incorrect. Answer c (**nfsmounts**) does not exist. **mountall** is used to mount resources, not to list NFS resources. Therefore, answer d is incorrect.

Question 8

When using NFS, which of the following results are true? [Select all that apply]

☐ a. Introduces redundancy

☐ b. Improves consistency

☐ c. Reduces administration

☐ d. Reduces network traffic

The correct answers are b and c. Answer a is incorrect because NFS eliminates redundancy by making a single copy of data available to multiple clients. Answer d is incorrect because NFS is a network application and using it will increase network traffic.

Question 9

Identify the NFS-specific option used with the **-o** command line argument of the **share** command to change the public file handle.

The correct answer is **public.**

Question 10

> Which file contains one or more **share** commands used with the **shareall** command?
>
> ○ a. /etc/nfs/nfstab
>
> ○ b. /etc/nfs/shares
>
> ○ c. /etc/dfs/dfstab
>
> ○ d. /etc/dfs/sharetab

The correct answer is c. Answers a and b do not exist. Answer d is the file that contains information on shared resources.

Need To Know More?

 Stern, Hal, *Managing NFS and NIS* (O'Reilly & Associates, Sebastopol, CA, 1991) ISBN 0-937175-75-7.

 Sun Microsystems, *NFS Administration Guide*, is available in printed form (ISBN 805-3479-10), on the Web at **docs.sun.com**, and from the online documentation, AnswerBook2, provided with the Solaris 7 operating system.

 Sun Microsystems, *System Administration Guide, Volume 1*, is available in printed form (ISBN 805-3727-10), on the Web at **docs.sun.com**, and from the online documentation, AnswerBook2, provided with the Solaris 7 operating system.

 Sun Microsystems, *System Reference Manual, Section 1M - Administration Commands*, is available in printed form (ISBN 805-3173-10), on the Web at **docs.sun.com**, and from the online documentation, AnswerBook2, provided with the Solaris 7 operating system.

  Sun Microsystems, *System Reference Manual, Section 4 - File Formats*, is available in printed form (ISBN 805-3176-10), on the Web at **docs.sun.com**, and from the online documentation, AnswerBook2, provided with the Solaris 7 operating system.

 Callaghan, B. J., Pawlowski, B., and Staubach, P., Request For Comments 1813, *NFS Version 3 Protocol Specification* (June 1995), is available at **www.nic.mil/ftp/rfc/rfc1813.txt**.

 Callaghan, B. J., Request For Comments 2054, *WebNFS Client Specification* (October 1996), is available at **www.nic.mil/ftp/rfc/rfc2054.txt**.

Callaghan, B. J., Request For Comments 2055, *WebNFS Server Specification* (October 1996), is available at **www.nic.mil/ftp/rfc/ rfc2055.txt.**

 Callaghan, B. J., *WebNFS* (April 1997), is available at **www.sun.com/ webnfs.**

Name Services

Terms you'll need to understand:

√ Name services

√ The /etc files configuration

√ Domain Name System (DNS)

√ Network Information Service (NIS)

√ Network Information Service Plus (NIS+)

√ Authentication and authorization

√ The name service switch

Techniques you'll need to master:

√ Configuring the name service switch

√ Configuring NIS master and slave servers

√ Configuring NIS clients

√ Updating and adding NIS maps

This chapter describes the name services supported by the Solaris 7 operating system. The first part provides an overview. The second part covers the Network Information Service (NIS) in more detail. The third part summarizes the Network Information Service Plus (NIS+).

Solaris Name Services

A *name service* or *naming service* provides a centralized location for information used by users and systems to communicate with each other across the network. The name service not only stores the information but also provides mechanisms to manage and access that information.

The information is referred to as a *namespace* and typically includes the following:

➤ Hostnames and their IP addresses

➤ User accounts and their passwords

➤ Access permissions

Without a centralized name service, each system would have to maintain its own copy of the information. For example, by default the Solaris 7 system uses the /etc/hosts file to resolve hostnames to IP addresses. This is fine for a small number of systems, but for a large number of systems this approach becomes a maintenance nightmare. A centralized name service eliminates redundancy, improves consistency, and reduces administration.

Supported Naming Services

The Solaris 7 operating system supports five naming services:

➤ The original Unix name configuration, referred to as the */etc files*

➤ The Domain Name Service (DNS)

➤ The Network Information Service (NIS)

➤ The Network Information Service Plus (NIS+)

➤ The Federated Naming Service (FNS), which conforms to the X/Open Federated Naming Specification (XFN)

Of these naming services, NIS and NIS+ are covered in the most detail on the exam. The /etc files are also covered, but from the context of configuring TCP/IP. DNS is covered briefly. FNS probably will only be mentioned.

Domain Name System (DNS)

DNS is part of the TCP/IP protocol suite and is the name service used by the Internet. It provides hostname-to-IP-address resolution as well as IP-address-to-hostname resolution. The DNS namespace is divided into domains that in turn are divided into subdomains (or zones). One or more DNS servers can be responsible (authoritative) for a zone. All the DNS servers work together to provide name resolution services across the entire namespace.

The DNS server provided with Solaris 7 is version 8.1 of the Berkeley Internet Name Domain (BIND) program that is referred to as the *Internet name daemon* (in.named).

Information on the namespace is stored in text files using a predefined syntax known as *records*. The in.named program uses the following data files:

➤ */etc/named.conf*—The BIND configuration file that identifies zones over which the DNS server is authoritative and the associated data files

➤ */etc/resolv.conf*—When configured as a DNS client, a file that identifies the DNS server that should be used for name resolution

➤ *named.ca*—The names and IP addresses of the Internet root DNS servers

➤ *hosts*—The DNS address (A type) records used for resolving hostnames to IP addresses (not to be confused with the /etc/hosts file)

➤ *hosts.rev*—The DNS pointer (PTR type) records used for resolving IP addresses to hostnames

➤ *named.local*—The DNS records for the localhost or the loopback interface

The named.ca, hosts, hosts.rev, and named.local files are typically located under the /var/named directory but can be in any directory specified by the /etc/named.conf file.

Network Information Service (NIS)

NIS is a distributed name service. It is a mechanism for identifying and locating network objects and resources. It provides a uniform storage and retrieval method for networkwide information in a platform-independent manner. The data files (called *maps*) can be distributed among NIS servers to improve availability but can still be managed and updated from a central location. The second part of this chapter provides additional details regarding NIS.

Network Information Service Plus (NIS+)

NIS+ is very similar to NIS but includes many more features. Unlike NIS, the NIS+ namespace is dynamic because updates can take effect at any time by any authorized user.

The NIS+ namespace is hierarchical and is similar to a Unix file system. This structure allows the namespace to conform to the hierarchy of an organization and can be divided into multiple domains that can be administrated separately.

Whereas NIS has weak security, NIS+ includes a security system that uses both authentication and authorization to maintain the integrity of its namespace. *Authentication* is a method to restrict access to specific users when accessing a remote system. Authentication can be set up at both the system level and the network level. Credentials are used to verify the identity of a user. For NIS+, every request for access is authenticated by checking the credentials of the user. *Authorization* is a method to restrict the operations that a user can perform on the remote system once the user has gained access (been authenticated). For NIS+, every component in the namespace specifies the type of operations that it will accept from each user.

The Name Service Switch

Because Solaris 7 supports five different naming services, a method is needed to select which name services should be used and in which order. This capability is provided by the *name service switch*, which consists of the /etc/nsswitch.conf file and three templates that can be used to simplify the setup of the nsswitch.conf file.

Applications use standardized routines to obtain name resolution and other system and network information. These routines consult the /etc/nsswitch.conf file to determine which name service(s) should be queried.

The /etc/nsswitch.conf file contains entries for each type of data supported by the name services. An entry consists of a keyword that identifies the type of information, followed by one or more information sources. The source keywords are separated from the information keyword and other source keywords by one or more space characters. Table 19.1 lists the 15 types of information keywords, and Table 19.2 lists the 5 information source keywords.

When these name services (DNS, /etc files, and NIS or NIS+) are queried or searched, they will return one of four search status messages:

➤ *SUCCESS*—The requested information was located.

➤ *UNAVAIL*—The service is not responding.

Table 19.1 The /etc/nsswitch.conf information keywords.	
Information Keyword	**Description**
aliases	Mail aliases
automount	Information on the Auto File System (AutoFS) configuration
bootparams	Location of root, swap, and dump partitions for diskless workstations
ethers	Ethernet addresses of systems
group	Group name and member information
hosts	Hostnames and network (IP) addresses
netgroup	Network groups and members defined in the domain
netmasks	Netmasks associated with known networks
networks	Networks and their associated names
passwd	Password information for user accounts
protocols	IP protocols used within the domain
publickey	Public keys used for authentication
rpc	Remote Procedure Call (RPC) program numbers for RPC services used within the domain
sendmailvars	Variables used by the **sendmail**(1M) program
services	Names of IP services and their port numbers

Table 19.2 The /etc/nsswitch.conf source keywords.	
Source Keyword	**Description**
compat	Uses old-style syntax for password and group information
dns	Uses DNS to resolve queries
files	Uses /etc/ files to resolve queries
nis	Uses NIS to resolve queries
nisplus	Uses NIS+ to resolve queries

➤ *NOTFOUND*—The requested data does not exist.

➤ *TRYAGAIN*—The service is busy; try again later.

For each of these four search status messages, an action can be associated with each source. The action is either *return* (stop looking) or *continue* (try the next source). For example, the following listing shows a hosts entry in the /etc/nsswitch.conf file:

```
hosts:    nisplus dns files
```

The default action for a SUCCESS status message is to return the information. The default action for the other status messages (NOTFOUND, TRYAGAIN, and UNAVAIL) is to continue to the next source if one exists or to return if one does not exist.

When an application attempts to resolve a hostname to an IP address, first NIS+ is searched. If the information is found, it is returned to the application. If it is not found, DNS is searched. If the information is found, it is returned to the application. If it is not found, the /etc files configuration (/etc/hosts file) is searched. If the information is found, it is returned to the application; otherwise, an error is returned.

Three templates are included with the Solaris 7 distribution to simplify setting up the /etc/nsswitch.conf file. These templates provide a standardized setup for the most commonly used name services in the Solaris 7 environment. These are:

➤ NIS (/etc/nsswitch.nis)

➤ NIS+ (/etc/nsswitch.nisplus)

➤ Original Unix /etc files configuration (/etc/nsswitch.files)

Listing 19.1 shows the default contents of the /etc/nsswitch.nisplus file. To use this configuration, copy this file to the /etc/nsswitch.conf file. Comments are preceded by the pound (#) character. An action can be defined for a status message by using a *message=action* statement within square brackets ([]) after the source keyword.

Listing 19.1   The contents of the /etc/nsswitch.nisplus file.

```
# Check /etc/passwd and /etc/group files first.
passwd:      files nisplus
group:       files nisplus

# consult /etc files only if nisplus is down.
hosts:       nisplus [NOTFOUND=return] files

services:    nisplus [NOTFOUND=return] files
networks:    nisplus [NOTFOUND=return] files
```

```
protocols:      nisplus [NOTFOUND=return] files
rpc:            nisplus [NOTFOUND=return] files
ethers:         nisplus [NOTFOUND=return] files
netmasks:       nisplus [NOTFOUND=return] files
bootparams:     nisplus [NOTFOUND=return] files
publickey:      nisplus
netgroup:       nisplus
automount:      files nisplus
aliases:        files nisplus
sendmailvars:   files nisplus
```

Network Information Service (NIS)

NIS, like other network applications, follows the client/server architecture model. This section of the chapter describes the components of NIS, how to configure these components, and how to add and update NIS maps.

NIS Components

NIS consists of a master server, possibly slave servers, and one or more clients. The servers store NIS maps and make the information contained in the maps available to clients on request.

NIS Maps

NIS stores information in a set of files called *maps*, which are two-column tables. The first column is used as a key, and the second column is the information associated with that key. Because the maps are organized by key, the same information might appear in more than one map. For example, host and associated IP addresses appear in two maps: hosts.byname (where the hostname is the key and the IP address is the information) and hosts.byaddr (where the IP address is the key and the hostname is the information). Table 19.3 lists the NIS maps. These maps are physically located under the /var/yp directory along with several other NIS files.

Table 19.3 The NIS maps.		
Keyword	**Maps**	**Description**
aliases	mail.aliases, mail.byaddr	Mail addresses and aliases
bootparams	bootparams	Location of root, swap, and dump partitions for diskless workstations
ethers	ethers.byaddr, ethers.byname	Ethernet addresses of systems

(continued)

Table 19.3   The NIS maps (continued).

Keyword	Maps	Description
group	group.bygid, group.byname	Group name, group ID (GID), and member information
hosts	hosts.byaddr, hosts.byname	Hostnames and network (IP) addresses
netgroup	netgroup, netgroup.byhost, netgroup.byuser	Network groups and members defined in the domain
netmasks	netmasks.byaddr	Netmasks associated with known networks
networks	networks.byaddr, network.byname	Networks and their associated names
passwd	netid.byname, passwd.adjunct.byname, passwd.byname, passwd.byuid	Password information for user accounts
protocols	protocols.byname, protocols.bynumber	IP protocols used within the domain
rpc	rpc.bynumber	RPC program numbers for RPC services used within the domain
services	services.byname, services.byservice	IP services and their port numbers

NIS was previously known as Yellow Pages. This is the reason why many of the NIS files and commands contain the *yp* prefix.

NIS Master And Slave Servers

Each NIS environment, or domain, must have only one NIS master server. The NIS maps reside on the master server. To provide load distribution and redundancy, one or more slave servers can be configured. Whenever the NIS maps are updated on the master server, they are propagated to the slave servers.

NIS Clients

NIS clients request information contained in the maps from NIS servers. The clients do not make any distinction between the master server and slave servers. NIS servers can also be NIS clients, depending on the configuration of the /etc/nsswitch.conf file.

Configuring NIS Servers And Clients

The procedures that are used to configure an NIS master server, a slave server, and a client are somewhat similar. The steps to do each are given in this section.

NIS Master Server

Before an NIS master server can be configured, the data that is used to build the maps must be prepared. By default, the maps will be built from the /etc files. However, it is recommended that the /etc files be copied to another directory so that any necessary changes to these source files can be made without affecting the local system. The following procedure is used to prepare the data:

1. Verify that the /etc files are up-to-date. These files are auto_home, auto_master, bootparams, ethers, group, hosts, netgroup, netmasks, networks, passwd, protocols, rpc, service, and shadow.

2. Select a directory to be used to build most of the maps (the DIR directory) and another directory for building the passwd map (the PWDIR directory).

3. Copy all the files (except /etc/passwd) to the DIR directory and copy the /etc/passwd file to the PWDIR directory.

4. Verify that the /etc/mail/aliases file is up-to-date, but do not copy it to the DIR directory.

5. Remove comments and other unnecessary information from the copied source files. Verify that the file formats are correct.

6. Modify the /var/yp/Makefile to identify the selected DIR and PWDIR directories.

The following procedure is used to configure an NIS master server. As part of the procedure, the maps will be built automatically:

1. Be sure that the system is using the /etc files configuration for the name service switch by copying the /etc/nsswitch.files file to the /etc /nsswitch.conf file.

2. Add entries to /etc/hosts for each NIS slave server.

3. If necessary, use the **domainname**(1M) command to set the domain name.

4. Run the **ypinit**(1M) command to initialize the NIS master server and build the maps as shown here:

```
ypinit -m
```

5. Provide the information in response to the prompts from the **ypinit** command. This includes a list of NIS slave servers, and whether the **ypinit** command should exit if an error is encountered.

6. Enable NIS by copying the /etc/nsswitch.nis file to the /etc/nsswitch.conf file.

To start the NIS master server, either reboot the server or run the **ypstart**(1M) command as shown here:

```
/usr/lib/netsvc/yp/ypstart
```

NIS Slave Server
A system can be configured as an NIS slave server using the following procedure:

1. First, configure the system as an NIS client. If necessary, use the **domainname** command to set the domain name.

2. Update the /etc/nsswitch.conf file to use NIS either by copying the /etc/nsswitch.nis template file to it or by manually editing the appropriate configuration.

3. Log into the system as the root account and run the **ypinit** command as shown here:

```
ypinit -c
```

4. The **ypinit** command will prompt for one or more NIS servers. Enter the hostnames of the closest NIS servers. This completes the client setup.

5. Add an entry for the NIS master server to the /etc/hosts file.

6. If the **ypbind**(1M) command is running, stop it by using the following command:

```
/usr/lib/netsvc/yp/ypstop
```

7. Restart the **ypbind** command using the following command:

```
/usr/lib/netsvc/yp/ypstart
```

8. Run the **ypinit** command from the /var/yp directory as shown in the following listing (where *master* is the hostname of the NIS master server):

```
# cd /var/yp
# ypinit -s master
```

To start the NIS slave server, either reboot the system or repeat Steps 6 and 7.

NIS Client

A system can be configured as an NIS client using the following procedure:

1. If necessary, use the **domainname** command to set the domain name.

2. Update the /etc/nsswitch.conf file to use NIS either by copying the /etc/nsswitch.nis template file to it or by manually editing the appropriate configuration.

3. Log into the system as the root account and run the **ypinit** command as shown here:

```
ypinit -c
```

4. The **ypinit** command will prompt for one or more NIS servers. Enter the hostnames of the closest NIS servers.

Updating And Adding NIS Maps

Updating one of the default maps (one automatically generated when the master server is configured) is fairly straightforward. Edit the appropriate source file, then execute the **make(1)** command from the /var/yp directory. The name of the map being updated must be specified as a command line argument to the **make** command. The **make** command updates the map and automatically propagates the updated map to any slave servers. The following listing shows the commands used to update the hosts map and propagate it to slave servers:

```
# cd /var/yp
# make hosts
```

To add a new map (referred to as a *nondefault map*), create a text file in the /var/yp directory with the appropriate information. Then run the **makedbm(1M)** command to add the map. The **makedbm** command expects two command line arguments. The first is the name of the source file, and the second is the name of the map that should be created. The **ypxfr(1M)** command is used to distribute a new map that does not currently exist on the slave servers. The name of the new map is specified as a command line argument. The following shows creating the new map, apps, from the apps.txt source file:

```
# cd /var/yp
# makedbm apps.txt apps
# /usr/lib/netsvc/yp/ypxfr apps
```

To update and propagate a nondefault map, edit the source file, and then run the **makedbm** command to rebuild the map. To propagate the updated map, use the **yypush**(1M) command and specify the map name as a command line argument. The following shows rebuilding the apps map from the apps.txt source file and propagating it to the slave servers:

```
# cd /var/yp
# makedbm apps.txt apps
# /usr/lib/netsvc/yp/yppush apps
```

Verifying NIS Configuration

Several commands provide access to NIS configuration information. These commands can be used to verify a client configuration and check the contents of the maps. Consult the *System Reference Manual* for additional details:

➤ **ypcat**(1)—Lists the contents of the specified map.

➤ **ypmatch**(1)—Returns data that matches the specified key from the specified map.

➤ **ypwhich**(1)—Returns the name of the NIS server or map master. When used with the **-m** command line argument, the **ypwhich** command returns a list of all available maps.

Network Information Service Plus (NIS+)

NIS+ is similar to NIS but provides additional features. In addition to providing centralized administration and access to domain data, it also supports a hierarchical domain that can be configured to reflect the structure of an organization. NIS provides only a flat domain. Whereas NIS provides no authentication, NIS+ provides Data Encryption Standard (DES) authentication. In addition, whereas NIS propagates updated information in a batch mode, NIS+ propagates incremental updates immediately. Like NIS, NIS+ supports the optional use of redundant servers (referred to as *replicas*). These replicas provide load balancing and alternate servers in case the master NIS+ server fails.

Whereas NIS stores its data in files referred to as *maps*, NIS+ stores its data in files referred to as *tables*. NIS+ provides tables for all the data stored in NIS maps, plus some additional tables for credentials, time zone, and automount information. Table 19.4 lists the NIS+ tables.

The tables are stored under a directory by the name of the domain. This directory contains three other directories: ctx_dir.*domain*, which is used for xfn (FNS) data; org_dir.*domain*, which is used to store the tables; and groups_dir.*domain*, which is used for group information.

Table 19.4 NIS+ tables.	
Table	**Description**
auto_home	Location of user's home directories
auto_master	AutoFS map information
bootparams	Location of root, swap, and dump partitions for diskless workstations
cred	Credentials for NIS+ principals
ethers	Ethernet addresses of systems
group	Group name, GID, and member information
hosts	Hostnames and network (IP) addresses
mail_aliases	Mail addresses and aliases
netgroup	Network groups and members defined in the domain
netmasks	Netmasks associated with known networks
networks	Networks and their associated names
passwd	Password information for user accounts
protocols	IP protocols used within the domain
rpc	RPC program numbers for RPC services used within the domain
services	IP services and their port numbers
timezone	Time zone of workstations in the domain

Practice Questions

Question 1

> Which of the following naming services requires the data to be configured manually on every system on which it is used?
>
> ○ a. NIS
>
> ○ b. NIS+
>
> ○ c. DNS
>
> ○ d. /etc files

The correct answer is d. All the other naming services provide a means to update one master database and propagate changes to every system that needs them. Although using /etc files is simple and quick for a small number of systems, using NIS, NIS+, or DNS for a large number of systems reduces maintenance.

Question 2

> Enter the name of a method to restrict access to NIS+ resources based on the credentials of the user.
>
> _____

The correct answer is authentication.

Question 3

> Which of the following are features provided by NIS+? [Select all that apply]
>
> ❏ a. Authentication
>
> ❏ b. Time zone support
>
> ❏ c. Batch propagation of updates
>
> ❏ d. Hierarchical domain architecture
>
> ❏ e. Flat domain architecture

The correct answers are a, b, and d. Answers c and e (batch propagation of updates and flat domain architecture) are characteristics of NIS.

Question 4

> Which of the following name services are supported by the Solaris 7 operating system? [Select all that apply]
>
> ❑ a. NIS
>
> ❑ b. NIS+
>
> ❑ c. FNS
>
> ❑ d. DNS
>
> ❑ e. /etc files configuration

All the answers are correct.

Question 5

> Which of the following commands is used to configure an NIS client?
>
> ○ a. **ypinit -m**
>
> ○ b. **ypinit -c**
>
> ○ c. **ypinit -s**
>
> ○ d. **nisclient**
>
> ○ e. **nisinit -c**

The correct answer is b. **ypinit -m** is used to configure a master server. Therefore, answer a is incorrect. **ypinit -s** is used to configure a slave server. Therefore, answer c is incorrect. Answers d and e do not exist.

Question 6

> Which of the following is *not* a valid type of search status message?
>
> ○ a. SUCCESS
>
> ○ b. NOTFOUND
>
> ○ c. TRYLATER
>
> ○ d. UNAVAIL

The correct answer is c. TRYLATER does not exist. The correct keyword is TRYAGAIN.

Question 7

Identify the name of the BIND program used to provide DNS services.

_____

The correct answer is the in.named program.

Question 8

Which of the following are information-type keywords that can be used in the /etc/nsswitch.conf file? [Select all that apply]

❑ a. hosts

❑ b. ipaddr

❑ c. protocols

❑ d. services

The correct answers are a, c, and d. ipaddr is not a valid keyword. IP addresses are a portion of the hosts information. Therefore, answer b is incorrect.

Question 9

What are the files that NIS uses to store the information that NIS clients request collectively referred to as?

_____

The correct answer is maps.

Question 10

Which of the following commands is used to propagate a new NIS map to NIS slave servers?

○ a. **yppush**

○ b. **ypupdate**

○ c. **yppropagate**

○ d. **ypxfr**

○ e. **ypmaps**

The correct answer is d. **yppush** is used to propagate an existing map that has been updated. Therefore, answer a is incorrect. Answers b, c, and e do not exist.

Need To Know More?

Stern, Hal, *Managing NFS and NIS*. (O'Reilly & Associates, Sebastopol, CA, 1991) ISBN 0-937175-75-7.

Sun Microsystems, *Solaris Naming Administration Guide*, is available in printed form (ISBN 805-3736), on the Web at **docs.sun.com**, and from the online documentation, AnswerBook2, provided with the Solaris 7 operating system.

Sun Microsystems, *Solaris Naming Setup and Configuration Guide*, is available in printed form (ISBN 805-3738), on the Web at **docs.sun.com**, and from the online documentation, AnswerBook2, provided with the Solaris 7 operating system.

AdminSuite

Terms you'll need to understand:

√ AdminSuite

√ Host Manager

√ Storage Manager

√ Database Manager

√ Serial Port Manager

√ User Manager

√ Group Manager

√ Printer Manager

Techniques you'll need to master:

√ Identifying the functionality and capability of AdminSuite

√ Identifying the types of systems supported by the Host Manager

√ Identifying the functionality of two tools of the Storage Manager

√ Identifying the data managed by the Database Manager

This chapter describes the graphical management tool AdminSuite. AdminSuite is a collection of the following tools:

➤ *Host Manager*—Manages AutoClient servers, standalone servers, and diskless clients

➤ *Storage Manager*—Manages partitions and file systems

➤ *Database Manager*—Manages network-related data

➤ *Serial Port Manager*—Manages the configuration of serial ports

➤ *User Manager*—Manages user accounts

➤ *Group Manager*—Manages group accounts

➤ *Printer Manager*—Manages printers and print servers

Many of the functions performed by AdminSuite can also be performed by the **admintool** command. These include serial port management, user and group account management, and printer management. For these cases, the AdminSuite graphical user interfaces (windows) look very similar to the windows provided by the **admintool** command.

 The Solstice AdminSuite is not covered in detail on Part II of the exam. However, you should be familiar with the capabilities of the seven AdminSuite manager tools and the two tools that compose the Storage Manager.

Host Manager

The Host Manager provides the ability to add and maintain server and client support. This includes the following:

➤ Adding and modifying system support for all types of system configurations (AutoClients, diskless clients, operating system (OS) servers, and standalone systems), including converting system types

➤ Setting root passwords for AutoClients or diskless clients

System support includes providing software services such as boot and install services for installation and OS services for systems with limited disk space. The Host Manager provides the ability to convert a standalone system to an OS server, an AutoClient to a standalone system, and so on. In addition, Host Manager can be used to add OS services to an OS server (for example, to add support for another type of operating system) or to remove OS services that are no longer needed. Another function of Host Manager is to set up install, boot, and profile servers that are used to perform over-the-network installation.

AdminSuite provides command line equivalents for some of the operations of the Host Manager. These are the following:

➤ **admhostadd**—Adds support for a new system or OS server

➤ **admhostdel**—Deletes support for an existing system or OS server

➤ **admhostmod**—Modifies an existing system

➤ **admhostls**—Lists existing hosts

Storage Manager

The Storage Manager consists of two tools: the Disk Manager and the File System Manager. The Disk Manager allows viewing and editing of partition-related information. This includes the following:

➤ Viewing and modifying x86 and SPARC slice parameters (that is, changing the starting and ending addresses of the slices)

➤ Specifying a disk label

➤ Viewing and modifying x86 fdisk partitions

➤ Copying the characteristics of a disk to one or more similar disks

The File System Manager supports creating and modifying file systems. This includes the following:

➤ Creating file systems

➤ Creating mount points

➤ Mounting and unmounting file systems

➤ Sharing and unsharing Network File System (NFS) resources

➤ Modifying the /etc/vfstab file on one or more systems

➤ Adding entries to existing Auto File System (AutoFS) maps

The File Manager also provides the ability to select mount and share options, such as the NFS-specific mount options.

AdminSuite does not provide any command line equivalents for the Storage Manager, as standard Solaris commands can be used to perform disk and file system tasks.

Database Manager

The Database Manager is used to view and modify network-related system information. This information can be stored in /etc files on a selected host, Network Information Service (NIS), or Network Information Service Plus (NIS+). The Database Manager can be used to view and modify the files, maps, or tables (depending on name service) that contain the following types of information:

➤ aliases

➤ AutoFS

➤ bootparams

➤ ethers

➤ group

➤ hosts

➤ locale

➤ netgroup

➤ netmasks

➤ networks

➤ passwd

➤ protocols

➤ rpc

➤ services

➤ timezone

AdminSuite does not provide any command line equivalents for the Database Manager. For the /etc files name service, you can use any text editor to modify the information. For NIS and NIS+, use the appropriate procedures to modify the maps and tables as necessary.

Serial Port Manager

The Serial Port Manager provides AdminSuite with a graphical interface to view and modify the settings of serial ports on the selected host. Using the Serial Port Manager, the following operations can be performed:

➤ View serial port settings

➤ Add a terminal

➤ Add a modem

➤ Disable a port service

➤ Delete a port service

AdminSuite provides command line equivalents for some of the operations of the Serial Port Manager. These are the following:

➤ **admserialdel**—Deletes a port service

➤ **admserialls**—Lists a port service

➤ **admserialmod**—Modifies a port service

User Manager

The User Manager is used to view and modify user account information. This information can be stored in /etc files on the selected host, NIS, or NIS+. The User Manager can be used to view and modify the files, maps, or tables (depending on name service) that contain the following types of information:

➤ aliases

➤ AutoFS for home directories

➤ cred

➤ group

➤ passwd

➤ shadow

AdminSuite provides command line equivalents for the User Manager. These are the following:

➤ **admuseradd**—Adds a user account

➤ **admuserdel**—Deletes a user account

➤ **admuserls**—Lists user accounts

➤ **admusermod**—Modifies a user account

Group Manager

The Group Manager is used to view and modify group account information. This information is stored in the /etc/group file on the selected host, NIS map, or NIS+ table. AdminSuite provides command line equivalents for the Group Manager. These are the following:

➤ **admgroupadd**—Adds a group account

➤ **admgroupdel**—Deletes a group account

➤ **admgroupls**—Lists group accounts

➤ **admgroupmod**—Modifies a group account

Printer Manager

The Printer Manager provides AdminSuite with a graphical interface to perform the following operations:

➤ Install a printer on a print server

➤ Install a network printer

➤ Give print clients access to a printer

➤ Modify existing information for a printer

➤ Delete access to a printer

➤ Delete a printer from a print server

AdminSuite does not provide any command line equivalents for the Printer Manager. Printers can be managed using the Solaris LP Service commands on the appropriate system.

Practice Questions

Question 1

> Enter the name of one of the two tools that are included in the Storage Manager.
>
> _____

The correct answer is either Disk Manager or File System Manager.

Question 2

> AdminSuite consists of seven tools. Six of these are Printer Manager, Host Manager, User Manager, Database Manager, Storage Manager, and Serial Port Manager. Name the seventh tool.
>
> _____

The correct answer is Group Manager.

Question 3

> Which of the following AdminSuite managers is used to mount a file system?
>
> ○ a. Volume Manager
>
> ○ b. Disk Manager
>
> ○ c. File System Manager
>
> ○ d. Mount Manager
>
> ○ e. Partition Manager

The correct answer is c. Disk Manager is used to manage disk partitions. Therefore, answer b is incorrect. Answers a, d, and e do not exist.

Question 4

> Identify the name of the AdminSuite manager that can be used to modify the /etc/protocols file.
>
> _____

The correct answer is the Database Manager.

Question 5

> Which of the following is not a tool provided with AdminSuite?
>
> ○ a. Database Manager
>
> ○ b. Storage Manager
>
> ○ c. Parallel Port Manager
>
> ○ d. Printer Manager

The correct answer is c. AdminSuite includes a Serial Port Manager, not a Parallel Port Manager. Database Manager, Storage Manager, and Printer Manager all are included in AdminSuite. Therefore, answers a, b, and d are incorrect.

Question 6

> Which of the following tasks can be performed with Host Manager? [Select all that apply]
>
> ❑ a. Add OS services
>
> ❑ b. Remove OS services
>
> ❑ c. Convert an AutoClient to a standalone system
>
> ❑ d. Set up a boot server
>
> ❑ e. Set the root password of an AutoClient system

All the answers are correct.

Question 7

Which of the following commands is provided with AdminSuite?

○ a. **admsliceadd**

○ b. **admfilesysdel**

○ c. **admdbls**

○ d. **admserialmod**

○ e. **admprinteradd**

The correct answer is d. None of the other commands exists.

Need To Know More?

 Sun Microsystems, *Solstice AdminSuite 2.3 Administration Guide*, is available in printed form (ISBN 802-7048), on the Web at **docs.sun.com**, and from the online documentation, AnswerBook2, provided with the Solaris 7 operating system.

 Sun Microsystems, *Solstice AdminSuite 2.3 Installation and Release Notes* is available in printed form (ISBN 805-3027), on the Web at **docs.sun.com**, and from the online documentation, AnswerBook2, provided with the Solaris 7 operating system.

Network Clients

Terms you'll need to understand:

√ Network clients

√ Diskless client

√ Dataless client

√ AutoClient

√ OS server

√ OS services

√ Solstice AdminSuite Host Manager

Techniques you'll need to master:

√ Identifying different network clients

√ Determining advantages of different network clients

√ Adding OS services

√ Adding network client support

√ Booting a network client

This chapter describes one of the least understood topics in the Solaris environment, that of network clients. Although network clients are not covered in detail on the exam, a thorough understanding of network clients and how to support them is required to answer the exam questions correctly. This chapter provides additional background information to assist in understanding network clients.

Network clients were briefly described in Chapter 13. This information is repeated and expanded in this chapter. In addition, Chapter 20 briefly described the use of the Host Manager (provided with Solstice AdminSuite), which is used to support network clients. Again, this information is repeated and expanded to provide a more comprehensive description. Finally, supporting network clients requires the use of Network File System (NFS), Cache File System (CacheFS), and Auto File System (AutoFS) (all of which are discussed in Chapter 18) and naming services (which is discussed in Chapter 19). Network clients can be thought of as a sophisticated network architecture built on top of these capabilities.

Network Clients

Solaris 7 supports three types of *network clients*: diskless, dataless, and AutoClients. These network clients are described separately in the following sections and then compared.

Although all three types of network clients are different, they have one thing in common: They are all dependent on one or more other systems (servers) to function properly and cannot operate completely independently.

Diskless Client

As the name implies, a *diskless client* does not have a local disk. The necessary boot and kernel files (the root file system) along with system commands (the /usr file system), applications (the /opt file system), and user data (the /home file system) are located on one or more network servers that are accessed via the network. This is also true for virtual memory (the swap space).

A diskless client is completely dependent on the network and the network servers for booting and operation. This generates a large amount of network traffic the entire time the diskless client is in operation.

Because a diskless client does not have a hard disk, it is less expensive than a system with a disk. In addition, it is easy to replace, as no permanent data, other than the Programmable Read-Only Memory (PROM) settings, is stored on the system. This easily replaced system is referred to as a *field-replaceable unit (FRU)*.

Dataless Client

A *dataless client* has a small local disk that is used to permanently store the root (/) file system. Thus, a dataless client has the necessary files to boot and start the operating system (kernel). System commands (the /usr file system) along with applications (the /opt file system) and user data (the /home file system) are located on one or more network servers that are accessed via the network. The local hard disk is used for the swap space as well.

A dataless client is partially dependent on the network and the network servers. It can boot independently but cannot operate by itself after booting. This generates a large amount of network traffic from the time it completes booting until it is powered down or rebooted. However, the amount of traffic is less than that of a diskless client.

Because a dataless client has a small disk, it is less expensive than a system with a large disk. In addition, the client is fairly easy to replace, as only a small amount of data needs to be restored to return it to service.

> *Note: Sun Microsystems is phasing out the use of the dataless client. In the near future, it will not be supported or probably even mentioned in system documentation. Sun has selected AutoClient as the network client of choice.*

AutoClient

An *AutoClient* has a local disk that is used to store the root (/) file system and system commands (the /usr file system). An AutoClient uses the local disk for caching via CacheFS. After the initial access of data from the network server, the AutoClient has the necessary files to boot, start the operating system (kernel), and perform most of the functions of a networked standalone system. However, because these files are actually copied from a network server when needed and cached using the local disk, the CacheFS mechanism is used to resync the cached data with the data on the network server.

Applications (the /opt file system) and user data (the /home file system) are located on one or more network servers that are accessed via the network. The local hard disk is used for the swap space as well.

An AutoClient is partially dependent on the network and the network servers. Initially, it boots using data from a server and caches the necessary files locally. As long as the cache remains up-to-date, it can be used, and the system can even be rebooted. After the necessary files are cached, the amount of network traffic generated by the AutoClient decreases and remains low even if the system is powered down or rebooted.

Because no permanent data is stored on the system, an AutoClient is easily replaced and is considered an FRU.

> An AutoClient requires a 100MB or larger local disk. This disk is used for caching the root and /usr file systems using the CacheFS capability. The local disk is used for swap space as well.

Comparison Of Network Clients

Table 21.1 provides a comparison of a diskless client, a dataless client, and an AutoClient.

> *Note: Solaris 7 also supports a JavaStation client that is optimized for Java and designed for zero administration. However, it is not an exam objective. For more information, see the Solstice AdminSuite 2.3 Administration Guide.*

Operating System Servers

Network clients obtain all or some of the operating system files from servers via the network. These servers are referred to as *operating system (OS) servers*.

Depending on the type of network client, an OS server may provide the root file system, the /usr file system, and swap space. An OS server can be set up using either the Solstice AdminSuite Host Manager or the commands provided with AdminSuite.

OS servers provide one or more types of *OS services*. The type of OS service required to support a particular network client is based on the platform, architecture, and OS release of the network client. This is because the contents and structure of the binary files that are executed are different between platforms, architectures, and OS releases. For example, the i386 i86pc Solaris 2.6 OS service supports x86 platforms running Solaris 2.6, and the SPARC sun4c Solaris 7 OS service supports SPARC sun4c platforms running Solaris 7.

Table 21.1 Comparison of network clients.

System Type	Local Swap	Local File Systems	Remote File Systems
Diskless client	No	None	root, /usr, /opt, /home
Dataless client	Yes	root	/usr, /opt, /home
AutoClient	Yes	cached root, cached /usr	root, /usr, /opt, /home

Each required type of OS service must be added to an OS server before support for that type of network client can be added. An OS service can be added to an OS server using either the Solstice AdminSuite Host Manager or the commands provided with AdminSuite. The Host Manager is started from the Solstice Launcher, which is displayed by entering the **solstice** command. The Solstice Launcher is shown in Figure 21.1.

Network Client Support Operations

The following operations are required to support network clients:

➤ Setting up an OS server

➤ Adding an OS service to an OS server

➤ Adding support for a network client on the OS server by defining information regarding the network client

➤ Booting the network client

In addition, support can be modified or deleted, but these operations are not covered here. For information on these operations, see the *Solstice AdminSuite 2.3 Administration Guide*.

Setting Up An OS Server

A system can be added to the name service (/etc files, NIS, or NIS+) initially as an OS server, or an existing system can be converted to an OS server. Of course,

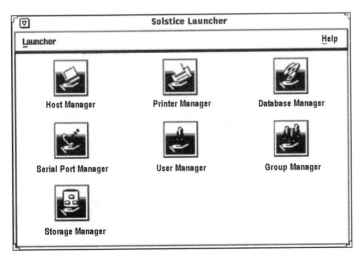

Figure 21.1   The Solstice Launcher.

the system must be networked and have adequate disk space. An OS server can support any mixture of diskless clients, dataless clients, and AutoClients.

Systems can be added or converted by using either the Solstice AdminSuite Host Manager or the equivalent commands provided with AdminSuite.

Adding An OS Server Using AdminSuite Host Manager

Use the following procedure to add a system to the name service as an OS server:

1. Start Host Manager from the Solstice Launcher and select the name service being used. The Host Manager main window is displayed (see Figure 21.2). This window lists the systems currently defined in the name service.

2. Select Add from the Edit pull-down menu. The Host Manager: Add window is displayed as shown in Figure 21.3.

3. Fill in the Host Name, IP Address, and Ethernet Address fields. The Ethernet address is entered as six two-digit hexadecimal numbers separated by colons.

4. Select Solaris OS Server from the System Type pull-down menu.

5. Select the appropriate time zone region from the Timezone Region pull-down menu. Select the appropriate time zone from the Timezone pull-down menu.

6. If the system is not already installed, it can be set up for over-the-network installation by clicking on the Enable Remote Install checkbox and providing information on the Install Server, Set Path, OS Release, Boot

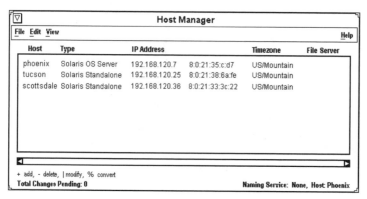

Figure 21.2   The Host Manager main window.

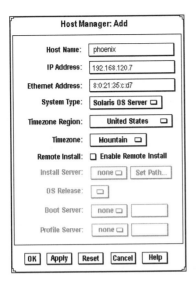

Figure 21.3 The Host Manager: Add window.

Server, and Profile Server. If you do not select the Enable Remote Install option, it is assumed that the system has already been installed using one of the four installation methods (covered in Chapters 3 and 14).

7. Click on OK. The Host Manager: Add window is closed.

8. On the main Host Manager window, select Save Changes from the File pull-down menu. An entry for the OS server is displayed in the list of currently defined systems.

Adding An OS Server Using Commands

An OS server can be added using the **admhostadd** command. The **-i** command line argument is used to specify the IP address, **-e** to specify the Ethernet address, **-x type** to specify that the system is a type OS_SERVER, and **-x tz** to specify the time zone. The hostname is specified as the last command line argument. The following listing shows using the **admhostadd** command to add the phoenix system to the name service that has an IP address of 192.168.120.7 and an Ethernet address of 08:00:21:35:0c:d7, and is located in the Mountain time zone. In this example, the line is wrapped to improve readability, but it should be entered on a single line:

```
# admhostadd -i 192.168.120.7 -e 8:0:21:35:c:d7 -x type=OS_SERVER
  -x tz=US/Mountain phoenix
```

Converting A System To An OS Server Using Host Manager

Only standalone, generic, or dataless client systems can be converted to an OS server. Use the following procedure to convert a system to an OS server:

1. Start Host Manager from the Solstice Launcher and select the name service being used. The Host Manager main window is displayed (see Figure 21.2 earlier in the chapter). This window lists the systems currently defined in the name service.

2. Highlight the desired server and select Convert To OS Server from the Edit pull-down menu. The Host Manager: Convert window is displayed as shown in Figure 21.4.

3. The Host Name, System Type, Timezone Region, and Timezone fields should display the appropriate settings.

4. If the system is not already installed, it can be set up for over-the-network installation by clicking on the Enable Remote Install checkbox and providing information on the Install Server, Set Path, OS Release, Boot Server, and Profile Server. If you do not select the Enable Remote Install option, it is assumed that the system has already been installed using one of the four installation methods.

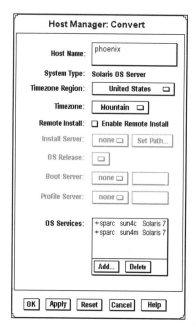

Figure 21.4 The Host Manager: Convert window.

5. The OS services field will display a list of available services. Each entry identifies the platform, architecture, and OS release. These can be added now or later. To add support for an OS service, highlight the entry and click on the Add button. A plus sign (+) will be shown in front of the entry. For each OS service added, the path to the Solaris CD or CD image (CD copied onto disk) must be specified. To delete an OS service, high-light an entry and click on the Delete button. A minus sign (-) will be shown in front of the entry.

6. Click on OK. The Host Manager: Add window is closed.

7. On the main Host Manager window, select Save Changes from the File pull-down menu. An entry for the OS server is displayed in the list of currently defined systems.

Converting A System To An OS Server Using Commands

A system can be converted to an OS server using the **admhostadd** command. The **-x type** command line argument is used to specify that the system is a type OS_SERVER. The hostname is specified as the last command line argument. The following shows using the **admhostadd** command to convert the phoenix system to an OS server:

```
# admhostadd -x type=OS_SERVER phoenix
```

When a system is added or converted to an OS server, it must have an /export file system with enough space to provide the OS services that will be required by the network clients. This file system also contains the /export/swap directory, which is used for network client swap space. The default amount of swap space is 32MB per diskless client (dataless clients and AutoClients provide their own swap space). The total amount of disk space required depends on the number of network clients and the number of OS services that must be supported.

Adding An OS Service

As previously described, each combination of platform (SPARC or i386), architecture (sun4c, sun4m, i86pc, and so on), and OS release (SunOS 4.5, Solaris 2.6, or Solaris 7) is a unique OS service. The OS services that are supported must match the platform, architecture, and OS release combinations of the network clients.

OS services can be added to an OS server using either the Solstice AdminSuite Host Manager or the equivalent commands provided with AdminSuite.

Note: The procedures to add SunOS 4.x OS services is significantly different from adding Solaris 2.x and Solaris 7 OS services. Because Sun Microsystems plans to remove support for SunOS 4.x releases, they are not covered here. For details on adding SunOS 4.x OS services, see the Solstice AdminSuite 2.3 Administration Guide.

Adding An OS Service Using AdminSuite Host Manager

Use the following procedure to add a Solaris 2.x or Solaris 7 OS service to an OS server:

1. Start Host Manager from the Solstice Launcher and select the name service being used. The Host Manager main window is displayed (see Figure 21.2 earlier in the chapter). This window lists the systems currently defined in the name service.

2. Highlight the desired OS server and select Modify from the Edit pull-down menu. The Host Manager: Modify window is displayed as shown in Figure 21.5.

3. The Host Name, IP Address, Ethernet Address, System Type, Timezone Region, and Timezone fields should display the appropriate settings.

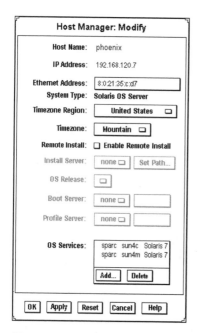

Figure 21.5 The Host Manager: Modify window.

4. If the system is not already installed, it can be set up for over-the-network installation by clicking on the Enable Remote Install checkbox and providing information on the Install Server, Set Path, OS Release, Boot Server, and Profile Server. If you do not select the Enable Remote Install option, it is assumed that the system has already been installed using one of the four installation methods.

5. The OS Services field will display a list of available services. Each entry identifies the architecture, platform, and OS release. To add support for OS service, highlight the entry and click on the Add button. A plus sign (+) will be shown in front of the entry. For each OS service added, the path to the Solaris CD or CD image (CD copied onto disk) must be specified. To delete an OS service, highlight an entry and click on the Delete button. A minus sign (-) will be shown in front of the entry.

6. Click on OK. The Host Manager: Modify window is closed.

7. On the main Host Manager window, select Save Changes from the File pull-down menu.

Adding An OS Service Using Commands

An OS service can be added to an OS server using the **admhostmod** command. The -x **mediapath** command line argument is used to specify the location of the Solaris CD or CD image. This takes the form of *server:path*, where *server* is the name or IP address of a remote system and *path* is the pathname to the Solaris CD or CD image. The -x **platform** command line argument is used to define the platform, architecture, and OS release of the OS service being added. The hostname of the OS server is specified as the last command line argument.

The following shows using the **admhostmod** command to add the OS service for a SPARC sun4c Solaris 7 network client to the phoenix OS server using the Solaris distribution CD mounted in the CD-ROM drive on the scottsdale system. In this example, the line is wrapped to improve readability, but it should be entered on a single line:

```
# admhostmod -x mediapath=scottsdale:/cdrom/cdrom0/s0
  -x platform=sparc.sun4c.Solaris_7 phoenix
```

Adding Support For A Network Client

The OS server must recognize and have information related to the network clients that they support. Support for a network client can be added to an OS server using either the Solstice AdminSuite Host Manager or the equivalent commands provided with AdminSuite.

Table 21.2	The /etc files modified to support network clients.
File	Description
/etc/bootparams	A database that contains the servers (and paths) that provide boot, root, and swap areas for network clients
/etc/dfs/dfstab	The **share** commands that share resources for network clients through NFS
/etc/ethers	A database of Ethernet addresses for the network clients
/etc/hosts	A database of IP addresses and hostnames
/etc/timezone	A database of time zones associated with the network clients

To support network clients, both Host Manager and the AdminSuite commands modify the /etc files listed in Table 21.2.

Adding Support For A Diskless Client

Use the following procedure to add support for a diskless client using the AdminSuite Host Manager:

1. Start Host Manager from the Solstice Launcher and select the name service being used. The Host Manager main window is displayed (see Figure 21.2 earlier in the chapter). This window lists the systems currently defined in the name service.

2. Select Add from the Edit pull-down menu. The Host Manager: Add window is displayed. Select Solaris Diskless from the System Type pull-down menu as shown in Figure 21.6.

3. Fill in the Host Name, IP Address, and Ethernet Address fields. The Ethernet address is entered as six two-digit hexadecimal numbers separated by colons.

4. Select the appropriate settings from the Timezone Region, Timezone, and File Server pull-down menus. The File Server is the OS server that will support the network client. Select the appropriate OS service from the OS Release pull-down menu.

5. Define the path of the root file system and the path of the swap space that will be used by the network client. In addition, define the amount of swap space (default 32MB).

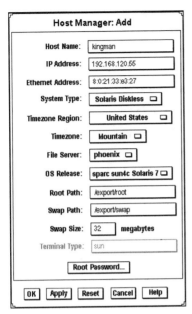

Figure 21.6   The Host Manager: Add diskless client window.

6. Click on the Root Password button to set the root password of the network client.

7. Click on OK. The Host Manager: Add window is closed.

8. On the main Host Manager window, select Save Changes from the File pull-down menu. An entry for the diskless client is displayed in the list of currently defined systems.

Support for a diskless client can be added using the **admhostadd** command. Table 21.3 lists the command line arguments used with the **admhostadd** command.

The following shows using the AdminSuite command line equivalent to add support for the diskless client named kingman. The last command line argument specifies the name of the diskless client. In this example, the line is wrapped to improve readability, but it should be entered on a single line:

```
# admhostadd -i 192.168.120.55 -e 8:0:21:33:e3:27 -x type=DISKLESS
  -x tz=US/Mountain -x fileserv=phoenix -x os=sparc.sun4c.Solaris_7
  -x passwd=abc123 -x root=/export/root -x swap=/export/swap
  -x swapsize=32 kingman
```

Table 21.3   The admhostadd command line arguments.

Argument	Description
-e *address*	Specifies the network client's Ethernet address
-i *ip_address*	Specifies the network client's IP address
-x diskconfig=*config*	Specifies the disk configuration
-x disconn=*mode*	Specifies whether disconnectability is supported
-x fileserv=*system*	Specifies the OS server
-x os=*service*	Specifies the platform, architecture, and OS release of the OS service
-x passwd=*password*	Specifies the network client's root password
-x root=*root_path*	Specifies the path for the network client's root file system
-x swap=*swap_path*	Specifies the path for the network client's swap space
-x swapsize=*size*	Specifies the swap space size (in MB)
-x type=*type*	Specifies the type of network client (dataless, diskless, or AutoClient)
-x tz=*timezone*	Specifies the network client's time zone

Adding Support For A Dataless Client

Use the following procedure to add support for a dataless client using the AdminSuite Host Manager:

1. Start Host Manager from the Solstice Launcher and select the name service being used. The Host Manager main window is displayed (see Figure 21.2 earlier in the chapter). This window lists the systems currently defined in the name service.

2. Select Add from the Edit pull-down menu. The Host Manager: Add window is displayed. Select Solaris Dataless from the System Type pull-down menu as shown in Figure 21.7.

3. Fill in the Host Name, IP Address, and Ethernet Address fields. The Ethernet address is entered as six two-digit hexadecimal numbers separated by colons.

4. Select the appropriate settings from the Timezone Region, Timezone, and File Server pull-down menus. The File Server is the OS server that will support the network client. Select the appropriate OS service from the OS Release pull-down menu.

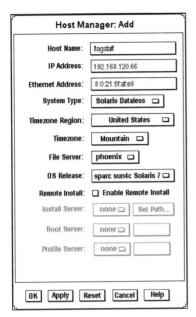

Figure 21.7   The Host Manager: Add dataless client window.

5. If the system is not already installed, it can be set up for over-the-network installation by clicking on the Enable Remote Install checkbox and providing information on the Install Server, Set Path, OS Release, Boot Server, and Profile Server. If you do not select the Enable Remote Install option, it is assumed that the system has already been installed using one of the four installation methods.

6. Click on OK. The Host Manager: Add window is closed.

7. On the main Host Manager window, select Save Changes from the File pull-down menu. An entry for the diskless client is displayed in the list of currently defined systems.

Support for a dataless client can be added using the **admhostadd** command. Table 21.3 lists the command line arguments used with the **admhostadd** command. The following shows using the AdminSuite command line equivalent to add support for the dataless client named flagstaff. The last command line argument specifies the name of the dataless client. In this example, the line is wrapped to improve readability, but it should be entered on a single line:

```
# admhostadd -i 192.168.120.66 -e 8:0:21:5f:af:e8 -x type=DATALESS
  -x tz=US/Mountain -x fileserv=phoenix -x os=sparc.sun4c.Solaris_7
  flagstaff
```

Adding Support For An AutoClient

Use the following procedure to add support for an AutoClient using the AdminSuite Host Manager:

1. Start Host Manager from the Solstice Launcher and select the name service being used. The Host Manager main window is displayed (see Figure 21.2 earlier in the chapter). This window lists the systems currently defined in the name service.

2. Select Add from the Edit pull-down menu. The Host Manager: Add window is displayed. Select Solstice AutoClient from the System Type pull-down menu as shown in Figure 21.8.

3. Fill in the Host Name, IP Address, and Ethernet Address fields. The Ethernet address is entered as six two-digit hexadecimal numbers separated by colons.

4. Select the appropriate settings from the Timezone Region, Timezone, and File Server pull-down menus. The File Server is the OS server that will support the network client. Select the appropriate OS service from the OS Release pull-down menu.

5. Define the path of the root file system that will be used by the network client. In addition, define the amount of local swap space (default 32MB).

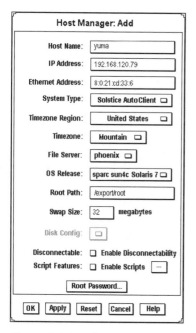

Figure 21.8 The Host Manager: Add AutoClient window.

6. Select the appropriate disk configuration option from the Disk Config pull-down menu. If the system has only a single physical disk, the Disk Configuration option is unavailable.

7. Select the Enable Disconnectability option to allow the system to continue to operate from the cache if the OS server is unavailable. Select the Enable Scripts option to set up custom scripts to run as part of the boot process.

8. Click on the Root Password button to set the root password of the network client.

9. Click on OK. The Host Manager: Add window is closed.

10. On the main Host Manager window, select Save Changes from the File pull-down menu. An entry for the diskless client is displayed in the list of currently defined systems.

Support for an AutoClient can be added using the **admhostadd** command. Table 21.3 earlier in the chapter lists the command line arguments used with the **admhostadd** command. The following listing shows using the AdminSuite command line equivalent to add support for the AutoClient named yuma. The last command line argument specifies the name of the AutoClient client. In this example, the line is wrapped to improve readability, but it should be entered on a single line:

```
# admhostadd -i 192.168.120.79 -e 8:0:21:cd:33:6 -x type=AUTOCLIENT
  -x tz=US/Mountain -x fileserv=phoenix -x os=sparc.sun4c.Solaris_7
  -x root=/export/root -x swapspace=32 -x disconn=N
  -x diskconf=1disk -x pass=abc123 yuma
```

Booting A Network Client

The procedure for booting diskless clients, dataless clients, and AutoClients is identical. However, the procedure varies depending on the platform (SPARC or x86).

Before booting the network client, the appropriate OS services must be added along with support for the network client.

Network clients are identified by their Ethernet address. They broadcast this information to OS servers. The OS server that has been set up to support the network client responds to the network client and begins downloading the information necessary to boot the network client and mount the remote file systems.

Booting A SPARC Network Client

To boot a SPARC network client, power up the system and put the system in the PROM monitor environment. The **ok** prompt should be displayed on the screen. If the > prompt is displayed instead, press the "N" key followed by the Enter key. Enter the **boot net** command and press the Enter key. The following listing shows booting the diskless client named kingman that is supported by the phoenix OS server:

```
> n
ok
.

.

.

ok boot net
Booting from: le (0,0,0)
2bc00 hostname: kingman
domainname: solaris.com
root server: phoenix
root directory: /export/root/kingman
SunOS Release 5.7 Version [2.4] [UNIX(R) System V Release 4.0]
Copyright (c) 1983-1997, Sun Microsystems, Inc.
configuring network interfaces: le0.
Hostname: kingman
Configuring cache and swap:.....done.
The system is coming up. Please wait.
NIS domain is solaris.com
starting rpc services: rpcbind keyserv ybind kerbd done.
Setting netmask of le0 to 255.255.255.0
.

.

.

The system is ready.
login:
```

To set up a SPARC system to boot from the network automatically, set the **boot-device** OpenBoot parameter. At the PROM monitor **ok** prompt, enter the following command:

```
ok setenv boot-device net
```

Booting An x86 Network Client

To boot an x86 network client, insert the Solaris boot diskette in the diskette drive and power on the system. When the Multiple Device Boot menu is displayed, enter the device code associated with using the network (NET) as a boot device, typically 12. After briefly displaying the secondary boot subsystem, the system boots from the network. The following listing shows booting the AutoClient named yuma that is supported by the phoenix OS server:

```
Solaris 7 for x86                      Multiple Device Boot

                  Solaris/x86 Multiple Device Boot Menu

        Code    Device    Vendor            Model/Desc
        =================================================================
         10      DISK      WESTERN DIGITAL   WD 3001
         11      CD        SONY              CD-ROM
         12      NET       3COM              I/O=300 IRG=5
12
.
.
.

Solaris 7 for 86                       Secondary Boot Subsystem

                     << Current Boot Parameters >>
     Boot path: /pci@0,0/pci-ide@7,1/ata@0/cmdk@0,0
     Boot args: /kernel/unix

Type b [file-name] [boot-flags] <ENTER> to boot with options
or   i <ENTER>                          to enter boot interpreter
or   <ENTER>                            to boot with default

                   << timeout in 60 seconds >>
     Select (b)oot or (i)nterpreter
     .
     .
     .

Booting from: elx (0,0,0)
2bc00 hostname: yuma
domainname: solaris.com
root server: phoenix
root directory: /export/root/yuma
SunOS Release 5.7 Generic 106542 [UNIX(R) System V Release 4.0]
Copyright (c) 1983-1997, Sun Microsystems, Inc.
configuring network interfaces: le0.
Hostname: yuma
The system is coming up. Please wait.
starting rpc services: rpcbind keyserv ybind kerbd done.
Setting netmask of elx0 to 255.255.255.0
.
.
.

The system is ready.
login:
```

Use the following procedure to create a boot diskette that will automatically boot from the network:

1. Obtain the Solaris boot diskette and a blank 1.44MB diskette.

2. Change to the /opt/SUNWadm/2.3/floppy directory.

3. As the root user account, execute the **mk_floppy** command.

4. When prompted, insert either the Solaris boot diskette or the blank diskette into the diskette drive. The required files are copied from the Solaris boot diskette to the blank diskette.

When you are finished, leave the new diskette in the diskette drive so that it will boot from the network automatically when the system boots.

Practice Questions

Question 1

Which of the following is not an attribute of an OS service?

○ a. OS release

○ b. OpenBoot PROM version

○ c. Platform

○ d. Architecture

The correct answer is b. The version of the OpenBoot PROM software does not affect the OS service. The OS release, platform, and architecture are all an attribute of an OS service. Therefore, answers a, c, and d are incorrect.

Question 2

Which of the following are types of network clients? [Select all that apply]

❑ a. Dataless

❑ b. OS server

❑ c. Diskless

❑ d. CacheFS

❑ e. AutoClient

The correct answers are a, c, and e. An OS server is required to support network clients. Therefore, answer b is incorrect. CacheFS is the type of file system used by AutoClients. Therefore, answer d is incorrect.

Question 3

Enter the name of the AdminSuite tool that is used to support network clients.

_____

The correct answer is Host Manager.

Question 4

> Which type of client does not have any local swap space?
>
> ○ a. Dataless
>
> ○ b. Diskless
>
> ○ c. AutoClient

The correct answer is b. A diskless client does not have a disk. Both dataless clients and AutoClients have a disk and use it for local swap space. Therefore, answers a and c are incorrect.

Question 5

> Enter the name of the AdminSuite command line equivalent used to add an OS service to an OS server.
>
> _____

The correct answer is **admhostmod**.

Question 6

> What is the default amount of swap space used for a diskless client?
>
> ○ a. 8MB
>
> ○ b. 16MB
>
> ○ c. 32MB
>
> ○ d. 64MB

The correct answer is c. This provides a reasonable amount of virtual memory without wasting storage space on the server.

Question 7

Enter the minimum size (in MB) of a local AutoClient disk.

The correct answer is 100.

Question 8

Which of the following functions cannot be performed using Host Manager?

○ a. Setting up an OS server

○ b. Adding an OS service

○ c. Adding support for a network client

○ d. Booting a network client

The correct answer is d. The Host Manager cannot force a network client to boot. The Host Manager can be used to set up an OS server, add an OS service, and add support for a network client. Therefore, answer a, b, and c are incorrect.

Question 9

Which of the /etc files are modified to support a network client? [Select all that apply]

❑ a. bootparams

❑ b. ethers

❑ c. timezone

❑ d. hosts

❑ e. vfstab

The correct answers are a, b, c, and d. The /etc/dfs/dfstab file is modified as well. The vfstab is used to mount local file systems and does not affect network clients. Therefore, answer e is incorrect.

Need To Know More?

Sun Microsystems, *Solstice AdminSuite 2.3 Administration Guide*, is available in printed form (ISBN 802-7048), on the Web at **docs.sun.com**, and from the online documentation, AnswerBook2, provided with the Solaris 7 operating system.

Sun Microsystems, *Solstice AdminSuite 2.3 Installation and Release Notes*, is available in printed form (ISBN 805-3027), on the Web at **docs.sun.com**, and from the online documentation, AnswerBook2, provided with the Solaris 7 operating system.

Sun Microsystems, *Solstice AutoClient 2.1 Administration Guide*, is available in printed form (ISBN 805-3167), on the Web at **docs.sun.com**, and from the online documentation, AnswerBook2, provided with the Solaris 7 operating system.

Sun Microsystems, *System Administration Guide, Volume 1*, is available in printed form (ISBN 805-3727-10), on the Web at **docs.sun.com**, and from the online documentation, AnswerBook2, provided with the Solaris 7 operating system.

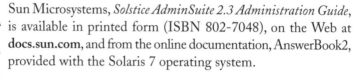

Managing The CDE

Terms you'll need to understand:

√ The Common Desktop Environment (CDE)

√ The Login Manager

√ The login screen

√ The Session Manager

√ The Workspace Manager

√ The Front Panel

Techniques you'll need to master:

√ Configuring the Login Manager

√ Customizing the Session Manager

√ Customizing Front Panel subpanels

√ Customizing Front Panel controls

This chapter describes managing the Common Desktop Environment (CDE). Because the exam objectives focus on configuring the CDE, only a brief overview of the CDE components is provided. These components include the Login Manager, the Session Manager, and the Workspace Manager, which includes the Front Panel.

The Login Manager

The Login Manager (also referred to as the Login Server or the Login Manager Server) displays a login screen, authenticates the user, and starts the user's session. This service can be provided by a locally attached display (a local display) or an X terminal or workstation on the network (a network display).

For configured local displays, the Login Server will automatically start an X server and display the login screen. Authorized network displays can request a login screen using the X Display Manager Control Protocol (XDMCP).

The Login Server is actually the **/usr/dt/bin/dtlogin** command. When the **dtlogin** command receives a request for service, it creates a copy of itself to handle the request. The **/usr/dt/bin/dtconfig** command is used to control the Login Server. The **dtconfig** command line arguments are listed in Table 22.1.

Login Server Configuration Files

Several files are used to control the configuration and behavior of the **dtlogin** command. These are the Xconfig file, the Xservers file, and the Xaccess file.

The Xconfig File
The default configuration file for the Login Server is /usr/dt/config/Xconfig. By convention, this file should not be modified. This file provides a consistent Login Server behavior for all systems. To customize the configuration of the

Table 22.1 The dtconfig command line arguments.	
Argument	**Description**
-d	Disables starting the Login Server automatically on the next system boot
-e	Enables starting the Login Server automatically on the next system boot
-kill	Stops the Login Server (all user sessions created using the **dtlogin** command are terminated)
-reset	Instructs the Login Server to re-read and process its configuration file (Xconfig)

Login Server, copy the /usr/dt/config/Xconfig file to the /etc/dt/config/Xconfig file and modify the /etc copy.

When the **dtlogin** command starts (or is instructed to re-read its configuration file by the **dtconfig** command), it first checks for the existence of the /etc/dt/config/Xconfig file. If it exists, that file is used to configure the behavior of the Login Server. Otherwise, the /usr/dt/config/Xconfig file is used. This allows the Login Server to be configured differently for each system but preserves the default configuration file.

Entries in the Xconfig file consist of a keyword followed by a value. The Xconfig keywords and their default values are listed in Table 22.2. Unless otherwise specified, the default path for files and scripts is first /etc/dt/config and then /usr/dt/config. The default value for %L is the uppercase letter "C."

In addition, the Xconfig file is used to define environmental variables used by the Xservers and other X-related scripts. These are listed in Table 22.3.

Table 22.2 The default Xconfig entries.		
Keyword	**Default**	**Description**
Dtlogin.accessFile:	Xaccess	Configuration file for controlling Login Server access
Dtlogin.errorLogFile:	/var/dt/Xerrors	File for logging error messages
Dtlogin.pidFile:	/var/dt/Xpid	File for the process ID (PID) of the **dtlogin** command
Dtlogin.servers:	Xservers	Configuration file for local and network displays
Dtlogin*Environment:	*variable=value*	One or more variables to be exported to the environment
Dtlogin*failsafeClient:	Xfailsafe	Fail-safe session script
Dtlogin*reset:	Xreset	Session reset script
Dtlogin*resources:	%L/Xresources	Configuration file for the login screen
Dtlogin*setup:	Xsetup	Setup script
Dtlogin*startup:	Xstartup	Session startup script
Dtlogin*terminateServer:	True	Terminate and restart the Xserver at user logout

Table 22.3 The Xconfig environment variables.	
Keyword	**Description**
Dtlogin.timezone:	The TZ variable
Dtlogin*systemPath:	System PATH variable
Dtlogin*systemShell:	System SHELL variable
Dtlogin*userPath:	User PATH variable

The Xservers File

When the Login Server starts up, it checks the Xservers file to determine whether any Xservers should be started and how login screens should be displayed on local and network displays.

Like the Xconfig file, the default Xservers file is located under the /usr/dt/ config directory. To customize the Xservers file, first copy it to the /etc/dt/ config directory and modify the /etc copy.

Each entry defines a local or network display on which the login server should display a login screen. The format of an entry consists of the following fields:

➤ *Display name*—A connection name used to identify the display

➤ *Display class*—Identifies resources associated with the display (typically local)

➤ *Display type*—Identifies whether the display is local or network (foreign) and how to manage the command line login option

➤ *User ID*—Optional field used to specify the user ID (UID) of the Xserver if the display type field is local_uid

➤ *X Server command*—The command used to start an Xserver for the display

By default, the Xservers file contains only one entry for the local display (typically the console). This can be disabled by placing the shell comment character (#) before the entry. Usually, network displays request a login screen. However, an entry can be added to the Xservers file to automatically display a login screen on a network display when the Login Server is started. The following listing shows the default contents of the Xservers file:

```
:0 Local local_uid@console root /usr/openwin/bin/Xsun :0 -nobanner
```

The Xaccess File

By default, any host on the network can request the Login Server to display a login screen. This can be modified by using the Xaccess file.

Like the Xconfig file, the default Xaccess file is located under the /usr/dt/ config directory. To customize the Xaccess file, first copy it to the /etc/dt/ config directory and then modify the /etc copy.

Each entry identifies a host that is allowed access. If the entry is preceded by an exclamation mark (!), the host is denied access. For example, if the name phoenix.system.com is an entry in the Xaccess file, that system is allowed access. Wildcard characters can be used to specify groups of systems. The asterisk (*) can be used to match zero or more characters, whereas the question mark (?) can be used to match a single character. For example, the entry *.system.com allows access to the Login Server for any host that is a member of the system.com domain.

The Login Screen

The login screen is a graphical window used to prompt for and accept a user account name and password. It is displayed automatically on any local or network displays specified in the Xservers file when the Login Server starts. In addition, network displays can request a login screen if they are allowed access per the Xaccess file. The default login screen is shown in Figure 22.1.

The Xresources File

The Xresources configuration file controls the appearance of the login screen. The default file is located under the /usr/dt/config/C directory. To customize the login screen, copy the Xresources file to the /etc/dt/config/C directory and modify the /etc file. The Xresources file contains keywords that identify attributes of the login screen and values that define the setting of the attribute. Table 22.4 lists the more significant keywords of the Xresources file. Examine the Xresources file for more details.

Figure 22.1   The default CDE login screen.

Table 22.4   Xresources keywords.

Keyword	Description
Dtlogin*background:	Background color
Dtlogin*foreground:	Foreground color
DTlogin*greeting*fontList:	Font used for welcome messages
Dtlogin*greeting*LabelString:	Welcome message
Dtlogin*greeting*persLabelString:	Personalized welcome message
Dtlogin*logo*bitmapFile:	Image to display as logo

Keep in mind that the CDE configuration files under /usr/dt /config and, in the case of Xresources, under /usr/dt/config /C should not be modified. To customize the Login Server and login screen, copy the appropriate files to the /etc/dt/config (in the case of Xresources to the /etc/dt/config/C) directory. Then modify the /etc copies. When the Login Server is started, it first will check for files under the /etc/dt/config directory and then, if they are not present there, under the /usr/dt/config directory.

The Session Manager

The Session Manager starts a session for a user. A session is associated with a display and consists of not only the displayed graphical desktop and its settings (fonts, colors, and so on) but also mouse behavior, keyboard click (the small noise made to provide feedback that a key was depressed), and applications or other resources present on the desktop.

When a user exits, the Session Manager can automatically save the current configuration of the session and restore it when the user logs in at a later time. Alternatively, the user can choose to have a default desktop whenever logging into the system.

Several types of sessions are based on context. These are the initial session, the current session, the home session, and the display-specific session. These sessions are summarized in Table 22.5.

Session Startup Sequence

When a user logs in using the Login Screen provided by the Login Manager, the Session Manager **/usr/dt/bin/Xsession** command is started. The **Xsession** command performs the following actions:

1. Reads and executes the .dtprofile script under the user's home directory.

Table 22.5 Types of CDE sessions.	
Type	**Description**
Initial	Occurs only once per user account; the first time the account is used. The Session Manager creates the session using the system defaults. This includes automatically starting a File Manager window and a Help Volume window.
Current	The session the user is currently using, whether it is an initial session, a home session, or a display-specific session.
Home	A custom session that the user account always receives when logging in. The other choice is to restore the session that was saved when the user account last logged out.
Display-specific	A custom session used for a specific display. When the display is used, it always receives the same session.

2. Reads and executes any scripts under the /usr/dt/config/Xsession.d directory. These scripts set additional environmental variables and execute optional commands.

3. Displays the welcome message. To change the welcome message, create a script that defines the dtstart_hello[0] variable with the text of the new message. Custom scripts or changes to the default scripts should be added under the /etc/dt/config/Xsession.d directory.

4. Sets up desktop search paths using the **/usr/dt/bin/dtsearchpath** command.

5. Locates the available applications using the **/usr/dt/bin/dtappgather** command by searching through the desktop search paths.

6. Reads and executes the login initialization file (.profile or .login, depending on login shell) if the DTSOURCEPROFILE variable in the .dtprofile is set to true.

7. Starts the ToolTalk messaging system. This allows applications to communicate with each other.

8. At this point, the **/usr/dt/bin/dtsession** command is started and takes over the session startup process.

9. Loads the system default session resources (specified by the /usr/dt/config/C/sys.resources file) and merges them with any systemwide defaults (specified by the /etc/dt/config/C/sys.resources file) and user-specified resources (specified by the .Xdefaults file under the user's home directory).

10. Starts the color server that manages the foreground and background colors. These can be specified in the sys.resources file.

11. Starts the Workspace Manager (described in the next section).

12. Starts the session applications. Any applications identified by the /etc/
    dt/config/C/sys.session file or the /usr/dt/config/C/sys.session file are
    started.

Customizing The Session Manager

This section summarizes the files used to customize the Session Manager. This
includes setting environment variables, defining resources, changing applications, and executing additional commands.

Systemwide variables can be set by creating an executable script under the
/etc/dt/config/Xsession.d directory. This script should set and export the variables. Variables for users can be set by using the .dtprofile script under the
user's home directory.

Systemwide resources are added by modifying the /etc/dt/config/C
/sys.resources file. In addition, display-specific resources can be defined using the /etc/dt/config/C/sys.resources file. Users can define display-specific
resources by using the .Xdefaults file under the user's home directory. The
applications of the initial session can be changed by modifying the /etc/dt/
config/C/sys.session file.

Additional commands can be executed whenever a user logs into or out of a
desktop session. This can be used to customize the desktop session. To execute
commands at session startup, create the sessionetc file under the .dt/sessions
directory of the user's home directory ($HOME/.dt/sessions). Then enter the
commands in the file using a text editor. This file must have execution permission because it is treated as a shell script. To execute commands at session exit,
create the sessionexit file under the $HOME/.dt/sessions directory. Then enter
the commands in the file using a text editor. This file must have execution permission because it is treated as a shell script.

The Workspace Manager

The Workspace Manager is a desktop window manager that controls the appearance of window components and supports the ability to modify the window
appearance and behavior, such as stacking and focus. The Workspace Manager
controls the workspaces (four by default), the background wallpaper (backdrop) of the workspaces through the Style Manager, and the Front Panel.

A workspace is a display consisting of the Front Panel and any windows
created or applications started by the user. A different workspace can be displayed by using the mouse to click on a workspace button. Each workspace is

independent of the other workspaces. The workspace buttons are part of the Workspace switch, described in the next section.

The default configuration file for the Workspace Manager is the /usr/dt/config /C/sys.dtwmrc file, whereas the customized system configuration file is the /etc/dt/config/C/sys.dtwmrc file. A customized configuration for a user account would be the $HOME/.dt/dtwmrc file.

The Workspace Manager has three menus:

➤ *Workspace*—Referred to as the root menu, this menu provides access to applications and a windows submenu that is used to manage the workspace and Front Panel. It is accessed by moving the mouse pointer over the backdrop and holding down the rightmost mouse button.

➤ *Window*—This menu provides control for moving, resizing, maximizing, minimizing, and closing a window. To access the Window menu, position the mouse cursor over the upper-left corner of a window and click the rightmost mouse button.

➤ *Front Panel*—This menu provides control for moving, minimizing, refreshing, and logging out of the Front Panel. To access the Front Panel menu, position the mouse cursor over the upper-left corner of the Front Panel and click the rightmost mouse button.

The Workspace menu can be modified by using either the Add Item To Menu or Customize Menu items from the Workspace menu. For more details, see *Solaris Common Desktop Environment: Advanced User's and System Administrator's Guide.*

 Whenever a change is made to the Workspace menu or the Front Panel, select Windows from the Workspace menu item and then select Restart Workspace Manager. This causes the Workspace Manager to re-read its configuration file and the Front Panel configuration files.

Front Panel

The Solaris 7 Front Panel is shown in Figure 22.2. The Front Panel is actually a collection of containers and objects within the containers. The *panel* is the top-level container, or parent, for all the other containers. The panel is divided into the *main panel* and several *subpanels*. The main panel is the large rectangular window that is positioned across the bottom of the display. The subpanels are menus that pop up when a button on the main panel is selected. The Hosts subpanel is also shown in Figure 22.2.

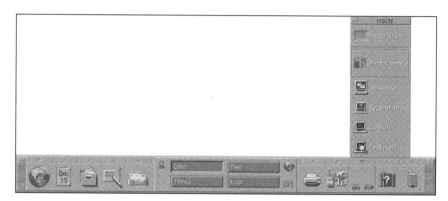

Figure 22.2 The Solaris Front Panel and the Hosts subpanel.

The main panel is divided into two containers: the *box* and the *switch*. The switch is the rectangular window in the center of the main panel. The box is the area to the left and right of the switch.

The box, the switch, and the subpanels contain controls, which are graphical icons or buttons. When the mouse is used to click on these icons or buttons, various events occur, such as displaying a subpanel, starting an application, or displaying a window for an existing application. Most of the controls on the box and subpanels are graphical icons used to display or start applications. Most of the controls on the switch (referred to as the *Workspace switch*) are buttons used to select the workspace that should be displayed.

The Front Panel Configuration Files

The characteristics of the Front Panel are controlled by a set of configuration files. The default Front Panel is defined by the /usr/dt/appconfig/types/C /dtwm.fp file. To create a customized systemwide Front Panel, copy the dtwm.fp file to the /etc/dt/appconfig/types/C directory and modify the /etc copy. To create a user-specified Front Panel, copy the dtwm.fp file to the $HOME/.dt/types directory and modify the copy under the user's home directory.

 Although the default Front Panel is defined by a single file, the systemwide and user-specified Front Panel definitions may actually consist of more than one file. However, regardless of the number of files, all file names will end with the .fp extension.

As with the other portions of the CDE, user-specific configuration files override systemwide configuration files, which in turn override the default configuration files.

The containers and controls of the Front Panel are defined by a plain-text scripting language. The syntax for definitions is shown in the following listing:

```
OBJECT name
{
KEYWORD value
KEYWORD value

   ...

}
```

OBJECT identifies the type of object and can be **PANEL, SUBPANEL, BOX, SWITCH,** or **CONTROL.** *name* is a unique name assigned to the object. *KEYWORD* is an attribute of the object, and *value* defines the setting for the *KEYWORD.*

There is only one **PANEL,** one **BOX,** and one **SWITCH** container definition. These define the behavior and positioning of the controls that are included in the container. The following shows the default definitions of these objects:

```
PANEL FrontPanel
{
  DISPLAY_HANDLES         True
  DISPLAY_MENU            True
  DISPLAY_MINIMIZE        True
  CONTROL_BEHAVIOR        single_click
  DISPLAY_CONTROL_LABELS False
  HELP_TOPIC              FPOnItemFrontPanel
  HELP_VOLUME             FPanel
}
BOX Top
{
  CONTAINER_NAME          FrontPanel
  POSITION_HINTS          first
  HELP_TOPIC              FPOnItemBox
  HELP_VOLUME             FPanel
}
SWITCH Switch
{
  CONTAINER_NAME          Top
  POSITION_HINTS          7
  NUMBER_OF_ROWS          2
  HELP_TOPIC              FPOnItemSwitch
  HELP_VOLUME             FPanel
}
```

Note that both the **BOX** and the **SWITCH** objects include a **CONTAINER_ NAME** keyword. These specify that the switch named Switch is contained in the container named Top and that the box named Top is contained in the container named FrontPanel.

One or more **SUBPANEL**s can be defined, each of which is associated with a control located on the **BOX**. In this case, the name of the control is specified as the value for the **CONTAINER_NAME**. The following listing shows the definition of the Applications subpanel, which is titled Hosts:

```
SUBPANEL Applications
{
    CONTAINER_NAME      PerformanceMeter
    TITLE               Hosts
}
```

Note that the Hosts subpanel shown in Figure 22.2 is positioned over the up/down arrow located above the Performance Meter control.

Controls are defined using the **CONTROL** object and can be placed in the **BOX**, the **SWITCH**, or a **SUBPANEL** container. The **CONTROL** object defines the icon that should be displayed, the action that should be performed when it is selected by clicking on the icon with the mouse, and other attributes, such as its position within the container. The following shows the definition of the Console control, which is placed in the Applications subpanel (see Figure 22.2):

```
CONTROL Console
{
        TYPE            icon
        CONTAINER_NAME  Applications
        CONTAINER_TYPE  SUBPANEL
        POSITION_HINTS  4
        ICON            Fpterm
        LABEL           Console
        PUSH_ACTION     DttermConsole
        HELP_TOPIC      TourSubpanels
        HELP_VOLUME     FPanel
}
```

Some of the more commonly used attribute keywords are listed in Table 22.6.

Details on the attribute keywords and values are described in the Solaris CDE guides listed at the end of this chapter.

Table 22.6 Front Panel attribute keywords.	
Keyword	**Description**
CONTAINER_NAME	Name of container in which an object is placed
CONTAINER_TYPE	Type of container
HELP_TOPIC	Help topic to display when help is selected
HELP_VOLUME	Help volume that contains the help topic
ICON	A small graphical image used to represent and select the control
LABEL	Display name of the control
POSITION_HINTS	Position of the control icon within the container
PUSH_ACTION	Name of the application to execute when an icon is selected
TITLE	Display name of the subpanel
TYPE	Type of control

Modifying A Subpanel

Follow these steps to make a systemwide modification to an existing subpanel:

1. Copy the **SUBPANEL** object from the /usr/dt/appconfig/types/C/ dtwm.fp file to a file under the /etc/dt/appconfig/types/C directory. The file should be named using the name of the subpanel followed by the .fp extension. For example, to modify the Applications subpanel, copy the **SUBPANEL Applications** object to the /etc/dt/appconfig/ types/C/Applications.fp file.

2. Edit the Applications.fp file and save the changes.

3. Select Restart Workspace Manager from the Workspace menu.

For example, to rename the Applications subpanel from "Hosts" to "My Applications," the /etc/dt/appconfig/types/C/Applications.fp file should look similar to the following listing:

```
SUBPANEL Applications
{
    CONTAINER_NAME      PerformanceMeter
    TITLE               My Applications
}
```

To modify the subpanel for a user account, use the same procedure, but this time copy the **SUBPANEL** object to the $HOME/.dt/types directory.

Creating A Subpanel

Follow these steps to create a new systemwide subpanel:

1. Examine the /usr/dt/appconfig/types/C/dtwm.fp file to determine the name of a control in the main panel with which to associate the subpanel.

2. Create a file under the /etc/dt/appconfig/types/C directory with a name of the subpanel followed by the .fp extension. For example, to create the Services subpanel, edit the /etc/dt/appconfig/types/C/Services.fp file and define a **SUBPANEL** object using existing **SUBPANEL** objects as a guide. Then save the contents of the file.

3. Select Restart Workspace Manager from the Workspace menu.

At a minimum, a **CONTAINER_NAME** (control on the panel) must be defined. For example, to create the Services subpanel, the /etc/dt/appconfig/types/C/Services.fp file should look similar to the following listing:

```
SUBPANEL Services
{
    CONTAINER_NAME      PerformanceMeter
}
```

To create a new subpanel for a user account, use the same procedure, but this time create the new **SUBPANEL** object file in the $HOME/.dt/types directory.

Deleting A Subpanel

Follow these steps to remove an existing subpanel on a systemwide basis:

1. Copy the **SUBPANEL** object from the /usr/dt/appconfig/types/C/dtwm.fp file to a file under the /etc/dt/appconfig/types/C directory. The file should be named using the name of the subpanel followed by the .fp extension. For example, to remove the Applications subpanel, copy the **SUBPANEL Applications** object to the /etc/dt/appconfig/types/C/Applications.fp file.

2. Edit the Applications.fp file and add "DELETE True" as a keyword and value to the **SUBPANEL** object, then save the changes.

3. Select Restart Workspace Manager from the Workspace menu.

For example, to delete the Applications subpanel, the /etc/dt/appconfig/types/ C/Applications.fp file should look similar to the following:

```
SUBPANEL Applications
{
   CONTAINER_NAME      PerformanceMeter
   TITLE               Hosts
   DELETE              True
}
```

To delete a subpanel for a user account, use the same procedure, but this time copy the **SUBPANEL** object to the $HOME/.dt/types directory.

Modifying A Control

Follow these steps to make a systemwide modification to an existing panel control or subpanel control:

1. Copy the **CONTROL** object from the /usr/dt/appconfig/types/C/ dtwm.fp file to a file under the /etc/dt/appconfig/types/C directory. The file should be named using the name of the control followed by the .fp extension. For example, to modify the Console control on the Applications subpanel, copy the **CONTROL Console** object to the /etc/dt/appconfig/types/C/Console.fp file.

2. Edit the Console.fp file and save the changes.

3. Select Restart Workspace Manager from the Workspace menu.

For example, to change the **LABEL** of the Console control to "System Console," the /etc/dt/appconfig/types/C/Console.fp file should look similar to the following:

```
CONTROL Console
{
        TYPE            icon
        CONTAINER_NAME  Applications
        CONTAINER_TYPE  SUBPANEL
        POSITION_HINTS  4
        ICON            Fpterm
        LABEL           System Console
        PUSH_ACTION     DttermConsole
        HELP_TOPIC      TourSubpanels
        HELP_VOLUME     FPanel
}
```

To modify the subpanel for a user account, use the same procedure, but this time copy the **CONTROL** object to the $HOME/.dt/types directory.

Creating A Control

Follow these steps to create a new systemwide control:

1. Create a file under the /etc/dt/appconfig/types/C directory with the name of the control followed by the .fp extension. For example, to create the Whatsup control, edit the /etc/dt/appconfig/types/C/Whatsup.fp file.

2. Define the **CONTROL** object. Use an existing **CONTROL** object as a model. If the object is being added to the panel, the **CONTAINER_ NAME** must be defined as **Top**, and **CONTAINER_TYPE** must be defined as **BOX**. If the control is being added to a subpanel, the **CONTAINER_NAME** must be defined as the name of the subpanel, and the **CONTAINER_TYPE** must be defined as **SUBPANEL**. The **POSITION_HINTS** should be specified to identify the placement of the control within the panel. When completed, save the contents of the file.

3. If necessary, create an icon for the control using the procedures described in *Solaris Common Desktop Environment: Advanced User's and System Administrator's Guide*.

4. Select Restart Workspace Manager from the Workspace menu.

For example, to create a remote console control, the /etc/dt/appconfig/types/ C/rconsole.fp file should look similar to the following:

```
CONTROL RemoteConsole
{
        TYPE            icon
        CONTAINER_NAME  Applications
        CONTAINER_TYPE  SUBPANEL
        POSITION_HINTS  4
        ICON            Fpterm
        LABEL           Remote Console
        PUSH_ACTION     DttermRConsole
        HELP_TOPIC      TourSubpanels
        HELP_VOLUME     FPanel
}
```

Note that this is only an example to illustrate creating a **CONTROL** object. The application that is called when the icon is clicked (DttermRConsole) does not exist.

To create a new control for a user account, use the same procedure, but this time create the new **CONTROL** object file in the $HOME/.dt/types directory.

Deleting A Control

Follow these steps to remove an existing control on a systemwide basis:

1. Copy the **CONTROL** object from the /usr/dt/appconfig/types/C/ dtwm.fp file to a file under the /etc/dt/appconfig/types/C directory. The file should be named using the name of the control followed by the .fp extension. For example, to remove the Console control from the Applications subpanel, copy the **CONTROL Console** object to the /etc/dt/appconfig/types/C/Console.fp file.

2. Edit the Console.fp file and add "DELETE True" as a keyword and value to the **CONTROL** object, then save the changes.

3. Select Restart Workspace Manager from the Workspace menu.

For example, to delete the Console control from the Applications subpanel, the /etc/dt/appconfig/types/C/Console.fp file should look similar to the following:

```
CONTROL Console
{
        CONTAINER_NAME  Applications
        CONTAINER_TYPE  SUBPANEL
        DELETE          True
}
```

Note that when deleting a control, it is not necessary to define the entire **CONTROL** object. At a minimum, the **CONTAINER_NAME** and **CONTAINER_TYPE** must be defined.

To delete a control for a user account, use the same procedure, but this time copy the **CONTROL** object to the $HOME/.dt/types directory.

In all the procedures for modifying, adding, and deleting both subpanels and controls, the /usr/dt/appconfig/types /C/dtwm.fp file has been used as the source for obtaining information. This is the default Front Panel configuration. If the Front Panel has been customized for the system using the /etc/dt/appconfig/types/C/dtwm.fp file, this configuration file under /etc should be used instead as the source for information.

Modifying The Workspace Switch

Like the box portion of the panel and the subpanels, the Workspace Switch can be modified by changing the **SWITCH** object named Switch or the **CONTROL** objects placed in the **SWITCH** container.

However, the number of workspaces is defined in the sys.dtwmrc file as part of the Workspace Manager configuration. For each defined workspace, a **CONTROL** object to select each workspace should be included in the **SWITCH** container.

Practice Questions

Question 1

Enter the name of the CDE Login Manager command.

The correct answer is **dtlogin**.

Question 2

Enter the name of the file used to execute commands when the user starts a CDE session.

The correct answer is sessionetc.

Question 3

What is the name of the default Front Panel configuration file?

○ a. /etc/dt/appconfig/config.fp

○ b. /usr/dt/appconfig/types/C/dtwm.fp

○ c. /usr/dt/config/dtwm.fp

○ d. /etc/dt/config/C/config.fp

The correct answer is b. None of the other files exist.

Question 4

Name the file under the .dt/sessions directory of the user's home directory that contains the command to be executed when the user exits the session.

The correct answer is sessionexit.

Question 5

Which of the following files will the Login Manager use to obtain its configuration? [Select all that apply]

- ❑ a. /etc/dt/Xconfig
- ❑ b. /etc/dt/config/Xconfig
- ❑ c. /usr/dt/config/Xconfig
- ❑ d. /usr/dt/Xconfig

The correct answers are b and c. /etc/dt/config/Xconfig will be used initially, and /usr/dt/config/Xconfig will be used if the /etc/dt/config/Xconfig file does not exist. Answers a and d do not exist.

Question 6

Which of the following directories contain scripts executed by the Session Manager? [Select all that apply]

- ❑ a. /etc/config/C
- ❑ b. /etc/dt/config/Xsession.d
- ❑ c. /usr/dt/config/Xsession.d
- ❑ d. User's home directory
- ❑ e. /usr/config/C

The correct answers are b, c, and d. Answers a and e do not exist.

Question 7

Which of the following is not a type of Front Panel container?

- ○ a. Box
- ○ b. Switch
- ○ c. Subpanel
- ○ d. Control

The correct answer is d. Controls are placed in the box, the switch, or a subpanel. When a subpanel is attached to the main panel, the name of a control is specified in the place of a container; however, it is not a container.

Question 8

Which of the following are Login Manager–related configuration files? [Select all that apply]

❏ a. Xconfig

❏ b. Xaccess

❏ c. Xservers

❏ d. Xlogins

❏ e. Xresources

Answers a, b, c, and e are correct. Answer d does not exist.

Question 9

Which Workspace Manager menu item must be selected after a change has been made to the Front Panel configuration?

○ a. Update Workspace Menu

○ b. Customize Menu

○ c. Restart Workspace Manager

The correct answer is c. Answers a and b are used to modify the Workspace menu, not the Front Panel.

Need To Know More?

Sun Microsystems, *Solaris Common Desktop Environment: Advanced User's and System Administrator's Guide*, is available in printed form (ISBN 805-3900-10), on the Web at **docs.sun.com**, and from the online documentation, AnswerBook2, provided with the Solaris 7 operating system.

Sun Microsystems, *Solaris Common Desktop Environment: User's Guide*, is available in printed form (ISBN 805-3899-10), on the Web at **docs.sun.com**, and from the online documentation, AnswerBook2, provided with the Solaris 7 operating system.

Sun Microsystems, *Solaris Common Desktop Environment: User's Transition Guide*, is available in printed form (ISBN 805-3903-10), on the Web at **docs.sun.com**, and from the online documentation, AnswerBook2, provided with the Solaris 7 operating system.

Sample Test II

This chapter provides 94 questions on the topics that pertain to Exam 310-010, "Certified Solaris Administrator Examination for Solaris 7." This exam must be completed in 120 minutes.

Keep in mind that to become certified, you must pass both the 310-009 exam and this one. The sample test for the other exam is in Chapter 11. See that chapter for test-taking tips, as well.

Practice Questions

Question 1

Enter the name of the command used to control the Login Server.

_____

Question 2

Which of the following virtual devices or RAID levels does the DiskSuite support? [Select all that apply]

❑ a. Concatenated virtual device

❑ b. RAID level 0

❑ c. RAID level 1

❑ d. RAID level 5

❑ e. RAID level 10

Question 3

Which of the following information is displayed by the **whodo** command? [Select all that apply]

❑ a. Login accounts

❑ b. Controlling terminals

❑ c. Process IDs

❑ d. Process names

Question 4

Which of the following commands is used to set up a system to be installed over the network?

- ○ a. **setup_network_client**
- ○ b. **network_install**
- ○ c. **add_install_client**
- ○ d. **install_network_client**

Question 5

Which of the following /etc/nsswitch.conf file entries would cause DNS, then NIS+, followed by the /etc files to be searched when trying to resolve a hostname?

- ○ a. hosts: dns nisplus files
- ○ b. hosts: files nisplus dns
- ○ c. ipaddress: file nisplus dns
- ○ d. ipaddress: dns nisplus files

Question 6

Which of the following hard disk sizes can be used in an AutoClient? [Select all that apply]

- ❏ a. 100MB
- ❏ b. 50MB
- ❏ c. 250MB
- ❏ d. 3GB

Question 7

Which of the following commands can be used to mount the /export/home file system from the solaris system (IP address of 192.168.39.7) on the /mnt mount point? [Select all that apply]

☐ a. **mount solaris:/export/home /mnt**

☐ b. **mount 192.168.39.7:/export/home /mnt**

☐ c. **mount -F nfs solaris:/export/home /mnt**

☐ d. **mount -F nfs -o soft,retry=1000,ro 192.168.39.7:/export /home /mnt**

Question 8

Which of the following information is displayed by the **last** command? [Select all that apply]

☐ a. Login accounts

☐ b. Login terminals

☐ c. Date and time of login

☐ d. Date and time of logout

☐ e. Process IDs

Question 9

Which of the following modem access modes result in a modem being configured to answer an incoming call and to negotiate with the originating modem on the other end to establish a connection? [Select all that apply]

☐ a. Inbound

☐ b. Outbound

☐ c. Bidirectional

Question 10

Which of the following is a reason to set up a boot server on a separate system from an install server?

- ○ a. A boot server cannot reside on an install server.
- ○ b. One or more install clients are not on the same subnet as the install server.
- ○ c. All install clients are not on the same subnet.
- ○ d. NIS or NIS+ cannot locate a boot server that resides on an install server.

Question 11

Which of the following are virtual file system managers? [Select all that apply]

- ❑ a. Volume Manager
- ❑ b. File System Manager
- ❑ c. DiskSuite
- ❑ d. **format** command
- ❑ e. Disk Manager

Question 12

Which of the following types of system configuration would generate the most network traffic?

- ○ a. AutoClient
- ○ b. Diskless
- ○ c. Networked standalone
- ○ d. Nonnetworked standalone

Question 13

Enter the name of the file used to execute commands when the user starts a CDE session.

_____

Question 14

Which of the following can be considered Data Communication Equipment (DCE)? [Select all that apply]

❑ a. Modem

❑ b. Computer

❑ c. Terminal

❑ d. Access point to a network

❑ e. Parallel port

Question 15

An OS service is identified by OS release, platform, and what?

_____

Question 16

Which of the following commands is used to propagate an updated NIS map to NIS slave servers?

○ a. **yppush**

○ b. **ypupdate**

○ c. **yppropagate**

○ d. **ypxfr**

○ e. **ypmaps**

Question 17

What is the name of the default session resources file?

○ a. /etc/dt/config/sys.resources

○ b. /usr/dt/appconfig/types/C/sys.resources

○ c. /usr/dt/config/C/sys.resources

○ d. /etc/dt/config/sys.resources

Question 18

/home (or /export/home) is a local file system on which of the following system types? [Select all that apply]

- ❏ a. Diskless client
- ❏ b. OS server
- ❏ c. AutoClient
- ❏ d. Standalone system

Question 19

Enter the name of the directory found under the .dt directory of the user's home directory that is used for modifying the Front Panel.

_____

Question 20

Which of the following files will the Workspace Manager use to obtain its configuration?

- ○ a. /etc/dt/sys.dtwmrc
- ○ b. /etc/dt/config/sys.dtwmrc
- ○ c. /usr/dt/config/C/sys.dtwmrc
- ○ d. /usr/dt/config/sys.dtwmrc

Question 21

Where is CacheFS used—on the NFS server or on the NFS client?

_____

Question 22

Which of the following AdminSuite tools is used to convert an AutoClient to a standalone system?

○ a. Host Manager

○ b. Database Manager

○ c. Group Manager

○ d. Printer Manager

Question 23

Enter the name of the command (without command line arguments) used to add install client information to an install or a boot server.

_____

Question 24

Which of the following commands could be used to execute the **who** command on the remote system "there"?

○ a. **rsh there who**

○ b. **rsh who@there**

○ c. **rsh who there**

○ d. **rsh -c who -s there**

Question 25

Which of the following steps are *not* used to add a new NIS map? [Select all that apply]

❑ a. Create a text file with the appropriate information

❑ b. Use the **make** command

❑ c. Use the **makedbm** command

❑ d. Use the **yppush** command

Question 26

Which of the following types of network clients have a disk? [Select all that apply]

- ❑ a. Dataless
- ❑ b. Diskless
- ❑ c. AutoClient

Question 27

Which of the following are valid entries for an AutoFS direct map? [Select all that apply]

- ❑ a. /usr/local/bin nfsserver:/usr/local/bin
- ❑ b. /usr/games -ro nfsserver:/usr/games
- ❑ c. /usr/bin nfsserver1:/usr/bin nfsserver2:/usr/bin
- ❑ d. /- nfsserver:/usr/data
- ❑ e. /usr/data nfsserver:/usr/data -ro

Question 28

Identify the prefix used with most of the commands associated with the Volume Manager command line interface.

_____

Question 29

Which of the following are features of a virtual disk management system? [Select all that apply]

- ❑ a. Graphical administration tool
- ❑ b. Improved reliability
- ❑ c. Improved performance
- ❑ d. Overcomes physical disk limitations

Question 30

Which of the following commands could be used to copy the "data" file to the remote system "remote"?

O a. **rcp data remote**

O b. **rcp data remote:/tmp**

O c. **rcp -f data -s remote**

O d. **rcp data@remote**

Question 31

Which of the following are fields in a custom JumpStart rules file? [Select all that apply]

❑ a. Rule keyword

❑ b. Rule value

❑ c. Begin script

❑ d. Profile script

❑ e. End script

Question 32

Which type of network client requires a 100MB (minimum) hard disk?

_____

Question 33

Which of the following functions can be performed using the AdminSuite Host Manager?

O a. Mounting a local hard disk

O b. Editing any NIS+ table

O c. Adding support for a network client

O d. Booting a network client

Question 34

Identify the file that contains the definition of host systems that can be accessed via the **tip** command.

_____

Question 35

Which of the following situations do not require the **automount** command to be executed manually? [Select all that apply]

❑ a. Addition to auto_master

❑ b. Addition to direct map

❑ c. Addition to indirect map

❑ d. Deletion from auto_master

❑ e. Deletion from direct map

❑ f. Deletion from indirect map

Question 36

Which of the following information is displayed by the **logins** command? [Select all that apply]

❑ a. Login accounts

❑ b. User IDs

❑ c. Login shells

❑ d. Group IDs

❑ e. Contents of the comment field from the /etc/passwd file

❑ f. Group names

Question 37

Which of the following files controls the appearance of the login screen?

○ a. Xresources

○ b. Xaccess

○ c. Xlogin

○ d. Xconfig

○ e. Xwindow

Question 38

Which of the following information does the **finger** command display? [Select all that apply]

❑ a. User account

❑ b. Terminal

❑ c. Login time

❑ d. Logout time

Question 39

Enter the name of the AdminSuite tool used to view mount point and disk slice information.

_____

Question 40

Which of the following commands is used to start the **ypbind** program?

○ a. **ypinit**

○ b. **ypstop**

○ c. **ypstart**

○ d. **ypcrank**

○ e. **ypwhich**

Question 41

Which of the following is the default source facility for syslog messages if a source is not specified?

○ a. mail

○ b. auth

○ c. user

○ d. kern

Question 42

What are the files that NIS+ uses to store the information that NIS+ clients request collectively referred to as?

_____

Question 43

Which of the following **cfsadmin** command line arguments are required to create a CacheFS configuration? [Select all that apply]

❑ a. NFS server name and resource

❑ b. **-c**

❑ c. **-o**

❑ d. Full pathname of cache directory

❑ e. Name of local host

Question 44

Which of the following AdminSuite tools is used to add a user account to a group?

○ a. Host Manager

○ b. Group Manager

○ c. User Manager

○ d. Database Manager

Question 45

Which of the following are interactive installation methods? [Select all that apply]

- ❑ a. SunInstall
- ❑ b. Custom JumpStart
- ❑ c. WebStart
- ❑ d. JumpStart

Question 46

Which of the following is considered a lower-level SAF process or program? [Select all that apply]

- ❑ a. **sac**
- ❑ b. **ttymon**
- ❑ c. **listen**
- ❑ d. **sacadm**

Question 47

Enter the name of the command to control the enabling and disabling of port monitors.

_____

Question 48

Which of the following are valid command line arguments for the **who** command? [Select all that apply]

- ❑ a. **-H** (displays headings above the output columns)
- ❑ b. **-q** (displays only account names and number of accounts)
- ❑ c. **-i** (displays accounts that are idle)
- ❑ d. **-g _group_** (displays login accounts that are a member of the specified group)

Question 49

Which of the following naming services uses ASCII text files, supports hostname-to-IP-address resolution and IP-address-to-hostname resolution, and is used on the Internet?

○ a. NIS

○ b. NIS+

○ c. DNS

○ d. /etc files

Question 50

Which of the following manages the Front Panel?

○ a. Login Server

○ b. Workspace Manager

○ c. Session Manager

○ d. Front Panel Manager

Question 51

Which of the following is a name for a virtual file system that is composed of several partitions that are allocated and used in an interleaved fashion?

○ a. RAID 1

○ b. Striped

○ c. Concatenated

○ d. Hot spare

Question 52

Which of the following are valid actions that can be specified in the /etc/syslog.conf file? [Select all that apply]

❑ a. The name of a file

❑ b. An exclamation mark (!)

❑ c. The name of a host

❑ d. The name of a user account

Question 53

Which of the following commands can be used to determine shared NFS resources? [Select all that apply]

❑ a. **share**

❑ b. **dfmounts**

❑ c. **dfshares**

❑ d. **mountall**

❑ e. **mount**

Question 54

Which of the following AdminSuite tools is used to view mount points?

○ a. Volume Manager

○ b. Disk Manager

○ c. Mount Manager

○ d. Partition Manager

○ e. File System Manager

Question 55

Which of the following files does the **ttymon** command use to determine the services that should be provided?

○ a. _pmtab

○ b. _sactab

○ c. _sysconfig

○ d. /etc/saf/pmconfig

Question 56

Identify the file used by Custom JumpStart installation to define which profile a system or group of systems should use for installation.

_____

Question 57

Identify one of the two standard serial devices supported by the Solaris 7 operating system.

_____

Question 58

Enter the word used to describe the technique of writing data across multiple disks to improve performance and to overcome disk limitations.

_____

Question 59

Identify the command used to list a description of login accounts.

_____

Question 60

Identify the command used to make an NFS resource unavailable for mounting.

_____

Question 61

Enter the name of a method to restrict operations on NIS+ resources once a user has gained access.

_____

Question 62

Which types of network clients have any local swap space? [Select all that apply]

❑ a. Dataless

❑ b. Diskless

❑ c. AutoClient

Question 63

The Solaris 7 operating system supports five types of name services. Four of these are /etc files, DNS, NIS, and NIS+. Enter the name of the fifth name service.

_____

Question 64

Which of the following is the most severe level of syslog message?

○ a. alert

○ b. notice

○ c. emerg

○ d. crit

Question 65

Which of the following commands is used to configure an NIS master?

○ a. **ypinit -m**

○ b. **ypinit -c**

○ c. **ypinit -s**

○ d. **nisclient**

○ e. **nisinit -c**

Question 66

Which file is used to automatically mount NFS resources during system boot or when the **mountall** command is used?

○ a. /etc/dfs/dfstab

○ b. /etc/vfstab

○ c. /etc/mnttab

○ d. /etc/dfs/sharetab

Question 67

Which of the following directories are used for CDE configuration files? [Select all that apply]

❏ a. /usr/dt/config

❏ b. /usr/dt/config/C

❏ c. /usr/dt/config/Xsession.d

❏ d. /usr/dt/appconfig/types/C

❏ e. /etc/dt/config

Question 68

Which of the following pathnames is associated with the Volume Manager?

○ a. /dev/dsk

○ b. /dev/vx/dsk

○ c. /dev/md/dsk

○ d. /dev/ds/dsk

Question 69

Identify the name of the NIS+ table that contains the Ethernet addresses of systems in the domain.

_____

Question 70

AdminSuite consists of seven tools. Six of these are Printer Manager, Host Manager, User Manager, Group Manager, Storage Manager, and Serial Port Manager. Name the seventh tool.

_____

Question 71

Which command is used to add support to an OS server for a diskless client?

○ a. **admhostadd -x client=DISKLESS**

○ b. **admhostadd -x type=NODISK**

○ c. **admhostadd -x type=DISKLESS**

Question 72

Which /etc file contains a list of the servers (and paths) that provide boot, root, and swap areas for network clients?

○ a. bootparams

○ b. ethers

○ c. timezone

○ d. hosts

○ e. vfstab

Question 73

Identify the NFS-related protocol that can be used to access NFS resources using a Web browser.

_____

Question 74

Which of the following commands is used to check and repair a file system?

○ a. **mount**

○ b. **newfs**

○ c. **fsck**

○ d. **format**

Question 75

From which of the following system run levels will the **sac** program be started? [Select all that apply]

❑ a. 0

❑ b. s

❑ c. 2

❑ d. 3

❑ e. 6

Question 76

Which of the following are Solaris 7 software groups? [Select all that apply]

- ❑ a. Entire Distribution
- ❑ b. Entire Distribution Plus OEM System Support
- ❑ c. End User Support
- ❑ d. Developer System Support

Question 77

Name the collection of graphical tools that includes the Host Manager.

_____

Question 78

Which Front Panel keyword and value is used to remove a control or subpanel from the Front Panel configuration?

- ○ a. **REMOVE object**
- ○ b. **REMOVE true**
- ○ c. **DELETE object**
- ○ d. **DELETE true**

Question 79

Enter the name of the AdminSuite command line equivalent used to delete an OS service from an OS server.

_____

Question 80

Identify the name of the AdminSuite manager that can be used to modify the serial port settings.

_____

Question 81

Which of the following is included with Volume Manager but not Disk Suite? [Select all that apply]

❏ a. Graphical administration tool

❏ b. Command line utilities

❏ c. Performance analysis tools

❏ d. Dynamic online tuning

Question 82

Enter the command line argument used with the **setup_install_server** command to set up a boot server.

_____

Question 83

Enter the name of the file used to configure the syslog facility.

_____

Question 84

Which of the following configurations can be set up using the **admintool** command? [Select all that apply]

❏ a. Inbound modem

❏ b. Outbound modem

❏ c. Bidirectional modem

❏ d. Hardwired terminal

Question 85

Which of the following is not a tool provided with AdminSuite?

○ a. Database Manager

○ b. Storage Manager

○ c. Network Client Manager

○ d. Serial Port Manager

Question 86

Which file should always contain the currently shared NFS resources?

○ a. /etc/nfs/nfstab

○ b. /etc/nfs/shares

○ c. /etc/dfs/dfstab

○ d. /etc/dfs/sharetab

Question 87

Which of the following pathnames is associated with standard Solaris file systems?

○ a. /dev/dsk

○ b. /dev/vx/dsk

○ c. /dev/md/dsk

○ d. /dev/ds/dsk

Question 88

Identify the facility used to capture and log messages from system components and user programs.

_____

Question 89

Which of the following programs can be used to set up an OS server? [Select all that apply]

❑ a. AdminSuite

❑ b. DiskSuite

❑ c. Volume Manager

❑ d. Admintool

Question 90

Which of the following commands are used to access remote systems? [Select all that apply]

❑ a. **rcp**

❑ b. **rsh**

❑ c. **telnet**

❑ d. **rlogin**

Question 91

Which of the following fields must be defined in a custom JumpStart rules file? [Select all that apply]

❑ a. Rule keyword

❑ b. Rule value

❑ c. Begin script

❑ d. Profile script

❑ e. End script

Question 92

Enter the type of network client that Sun plans to discontinue supporting.

_____

Question 93

Which of the following functions can be performed using the AdminSuite
Database Manager?

- ❑ a. View time zone data
- ❑ b. Edit ethers data
- ❑ c. Edit host IP addresses
- ❑ d. View group data

Question 94

Identify the file that contains phone numbers for host systems that can be
accessed via the **tip** command.

_____

Answer Key II

1. **dtconfig**
2. a, b, c, d
3. a, b, c, d
4. c
5. a
6. a, c, d
7. a, b, c, d
8. a, b, c, d
9. a, c
10. b
11. a, c
12. b
13. sessionetc
14. a, d
15. architecture
16. a
17. c
18. b, d
19. types
20. c
21. NFS client
22. a
23. **add_install_ client**
24. a

25. b, d
26. a, c
27. a, b, c
28. **vx**
29. a, b, c, d
30. b
31. a, b, c, d, e
32. AutoClient
33. c
34. /etc/remote
35. c, f
36. a, b, d, e, f
37. a
38. a, b, c
39. Storage Manager
40. c
41. c
42. tables
43. b, d
44. b
45. a, c
46. b, c
47. **sacadm**
48. a, b

49. c
50. b
51. b
52. a, c, d
53. a, c
54. e
55. a
56. rules
57. /dev/term/a or /dev/term/b
58. striping
59. **logins**
60. **unshare**
61. authorization
62. a, c
63. FNS
64. c
65. a
66. b
67. a, b, c, d, e
68. b
69. ethers
70. Database Manager
71. c

72. a
73. WebNFS
74. c
75. c, d
76. a, b, c, d
77. AdminSuite
78. d
79. **admhostdel**
80. Serial Port Manager
81. c, d
82. **-b**
83. /etc/syslog.conf
84. a, b, c, d
85. c
86. d
87. a
88. syslog or syslogd
89. a
90. a, b, c, d
91. a, b, d
92. Dataless client
93. a, b, c, d
94. /etc/phones

Question 1

The correct answer is **dtconfig**.

Question 2

Answers a, b, c, and d are correct. DiskSuite does not support RAID level 10.

Question 3

All the answers are correct. The **whodo** command displays a listing of active processes that consist of the controlling terminal, the process ID, and the process name. This process listing is grouped by login account so that you can easily determine which processes each account is running.

Question 4

The correct answer is c, **add_install_client**. None of the other answers exist.

Question 5

The correct answer is a. hosts: files nisplus dns has all the name services, but in the incorrect order. The search order is left to right; therefore, answer b is incorrect. Answers c and d use an invalid keyword (ipaddress) and therefore are incorrect.

Question 6

The correct answers are a, c, and d. Answer b is incorrect because an AutoClient requires a minimum of 100MB hard disk. Answers c and d are correct, but the extra storage space beyond 100MB may not be used.

Question 7

All the answers are correct. The system sharing an NFS resource can be identified by either hostname or IP address. If the file system type is not specified using the -F command line argument, NFS is assumed. NFS-specific options can be specified using the -o command line argument.

Question 8

Answers a, b, c, and d are correct. Each entry consists of a login account, login terminal, date and time of login, and date and time of logout (or, if the user is still logged in, the phrase "still logged in"). No information regarding processes is displayed. Therefore, answer e is incorrect.

Question 9

The correct answers are a and c. Inbound and bidirectional both support incoming calls. Answers b only supports outgoing calls.

Question 10

The correct answer is b. Answer a is incorrect because a boot server can reside on an install server. Answer c is incorrect because the location of clients in relation to other clients does not determine the need for boot servers. It is the location of the clients in relation to the install server that determines the need for a separate boot server. Answer d is incorrect because NIS and NIS+ do not locate things but serve only as a database of information.

Question 11

The correct answers are a and c. The File System Manager and Disk Manager are disk management tools provided with AdminSuite, but they do not support virtual file systems. Therefore, answers b and e are incorrect. Likewise, the **format** command does not support virtual file systems. Therefore, answer d is incorrect.

Question 12

The correct answer is b. Because the diskless configuration requires everything, including swap space, to be accessed via the network, this configuration generates the most network traffic. AutoClients cache root and /usr along with providing their own swap space. Therefore, answer a is incorrect. Standalone systems access all necessary data from local hard disks. Therefore, answers c and d are incorrect.

Question 13

The correct answer is sessionetc.

Question 14

The correct answers are a and d. Answers b, c, and e are types of Data Termination Equipment (DTE).

Question 15

The correct answer is architecture.

Question 16

The correct answer is a. Answer d is used to propagate a new map. Answers b, c, and e do not exist.

Question 17

The correct answer is c. None of the other files exist.

Question 18

Answers b and d are correct. Standalone systems have local file systems, including /export/home. Both diskless clients and AutoClients access /home remotely from an OS server. Therefore, answers a and c are incorrect.

Question 19

The correct answer is types.

Question 20

The correct answer is c. None of the other files exist.

Question 21

The correct answer is NFS client.

Question 22

The correct answer is a. The Database Manager is used to view and modify data in the /etc files, NIS maps, or NIS+ tables. Therefore, answer b is incorrect. The Group Manager is used to view and modify group accounts. Therefore, answer c is incorrect. The Printer Manager is used to view and modify printer configurations. Therefore, answer d is incorrect.

Question 23

The correct answer is **add_install_client**.

Question 24

The correct answer is a. The name of the remote system is specified as a separate command line argument before the name of the command to execute. Therefore, answers b, c, and d are incorrect.

Question 25

The correct answers are b and d. The **make** command is used when updating a default map. The **yypush** command is used for propagating an updated nondefault map. Answer a is incorrect because the text file is used to add a new map. Likewise, the **makedbm** command is used for new maps. Therefore, answer c is incorrect.

Question 26

Answers a and c are correct. Answer b does not have a disk.

Question 27

The correct answers are a, b, and c. If more than one NFS server provides the same resource, as in answer c, multiple servers can be listed (separated by spaces). The first available resource is used. /- nfsserver:/usr/data does not provide a valid mount point. Therefore, answer d is incorrect. The format for a direct map entry is mount point, options, and then resource. The format of answer e is mount point, resource, and then options. Therefore, answer e is incorrect.

Question 28

The correct answer is **vx**.

Question 29

All the answers are correct. Virtual disk management systems provide all these features.

Question 30

The correct answer is b. The name of the file is specified as a separate command line argument before the name of the remote system and the target directory on the remote system. The remote system and target directory are separated by a colon. None of the other answers use this syntax. Therefore, answers a, c, and d are incorrect.

Question 31

All the answers are correct. A rules entry consists of one or more rule keywords and rule values followed by the name of a begin script and then a profile script and an end script. If the begin script or end script is not specified, a hyphen (-) is used in place of the script name.

Question 32

The correct answer is AutoClient.

Question 33

The correct answer is c. The Host Manager cannot be used to mount a disk. Therefore, answer a is incorrect. It also cannot edit any NIS+ table or boot a network client. Therefore, answers b and d are also incorrect.

Question 34

The correct answer is /etc/remote.

Question 35

Answers c and f are correct. Changes to indirect maps do not require running the **automount** command. Changes to the auto_master and direct maps require that the **automount** command be executed manually. Therefore, answers a, b, d, and e are incorrect.

Question 36

Answers a, b, d, e, and f are correct. The **logins** command displays entries that consist of the login account, user ID, group name, group ID, and comment field. The login shell is not displayed. Therefore, answer c is incorrect.

Question 37

Answer a is correct. Xaccess controls the access to the Login Server. Therefore, answer b is incorrect. Xconfig controls the configuration of the Login Server. Therefore, answer d is incorrect. Answers c and e do not exist.

Question 38

Answers a, b, and c are correct. The **finger** command displays information about logged-in users. Therefore, answer d is incorrect.

Question 39

The correct answer is Storage Manager. The Storage Manager consists of the Disk Manager, which is used to view disk slice information, and the File System Manager, which is used to view mount point information.

Question 40

The correct answer is c. **ypinit** is used to initialize NIS servers and clients. Therefore, answer a is incorrect. **ypstop** is used to stop the **ypbind** program. Therefore, answer b is incorrect. **ypcrank** does not exist. Therefore, answer d is incorrect. **ypwhich** is used to identify the NIS server. Therefore, answer e is incorrect.

Question 41

The correct answer is c. user is used for messages from user programs. mail is used for messages related to mail. Therefore, answer a is incorrect. auth is used for messages related to login authentication. Therefore, answer b is incorrect. kern is used for messages related to the kernel. Therefore, answer d is incorrect. If a source is not specified, user is assumed.

Question 42

The correct answer is tables.

Question 43

The correct answers are b and d. The NFS server name and resource, along with the name of the local host, cannot be specified using a command line argument. Therefore, answers a and e are incorrect. The -o command line argument can be used to specify options but is not required. Therefore, answer c is incorrect.

Question 44

The correct answer is b. Host Manager is used to modify information about systems. Therefore, answer a is incorrect. User Manager is used to view and modify information regarding user accounts. Therefore, answer c is incorrect. Database Manager is used to modify information in /etc files, NIS maps, or NIS+ tables. Therefore, answer d is incorrect.

Question 45

The correct answers are a and c. Custom JumpStart and JumpStart are automatic installation methods. Therefore, answers b and d are incorrect.

Question 46

The correct answers are b and c. **sac** is the top-level SAF program. Therefore, answer a is incorrect. **sacadm** is not considered part of the two-level SAF but is a command used to configure the lower-level SAF programs. Therefore, answer d is incorrect.

Question 47

The correct answer is **sacadm**.

Question 48

The correct answers are a and b. Answers c and d do not exist.

Question 49

The correct answer is c. Although some of the name services use ASCII files and/or provide both hostname and IP address resolution, DNS is the only one used on the Internet. Therefore, answers a, b, and d are incorrect.

Question 50

The correct answer is b. The Front Panel is part of the workspace. The Login Server controls the login process. Therefore, answer a is incorrect. The Session Manager manages the setup of the session. Therefore, answer c is incorrect. The Front Panel Manager does not exist. Therefore, answer d is incorrect.

Question 51

The correct answer is b. RAID 1 is a configuration that uses mirroring in an identical (not interleaved) fashion. Therefore, answer a is incorrect. A concatenated virtual file system uses one partition at a time. Therefore, answer c is incorrect. Hot spare is not a type of virtual file system. Therefore, answer d is incorrect.

Question 52

The correct answers are a, c, and d. If a file name is specified, the message is appended to the file. If a hostname is specified, the message is sent to the host. If a user account name is specified, the message is displayed on the standard output of the logged-in user. The only other valid action is an asterisk (*), which causes the message to be displayed on the standard output device of all logged-in user accounts. Therefore, answer b is incorrect.

Question 53

The correct answers are a and c. The **share** command, used without arguments, lists all locally shared NFS resources. The **dfshares** command can be used to list locally or remotely shared resources. The **dfmounts** command is used to list locally or remotely mounted resources. Therefore, answer b is incorrect. The **mountall** command is used to mount local file systems. Therefore, answer d is incorrect. The **mount** command is used to mount or list currently mounted local file systems and NFS resources. Therefore, answer e is incorrect.

Question 54

The correct answer is e. Volume Manager is not an AdminSuite Tool. Therefore, answer a is incorrect. Disk Manager is used to manage disk partitions. Therefore, answer b is incorrect. Mount Manager and Partition Manager do not exist. Therefore, answers c and d are incorrect.

Question 55

The correct answer is a. _sactab defines the port monitors to be started. Therefore, answer b is incorrect. _sysconfig is used to define configuration parameters that control the behavior of the **sac** command. Therefore, answer c is incorrect. Answer d is incorrect because it does not exist.

Question 56

The correct answer is rules.

Question 57

The correct answer is either /dev/term/a or /dev/term/b.

Question 58

The correct answer is striping.

Question 59

The correct answer is **logins**.

Question 60

The correct answer is **unshare**.

Question 61

The correct answer is authorization.

Question 62

The correct answers are a and c. The diskless client does not have a disk; therefore, it cannot have local swap space. So answer b is incorrect.

Question 63

The correct answer is FNS.

Question 64

The correct answer is c. The rank order of severity levels is emerg, alert, crit, err, warning, notice, info, debug, and none.

Question 65

The correct answer is a. Answer b is used to configure a NIS client, and answer c is used to configure a NIS slave server. Answers d and e do not exist.

Question 66

The correct answer is b. The /etc/dfs/dfstab file is used to automatically share NFS resources. Therefore, answer a is incorrect. The /etc/mnttab file lists the currently mounted file systems and NFS resources. Therefore, answer c is incorrect. The /etc/dfs/sharetab file lists the NFS resources currently shared. Therefore, answer d is incorrect.

Question 67

All the answers are correct. Answer a, /usr/dt/config, is used for the default Login Manager configuration files. Answer b, /usr/dt/config/C, is used for the login screen configuration file and the Session Manager resource configuration file. Answer c, /usr/dt/config/Xsession.d, is used for Session Manager scripts. Answer d, /usr/dt/appconfig/types/C, is used for Front Panel configuration files. Answer e, /etc/dt/config, is used for the system wide Login Manager configuration files.

Question 68

The correct answer is b. /dev/dsk is associated with the standard file systems. Therefore, answer a is incorrect. /dev/md/dsk is associated with Disk Suite virtual file systems. Therefore, answer c is incorrect. Answer d does not exist.

Question 69

The correct answer is ethers.

Question 70

The correct answer is Database Manager.

Question 71

The correct answer is c. The **-x type** command line argument is used to identify the type of network client.

Question 72

The correct answer is a. ethers contains network client Ethernet addresses. Therefore, answer b is incorrect. timezone contains network client time zone information. Therefore, answer c is incorrect. hosts contains system hostnames and IP addresses. Therefore, answer d is incorrect. vfstab contains a list of file systems to be mounted automatically. Therefore, answer e is incorrect.

Question 73

The correct answer is WebNFS.

Question 74

The correct answer is c. The **mount** command is used to mount the file system. Therefore, answer a is incorrect. The **newfs** command is used to create a file system after the disk has been formatted. Therefore, answer b is incorrect. The **format** command is used to format a file system. Therefore, answer d is incorrect.

Question 75

The correct answers are c and d. Run level 0 is the power down state. Services are being shut down in this state. Therefore, answer a is incorrect. Run level s is used for administration, and users are not allowed to access the system. Therefore, answer b is incorrect. Run level 6 is the reboot state, and the system is being restarted. Therefore, answer e is incorrect.

Question 76

All the answers are correct. From smallest to largest, they are End User Support, Developer System Support, Entire Distribution, and Entire Distribution Plus OEM System Support.

Question 77

The correct answer is AdminSuite.

Question 78

The correct answer is d. **REMOVE** is an invalid keyword. Therefore, answers a and b are incorrect. **object** is an invalid value. Therefore, answer c is incorrect.

Question 79

The correct answer is **admhostdel**.

Question 80

The correct answer is Serial Port Manager.

Question 81

The correct answers are c and d. Both Volume Manager and Disk Suite provide a graphical administration tool and command line utilities. Therefore, answers a and b are incorrect.

Question 82

The correct answer is **-b**

Question 83

The correct answer is /etc/syslog.conf.

Question 84

All the answers are correct. The **admintool** command can be used to configure a port to answer inbound calls, originate outbound calls, handle both, and support a hardwired connection to a terminal.

Question 85

The correct answer is c. AdminSuite includes a Host Manager that is used to manage network clients, not a Network Client Manager. Database Manager, Storage Manager, and Serial Port Manager all are included in AdminSuite. Therefore, answers a, b, and d are incorrect.

Question 86

The correct answer is d. Answers a and b do not exist. Answer c is the file that contains resources that should be shared automatically during system boot or when the **shareall** command is used.

Question 87

The correct answer is a. /dev/vx/dsk is associated with the Volume Manager virtual file systems. Therefore, answer b is incorrect. /dev/md/dsk is associated with Disk Suite virtual file systems. Therefore, answer c is incorrect. Answer d does not exist.

Question 88

The correct answer is syslog or syslogd.

Question 89

The correct answer is a. DiskSuite and Volume Manager are virtual file system managers and have nothing to do with supporting network clients. Therefore, answers b and c are incorrect. Admintool provides a limited set of system administration capabilities; network client support is not included. Therefore, answer d is incorrect.

Question 90

All the answers are correct. The **rcp** command is used to copy a file to a remote system. The **rsh** command is used to execute a command on the remote system. The **telnet** and **rlogin** commands are used to log in to a remote system.

Question 91

The correct answers are a, b, and d. The begin and end scripts are optional. Therefore, answers c and e are incorrect. If the begin script or end script is not specified, a hyphen (-) is used in place of the script name.

Question 92

The correct answer is dataless client.

Question 93

All the answers are correct. The Database Manager can view and edit data in /etc files, NIS maps, or NIS+ tables.

Question 94

The correct answer is /etc/phones.

Appendix
Configuration Files
And Formats

This appendix provides a quick reference for important system configuration files that should be known not only for the exams but also for Solaris 7 system administration. This includes files relating to account administration, the CDE, the kernel, the LP Print service, name services, and NFS.

Also included in this section are the formats of selected files. These include the account administration files and name service switch.

Configuration Files

Table A.1 Account administration files.

File	Description
/etc/passwd	Information regarding user accounts
/etc/shadow	Information regarding user account passwords
/etc/group	Information regarding group accounts

Table A.2 CDE configuration files.

File	Description
/usr/dt/appconfig/types /C/dtwm.fp	Front Panel configuration file
/usr/dt/config/Xaccess	Login Server access control file
/usr/dt/config/Xconfig	Login Server configuration file
/usr/dt/config/Xservers	Local display configuration file

(continued)

449

Table A.2   CDE configuration files (continued).

File	Description
/usr/dt/config/C/sys.dtwmrc	Workspace Manager configuration file
/usr/dt/config/C/sys.resources	System default session resources
/usr/dt/config/C/Xresources	Login Screen configuration file

Table A.3   DNS configuration files.

File	Description
/etc/named.conf	BIND configuration file that identifies zones over which the DNS server is authoritative and identifies the associated data files
/etc/resolv.conf	When configured as a DNS client, a file that identifies the DNS server that should be used for name resolution
hosts	The DNS address (A type) records used for resolving hostnames to IP addresses (not to be confused with the /etc/hosts file)
host.rev	The DNS pointer (PTR type) records used for resolving IP addresses to hostnames
named.ca	The names and IP addresses of the Internet root DNS servers
named.local	The DNS records for the localhost or the loop-back interface

Table A.4   Kernel configuration files.

Directory Or File	Description
/etc/system	Controls the kernel configuration
/kernel	Directory used for common kernel modules required for booting
/platform/i86pc/kernel	Directory used for modules that are specific to the platform (Intel x86 only)
/platform/sparc/kernel	Directory used for modules that are specific to the platform (SPARC only)
/usr/kernel	Directory used for common kernel modules used by platforms with a particular instruction set

Table A.5   LP Services configuration files.

File	Description
/etc/lp/model/netstandard	Print model for remote printers
/etc/lp/model/standard	Print model for local printers
/usr/share/lib/terminfo	Location of terminfo database

Table A.6   Name Service Switch files.

File	Description
/etc/nsswitch.conf	Name Service Switch configuration file
/etc/nsswitch.files	Template for /etc files configuration
/etc/nsswitch.nis	Template for NIS configuration
/etc/nsswitch.nisplus	Template for NIS+ configuration

Table A.7   NFS configuration files.

File	Description
/etc/dfs/dfstab	NFS resources to be shared automatically on boot or when the **shareall**(1M) command is executed
/etc/dfs/dfstypes	Default type of shared resources (NFS)
/etc/dfs/sharetab	List of NFS resources currently shared
/etc/vfstab	File systems and NFS resources to be mounted automatically on boot or when the **mountall**(1M) command is executed

Table A.8   NIS maps.

Keyword	Maps	Description
aliases	mail.aliases, mail.byaddr	Mail addresses and aliases
bootparams	bootparams	Location of root, swap, and dump partitions for diskless workstations
ethers	ethers.byaddr, ethers.byname	Ethernet addresses of systems
group	group.bygid, group.byname	Group name, group ID (GID), and member information

(continued)

Table A.8   NIS maps (continued).

Keyword	Maps	Description
hosts	hosts.byaddr, hosts.byname	Hostnames and network (IP) addresses
netgroup	netgroup, netgroup.byhost, netgroup.byuser	Network groups and members defined in the domain
netmasks	netmasks.byaddr	Netmasks associated with known networks
networks	networks.byaddr, network.byname	Networks and their associated names
passwd	netid.byname, passwd.adjunct.byname, passwd.byname, passwd.byuid	Password information for user accounts
protocols	protocols.byname, protocols.bynumber	IP protocols used within the domain
rpc	rpc.bynumber	RPC program numbers for RPC services used within the domain
services	services.byname, services.byservice	IP services and their port Inumbers

Table A.9   NIS+ tables.

Table	Description
auto_home	Location of user's home directories
auto_master	AutoFS map information
bootparams	Location of root, swap, and dump partitions for diskless workstations
cred	Credentials for NIS+ principals
ethers	Ethernet addresses of systems
group	Group name, GID, and member information
hosts	Hostnames and network (IP) addresses
mail_aliases	Mail addresses and aliases
netgroup	Network groups and members defined in the domain
netmasks	Netmasks associated with known networks
networks	Networks and their associated names

(continued)

Table A.9   NIS+ tables (continued).

Table	Description
passwd	Password information for user accounts
protocols	IP protocols used within the domain
rpc	RPC program numbers for RPC services used within the domain
services	IP services and their port numbers
timezone	Time zone of workstations in the domain

Table A.10   SAF configuration files.

File	Description
/etc/saf/_sactab	The SAC administrative file used to list the port monitors that should be started
/etc/saf/_sysconfig	The SAC configuration file used to control the behavior of the **sac** command
/etc/saf/*port monitor*/_pmtab	The administrative file for a port monitor that defines the services that should be controlled by the port monitor
/etc/ttydefs	Contains information used to initialize the baud rate and terminal settings for serial ports

Table A.11   TCP/IP configuration files.

File	Description
/etc/inet/hosts	List of IP addresses and hostnames (also /etc/hosts)
/etc/nodename	Default hostname of the local system
/etc/hostname.*interface*	Hostname or IP address assigned to *interface*

Table A.12   tip configuration files.

File	Description
/etc/phones	Phone numbers of remote systems
/etc/remote	Information regarding remote systems accessible using the **tip** command

Formats Of Selected Files

Table A.13   Fields of the /etc/group files.

Field	Purpose
group name	The unique name of the group.
password	The password associated with the group. If a password is present, the **newgrp**(1) command prompts users to enter it.
GID	The unique numeric group identification.
users	A comma-separated list of users that belong to the group.

Table A.14   The /etc/nsswitch.conf information keywords.

Information Keyword	Description
aliases	Mail aliases
automount	Information on the Auto File System (AutoFS) configuration
bootparams	Location of root, swap, and dump partitions for diskless workstations
ethers	Ethernet addresses of systems
group	Group name and member information
hosts	Hostnames and network (IP) addresses
netgroup	Network groups and members defined in the domain
netmasks	Netmasks associated with known networks
networks	Networks and their associated names
passwd	Password information for user accounts
protocols	IP protocols used within the domain
publickey	Public keys used for authentication
rpc	Remote Procedure Call (RPC) program numbers for RPC services used within the domain
sendmailvars	Variables used by the **sendmail**(1M) program
services	Names of IP services and their port numbers

Table A.15   The /etc/nsswitch.conf source keywords.

Source Keyword	Description
compat	Uses old-style syntax for password and group information
dns	Uses DNS to resolve queries
files	Uses /etc files to resolve queries
nis	Uses NIS to resolve queries
nisplus	Uses NIS+ to resolve queries

Table A.16   The /etc/nsswitch.conf search status messages.

Search Status Message	Description
SUCCESS	The requested information was located.
UNAVAIL	The service is not responding.
NOTFOUND	The requested data does not exist.
TRYAGAIN	The service is busy; try again later.

Table A.17   The /etc/nsswitch.conf action keywords.

Action Keyword	Description
continue	Try the next source.
return	Stop looking.

Table A.18   Fields of the /etc/passwd file.

Field	Purpose
user name	The unique name assigned to the user account.
password	In earlier versions of Unix, the password field contained the encrypted account password. For security reasons, the passwords have been moved to the /etc/shadow file. The letter "x" is typically placed in this field to indicate that the password is in /etc/shadow.

(continued)

Table A.18 Fields of the /etc/passwd file (continued).

Field	Purpose
UID	A unique user numeric identification assigned to the user account. Any processes or files created by the user account will be owned by this UID. The system administrator account, root, is assigned the UID of 0. This is the UID of a superuser account. System maintenance accounts are usually assigned a UID of less than 100, whereas user accounts typically start at 1001.
GID	The numeric identification of the default group that the user account has been assigned to as a member. Groups are defined in the /etc/group file.
comment field	Information about the owner of the user account, such as real name, phone number, mailing address, and so on. An ampersand (&) in this field is interpreted as the contents of the Username field.
home directory	The full path to the directory where the user is initially located after logging in.
login shell	The full pathname of the initial shell used as a command interpreter. If empty, the default is /usr/bin/sh.

Table A.19 Fields of the /etc/shadow file.

Field	Purpose
UID	Used to relate the /etc/shadow entry to a user account defined in the /etc/passwd file.
password	A 13-character encrypted password for the associated user account. If the field contains "NP," this account is used only to own processes or files (setuid) and cannot be used to log into the system. If the field contains "*LK*," the account is locked and cannot be used to access the system. If the field is empty, no password exists, and the user is forced to enter a password the first time the account is used.
last changed	The number of days between January 1, 1970, and the last date the password was changed.

(continued)

Table A.19   Fields of the /etc/shadow file (continued).

Field	Purpose
minimum	The minimum number of days required to pass before the user is allowed to change the password again.
maximum	The maximum number of days the password is valid.
warning	The number of days the user is warned before the password expires.
inactivity	The number of days the account can be inactive before the password must be changed.
expiration	The number of days between January 1, 1970, and the date on which the account expires.
flag	Reserved for future use.

Glossary Of Terms

. . . .

absolute file permissions mode—A numeric notation used to represent the standard file permissions for owner, group, and other. The access mode of a file is determined by adding these absolute modes together. The following lists the absolute file permission modes:

➤ 001—Other execution

➤ 002—Other write

➤ 004—Other read

➤ 010—Group execution

➤ 020—Group write

➤ 040—Group read

➤ 100—User execution

➤ 200—User write

➤ 400—User read

Access Control List (ACL)—Solaris 7 extends the standard Unix file permissions by adding an Access Control List capability. ACLs provide the ability to add permissions for specific users and groups along with a default permission (mask). In addition to supporting the standard read/write/execute permission for owner, group, and other, ACLs can be used to set read/write/execute permissions for additional user accounts and group accounts and to define a mask capability that controls the maximum allowed permissions given to user and group accounts. The ACL for a directory includes default entries that determine the permissions assigned to files and subdirectories created under the directory. The **setfacl**(1M) command is used to set ACLs, and the **getfacl**(1M) command is used to display ACLs.

AdminSuite—A collection of graphical tools used to administer a system or several systems. AdminSuite supports several name service environments, including /etc files, NIS, and NIS+. It consists of the Database Manager, Group Manager, Host Manager, Printer Manager, Serial Port Manager, Storage Manager, and User Manager.

Admintool—An administrative tool used to manage user and group accounts, install software packages, and manage printers.

aliasing—The ability of a shell to assign a name or an alias to a set of commands and to use the alias to execute the commands.

architecture—The variation of the platform. For SPARC platforms, this includes types such as sun4c and sun4m.

authentication—A method to restrict access to specific users when accessing a remote system.

authorization—A method to restrict the operations that a user can perform on the remote system once the user has gained access (been authenticated).

AutoClient—A type of network client that uses a small local disk for swap space and a cached copy of the root and user file systems.

AutoFS—A network service and type of file system. AutoFS resources are mounted automatically when an attempt is made to access them and are then unmounted automatically after a period of being idle.

AutoFS map—A file used to configure the AutoFS service. The three types of AutoFS maps are the /etc/auto_master file that identifies other maps, direct maps that identify full pathnames to mount points and associated NFS resources, and indirect maps that identify partial pathnames to mount points and associated NFS resources.

Berkeley Software Distribution (BSD)—The version of the Unix operating system developed by the University of California at Berkeley.

bidirectional modem access—A modem configuration that is a combination of the inbound and outbound configurations. It can answer incoming calls and originate outgoing calls.

boot server—A network server that provides the files necessary to boot an install client over the network during an over-the-network installation. After an install client has booted, the boot server has completed its function. The remainder of the installation is supported by an install server. Typically, an install server and a boot server reside on the same system. However, if install clients are on a different subnet than an install server, a boot server must be set up on the same subnet as the install clients.

Bourne shell—A version of the Unix shell developed by Steven Bourne from AT&T Bell Labs. It is referred to as *sh*. The Bourne shell is the default shell for the Solaris operating system.

box—A container of the Front Panel that contains controls and is located on the main panel to the left and right of the switch.

C shell—A version of the Unix shell developed at the University of California at Berkeley. It is referred to as *csh*.

CacheFS—A storage service and a type of file system. CacheFS is used to locally store a copy of a remote NFS resource. This allows faster access and less network traffic.

client—A networked computer system that uses services provided by a server.

client/server—An operation model used by computer systems where services are centralized on a server and accessed by one or more clients via a network.

Common Desktop Environment (CDE)—The graphical user interface consisting of the login screen, workspaces, and Front Panel.

concatenated striped virtual device—A striped virtual device that has been expanded by concatenating additional slices to the end of the device.

concatenated virtual device—A device consisting of two or more slices. The slices can be on the same physical disk or on several physical disks. The slices also can be of different sizes. The slices are addressed in a sequential manner; that is, as space is needed, it is allocated from the first slice in the concatenation. Once this space is completely used, space is allocated from the second slice, and so on.

crontab files—Files stored under /var/spool/cron/crontabs that specify commands to be executed along with a time and frequency of execution. Commands can be executed daily, weekly, or monthly at any time of the day. A crontab entry consists of six fields separated by spaces or tabs. An asterisk (*) is used as a placeholder in a field that is not used. The following are the fields of a crontab entry:

➤ *minute*—This field specifies the minutes of the hour. The values can be 0–59.

➤ *hour*—This field specifies hours of the day. The values can be 0–23.

➤ *day*—This field specifies the day of the month. The values can be 1–31.

➤ *month*—This field specifies the month of the year. The values can be 1–12.

➤ *weekday*—This field specifies the day of the week. The values can be 0–6 (0=Sunday).

➤ *command*—This field specifies the command to execute.

csh—See **C shell**.

Custom JumpStart—An automated installation method that uses a predefined rules file and one or more profile files to determine the system configuration to install, depending on architecture, equipped hardware, or other defined characteristics. These files are located in the JumpStart Configuration directory.

Data Carrier Detect (DCD)—One of the interchange circuits defined by the RS-232 standard and transmitted on one of the wires in a serial cable. The DCE (typically a modem) will inform the attached DTE that it has detected a carrier signal from the DCE at the other end of the communication path by placing a voltage on (asserting) the DCD circuit. This informs the DTE that the remote device is present and has answered the call (but is not necessarily ready, which is indicated by a different signal).

Data Communication Equipment (DCE)—The most widely used DCE is probably the modulator/demodulator (modem) used for communication through the Public Switched Telephone Network (PSTN), otherwise known as the phone system.

data set—A grouping of data on a magnetic tape.

Data Terminal Equipment (DTE)—The most commonly used DTE devices are terminals and computers. Technically, the serial communication port on the terminal or computer that interfaces to the DCE is considered the DTE, but opinions vary, and most accept either view. Almost every computer made in the last 15 years has at least one serial communication port; most personal computers and desktops have two. These can be used to interface to communication devices such as modems, input devices such as mice, output devices such as printers, and even other computers.

Database Manager—A graphical tool included with AdminSuite that's used to modify the data associated with systems, such as hostnames, IP addresses, Ethernet addresses, time zones, and so on.

dataless client—A type of network client that uses a small local disk for swap space and a root file system. Other file systems are accessed remotely.

default file permissions—When a file is created, a set of default permissions are assigned to it. The default permissions are defined using the **umask(1M)**

command and are typically added to the user's login initialization file to provide a consistent permission mask.

default printer—The printer used for a print request if no printer is specified. The two types of default printers are a *system default printer* and a *user/application-defined default printer.*

device aliases—An OpenBoot feature that allows assigning a short, easy-to-use name to a full physical device pathname.

device driver—Software modules that interface with physical resources and understand how to communicate with hardware devices and control their operation. Typically, each device has a unique driver that is provided with the hardware and identified by hardware manufacturer, model, and sometimes hardware version.

direct map—A type of AutoFS configuration file that identifies the full path to mount points and associated NFS resources.

directory—A folder used to organize files.

disk group—A collection of Volume Manager (VM) disks that share a common configuration.

disk label—See **volume table of contents**.

Disk Manager—A graphical tool used to create and format partitions. One of two tools that compose the AdminSuite Storage Manager.

diskless client—A type of network client that does not have any local storage, so all file systems along with swap space are accessed remotely.

DiskSuite—A virtual disk management system that supports disk mirroring and several RAID configurations.

domain—A group of systems managed as a single entity using a name service such as NIS or NIS+.

Domain Name Service (DNS)—The name service used on the Internet to resolve hostnames to IP addresses and IP addresses to hostnames.

duplexing—The technique of copying data being written to one online device to another, offline device. This provides a realtime backup of data that can be brought online to replace the original device in the event that it fails. Each disk has its own controller.

End Of File (EOF) mark—The mark placed on a magnetic tape to signify the end of a file or set of records.

Enterprise Volume Manager—A virtual disk management system. In addition to supporting disk mirroring and several RAID configurations, it provides statistics and dynamic tuning capability.

/etc files—The original name service provided with the Unix operating system. Information about other systems is stored in files located under the /etc directory.

extended file permissions—See **Access Control List (ACL)**.

Federated Naming Service (FNS)—A name service that conforms to the X/Open Federated Naming Specification (XFN).

field-replaceable unit (FRU)—An AutoClient or diskless client that can be easily replaced.

file—A group of bytes treated as a unit for storage, retrieval, and manipulation.

file access modes—See **standard file permissions**.

file server—A networked standalone system used to provide remote access to shared or common data.

file system—A logical collection of files and directories contained in a partition. It can be treated as a single entity when making it available for use (mounting), checking, and repairing. The following summarizes the default Solaris 7 file systems:

➤ *root (/)*—The top of the hierarchical file system tree; contains critical system files, such as the kernel and device drivers

➤ */usr*—System files, such as commands and programs, for administering and using the system

➤ */home*—User home directories; on some systems, it might be /export/home or a network-based file system

➤ */var*—System files to change or grow, such as logs, queues, and spooling areas

➤ */opt*—Third-party software and applications

➤ */tmp*—Temporary files cleared each time the system boots

➤ */proc*—Information on active processes

file system formats—Disk-based file systems are stored on physical disks, CD-ROMs, and diskettes. The following are the formats of the disk-based file systems:

➤ *HSFS (High Sierra File System)*—The default format for CD-ROM file systems

➤ *PCFS (PC File System)*—The default format for diskette file systems; same as the DOS disk format

➤ *S5 (System V File System)*—An older format used for hard disk file systems

➤ *UFS (Unix File System)*—The default format for hard disk file systems

File System Manager—A graphical tool used to create and manage file systems. One of the two tools that compose the AdminSuite Storage Manager.

Front Panel—A collection of containers and objects (controls) within the containers. The Front Panel is divided into the main panel and subpanels. The main panel is divided into the box and the switch. The box, switch, and subpanels contain controls that are graphical icons or buttons that start applications or display windows.

Front Panel menu—A Workspace menu that provides move, minimize, refresh, and logout control over the Front Panel. To access the Front Panel menu, position the mouse cursor over the upper-left corner of the Front Panel and click the rightmost mouse button.

group account—A unique name and associated group ID used to manage a collection of user accounts.

group ID (GID)—A unique numeric ID assigned to a group account used for group ownership and permissions.

Group Manager—A graphical tool included with AdminSuite that is used to create and modify group accounts.

host—A computer system that provides resources to locally and/or remotely logged-on users.

Host Manager—A graphical tool included with AdminSuite that is used to create and configure OS servers and provide support for network clients.

hostname—A name assigned to a host. To provide interoperability on the Internet, the hostname should conform to RFC 952, DOD Internet Host Table Specification.

hot relocation—The process that the Volume Manager uses to reconstruct a failed subdisk on a spare disk or free space within a disk group and then substitute the rebuilt subdisk for the failed subdisk.

hot spare—A disk slice that DiskSuite automatically substitutes for a slice that has failed.

hot spare pool—A collection of hot spares managed by DiskSuite.

inbound modem access—The modem is configured to answer incoming calls and negotiate with the originating modem to establish a connection. Once a connection is established, a process such as the **login** command or the Unix-To-Unix Copy Protocol (UUCP) uses the connection to perform some operation.

indirect map—A type of AutoFS configuration file that identifies partial pathnames to mount points and associated NFS resources. The partial pathnames are relative to directory identified in the /etc/auto.master file.

initialization file templates—Login and shell startup initialization files for each user account are copied from templates under the /etc/skel directory when the home directory for the user account is created. The following are the available templates:

➤ */etc/skel/local.cshrc*—csh shell startup file

➤ */etc/skel/local.login*—csh login initialization file

➤ */etc/skel/local.profile*—ksh and sh login initialization file

initialization files—Several initialization files are associated with each user account home directory. These files are used to specify commands to be executed when the associated event occurs. Depending on the login shell being used, there might be a login initialization file, a shell startup file, or a logout file. Commands in the login initialization file are executed when the user logs in. All three common shells provide a login initialization file. Commands in the shell startup file are executed whenever the logged-in user starts a shell. Both csh and ksh provide this capability. The ENV parameter is used to define the ksh shell startup initialization file. Only csh provides a file for automatic execution of commands when a user logs out. The following are the various initialization files:

➤ *Login initialization file*—The login initialization file for sh and ksh is .profile. The file for csh is .login.

➤ *Shell startup initialization file*—There is no shell startup file for sh. The shell startup file for csh is .cshrc, and the file for ksh is user-defined.

➤ *Logout file*—There is no logout file for sh or ksh. The logout file for csh is .logout.

install client—A system that will be installed over the network. Basic information about the install clients needs to be available through a name service (NIS/NIS+) or in the files under the /etc directory on the install server or boot server.

install server—A network server that provides the distribution files necessary for the installation of the Solaris operating system on an install client during an over-the-network installation. The files can be provided directly from the Solaris distribution CD mounted in a local CD-ROM drive or from the local hard disk.

installation—The four installation methods are SunInstall, WebStart, JumpStart, and Custom JumpStart. All four methods can use either a local CD-ROM or over-the-network installation resources to obtain the distribution files. The installation process is divided into three phases: system configuration, system installation, and postinstallation.

instance name—Abbreviated names that are mapped to or associated with the physical device names of devices. These allow devices to be quickly and easily identified without requiring the use of the long and typically complicated physical device names. An instance name typically consists of a short driver binding name and an instance number. The mapping of physical device names (also known as *full device pathnames*) with instance names is accomplished using the /etc/path_to_inst file.

interprocess communication—The cooperative communication between processes.

IP address—A unique 32-bit (4-byte or 4-octet) address assigned to a networked computer using the IP addressing scheme as defined by Internet RFC 1700, Assigned Numbers. The IP address consists of four numbers between 0 and 255 and typically is written in dotted decimal notation, such as 192.168.99.27. The IP addresses are grouped into five network classes on the basis of the value of the first octet.

JumpStart—An automated installation process that uses standardized configurations based on system architecture and hardware to determine the system configuration to install.

JumpStart configuration directory—A directory that contains the files used to customize a JumpStart installation. It provides a means to automate the system configuration phase of an installation for groups of similar systems. This directory can reside either on a floppy diskette, referred to as a *profile diskette*, or on a network server, referred to as a *profile server*. The two basic types of files in the JumpStart directory are a rules file and one or more profile files.

kernel—A collection of software that manages the physical and logical resources of a computer. These management services include controlling the allocation of memory and other storage devices, controlling the access to peripheral devices (input/output), and controlling the scheduling and execution of processes or tasks. One of the three parts of an operating system (the other parts are the shell and the file system).

kernel modules—Kernel software divided into groups of related functions. Some modules are part of a small, common core of the operating system, some modules provide platform-specific operations, and other modules are device drivers. This architecture allows portions of the kernel to be included or excluded on the basis of the desired functionality or allows portions of the kernel to be updated without replacing the entire kernel. The device drivers are loaded when the device is accessed.

Korn shell—A version of the Unix shell developed by David Korn from AT&T Bell Labs and referred to as *ksh*. It combines the best features of the Bourne shell and the C shell.

Line Printer (LP) Service—A service that allows users to print files. It provides the ability to add, modify, and delete printer definitions; provides print scheduling; and supports both local and remote printers.

local printer—A printer attached directly to the local system by means of a serial or parallel communication port.

localhost—The loopback IP address for the local system; typically 127.0.0.1, but can be any address starting with 127.

logical device name—A naming convention used to identify disk, tape, and CD-ROM devices and provide either raw access (one character at a time) or block access (via a buffer for accessing large blocks of data). All logical device names reside under the /dev directory, and the /dev/dsk subdirectory identifies the device as a block disk device (the /dev/rdsk subdirectory indicates a raw disk).

Login Manager—A program that displays a login screen, authenticates the user, and starts the user's session. This service can be provided as a locally attached display (a local display) or as an X terminal or workstation on the network (a network display). Also referred to as the *Login Server* or the *Login Manager Server*.

Login Manager Server—See **Login Manager**.

login screen—A graphical window used to prompt for and accept a user account name and password. It is displayed automatically on any local and/or network displays specified in the Xservers file when the Login Server starts. In addition, network displays can request a login screen if they are allowed access per the Xaccess file.

Login Server—See **Login Manager**.

main panel—A container of the Front Panel that is divided into the box and the switch. The box and the switch contain controls that are graphical icons or buttons that start applications or display windows.

memory management—Memory management involves keeping track of available memory, allocating it to processes as needed, and reclaiming it as processes release it or terminate.

metadevice—The basic virtual disk used by DiskSuite to manage physical disks. The following types of metadevices are supported:

➤ *Simple*—Used directly or as a building block for mirror and trans metadevices. (The three types of simple metadevices are stripes, concatenations, and concatenated stripes.)

➤ *Mirror*—Used to replicate data between simple metadevices to provide redundancy.

➤ *RAID5*—Used to replicate data with parity, allowing regeneration of data.

➤ *Trans*—Used for UFS file system logging.

mirroring—The technique of copying data being written to one online device to another, offline device. This provides a realtime backup of data that can be brought online to replace the original device in the event that the original device fails. Typically, the two disks share the same controller.

modem—Converts digital data to and from electrical analog signals. These signals can be transmitted over the PSTN or dedicated lines.

modem access modes—Solaris supports three types of modem access: inbound, outbound, and bidirectional.

mount—The process of associating a file system or NFS resource with a directory (mount point) so that it can be accessed by users and programs.

mount point—A directory in a mounted file system that serves as an access point for another file system.

multitasking—The ability to execute more than one process or task at a time.

multiuser—The ability of a system to support multiple simultaneous users.

name service—A network service that provides a centralized location for information used by users and systems to communicate with each other across the network. The name service not only stores the information but also provides mechanisms to manage and access that information.

name service switch—A configuration file that is used to select which name services to use and in what order.

namespace—A collection of information regarding systems within the domain of a name service.

network classes—The five classes of networks are based on the first octet of the IP address. These are:

➤ *A*—Used for large networks. The first octet is 1–126. The default subnet mask is 255.0.0.0.

➤ *B*—Used for medium networks. The first octet is 128–191. The default subnet mask is 255.255.0.0.

➤ *C*—Used for small networks. The first octet is 192–223. The default subnet mask is 255.255.255.0.

➤ *D*—Used for multicasting. The first octet is 224–239.

➤ *E*—Reserved for future use. The first octet is 240–255.

network client—A system that contains little to no local storage space. Some or all of the necessary files for booting and operation are accessed remotely via the network. The following describes the types of network clients:

➤ *Diskless client*—This has no local swap and no local file systems. The remote file systems are root, /usr, /opt, and /home.

➤ *Dataless client*—This has local swap. The local file system is root and the remote file systems are /usr, /opt, and /home.

➤ *AutoClient*—This has local swap. The local file systems are cached root and cached /usr. The remote file systems are root, /usr, /opt, and /home.

Network File System (NFS)—A network service and type of file system. This service allows local storage, such as file systems, to be accessible by other systems via the network. The version 3 of the NFS protocol is defined by RFC 1813.

Network Information Service (NIS)—A name service that stores information in maps and makes it available to NIS clients that request it.

Network Information Service Plus (NIS+)—An enhanced version of NIS that stores information in tables. Security is provided using authentication and authorization.

NFS client—A system that mounts remote NFS resources made available by NFS servers via the network.

NFS server—A system that shares NFS resources so that they can be accessed via the network.

NIS client—A system configured to use NIS as a name service.

NIS map—A file used by an NIS server to store a particular type of information.

NIS master server—The NIS server that is the master for a domain. It maintains the maps that define the namespace.

NIS slave server—An NIS server that provides redundancy in the event that the NIS master server fails. It obtains copies of the NIS maps from the master server.

NIS+ client—A system configured to use NIS+ as a name service.

NIS+ master server—The NIS+ server that is the master for a domain. It maintains the tables that define the namespace.

NIS+ replica—An NIS+ server that provides redundancy in the event that the NIS+ master server fails. It obtains copies of the NIS+ tables from the NIS+ master server.

NIS+ table—A file used by an NIS+ server to store a particular type of information.

Nonvolatile Random Access Memory (NVRAM)—Area of memory used to store OpenBoot parameters that is not affected by powering down or rebooting the system.

null modem cable—A cable that allows two DTE devices (such as computers) to communicate via serial ports. This is accomplished by cross-wiring the cable so that each DTE appears as a DCE device (or modem) to the other one. This makes it appear as if a modem is being used when actually no (or null) modems are being used.

OpenBoot—The standard firmware for Sun Systems. OpenBoot is used to boot the operating system, run diagnostics, and modify boot-related parameters stored in nonvolatile RAM (NVRAM), and provides a Forth interpreter. OpenBoot firmware pertains only to SPARC platforms, but some limited functionality is available on Intel x86 platforms.

operating system release—The version of an operating system, such as 2.6 or 7 for Solaris.

operating system (OS) server—A network server that provides network clients access to operating system files as required.

operating system (OS) service—A set of files needed to support a particular network client. An OS service is identified and configured for a combination of platform, system architecture, and OS release.

outbound modem access—With the outbound configuration, the modem is configured to originate an outgoing call on behalf of a service. An outbound configuration can be used to connect to an Internet Service Provider (ISP) or send files using the UUCP capability.

over-the-network installation—Solaris can be installed over the network using an install server that has either the Solaris distribution CD in its CD-ROM drive or a copy of the files from the Solaris distribution CD on its hard disk. A boot server may also be required.

partition—A contiguous collection of disk sectors as defined by the partition table. Once a partition is defined in the partition table, a file system can be created within the partition.

partition table—A table in the VTOC that contains an entry for each partition on the disk. The following describes the fields of the partition table:

➤ *Partition Name*—Single hexadecimal character used as a name for the partition (0 through f)

➤ *Tag*—Intended use of the partition; obsolete

➤ *Flags*—A value of 1 indicates that the partition is not mountable; a value of 10 indicates that the partition is read-only; obsolete

➤ *First Sector*—Number of the first sector in the partition

➤ *Sector Count*—Number of sectors in the partition

➤ *Last Sector*—Number of the last sector assigned to the partition

➤ *Mount Directory*—The directory where the partition (actually, the file system) was last mounted

password aging—The parameters of the /etc/shadow file determine the password aging policy. This includes how long a password is valid (Max Change), how often it can be changed (Min Change), and how long an account can be inactive before the password must be changed (Max Inactive). These parameters enforce a policy for protecting the integrity of passwords.

physical device name—The name assigned to a device based on the system bus that it is attached to and where on the bus it is attached. The name represents its location on the device tree.

platform—The particular type of hardware—either SPARC or Intel x86 compatible.

plex—A collection of Volume Manager subdisks organized to support various levels of RAID.

port—A controlled physical device that can transfer data between entities. The port can be used for input, output, or both.

port monitor program—A program that monitors the RS-232 interchange circuits (such as DCD) on the serial ports of the system and provides information to applications as to the status of the interchange circuits.

postinstallation phase—The installation phase when any appropriate patches and applications are installed or when custom configurations such as user accounts and environments are set up.

preconfigured system information—There are two methods for preconfiguring system information: using the sysidcfg file and using a name service.

print client—A system that sends its print requests to a print server. Solaris 2.x, Solaris 7, SunOS 4.x, SunOS 5.x, and HP-UX systems are supported as print clients.

print model—A script that defines how the LP Print Service interfaces with printers. The print model is responsible for initializing the printer port and the printer based on information provided by the terminfo database, printing a banner page and multiple copies if requested. Generic print models are provided with the Solaris operating system. To make full use of printer capability, a model might be provided with the printer, or a custom model can be written. The default print model for a local printer is /etc/lp/model/standard, and the default model for a remote printer is /etc/lp/model/netstandard.

print queue—A list of print requests waiting to be printed. By default, the print requests will be printed in the order they were submitted, unless commands are used to modify print request priorities.

print request—One or more files submitted to a print queue to be printed.

print server—A system that has a local printer attached to it and makes it available to other systems on the network.

printer class—A group of one or more printers assigned to a printer class name. When a print request is submitted to a printer class instead of a printer, the first available printer in the class is used to print the request.

Printer Manager—A graphical tool included with AdminSuite that is used to define and configure local and remote printers.

process—A task or program currently being executed by the computer system.

profile diskette—A diskette that contains the JumpStart configuration directory; that is, a rules file and one or more profile files.

profile file—A text file that defines how to install the Solaris 7 software on a system. Like the rules file, a profile file contains keywords and associated values that guide the installation.

profile server—Provides access to a custom JumpStart configuration directory over the network and eliminates the need to create and distribute multiple profile diskettes during installation of large numbers of systems.

RAID—Redundant Array of Inexpensive Disks. The following are the various RAID levels:

➤ *0*—Striping or concatenation

➤ *1*—Mirroring and duplexing

➤ *2*—Hamming Error Code Correction (ECC), used to detect and correct errors

➤ *3*—Bit-interleaved striping with parity information (separate disk for parity)

➤ *4*—Block-interleaved striping with parity information (separate disk for parity)

➤ *5*—Block-interleaved striping with distributed parity information

➤ *6*—Block-interleaved striping with two independent distributed parity schemes

➤ *7*—Block-interleaved striping with asynchronous I/O transfers and distributed parity information

➤ *10*—Mirrored striping or striped mirroring (combination of RAID 0 and RAID 1)

➤ *53*—Similar to RAID 5 except data is taken from RAID 3 disks. (The data on a set of RAID 3 disks is copied to another set of disks using RAID 5 methodology.)

remote authentication database—Used to determine which remote hosts and users are considered as being trusted. The **rlogin, rsh,** and **rcp** commands use the remote authentication database. This database consists of two types of files:

the /etc/host.equiv file, which applies to the entire system, and the .rhosts files, which apply to individual user accounts and are located in the home directories of user accounts.

remote printer—A printer attached to a system (or network interface device) that functions as a print server. Accessing a remote printer from a local system requires defining the local system as a print client to the remote printer.

Request For Comment (RFC)—A document used to publish networking-related policies and protocols so that interested parties can submit comments and recommend changes. After a period of time, the RFC is adopted as a standard by the U.S. government and industry. Protocols such as TCP/IP and NFS have been defined by RFCs.

RS-232—An Electronics Industries Association (EIA) standard that defines the interface between the DCE and DTE in terms of electrical signal characteristics, the mechanical interface (connector), and a functional description of the interchange circuits.

rules file—A text file that contains an entry or rule for each system or group of systems that are to be automatically installed. Each rule identifies the system (or group of systems) based on one or more attributes and identifies a unique profile file that provides the configuration details for that system or group of systems. Each rule consists of one or more keywords and values followed by the name of the profile file.

run control (RC) script—A shell script (typically Bourne) written to start and stop various processes and services. An rc script is usually written in two portions: a start portion and a stop portion. The appropriate portion is executed when the system is booted or shut down.

serial device—A device that communicates using the RS-232 standard. This includes communication devices such as modems, input devices such as mice, output devices such as printers, and, in some contexts, other computers.

serial port—A port that conforms to the RS-232 standard. This includes not only the electrical signaling and interchange circuits but also connectors and cables.

Serial Port Manager—A graphical tool included with AdminSuite that is used to configure settings of serial ports.

server—A computer system that provides resources to remote clients.

service access facility (SAF)—A two-level facility that provides services for serial ports and network connections. A *service* is defined as a program that monitors and sets up connections using the serial ports and network interfaces.

The first, or top-level, SAF program is the Service Access Controller, or **sac**(1M) command. It is responsible for starting and controlling the lower-level SAF programs, or port monitors, which monitor one or more ports to handle requests for services.

Session Manager—A program that starts a session for a user. A session is associated with a display and consists of not only the graphical desktop and its settings (fonts, colors, and so on) but also mouse behavior, keyboard click, applications, and other resources present on the desktop.

setgid—A special file access mode that sets the effective GID of the user account executing a program to the GID of the program group owner. The setgid permission has an absolute mode of 2000 and a symbolic mode of **s**.

setuid—A special file access mode that sets the effective UID of the user account executing a program to the UID of the program owner. The setuid permission has an absolute mode of 4000 and a symbolic mode of **s**.

sh—See **Bourne shell**.

share—The process of making an NFS resource available for mounting by remote NFS clients.

shell—A software module that provides the interface between users and the kernel. One of the three parts of an operating system (the other parts are the kernel and the file system).

signal—A notification sent to a process to indicate an event or an action that should be performed. Signals are used to terminate processes. The following shows the most frequently used signals to terminate a process:

➤ *SIGHUP*—This is a hang-up. It has a value of 1.

➤ *SIGINT*—This is an interrupt. It has a value of 2.

➤ *SIGKILL*—This is a kill. It has a value of 9.

➤ *SIGTERM*—This is a terminate. It has a value of 15.

slice—See **partition**.

software cluster—A logical grouping of software packages. Clusters are necessary because some software is distributed in more than one package, but all the packages need to be distributed and installed as a unit.

software configuration cluster—See **software group**.

software group—A collection of software clusters. Depending on the intended use of the system, the most appropriate software group should be selected for installing an operating system. The following are the five software groups:

➤ *Core*—Minimum files required for the operating system.

➤ *End User Support System*—This is the typical configuration for a system that supports general users. Consists of the Core software group plus windowing software (Common Desktop Environment [CDE] and Openwindows), basic networking and printer support, standard Unix and patch utilities, and Java Virtual Machine.

➤ *Developer System Support*—Intended as a software development environment. Consists of the End User Support System plus programming tools and libraries; Extended terminal, X, and kernel probing support; CDE/Motif developer software and runtimes; and online manual pages.

➤ *Entire Distribution*—All files included with the Solaris 7 distribution. Consists of the Developer System Support plus AnswerBook2 (online Web-based documentation), enhanced security features (including disk quotas and system accounting), and enhanced network support, (including UUCP, DHCP server, PPP, and NIS.

➤ *Entire Distribution Plus OEM System Support*—Includes modules and drivers for optional hardware components. Consists of the Entire Distribution plus PCI drivers and Sun FastEthernet and FastWide SCSI adapter drivers.

software package—An easily installable collection of Solaris 7 system and application software. These packages consist of files and directories and can be copied onto the system from CD-ROM or magnetic tape as a single compressed file and then uncompressed for installation. Included with the package is information regarding the package, such as title, storage requirements, and version. Also included are any custom scripts needed to properly install the software.

software patch—An easily installable collection of file and directories intended to update or fix a problem with an installed software package.

SPARC—A computer architecture developed by Sun Microsystems that uses a reduced instruction set processor that provides superior performance over processors that operate using a standard instruction set.

standalone system—A system that has local disk space used to store all operating system files, applications, and user data. This includes the root (/), /usr,

/export/home, and /var file systems. Likewise, it provides local swap for the system's virtual memory. A standalone system can function autonomously and can be either networked or non-networked.

standard file permissions—Files and directories can have read, write, and execution permissions. Permissions can be assigned to three classes of system accounts: the user account that owns the file, the group account that has group permissions, and everyone else. These are referred to as user, group, and other permissions. The read, write, and execution for user, group, and other can be set independently of one another.

sticky bit—A special file permission that, when set on a directory that allows write permission for everyone, allows only the user account that created the files and subdirectories under that directory to remove those files and subdirectories. This is especially useful for the /tmp directory, which is available from any user account. The sticky bit permission has an absolute mode of 1000 and a symbolic mode of **t**.

Storage Manager—A graphical tool included with AdminSuite that is used to manage physical disks and file systems. The Storage Manager consists of two graphical tools: the Disk Manager and the File System Manager.

striped virtual device—A device consisting of two or more slices. The slices can be on the same physical disk or on several physical disks. The slices also can be of different sizes. The slices are addressed in an interleaved manner. That is, as space is needed, it is allocated as a block from the first slice, then a block from the second slice, and so on.

subdisk—The basic unit used by the Volume Manager to allocate storage. It is a portion of the public region of a VM disk.

subnet mask—A mask used to separate the network portion of an IP address from the host portion. See **network classes**.

subpanel—A pop-up menu associated with a button on the main panel. It contains graphical icons or buttons that start applications or display windows.

superuser—A special administrative account that provides the ultimate in terms of access to data and services, as it can override any file permissions on the system.

swap space—Disk space used as virtual memory. Swap space can be on a local disk or a remote disk that is accessed via the network.

switch—A container of the Front Panel that contains controls and is located in the center of the main panel.

symbolic file permission mode—An alphabetic notation used to represent the standard file permissions for owner, group, and other. Read access is represented by the letter "r," write by the letter "w," and execution by the letter "x."

sysadmin group—User accounts that are a member of the sysadmin group (numerical group 14) can perform some selected system administration activities using **admintool**(1M) without being granted full superuser privileges. This allows basic system administration (adding and deleting users, printers, software, and so on) to be performed by more than one person without compromising system security.

syslog—A facility used to collect messages from system programs and applications. These are identified by a source facility and priority level. The /etc/syslog.conf file assigns an action with each combination of source and priority level.

syslog actions—The action that should be performed when a syslog message of the identified *source.priority* is received by the **syslogd** daemon. The following actions can be defined in the /etc/syslog.conf file:

➤ */filename*—The identified syslog messages will be appended to the specified file (must begin with a slash [/] character).

➤ *@host*—The identified syslog messages will be forwarded to the **syslogd** daemon on the specified remote host (must begin with an at [@] character).

➤ *login account*—The identified syslog messages are written to the standard out (typically the monitor) associated with the specified login account if the account is currently logged onto the system. Multiple login accounts can be specified (separated by commas).

➤ ***—The identified syslog messages are written to the standard out of all login accounts currently logged onto the system.

syslog priority levels—A syslog message can be identified by priority level or severity. This provides a second mechanism (with finer granularity) for handling messages on the basis of importance. The following lists the keywords used in the /etc/syslog.conf to identify the severity of messages and control handling. These keywords are ordered on the basis of severity (from most severe to least severe):

➤ *emerg*—Panic conditions

➤ *alert*—Conditions that need immediate attention

➤ *crit*—Critical conditions

➤ *err*—Other errors

➤ *warning*—Warning messages

➤ *notice*—Conditions that might require special handling

➤ *info*—Nonurgent information

➤ *debug*—Typically information generated by debug messages in programs

➤ *none*—Special keyword used to prevent logging of messages generated by specified sources

syslog source facilities—The facilities generating syslog messages can be used to determine where the messages are sent or stored. This allows separate log files for different types of messages based on source. The following are the keywords used in the /etc/syslog.conf to identify the source of messages and control handling:

➤ *auth*—Login authentication

➤ *cron*—The **at**(1) and **cron**(1M) commands

➤ *daemon*—System daemons

➤ *kern*—The kernel

➤ *lpr*—The line printer spooling system

➤ *local0-7*—As defined locally

➤ *mail*—System mail

➤ *mark*—Timestamp produced by **syslogd**(1M)

➤ *news*—The USENET network news system

➤ *user*—User programs (default)

➤ *uucp*—The UUCP system

➤ ***—All facilities except mark

system configuration phase—The installation phase during which basic information about the system, such as hostname and domain, is identified. This information can optionally be set up ahead of time, or preconfigured.

system default printer—A printer identified as the default printer using the **lpadmin** command.

system installation phase—The installation phase during which the system software is installed. The system software is one of the Solaris 7 software groups.

system profile—For user accounts that use sh (Bourne shell) or ksh (Korn shell) as a login shell, commands in the system profile (/etc/profile) are executed before the user's login initialization file.

system run levels—Eight defined levels, each associated with specific functions used to shut down or reboot the system and control system services and resources. The following summarizes the eight run levels:

➤ *0*—Power Down. The system is being shut down.

➤ *s or S*—Single User. Single-user maintenance.

➤ *1*—Administrative. Multiuser maintenance.

➤ *2*—Multiuser. Normal operations.

➤ *3*—Multiuser with NFS. Normal operations plus NFS.

➤ *4*—Alternative Multiuser. Not used and is unavailable.

➤ *5*—Power Down. The system is being shut down.

➤ *6*—Reboot. The system is being restarted.

System V—The version of the Unix operating system developed by AT&T Bell Labs. It is the basis for the Solaris operating system.

terminfo database—A database that contains characteristics of both terminals and printers. Characteristics include control sequences that switch between typefaces (bold, underline, and so on) and other functionality, such as cursor/print head positioning.

UFS file system logging—Updates to a UFS file system are recorded in a log before they are applied. In the case of system failure, the system can be restarted, and the UFS file system can quickly use the log instead of having to use the **fsck** command.

user account—A unique name and User ID that control an individual's access to a computer and its resources.

user/application default printer—A default printer defined by the LPDEST or PRINTER environment variable. Usually specified in the .profile file.

user ID (UID)—A unique numeric ID assigned to a user account that is used for file and process ownership and access permissions.

User Manager—A graphical tool included with AdminSuite that is used to create and modify user accounts.

Veritas File System (vxfs)—The type of virtual file system supported by the Enterprise Volume Manager.

virtual disk management system—A software package that allows the use of physical disks in different ways that are not supported by the standard Solaris file systems. It can overcome disk capacity and architecture limitations and improve performance and reliability. In addition, manageability is enhanced by the use of a graphical management tool.

virtual file system—An enhanced file system that provides improved performance and data reliability.

volume—An Enterprise Volume Manager virtual disk device composed of up to 32 plexes. The volume is the virtual object that the operating system and applications view and manipulate.

Volume Manager (VM) disk—A physical disk partition or slice that has been assigned to the Enterprise Volume Manager.

volume table of contents (VTOC)—Contains the partition table and various geometry data about the disk, such as sectors per track, tracks per cylinder, available cylinders, and so on.

WebNFS—A protocol that allows Web browsers to access NFS resources. This protocol is defined by RFCs 2054 and 2055.

WebStart—An interactive installation method that uses a Web browser.

Window menu—A Workspace Manager menu that provides control over a window for moving, resizing, maximizing, minimizing, closing, and so on. To access the Window menu, position the mouse cursor over the upper-left corner of a window and click the rightmost mouse button.

workspace—A CDE display that consists of the Front Panel and windows created by the user. By default, four workspaces are created and can be used independently of one another.

Workspace Manager—A desktop window manager that controls the appearance of window components and supports the ability to modify the window appearance and window behavior, such as stacking and focus. The Workspace Manager controls the workspaces (four by default), the background wallpaper (backdrop) of the workspaces via the Style Manager, and the Front Panel.

Workspace menu—Provides access to applications and a windows submenu that is used to manage the workspace and Front Panel. It is accessed by moving the mouse pointer over the backdrop and holding down the rightmost mouse button. It is also referred to as the *root menu*.

X Display Manager Control Protocol (XDMCP)—The protocol used by network displays (X terminals and workstations) to request the Login Manager to display a login screen.

x86 Intel compatible—A computer architecture based on a microprocessor originally designed by the Intel Corporation that used the 286, 386, 486 series of numbers to denote versions.

X/Open Federated Naming Specification (XFN)—The specification for the Federated Naming Service (FNS) as defined by the X/Open Consortium.

zone—A portion of a domain delegated to a DNS server.

Glossary Of Commands

accept—Configures a printer to accept attempts to place print requests on its print queue.

add_install_client—Adds information about an install client to the /etc files of an install server or a boot server.

admgroupadd—Adds a group account. Provided with AdminSuite.

admgroupdel—Deletes a group account. Provided with AdminSuite.

admgroupls—Lists group accounts. Provided with AdminSuite.

admgroupmod—Modifies a group account. Provided with AdminSuite.

admhostadd—Adds support for a new system or OS server. Provided with AdminSuite.

admhostdel—Deletes support for an existing system or OS server. Provided with AdminSuite.

admhostls—Lists existing hosts. Provided with AdminSuite.

admhostmod—Modifies an existing host. Provided with AdminSuite.

admserialdel—Deletes a port service. Provided with AdminSuite.

admserialls—Lists port services. Provided with AdminSuite.

admserialmod—Modifies a port service. Provided with AdminSuite.

admuseradd—Adds a user account. Provided with AdminSuite.

admuserdel—Deletes a user account. Provided with AdminSuite.

admuserls—Lists user accounts. Provided with AdminSuite.

admusermod—Modifies a user account. Provided with AdminSuite.

at—Executes commands only once at a future time. The time and command are specified as command line arguments.

automount—Initializes the AutoFS service.

automountd—The daemon process that runs continuously and provides automatic mounting and unmounting.

cachefspack—Specifies files to be placed in the CacheFS cache.

cachefsstat—Provides usage statistics on the CacheFS cache.

cancel—Cancels one or more print requests: the request currently being printed or print requests from a specific user.

cfsadmin—Creates, checks, tunes, and deletes the cache associated with a CacheFS service.

check—Validates a custom JumpStart rules file.

chgrp—Changes file group account ownership.

chmod—Modifies the file access permissions of existing files and directories. Either absolute mode or symbolic mode can be used to specify the new permissions.

chown—Changes file user account ownership.

cron—A daemon started during system boot. It is responsible for executing commands at a future time and perhaps periodically on a scheduled basis. The commands to be executed are specified in a standardized tabular format and stored in files referred to as *crontab files*.

crontab—Creates, lists, edits, and deletes crontab files. Access to the **crontab** command is controlled by two files—cron.allow and cron.deny—both of which reside under the /etc/cron.d directory. These text files contain lists of user account names (one per line) that are allowed or denied access.

df—Displays the mount point, logical block device name, number of free 512-byte blocks, and number of files that can be created for each file system.

dfmounts—Lists mounted NFS resources on a local or remote system.

dfshares—Lists shared NFS resources on a local or remote system.

disable—Prevents use of a printer.

dmesg—Collects and displays diagnostic messages from the syslog (typically /var/adm/messages). These messages are generated during system boot and use instance names (and physical names) to identify devices.

domainname—Sets the domain name.

dtappgather—Locates available CDE applications.

dtconfig—Configures the Login Manager.

dtlogin—The Login Manager.

dtpathsearch—Sets CDE desktop search paths.

dtsession—Sets up the user CDE session.

du—Displays the number of 512-byte blocks allocated to each subdirectory and the total for the current directory.

eeprom—Displays and modifies OpenBoot parameters while using the Solaris 7 operating system.

enable—Allows use of a printer.

finger—Displays users logged into the local or a remote system.

fmthard—Creates and populates a partition table.

format—Creates and populates partition tables and formats partitions of a hard disk.

fsck—Checks (audits) the logical consistency of a file system and attempts to make the repairs necessary to eliminate any inconsistency.

getfacl—Displays the ACL for files and directories.

growfs—DiskSuite command used to expand a UFS file system make.

halt—Halts the system, logs the shutdown to the system log, writes a shutdown record to the system accounting file, performs a call to the **sync**(1M) command to write out any pending information to the disks, and halts the processor(s). Changes to run level 0 but does not execute the rc scripts associated with run level 0.

id—Displays the real and effective UID and GID for the invoking process or specified user account.

in.named—Implementation of the Berkeley Internet Name Domain (BIND) program, which is a DNS server.

inetd—The Internet services daemon, which is used to start the standard Internet services.

infocmp—Displays terminfo entries.

init—Changes to any of the eight run levels. The commands identified in the /etc/inittab for each run level are executed and any running process not in /etc/inittab is sent a SIGTERM and possibly a SIGKILL to cause them to terminate. For each run level, an entry in the /etc/inittab runs the appropriate rc scripts to start and stop processes.

kill—Terminates a process identified by its PID.

last—Displays login and logout information. This command can be used both to determine which accounts are logged into the system and to display the last time accounts were used (starting with the most recent).

listen—A network listener daemon. It listens for and accepts network service requests and then invokes a specified service and associates it with the network connection.

login—Logs onto the system.

logins—Displays user account information.

lp—Submits one or more files to be printed.

lpadmin—Defines a printer, a printer class, and a default system printer.

lpmove—Moves all queued print requests from one printer queue to another.

lpsched—Starts the LP Print Service.

lpshut—Stops the LP Print Service.

lpstat—Checks the status of print requests.

makedbm—Creates NIS maps.

mdlogd—DiskSuite daemon used to send SNMP messages.

metaclear—DiskSuite command used to delete metadevices and hot spare pools.

metadb—DiskSuite command used to create and delete database replicas.

metadetach—DiskSuite command used to detach a metadevice from a mirror.

metahs—DiskSuite command used to manage hot spares and hot spare pools.

metainit—DiskSuite command used to configure metadevices.

metaoffline—DiskSuite command used to place mirrors offline.

metaonline—DiskSuite command used to place mirrors online.

metaparam—DiskSuite command used to modify metadevices.

metarename—DiskSuite command used to rename metadevice names.

metareplace—DiskSuite command used to replace slices of mirrors and RAID 5 metadevices.

metaroot—DiskSuite command used to set up files for mirroring the root file system.

metaset—DiskSuite command used to administer disk sets.

metastat—DiskSuite command used to display status of metadevices or hot spare pools.

metasync—DiskSuite command used to resync metadevices during reboot.

metatool—DiskSuite command used to run the DiskSuite graphical user interface.

metattach—DiskSuite command used to attach a metadevice to a mirror.

mk_floppy—Creates a boot diskette for an Intel x86 network client.

mkfs—Creates a UFS type of file system.

mkfs_ufs—Creates a UFS type of file system.

mount—Makes a file system accessible.

mountall—Mounts all file systems and NFS resources listed in the /etc/vfstab file.

mt—Controls magnetic tape operations.

netstat—Displays network statistics.

newfs—Creates a UFS type of file system.

nlsadmin—Formats **listen**-specific data. Typically, the output of the **listen** command is captured and placed in a **listen** port monitor table (_pmtab).

patchadd—Installs an update to an installed software package.

patchrm—Removes an install patch and returns the updated software package to its original condition.

pgrep—Displays the PID of a process based on one or more attributes of the process.

ping—Used to verify both the connectivity between two hosts and the proper operation of the network interfaces and protocol stacks (of both hosts) up to the Internet layer where the Internet Protocol (IP) resides.

pkgadd—Installs a software package on the system.

pkgchk—Verifies the proper installation of a software package.

pkginfo—Displays information regarding an installed software package.

pkgparam—Displays specified parameters associated with an installed software package.

pkgrm—Removes an installed software package.

pkill—Terminates a process based on one or more attributes of the process.

pmadm—Provides administrative control over the lower level of the SAF, namely, the services provided by a port monitor.

poweroff—Changes the system to run level 5, logs the shutdown to the system log, writes a shutdown record to the system accounting file, performs a call to **sync(1M)** to write out any pending information to the disks, halts the processor(s), and, if possible, shuts the power off.

prtconf—Prints the current system configuration.

prtvtoc—Prints the VTOC of a hard disk.

ps—Displays information regarding the processes currently running on the system.

quot—Lists the number of 1,024-byte blocks of a file system owned by each user.

reboot—Used to change the system to run level 6; logs the reboot to the system log, writes a shutdown record to the system accounting file, performs a call to **sync** to write out any pending information to the disks, and initiates a multiuser reboot.

reject—Configures a printer to reject attempts to place print requests on its print queue.

rlogin—Remotely logs into a system through the network. If the remote authentication database has been set up properly, the user could log in without providing a valid user account name and password. If the database has not been set up properly, the user must provide a valid user account name and password as defined on the remote system.

rusers—Displays users logged into the local or a remote system.

sac—Starts and controls the lower-level SAF programs (port monitors).

sacadm—Provides administrative control over the top level of the SAF, namely, the SAC.

setfacl—Defines the ACL for files and directories.

setup_install_server—Sets up and configures install servers and boot servers used in over-the-network installations.

share—Makes an NFS resource available to NFS clients.

shareall—Shares all NFS resources listed in the /etc/dfs/dfstab file.

showrev—Displays the version information of the operating system and installed patches.

shutdown—Changes to any of the eight run levels.

spray—Sends a stream of User Datagram Protocol (UDP) packets to a host using the Remote Procedure Call (RPC) mechanism. On the remote end, the spray daemon, **sprayd**, accepts these packets and acknowledges receiving the packets. The **spray** command, along with the **sprayd** program, is used to verify both the connectivity between two hosts and the proper operation of the network interfaces and protocol stacks (of both hosts) up to the application layer.

sysdef—Displays the system configuration or definition that lists all hardware devices, including pseudo and system devices, loadable modules, and tunable kernel parameters.

sysidnet—Configures the network interface.

sysidnis—Sets up the NIS/NIS+ client configuration.

sysidpm—Configures the Power Management settings.

sysidroot—Sets the root password.

sysidsys—Configures date, time, and time zone.

sysidtool—A suite of five system configuration programs. These are the **sysidnet**, **sysidnis**, **sysidpm**, **sysidroot**, and **sysidsys** commands. They are executed as part of the System Configuration install phase.

syslogd—Accepts messages from system and user programs and handles them on the basis of the entries in the /etc/syslog.conf file. These messages can be reporting anything from emergency situations to debugging details. Common uses include monitoring logins and recording hacking attempts. A syslog message is categorized by its source, a source facility, and a priority (or severity) level.

SunInstall—A common interactive installation utility used to perform standard or customized installations.

tar—Creates tape archives and adds/extracts files from the archive.

telinit—See **init**.

telnet—Remotely logs into a system through the network. The user must provide a valid user account name and password as defined on the remote system, as the standard Unix login/password is used for authentication.

tip—Connects to a remote system through an RS-232 connection. It is a basic terminal emulator designed to communicate over a modem or hardwired serial port.

ttyadm—Formats **ttymon**-specific data. Typically, the output of the **ttyadm** command is captured and placed in the **ttymon** port monitor table (_pmtab).

ttymon—A port monitor that monitors serial ports to select terminal modes, baud rates, and other communication-related settings.

uadmin—Provides basic administrative functions, such as shutting down or rebooting a system. Typically, it is called by various system administration procedures and is not intended for general use.

ufsdump—Backs up a UFS file system.

ufsrestore—Restores a UFS file system or selected files and directories.

umask—Sets the default file permissions used when a file is created.

umount—Makes a file system inaccessible.

umountall—Unmounts all mounted file systems listed in the /etc/mnttab file.

unshare—Prevents NFS clients from accessing an NFS resource.

unshareall—Prevents NFS clients from accessing any locally provided NFS resources.

vxassist—Enterprise Volume Manager command used to manage volumes.

vxbootsetup—Enterprise Volume Manager command used to set up system boot information.

vxdctl—Enterprise Volume Manager command used to control Volume Manager daemons.

vxdg—Enterprise Volume Manager command used to manage disk groups.

vxdisk—Enterprise Volume Manager command used to manage disks.

vxdiskadd—Enterprise Volume Manager command used to add a disk.

vxdiskadm—Enterprise Volume Manager command used to administer disks.

vxdisksetup—Enterprise Volume Manager command used to set up disks.

vxedit—Enterprise Volume Manager command used to edit configuration records.

vxencap—Enterprise Volume Manager command used to encapsulate partitions on a new disk.

vxevac—Enterprise Volume Manager command used to evacuate all volumes on a disk.

vxinfo—Enterprise Volume Manager command used to print volume accessibility information.

vxiod—Enterprise Volume Manager command used to manage kernel daemons.

vxmake—Enterprise Volume Manager command used to create configuration records.

vxmend—Enterprise Volume Manager command used to mend problems with a configuration record.

vxmirror—Enterprise Volume Manager command used to mirror a volume on a disk.

vxnotify—Enterprise Volume Manager command used to display configuration events.

vxplex—Enterprise Volume Manager command used to manage plexes.

vxprint—Enterprise Volume Manager command used to display configuration records.

vxr5check—Enterprise Volume Manager command used to verify RAID 5 parity.

vxreattach—Enterprise Volume Manager command used to reattach a disk.

vxrecover—Enterprise Volume Manager command used to recover a volume.

vxrelocd—Enterprise Volume Manager command used to relocate failed disks.

vxresize—Enterprise Volume Manager command used to change the size of a volume.

vxrootmir—Enterprise Volume Manager command used to mirror a root volume.

vxsd—Enterprise Volume Manager command used to manage subdisks.

vxserial—Enterprise Volume Manager command used to manage licensing keys.

vxsparecheck—Enterprise Volume Manager command used to replace failed disks.

vxstat—Enterprise Volume Manager command used to display statistics.

vxtrace—Enterprise Volume Manager command used to run a trace operation.

vxva—Enterprise Volume Manager command used to start the Visual Administrator.

vxvol—Enterprise Volume Manager command used to manage a volume.

w—Lists user accounts currently logged into the local system.

who—Lists user accounts currently logged into the local system.

whodo—Displays the processes that each login account is executing.

xsession—The session manager that starts a CDE session for a user.

ypbind—NIS daemon that provides the NIS functionality.

ypinit—Initializes master NIS servers, slave NIS servers, and NIS clients.

yppush—Propagates updated NIS maps to NIS slave servers.

ypstart—Starts the NIS processes.

ypstop—Stops the NIS processes.

ypxfr—Distributes new NIS maps to NIS slave servers.

OpenBoot Commands

banner—Displays the power-on banner.

boot cdrom—Boots from the local CD-ROM.

boot disk—Boots from the default hard disk.

boot floppy—Boots from the diskette drive.

boot net—Boots from the network.

boot tape—Boots from the SCSI tape drive.

devalias—Creates a device alias or lists all device aliases.

.enet-addr—Displays Ethernet address.

.idprom—Displays formatted ID PROM contents.

module-info—Displays CPU speed (multiprocessor 2.x only).

nvalias—Creates a device alias in NVRAM.

nvunalias—Removes a device alias in NVRAM.

pcia-probe-list—Tests PCI.

printenv—Lists all NVRAM parameters and default values.

probe-scsi—Tests built-in SCSI for connected devices.

probe-scsi all—Tests all SCSI buses.

show-devs—Lists installed devices.

.speed—Displays CPU and bus speeds (3.x only).

stop—Bypasses the POST.

stop+a—Aborts the operating system or boot process (returns to OpenBoot OK prompt).

stop+d—Enters diagnostic mode.

stop+f—Enters the Forth Monitor on TTYA (instead of the system console).

stop+n—Resets NVRAM contents to default values.

test-all—Tests a group of install devices.

test floppy—Tests diskette drive.

test /memory—Tests system memory.

test net—Tests the on-board Ethernet interface.

.traps—Lists types of SPARC traps.

.version—Displays boot PROM version and data.

watch-clock—Monitors system clock.

watch-net—Monitors network connection.

Index

V

W

X

Y